The Indigenous Public Sphere

The Indigenous Public Sphere

The reporting and reception of Aboriginal issues in the Australian media

John Hartley and Alan McKee

OXFORD
UNIVERSITY PRESS

Great Clarendon Street, Oxford OX2 6DP
Oxford University Press is a department of the University of Oxford.
It furthers the University's objective of excellence in research, scholarship,
and education by publishing worldwide in

Oxford New York
Athens Auckland Bangkok Bogotá Buenos Aires Calcutta
Cape Town Chennai Dar es Salaam Delhi Florence Hong Kong Istanbul
Karachi Kuala Lumpur Madrid Melbourne Mexico City Mumbai
Nairobi Paris São Paulo Shanghai Singapore Taipei Tokyo Toronto Warsaw

and associated companies in Berlin Ibadan

Oxford is a registered trade mark of Oxford University Press
in the UK and certain other countries

Published in the United States
by Oxford University Press Inc. New York

© John Hartley and Alan McKee 2000
© The Individual Contributors, Chapters 4, 5, and 6.

The moral rights of the author have been asserted
Database right Oxford University Press (maker)

First published 2000

British Library Cataloguing in Publication Data
Data available

Library of Congress Cataloging in Publication Data
Data availavle

ISBN 0–19–815999–4

1 3 5 7 9 10 8 6 4 2

Typeset by Kolam Information Service Pvt. Ltd, Pondicherry, India
Printed in Great Britain
on acid-free paper by
Biddles Ltd,
Guildford and King's Lynn

To Patrick Dodson,

and to the memory of Rob Riley

Acknowledgements

The research upon which this book is based was supported by an Australian Research Council Large Grant, held between 1994 and 1997, first at Murdoch University and subsequently at Edith Cowan University in Western Australia. We are grateful to the ARC for this assistance.

Financial assistance for the National Media Forum, reported on in Part Two of this book, was received from JLV Industries, the Council for Aboriginal Reconciliation, the Louis Johnson Trust, and Edith Cowan University. We are delighted to acknowledge their assistance with thanks.

We are also grateful to Cardiff University and Edith Cowan University for allowing each of us time to concentrate on the project at crucial moments.

We are especially grateful to the many people whose ideas and commitment have helped us along the way, especially to Patrick Dodson and the late Rob Riley. Thanks to Steve Mickler, Alison Bunbury, Bill Johnson, and Robyn Quin in WA; to Sophie Goldsworthy at Oxford University Press; to Tina Horton in the Cymric gloom and to Marc Brennan in the Aussie sunshine—without them we could not have made this book. Heartfelt thanks, finally, go to all the participants in the National Media Forum, whose wise words you may read herein.

JH, Cardiff, Wales
AMcK, Perth, Western Australia
January 2000

CONTENTS

CONTENTS

Part Three: Reporting

List of Illustrations

List of Figures

1. Biddy, Aboriginal nursemaid, holding John Gordon, Brewon Station, Walgett, NSW, 1887. The picture was used in the 'Stolen Generations' Report, 1997 (see p. 250). Source: Bicentennial Copying Project, State Library of New South Wales.

2. Maurin Miller, Aboriginal father, holding his six-week old daughter outside King Edward Memorial Hospital for Women, Perth, WA, 1995. This still from ABC-TV news shows Miller moments before police rushed him, breaking the baby's arm (see pp. 286–7). Source ABC News, 13 July 1995—'Bail granted'. Courtesy Australian Broadcasting Corporation.

3. Aaron Pederson, Aboriginal actor, seen here in the hit TV drama series *Water Rats*, 2000 (see pp. 229–30). Source: Channel Seven.

COUNCIL FOR ABORIGINAL RECONCILIATION

HE COUNCIL'S VISION

A united Australia which respects this land of ours; values the Aboriginal and Torres Strait Islander heritage; and provides justice and equity for all.

Locked bag 14
Queen Victoria Terrace
PARKES ACT 2600
Telephone (Toll-free):
008 807 071

Together we can't lose

4. 'Together We Can't Lose'. Cathy Freeman, Aboriginal athlete, carrying the Aboriginal national flag, joins Melinda Gainsford-Taylor, who carries the Australian flag, 1996 (see pp. 236–40, 273–4). This picture was used by the Council for Aboriginal Reconciliation to promote the reconciliation process. Source: Council for Aboriginal Reconciliation.

Introduction: The 'Indigenous Public Sphere'

> At times it would seem as if all the culture of old Europe were being brought to bear upon our writers and artists in order to blot from their memories the crimes perpetrated upon Australia's first inhabitants. In recent years, however, both sides, black and white alike, have become increasingly aware of the continuing colonial crime, the locked cupboard of our history. It is this new awareness of what actually occurred that, it seems to me, constitutes a central problem for the integrity and authenticity of Australian culture today.
>
> (Bernard Smith, 1980: 10)

A 'locked cupboard of history' can only be kept locked anew each day, in a continuously unfolding present. If there is a 'new awareness', that too must be disseminated on a daily basis. If there is a 'central problem for the integrity and authenticity of Australian culture today', then that problem must be pondered and wrestled with 'today'. Responsibility for letting the skeleton out of the cupboard, for creating awareness, and for thinking through the central problems of a nation, is taken not only by the writers and artists to whom Bernard Smith referred in the passage quoted above, but also by the media of disclosure, the journalism of popular enlightenment, the reporting of governmental decision-making. The locked cupboard itself, awareness of its contents, and the subsequent condition of Australian integrity and authenticity, are all, in short, questions of media.

The Indigenous Public Sphere presents an original approach to the reporting of Aboriginal affairs in the media. Where previous work has often concentrated on finding examples of racist or 'negative' coverage, this is an attempt to retheorize the field, and to set questions of media, racism, and Indigenous representation into a larger context. Innovative aspects of the work include:

1

- By studying a much broader range of 'reporting' than is normally included in research of this kind, extending beyond hard news to include feature and lifestyle journalism and even some fiction, we attempt to map the Indigenous 'mediasphere' (Hartley, 1996). This means we are able to identify *generic* aspects of reporting, showing how coverage that attracts criticism for racism or negativity is often simply conforming to an established mode of news narration.

- Instead of gauging audiences' and readers' 'reception' of media by means of surveys, interviews, or ethnography (McKee, 1999), we have developed a *parliamentary* mode of conducting 'audience research', where Indigenous people may be understood to speak with a 'national' rather than an individual voice.

- We investigate how Indigeneity has been created and understood in academic writing as well as in the news media. Part of our purpose has been to show lines of continuity between the academic imagination on the one hand, and that of the media on the other. We do not accept the familiar scholarly role of standing at arm's length from media coverage and criticizing it. Scholarship is as much a part of the public domain as is news, and the two are in increasingly direct competition for the public's attention and assent.

- Our approach is interdisciplinary, derived from our own training in media, cultural, and journalism studies. However, within this disciplinary context, there are sometimes keenly contested debates about appropriate methods and purposes. We address these issues, seeking to contribute to the development of media studies, rather than simply applying established methods to a local example.

The research upon which this project is based was inspired by two sources. At the pragmatic end of the scale, we took our 'research questions' from the recommendations of the Royal Commission into Aboriginal Deaths in Custody (1991). Concern was expressed in that document about the hostility many Aboriginal people feel emanating towards them from the media, and that they in turn feel towards the media. Recommendations were put in place to deal with that problem in a practical, reconciliatory way. Dealing with the fact that many Indigenous people, far from seeing themselves as media victims, are enthusiastic and talented media producers, required moving beyond 'racist' models of media coverage. Commissioner Pat Dodson was also curious about our contention that news stories may be 'scripted' in advance of the events they seem to report, since that squared with his experience of coverage of Indigenous affairs. Without at all claiming that news is 'written before it happens', we do explore the *generic* quality of news narrative, which has focused on stories of 'correction and protection' of Aboriginal people, creating two domains that may be dubbed 'wedom' and 'theydom' (Hartley, 1992)—where Aboriginal people systematically appear as 'they' figures, outside the imagined community of readers and audiences of media.

Our second source of inspiration was at the theoretical end of the scale. We make extensive use of the work of Yuri M. Lotman, whose book *Universe of the Mind: A Semiotic Theory of Culture* (1990) introduces the concept of the 'semiosphere', and shows how stories and other narrative forms are organized within that 'semiotic space'. Taking his cue, we have attempted to map the narrative 'universe of Indigeneity' as it has been formed and reformed in a wide range of writing and story-telling during the 1990s. We have relied heavily on his distinction between 'law affirming' and 'anomalous' tales, since we think it explains the differentiation of stories at various levels of complexity, from academic treatises to individual news stories. One of the attractions of Lotman's work is that while he is firmly at the 'textual' end of cultural analysis, his writing is accessible, practical, and historical. Thus, his work encourages the pursuit of questions that inevitably lie at the heart of research such as this: the relations between 'text' and history, between narrative power and social power. Lotman's approach to sense-making, at the micro and macro levels alike, is resolutely 'dialogic', and we borrow that fundamental insight from him too.

The concept of the 'Indigenous public sphere' is intended to describe the highly mediated public 'space' for developing notions of Indigeneity, and putting them to work in organizing and governing the unpredictable immediacy of everyday events. Thus far, the Indigenous public sphere has hardly been under the control of Indigenous people. Indeed, it is a peculiar example of a public sphere, since it precedes any 'nation' that a public sphere normally 'expresses', as it were; it is the 'civil society' of a nation without borders, without state institutions, and without citizens. Strange though such a thing might be, it is becoming more common. Other writers have identified a 'feminist public sphere' for instance (Felski, 1989), and one might imagine that other 'virtual' or non-territorially defined communities, such as certain ethnic groups, people of particular sexual orientation (McKee, 1997b), environmentalists, peace and human rights activists, children, even taste constituencies of various kinds, may have developed 'public spheres' (or possibly 'sphericules', in Todd Gitlin's word; Gitlin, 1998), both in their own writing and public narration, and in the way their 'semiotic universe' is brought into being and structured in the writing of others.

It follows that we believe the 'Indigenous public sphere' stands as a model for other developments in late modern culture, not only in Australia, nor even only in countries with Indigenous populations, but in the developed Western world as a whole. New notions of citizenship have arisen that stress culture, identity, and voluntary belonging over previous definitions based on rights and obligations to a state (see Holston and Appadurai, 1996; Chesterman and Galligan, 1997; Davidson, 1997: 203–15; Peterson and Sanders (eds.), 1998; Stokes (ed.), 1997; Trigger; 1998, McKay, 1998). Political institutions are evolving in which commercial organizations take responsibility for democratic practice. Public participation is much higher and more enthusiastic in 'commercial democracy' than in the formal mechanics of representative politics. Economic activity is most heated beyond the traditional areas of manufacturing and industry, in new areas of culture, knowledge, information, and 'identity' consumerism, from tourism to fashion. The media are no longer explained as a secondary institution, reporting more or less accurately on events that originate and occur elsewhere. Media are primary and central institutions of politics and of idea-formation; they are the *locus* of the public sphere. Journalism has brought to the fore one of its own longstanding tendencies, making the discourse of private identity as central as the discourse of public decision-making. Within such a landscape of change, it is useful to identify how one particular 'public sphere' is handled.

Historically, European narratives have given agency to Europeans, construing 'natives' as passive recipients of good actions (development) and bad ones (extermination or coercive control), but only rarely and grudgingly giving agency and a 'speaking part' to the 'other' of their imaginings. This does describe the history of Indigeneity in Australia, but here too change is rapidly occurring. Indeed, it may be that the 'Indigenous public sphere' is evidence that 'Australia' is Indigenizing its narrative sense of self as a whole. Thus, the current period may be characterized as an intense dialogue between 'Aboriginal' and 'Australian' components of the overall Australian 'semiosphere', the outcome of which is not yet resolved. Will there develop an autonomous 'national' Indigenous 'region' of Australia? Or will Australia Indigenize its own history, politics, and community identity? There may be hope that the answer to *both* of those questions is in the affirmative.

One of the underlying motivations of this work is a longstanding discomfort with models of social and textual power that can be observed in media studies. Here too there is frequently found a victimized other, vulnerable to the influence of powerful agencies and incapable of self-determination or self-representation. This poor beast is 'the audience' of popular mass media. We think the general public of modern Western polities has too often been construed as an 'indigenous' other. Thus, study of the real thing may give pointers to media studies and thence to political practice, directing it towards a more 'dialogic' and active model of media 'reception' and thus public participation.

If democracy is to be democratized, as Anthony Giddens proposes (Giddens, 1998), then the relationships between populations, media, education, and government all need to be rethought and re-formed. Hence, the study that follows is intended as part of the work of democratization in conditions that some describe as postmodern. Its concern is as much practical and instrumental as it is theoretical and intellectual, however. While attitudes and general theoretical orientations among intellectuals, media professionals, and government agencies alike certainly need reform, very often rather small innovations would be of practical benefit. For instance, during the period of our research one of Australia's leading media directories boasted several pages of names and contact numbers for 'rugby correspondents' around Australia, but had no section listing Indigenous journalists and Indigenous media organizations. Making available to the media the resources required simply to phone the 'Indigenous public sphere' strikes us as a useful step forward (though since the time of writing even this modest project seems to have faltered).

Interdisciplinary Dialogues

Indigenous issues have largely remained the province of anthropology. Political change seems to be the province of history (from which Indigenous people were long excluded: see Griffiths, 1996: 25–7). Media studies, concerned on either horn of its own methodological dilemma with the endless present tense of 'popular culture' and 'public policy' respectively, has largely neglected questions of Indigeneity, with notable exceptions, especially the work of Michael Meadows and Steve Mickler (see their entries in the bibliography). Bringing these disciplines together allows a new perspective to emerge in which the role of the media in general, and the place of Indigenous issues in general, can be rethought.

A central feature of our approach is that it takes the relations between Indigeneity and media to be 'dialogic' in mode. The investigation of what at first sight may seem an exceptional or anomalous area of media coverage may yield generally applicable insights that help to explain how the media as a whole work, and what they do in modern societies. So Indigeneity 'speaks' to media studies. Equally, Indigenous people are far from passive recipients of media representations. They are themselves media producers, and are active participants in the processes of media production, dissemination, regulation, reception, and innovation. So Indigenous people 'speak' to media. At the same time, it is clear that media coverage is vitally important to Aboriginal and non-Aboriginal people alike—Indigeneity is a 'semiotic hot spot' of contemporary Australian political and cultural life. The media 'speak' to Indigeneity. Currently, a dialogue about the constitutional, cultural, and political future of Australia is centred on Indigenous issues. Aboriginal and non-Aboriginal Australians 'speak' to each other via media coverage of Aboriginal affairs. It may even be said that the Australian public sphere as a whole is being 'Indigenized', not always consensually, and that that is our principal research 'finding', though of course we didn't 'find it out': it was there for all to see.

Throughout the 1990s a crescendo of debate followed landmark legal decisions of the High Court. 'Mabo' (1991) revised common law to recognize Indigenous land ownership prior to European colonization; the doctrine of *terra nullius* (empty land) was overturned. 'Wik' (1996) extended native land title to include not only vacant Crown land but also land held by pastoralists. Meanwhile, the Labor government under Paul Keating enacted the first Federal land rights legislation (1993). The incoming (conservative) Coalition government (1996) took legislative powers to limit or extinguish 'native title' claims in the name of development (providing security to mining and pastoral industries) and equality (not giving Aboriginal people property rights unavailable to all). Simultaneously, an anti-Aboriginal populist political party, One Nation, waxed (in the Queensland State election of 1995) and waned (in the Federal election of 1996). All of these developments centred on the place of Indigenous people in Australia, and on the constitution of Australia as a nation with 'first peoples' with whom treaties had never been concluded. During the same period, the condition of Indigenous people was highlighted in successive official reports that were critical of their treatment at the hands of the state, especially in the crucial areas of 'correction'—prisons, police custody, juvenile detention, the justice system; and 'protection'—welfare, health, and care programmes. The landmark documents in this context were the Report of the Royal Commission into Aboriginal Deaths in Custody (1991), and the 'stolen generations' Report of the National Inquiry into the Separation of Indigenous Children from Their Families (1997).

There is far too much going on in all this to reduce it to a simple formula—least of all that media coverage is 'racist' or 'biased'. There is a serious need to move beyond notions of 'ideological atrocity' (Ray,

1995: 7) committed by all-powerful media against vulnerable populations. Indigenous people themselves actively use the media for self-
representation and community-building, as well as pursuing a political
agenda in the media designed to combat prejudicial coverage, and using
the media to get their ideas across to their own and other people.

Media Stars

What would you call a small group of people, proportionally insignificant as a percentage of the population as a whole, who are subjected to
compulsive, unrepresentative, continuous media coverage across all
media forms from the national daily press to fishing and fashion magazines? What do you call people who, in stories about their banal, everyday lives, are taken to embody (often in the breach) the core values and
major difficulties facing their society? What do you call people whose
image is largely created by media; who serve as character and plot in the
ongoing public narration of the story of who 'we' are?

Normally, such people are called 'stars' and 'celebrities'. But this is
also the role performed by Indigenous people in Australia in the 1990s.
Anomalous their place in the media may be, but it is by no means clear
that Aboriginal and Islander people occupy the classic position of media
'victims'. Coverage in news and documentary especially, but increasingly
in fictional forms too, is quite disproportionate to their actual numbers.
The stories in which they figure are central to the core values of Australian society. It is therefore impossible to conclude that Indigenous
people are merely victimized by, or portrayed as victims in, the media
coverage they receive. Even so, that coverage may be far from pleasant or
comforting for them or the consumers of particular shows and stories.
That's not really the point (doubtless stars and celebrities likewise feel
the embrace of the media as a mixed blessing at best). The point is that,
like stars, Indigenous people occupy a *structural* place in media stories.
They are 'scripted' in advance by their role in a dramatic narrative over
which they have little individual control, but which is nevertheless telling
their story.

Media coverage of Indigenous issues raises questions about core
values and processes for the whole society, and the way Indigenous
issues are covered does not result from racism or from poor journalism,
but precisely from journalists and other media story-tellers doing their
job well. The 'mediasphere' operates to think through intractable problems for 'reading publics' characterized by internal difference. Hence the
coverage of what is by far the most intractable of such problems for

contemporary Australia sheds light on the system as a whole, allowing new insights into the place of media and of the knowledge professions more generally in the government of society and the development of public discourse about cultural directions.

In proportional terms, Aboriginal people are seriously over-represented, not under-represented, in the Australian media (Mickler, 1998), and they attract an equally disproportionate interest in international coverage too (Miller, 1995). The cause is not only the actual circumstances of Aboriginal life, whether understood as culturally exotic, constitutionally unresolved, or as fourth-world scandal, but also the way these are made to stand for major conflicts in the symbolic domain of national identity-building. In an international media arena where questions of identity, control, citizenship, and sovereignty are newly controversial, a study of how such abstract issues are worked through in the 'practical reasoning' of everyday media coverage can contribute to wider debates, from questions of ethnicity and gender to new, 'post-identity' politics based on interactive media and 'semiotic self-determination'.

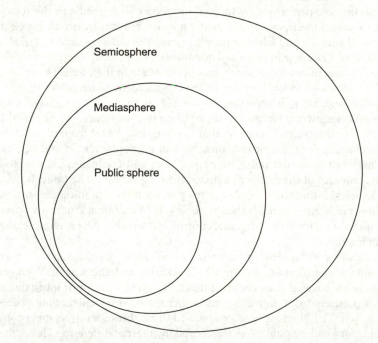

The 'Mediasphere'

The Indigenous Public Sphere

The book takes its inspiration from work on culture, text, and the 'semiosphere' by Yuri Lotman, and builds on a body of previous work by John Hartley that has attempted to rethink the place of popular media and journalism in modernity (Hartley 1992, 1996, 1999). In Part One, 'Research', we open the study with problems of knowledge, discussing issues of method and the place of 'Indigenous media studies' in relation to disciplines such as journalism education, media and cultural studies, anthropology, and history (Chapters 1 to 3). In a dialogue with other writing in the area, both scholarly and social, we elaborate our own positions, preferences, and biases. We show how the issues we have detailed in the Australian context are connected with developments in other countries, where race, class, and Indigeneity are important social and media issues. A two-way process of influence and borrowing has occurred. Australia has imported concepts of race and class from the USA and the UK, but has much to learn from Indigenous developments in Canada, Scandinavia, the Russian Federation, and Alaska. Equally, however, its experience has much to say to those far-flung and disparate environments. Meanwhile, a similar dialogue seems to have been inaugurated between the Aboriginal and 'Australian' components of the Australian semiosphere, and the working through of the terms of that dialogue in public discourses such as the news media and journalism of various kinds forms the basis of the rest of the book.

It is common for studies of media to address *production, text*, and *reception* as successive 'moments' in the construction, distribution, and consumption of meaning and knowledge. Although we do not maintain this tripartite structure, we do address issues of production and reception in addition to our main focus on textuality. In particular, in Part Two: 'Reception', we offer what we believe to be a serviceable innovation to the methods of 'reception' studies in general. Instead of relying on surveys, diaries, meters, interviews, focus groups, or ethnographic description for our 'audience research', we evolved a *parliamentary* method of gauging the reception of media by a particular community. We wanted to avoid the individuating tendencies of most audience research methods, and to elaborate instead a means of identifying and discussing the collective—in a word the *national*—mode of reception of media coverage of Indigenous people *by* Indigenous people.

This initiative took the form of a Media Forum called *Telling Both Stories: Indigenous Australia and the Media*, held biennially, in 1992, 1994,

1996, and 1998. The 1996 event was a national forum, designed with the project of this book in mind and organized in parallel with its research. What do Indigenous national and community leaders, ordinary Indigenous people, and Indigenous media producers, have to say on the coverage of Indigenous issues in the Australian media—and what are those issues? Chapters 4 to 6 report on some of the answers to those questions, in the words of the (mostly) Indigenous people who spoke at the 1996 National Media Forum. Chapter 4 is devoted to the contribution of those national leaders who may well have formed, had there been one, about half of the Cabinet of any national Indigenous government of that time. Chapter 5 is devoted to the voice of the community, in this case mostly a Western Australian voice (the Forum was held in Perth). And Chapter 7 combines producer perspectives (the speakers are all media producers) with 'reception' studies (they have much to say on the 'mediasphere' in general).

The book also relies on a large archive of media coverage, amassed as part of a project funded by the Australian Research Council. The archive includes an unusual range of media, encompassing not only the news and traditional print journalism, but also radio, television, and magazine journalism, and a sprinkling of fiction, collected from 1994 to 1997. In Part Three: 'Reporting', we report on some of the issues that arise from that archive in Chapters 7, 8, and 9. Finally, in Chapter 10 we survey existing policies and codes of practice relating to the coverage of Indigenous issues by Australian media, and the training of journalists.

Both the present research project and the parallel *Telling Both Stories* series of Media Forums, including the National Media Forum of 1996, were inspired directly by the recommendations of the Royal Commission into Aboriginal Deaths in Custody (1991). One of us had appeared before the Royal Commission as an 'expert witness' during its hearings into 'underlying issues' in Perth, chaired by WA Royal Commissioner Pat Dodson in 1990, before he went on to chair the Council for Aboriginal Reconciliation. The seed for the present research was planted during that hearing (Hartley, 1992: 197–217).

The aim of the Media Forum series, and of other work described in this book, has been to implement the media-related recommendations of the Royal Commission. While it is the responsibility of state and federal governments to implement the Royal Commission's main recommendations, it is impossible for any government agency to intervene in the conduct and content of journalistic practices such as newsgathering, editorial policies, comment and criticism, and so on. While Australia does not enjoy a 'First Amendment' constitutional guarantee of freedom of speech, it does practise a convention of keeping government and media at arm's length, especially in the area of content, news values, opinion, and the detail of how stories are told.

Nevertheless it is precisely in such areas of detail—of how stories are told, by whom, for what purpose, to what effect, and for whose benefit—that the main problems arise in the reporting of Indigenous issues in the mainstream Australian media. In order to implement the Royal Commission's media-related recommendations, then, it was necessary to go beyond the standard response of having a government department issue a statement, or set up a task force. It was necessary, and it still is, for media organizations, journalists, Indigenous people and their organizations, journalism educators, media researchers, funding agencies and regulators, all to get together to identify, work through, and where necessary reform some of the most fundamental assumptions and habits of industrial news-making. The National Media Forum was designed to assist this process.

The Royal Commission's recommendations on media issues are:

- **Recommendation 205.** That (a) Aboriginal media organisations should receive adequate funding where necessary in recognition of the importance of their function; (b) all media organisations should be encouraged to develop codes and policies relating to the presentation of Aboriginal issues, the establishment of monitoring bodies, and the putting into place of training and employment programs for Aboriginal employees in all classifications.

- **Recommendation 206.** That the media industry and media unions be requested to consider the establishment of and support for an annual award or awards for excellence in Aboriginal affairs reporting to be judged by a panel of media, union and Aboriginal representatives.

- **Recommendation 207.** That institutions providing journalism courses be requested to: (a) Ensure that courses contain a significant component relating to Aboriginal affairs, thereby reflecting the social context in which journalists work, and, (b) Consider, in consultation with the media industry and media unions, the creation of specific units of study dedicated to Aboriginal affairs and the reporting thereof.

- **Recommendation 208.** That in view of the fact that many Aboriginal people throughout Australia express disappointment in the portrayal of Aboriginal people by the media, the media industry and media unions should encourage formal and informal contact with Aboriginal organisations, including Aboriginal media organisations

> where available. The purpose of such contact should be the creation, on all sides, of a better understanding of issues relating to the media treatment of Aboriginal affairs. (Johnston, 1991)

The Royal Commission thus includes a general recommendation to promote better contacts between the media and Aboriginal people—a recommendation that we see as calling for the establishment of an Indigenous public sphere in the context of mediated political culture. It also makes specific suggestions about journalism training, monitored codes of practice, employment policies, the funding of Aboriginal media organizations, and the need for an award for journalistic excellence in the reporting of Aboriginal Affairs. The *Telling Both Stories* Media Forum series implemented all of the recommendations over a seven-year period after they were made. To our knowledge it was the only formal event ever to do this across the whole of Australia. A conference sponsored by the Aboriginal and Torres Strait Islander Commission on Indigenous issues and the media was held in Brisbane in 1993 (itself modelled on the first *Telling Both Stories* forum), but no other initiative has covered all of the recommendations, including the need for an award for excellence in the area. The Louis Johnson Media Awards were inaugurated at the 1994 Media Forum, thanks to Bill Johnson and the Louis Johnson Trust. In 1996, for the first time, these Awards, and the Media Forum as a whole, were extended to the national stage (Bunbury *et al.*, 1993, 1994; Hartley and McKee (eds.), 1996). The 1998 Forum specifically addressed the training component of the recommendations (McKee and Burns, 1999).

The present book is an attempt to give shape to the slower rhythms of some of those activities. Its main finding is that the over-representation of Indigeneity in the media is evidence neither of racist media nor of unequal 'privilege' for Aboriginal people compared to other demographic groups (Mickler, 1998), but a direct result of the *unresolved national status of Indigenous people.* Aboriginal and Islander people in Australia share this uncomfortable position with Indigenous people in many other countries, especially in North America, Scandinavia, and the Russian Federation. Their relationships with the state, with the dominant national group in that state, and with the media, are all at the cutting edge of evolving conceptualizations of citizenship and self in postmodern, mediated societies. To explore the 'universe of Indigneity' in the Australian 'mediasphere' is to observe directly how these important issues are being played out at the beginning of the twenty-first century.

Part One | **Research**

1 | Stubbie-Truth: Journalism, Media, Cultural Studies, and an Ethics of Reading

In a democracy everyone is a journalist. This is because, in a
democracy, everyone has the right to communicate a fact or a
point of view, however trivial, however hideous.

(Ian Hargreaves, 1999: 4)

Stubbie Dreaming?

It's hard to know where to start with a subject like this, so it might as well
be, Australian-style, with a beer. Two beers, in fact: two 'stubbies' of Emu
Bitter, brewed in Western Australia and purchased in the course of
research for this book. At the time, Emu Bitter were conducting an
on-going game of trivial pursuits for their consumers: each bottle had
a question and answer printed on the underside of the cap. Here's one:

Q. WHO WAS
THE FIRST MAN
TO EXPLORE THE
KIMBERLEYS?

Nothing here but a pleasant way to pass the time, and to learn some
interesting facts about the Great State of Western Australia, home of the
Swan Brewery and makers of Emu Bitter. The information was encountered in the everyday context of taking a beer out of the fridge; it was
routine, non-political, and the opposite of provocative, since no commercial organization (apart from talkback radio) would knowingly put
its customers offside in the very act of appealing to them. The question
betrayed an almost Reithian project of popular pedagogy; it was
educating the citizen-drinkers of WA by stealth, quenching thirst and

15

epistemophilia at once, combining the pleasure of sharing a beer with the comfort of sharing common knowledge. It was cementing the social with 'well-known facts'. It was, in microcosm, the public sphere. So what was the answer?

A. Alexander Forrest

Alexander Forrest was the brother of the first premier of Western Australia, and himself the first MLC (Member of the Legislative Council) for the Kimberley. He certainly explored there in the 1880s. But 'first man to explore the Kimberleys' he was not. He was not even the first *white* man to explore there, having been preceded by (Sir) George Grey, afterwards Governor of South Australia, New Zealand, and South Africa. But the honour of being first *human* (man or woman) to explore the Kimberleys obviously belongs to an Aboriginal person. 'We'—that is, common knowledge—don't know the name. So there's the rub. Two cultures fail to connect. A state history that knows individual names, rank, and dates fails to enter into dialogue with an Indigenous tradition of anonymous stories and songs, where 'first' might be tens of thousands of years ago but is (im)memorialized in 'dreamings' in which human ancestors fuse with supernatural beings and both with the natural features of the country. Stubbie-truth makes its own foundation myth for the modern state: Forrest was its 'first explorer' in the crucial category of land, country. But stubbie-truth 'forgets' the entire 'first people' in whose culture the 'firstness' of the ancestral dreaming might have meaning, and hence the force of law—law of the land (see Burnum, 1988: 196–8).

Opening a second stubbie; another question:

Q. Who was the first white man to walk across the Simpson Desert?

Obviously, someone over at the Swan Brewery, or at their promotions company's HQ, had cottoned on to the problems associated with 'firsts' in disputed country. So here was a 'white' foundation hero:

A. John Gibson, 1970

What was the difference between Forrest's 'first to explore' and Gibson's 'first to walk across'—and more to the point why should both have been more noteworthy than what another group of people have

5. Stubbie-truth. Common knowledge, or the literacy of the land-grab? *Source: Emu Bitter (beer caps), 1995.*

been doing more or less routinely for millennia? Among the law-forming foundational stories of the 'we' community addressed by the Emu Bitter stubbie-cap mode of discourse, 'explore' and 'walk across' seemed to imply rather different modes of travel; different kinds of 'first'. Forrest's was the 'opening-up of the land', colonizing type. Explorers tended to plant the flag, find the natural resources, tap the wealth, and subject the native people. Naming was part of this, so Forrest named the Kimberley after John Wodehouse, Earl of same, imperial Secretary for the Colonies at the time. And the Forrest River—location of massacres of Aboriginal people in 1926—was named after Alexander Forrest himself. But, as Burnum Burnum comments, since then 'the dreamtime names have long given way to names commemorating the invaders, their homelands, and sometimes their wives or girlfriends' (Burnum, 1988: 180). So much have they 'given way' that while Burnum gives the name 'Onmalmeri massacre' to the 1926 atrocities, as does Anna Haebich (Haebich, 1988: 267–8, 280), Klaus Neumann, writing in the *UTS Review*, uses the name Oombulgurri, referring to the same events at the Forrest River Mission, but does not use the name Onmalmeri at all (Neumann, 1998: 3 ff.).

John Gibson's exploit was different from Forrest's: 'walking across' the desert was personal, not imperial. The feat was noteworthy, but *his* fortitude is celebrated, not that of the state; it was a sporting feat of endurance, an individual achievement in a natural environment that is valued for its extreme properties, but not for its potential *as* property.

However, despite the difference in the *journeys*, something else made them equal as *common knowledge*. Everyone with the wit to read a bottle top is meant to understand why such different journeys shared the same significance: these foundation-feats were—and we quote—'*white*'. Alexander Forrest's 'whiteness' may differ from John Gibson's in just the way that an Established Church differed from an individual believer in a dissenting sect: Forrest was to Gibson as the Archbishop of York was to John Bunyan. Forrest's whiteness represented what may be seen as a racial equivalent of state religion; it bespoke an 'Established Race' on the model of the Established Church. His whiteness belonged to the state. Gibson, however, walked across the desert in a secular, individual 'pilgrim's progress'; inspiring to the onlooker perhaps, but not coercive or even representative. His whiteness belonged to himself, almost as an obstacle of the sort that Bunyan's Pilgrim had to overcome in order to complete his journey to 'grace abounding'.

Interesting, then, that stubbie-truth can accommodate such differences within whiteness, but not extend 'common-knowledge' to include Indigeneity as common to Australians. It appears that the Aboriginal relationship with the Kimberleys is not readily brought to mind as a 'well-known fact' of the bottle-top kind. Nevertheless such facts are well enough known. Was there ever a real, historical, militarily successful character, like Forrest, who was, like Gibson, simultaneously fleet of foot, resourceful, and successful in his land-crossing adventures? Well, how about this (see Burnum, 1988: 192):

Q. WHO LED ARMED
RESISTANCE TO THE
WHITE COLONISATION
OF THE KIMBERLEY?

Needless to say, Emu Bitter did not trouble its customers with this bit of trivia, the answer to which may still not be 'common knowledge':

A. 'PIGEON'
JUNDUMURRA

Tellingly, better known in the Australian mediasphere of the 1990s than Jundumurra (although rumour had it, via *The Age* web page, that Mel Gibson was producing a film on him), was the relationship between Aboriginality and alcohol. Marcia Langton writes: 'Of all the different constructs of "the Aborigine", or ways of imagining the native in Australia, the most vocal is the "drunken Aborigine"' (Langton, 1993*b*: 195). She points out that 'the rate of alcohol misuse in the Aboriginal community is actually less than in the general population' (196), but the facts are not the point. She concludes: 'the notion of the "drunken Aborigine" is *a myth of origin*. The virile white man needs a can or two after a long hard day. The black man, however, cannot hold his alcohol' (199, our emphasis). Here's another history-in-beer, of a kind quite unsuited to stubbie-cap memorialization. So the question of who might open a stubbie of Emu Bitter, and what they might think of what they find inside, is not a matter of racial indifference.

For those who know Western Australia, mention of the Swan Brewery during this period raises another spectre. A long-running dispute, over the future of the old Swan Brewery site on the banks of the Swan River in Perth, was waged between the developers, Multiplex, and members of the Swan Valley Fringe-dwellers' community led by Robert Bropho, Clarrie Isaacs, and their supporters. Should the site be recognized as an Aboriginal sacred site, home of the Waugal, the Rainbow Serpent, and thus be left undeveloped for Indigenous people to enjoy under its original name of Goonininup—as perhaps the only site in the Perth metropolitan area publicly dedicated to Aboriginal people's heritage? (see Mickler, 1991). Or should the former brewery be redeveloped as a leisure complex of bars and restaurants, serving Emu Bitter to those for whom Aboriginal culture is distant, forgotten, or unknown? The conclusion was by no means foregone; it took six years of political, legal, and direct action before an alliance of developers, the State government, and local radio talkback opinion-leaders won the day. The dispute was still unresolved when the Emu Bitter stubbies under discussion were released.

Is drinking an Emu Bitter an innocent pleasure, or a species of racist exclusionism? Is reading a stubbie-cap a trivial pursuit, or the literacy of the land-grab?

Reading Media: A Trivial Pursuit?

To begin any study, especially one on journalism and related media, with a 'reading' of a beer-cap, may seem unduly provocative. We do it however with a modest aim—to perform a technique of analysis we would like to defend, i.e. 'textual analysis', and to illustrate some fundamental issues. We seek to show that textual analysis is not abstract, decontextualized, or apolitical, but on the contrary is a form of historiography. It is a 'method' of demonstrating just how meanings are embedded in history, in a sense of who 'we' are, and in a network of other texts, contexts, meanings, and dialogue without which they cannot be explained. Indeed, we have chosen these impoverished scripts to show just how rich textuality is, but at the same time how analysis of it has to be anchored in actual 'documentary' objects that can be recovered for observation. We argue that textual analysis is among the most empirical, 'objective', and real-oriented 'methods' available, not only to today's students of media studies, but also to journalists since Johnson (see Hartley, 1992: 159–63) and to historians since the Whigs (see Osborne, 1998: 167).

Turning to the issues: first, it is in the context of everyday life, of routine pleasures and personal consumption, of corporate entertainment strategies and the privatized maintenance of common knowledge, that some of the most important political problems of the day are being thought through and fought out. This context is not immediately identifiable as political or controversial within the familiar terms of the journalistic public sphere, but is every bit as important as the formal institutional terrain of education and government. It is the domain of common-knowledge production and community law-formation, and so forms the context within which journalism now finds itself, as a contributor to the micro-meaningfulness of everyday life.

Of course the ephemera of consumer culture are not important in any pivotal way: it isn't *this* stubbie that 'causes' any given outcome, political or racial, any more than a single headline, story, or even a single outlet does. And as 'ideological atrocities' go, stubbie-racism is pretty minor—it doesn't bring tears of embarrassment, outrage, or despair into anyone's eyes, whatever their own ethnicity or politics. No one is going to picket the Swan Brewery over a stubbie-cap. Simply, it is an example of the pervasiveness of text about 'whiteness' in a country whose public rhetoric is non- or anti-racist.

The response to these stubbie-caps should, therefore, not be an adversarial politics directed towards the banning or revision of texts deemed to be offensive. Rather it should be to recognize a 'common' need for a form of comportment, *an ethics of reading* (see Osborne, 1998: 26) in relation to the inevitable encounters everyone will constantly have with the textuality of race, of indigeneity and of whiteness, in Australia and elsewhere. We are not arguing that there's a direct connection between this or any text and *behaviour*; it is not our contention that such texts are either caused by racism or causal of it. We maintain, however, that *readership* is an important part of individual and community life, and that even casual, consumerist entertainment is nevertheless textually significant both for individuals and communities. It is the very place where the public/private interface occurs, and where the 'common'—the 'we'—of 'common knowledge' is made so.

Second, readers and audiences make much less rigid distinctions between different media, and different genres or formats, than do researchers. People are themselves multi-generic: they are simultaneously readers, audiences, publics, and consumers, and as persons they are variously marked and active in relation to ethnicity, gender, and so on. They don't turn from freedom-loving, fact-seeking members of *the public* when reading or watching the news into fantasy-loving, thrill-seeking *consumers* when they become the audience for commercial entertainment. News is itself a form of commercial entertainment, and people take their news where they find it, which in any case is less and less on the front page of newspapers. Historically, daily newspapers are losing readers to other forms of media consumption, especially television and new media; and news as such is becoming more porous to other generic forms of entertainment as it competes with them for the attention of a decreasingly respectful audience (Franklin, 1997: 66, 104–5).

Demographically, some groups, especially young people, women, ethnic minorities, and Indigenous people, are abandoning news altogether, along with other more active forms of participation with the public sphere, such as voting. For people disaffected with moribund public-participation formats, information comes from other media, including TV, advertising, magazines, fiction, and music. To understand journalism it is important not to confine analysis to news media, but to include other factual and even some fictional forms. A social picture is built up across the whole 'mediasphere', which includes even stubbie-caps.

Third, these little beer bottles raise the issue of who 'we' might be. 'We' can refer to the imagined community of the culture as a whole (and thus to an implied 'they' of outsiders); it can refer to 'scholarly knowledge'; and it can refer to an authorial or personal 'we'. But during the act of reading it is impossible to separate 'we' as persons, 'we' as knowing subjects, and 'we' as community. And in 'communal' issues such as race, everyone is a 'we'— there's no neutral, scholarly space from which to observe. All types of 'we' have a stake in the making and public circulation of such meanings, and the meanings that circulate are frequently indifferent to boundaries between media forms. So 'the public' is first and foremost a reading public, and it is as a reading public that 'we' encounter, contribute to, and decide issues that cross between our personal, professional, and communal belongings. 'We' turn out to be a figure of the imagination (an 'imagined community' in Perry Anderson's famous phrase), created and circulated in innumerable stories, images, and texts. The degree to which communities, scholarship, or authors identify Indigenous people as part of a 'we' group or as a 'they' group is established in the textual minutiae of ordinary life.

Fourth, the interface between public and private is fluid. Whether we're in the public domain or the public bar, whether we're addressed by publisher or publican, 'public' meanings are circulated via 'private' activities. 'The public' is an idealization of what is assumed or hoped

21

to occur when perfect strangers join with each other via the act of reading. This in turn means that 'the public' is an unstable as well as a 'virtual' community: it is called into being by media which may be local, national, or international; it depends on taste boundaries as much as territorial ones; it can be indifferent to gender, race, family, region, age, and other demographic variables among its members or it can insist on them; and every single person is both part and not part of different publics at the same time, and from time to time.

'The public' is not, in this view, an aggregate of previously existing and fully formed individuals expressing some sort of relation with a state, but is a 'textual position' that can be 'peopled'—sometimes by a 'weak (gravitational) force' that sustains the taken-for-grantedness of 'our' membership of it; sometimes by a 'strong (magnetic) force' that can call real people out into the streets *as* the public. Different streets, different publics: any assembly *can* represent 'public opinion', but whether it does or not is contingent upon further textual 'struggles' between advocates for contending positions, and upon further acts of reading by people acting as, and speaking on behalf of, the public. Did the 1992 'Rally for Justice' in Perth represent the will of the people of Western Australia? Or did it represent rabble-rousing by unrepresentative talkback hosts and populist politicians? That question turns on the status of 'the public', and in this case (as always) it had serious political implications. But fundamentally it's a question of the relationship between texts and readers, addressees and addressers; of the *mediation* of public life.

It is necessary for there to be 'mediation' (dialogue) between citizens and various specialized groups in the community—from government and specialist experts to victims and advocates—for anything like a 'community' to exist, never mind to govern itself. The media perform this mediation, and they teach the 'critical literacy' through which readers can act as citizens. That's why they're important. But 'the media' must be understood to include more than the opinion columns of the broadsheet press; mediation extends even to brewers playing games with their customers. Having a couple of beers obviously doesn't amount to much in this world; it has about the same significance (and effect) as the proverbial hill of beans. But it is in this unworthy context that really weighty issues are invoked, if not decided: common knowledge is made common; communities are imagined for their own members (and outsiders are verbally excluded or fenced out); popular pedagogy is performed, political participation is provoked, publics are peopled.

This being so, in a sense it doesn't matter where one starts, but to start with a beer, and to ask what is at stake in reading it, is to begin with the question of the reader, the perspective of the audience, the form of common knowledge.

Perhaps now it's time to return to the more familiar location of academic discussion—the question of the producer, the perspective of the intellectual, the form of academic knowledge. Naturally, instead of a beer, here we find a 'war'.

Make Tea, Not War

Quite a vivid debate occurred during the late 1990s in Australia about the condition of journalism education—who should do it and, in particular, what media and cultural studies might have to do with it. One moment in the debate, to which an early version of this chapter was a contribution, was a seminar called 'Media Wars', organized by the Key Centre for Cultural and Media Policy in Brisbane (see *Media International Australia*, 90, February 1999). At first sight, this 'war' (between journalism education and cultural/media studies) looked more like 'no contest'. Journalism education is a specific activity for a specific purpose. Common sense dictates that journalism education ought to be done by journalism educators, possibly even by journalists (i.e. not by professional 'educators' at all). Not only is there a question about the practical utility of academic theories in the training of practitioners, there is also a widespread sense of exasperation among journalists that academic interest in their subject is dictated not by love but by contempt:

Communication theorists are not obsessed with journalism. They do not love it. Many of them despise it. They read, for preference, the newspapers designed for the affluent and educated. They believe that most television is for morons. Their attitude to the popular press is reminiscent of Lord Salisbury's celebrated gibe at the *Daily Mail*: 'produced by office boys for office boys.'... Their reaction to the popular press is to complain that it does not meet academic standards. Mass communication theorists do not seek to explain the success of Kelvin McKenzie [of the *Sun* newspaper in Britain] (or even Rupert Murdoch), a task which they find beneath their dignity. At heart they believe the mainstream press is a social problem...Mass communication theory...is a science which has become a scholasticism...This is mainly because the researchers really do not like their subject. (Hamlett, 1999: 68–9).

Tim Hamlett really does have a point; his frustration with a mode of enquiry that produces neither patentable discoveries about the object of study (like science), nor a language of appreciation for a loved textual form (like literary or film studies), is understandable. However, his practical response to the problem he identifies is not to challenge 'mass communication theorists' directly, but to tar them all with the same brush and retreat to the more congenial company of his peers. His conclusion, presented to an annual conference of a Journalism Education Association, is that 'A journalism theory could be useful. But it must come from within journalism' (70).

Unfortunately this commonsensical solution to the problem won't work. First, it won't make theory or theorists go away; it would be better to debate these important issues with those who are criticized, with a view to developing best practice out of the insights both sides may have to offer. Second, not all communication theorists (among whom the present authors presumably number) are disdainful of popular media (and they have publications going back to the 1970s to prove it). Indeed, they have consistently criticized academic prejudices and preferences in this very area. Alliances are necessary to reform not only journalism (where necessary), but the academy too (where necessary). And third, while it seems to be a truism that 'journalism theory' must come from 'within journalism' as Hamlett recommends, there is a serious danger at the heart of such a formula. We concur with Ian Hargreaves (professor of Journalism at Cardiff University, former Editor of the *New Statesman* and the *Independent*, deputy editor of the *Financial Times* and Director of News and Current Affairs at the BBC), whose view is that 'in a democracy everyone is a journalist. This is because, in a democracy, everyone has the right to communicate a fact or a point of view, however trivial, however hideous' (Hargreaves, 1999: 4). In other words, there is no 'inside' to journalism that can or should be protected from anyone, least of all harmless (if useless) theorists. There's no such place as 'within journalism'. Hargreaves cites J. S. Mill's defence of diversity of opinion: 'he who knows only his own side of the case knows little of that'. A theory of journalism ought not to be judged by the qualifications or occupation of its author. It ought to be judged by whether it is a good theory. And if it is, journalists of all people ought to give it house room.

Unfortunately, so suspicious are journalists of theory that they won't even give house room to their own. 'Common sense' and newspaper editors don't always coincide, in Britain at least. A recent survey showed that 'uncertainties about what constitutes appropriate training for journalists' resulted in low uptake even for the industry's own scheme: only 40 per cent of journalists held the National Council for the Training of Journalists qualification and a third received no in-house training at all.

Less than 2 per cent of editors believed that an understanding of journalism history was essential, but half thought shorthand was. Bob Franklin comments:

It is undoubtedly a telling indictment of the pedestrian and uncritical grind which much of the new journalism has become, that editors listed the ability to rewrite handouts as the most essential competence required of trainees after six months. (Franklin, 1997: 64).

Unsurprisingly, therefore, Franklin finds that editors systematically undervalue journalism education at universities:

Many editors seem hostile to the middle-class graduates entering journalism, preferring the 'streetwise council-estate youngsters': 'working class recruits with local knowledge'. Some editors still display the anti-intellectualism noted by an early study of journalism published in 1923. . . . A major complaint of trainees is that editors do not seem to attach too great a significance to any form of training. Journalists are born, not made. (Franklin, 1997: 65).

Small wonder that journalism educators feel embattled: their vocational, 'craft-skill' orientation sits uneasily within universities, while their academic orientation sits uneasily with employers, even in America, where J-schools have been established for a century (see Fedler *et al.*, 1998: 32). Fedler and his colleagues recommend 'eight strategies that journalism and mass communication programs can adopt to improve their status in academia'. Listed in their approximate order of importance, the strategies include:

(a) making themselves more central to the mission of their institution;
(b) serving larger numbers of students;
(c) recruiting more talented students;
(d) doing more to help the students find jobs;
(e) improving their record of scholarly activity;
(f) developing unique programmes, ones not duplicated elsewhere in their state;
(g) emphasizing intellectual rather than vocational training; and
(h) seeking accreditation. (Fedler *et al.* 1998: 39).

Media studies, for 'its' part, isn't even an 'it'. It's a portmanteau term for an eclectic array of different types of study, from different disciplinary perspectives, into different media. It grew out of the expansion and democratization of higher education, not out of a professional body or specialist industrial process. Its hybridity and interdisciplinarity is such that no single person can act as 'its' champion.

One response to the fact that media studies is just a convenient collective term has been to try to identify some unifying theory that might be said to organize such a disparate field. A culprit has evidently been found, in the shape of 'cultural studies'. Cultural studies has become a focus of debate in Higher Education. After the 'doorstopper'-phase of giant anthologies, it has recently attracted much more critical attention, even from its own practitioners, who perform self-reflexive critique with Daliesque auto-cannibalistic relish (see *Cultural Studies*, 1998; *Continuum*, 1998; Bennett, 1998). Critiques also abound from writers associated with social theory and public policy; so much so that one definition of cultural studies might be: 'that tendency in contemporary interdisciplinary academic work in the humanities and social sciences of which I (on behalf of my faction) *disapprove*.' Cultural studies is being 'named and shamed'; it is this season's fair game. And perhaps that's fair enough: at the 'Media Wars' event journalism professor Clem Lloyd characterized it as having a 'critique or "attack" approach'. If so, then of course it should expect the favour to be returned.

Certainly in the context of news, it has been a habit in cultural studies since the 1970s to criticize the media, not to assist them. But such analysis was done to reveal journalism's signifying strategies to its readers and audiences, not to benefit the industry's entrepreneurs, executives, or editors. Ever since the early days of the Birmingham Centre for Contemporary Cultural Studies (CCCS), the purpose of cultural studies has been *intellectual* not *instrumental*. If it 'attacked' news media this was not its primary purpose. In a perverse way, the original 'Birmingham' approach might be seen as a defence of the importance of journalism, because their aim was to understand how political communication actually works. They did the media the honour of taking their specific, discursive, contribution to political activity seriously, perhaps for the first time in the British academic context, by trying to show exactly how the *social* power claimed for the media was actualized *textually*.

The CCCS analysis was not confined to what journalists do, though it focused on the media's specific role in the 'production' of meaning. It was actually much more ambitious, seeking to describe the general process of sense-making in contemporary mediated societies, and to relate that to the political process and the operations of other forms of power based on class, economic interests, and the like. The classic form of cultural studies did not 'attack' journalism or media, rather it sought to intervene in the 'symbolic work' of *critical reading*, training its followers as intellectuals, and discovering how important the media have become in the general circulation of powerful ideas in contemporary societies. If they were 'attacking' anything, it was not journalists but 'power'. They discovered that in order to do *intellectual* work in the context of social and political *power*, it was necessary to think seriously about *media*.

This anti-instrumental intellectualism has remained a feature of cultural studies ever since. Perhaps this is not only a reason why it attracts criticism from all sides, but is also one of its attractions for those who do it. As James Donald has put it:

I am not going to start telling media executives how to plot their coups, nor politicians how to frame their laws. Why on earth should they take any notice if I did? They pay people a lot more than I get paid to do that for them. My job, it unfashionably seems to me, is not to do their thinking for them, but to think about the ways in which media regulation is thought about. (Donald, 1998: 217–18; see also Morrison, 1998: 253–73).

However, Donald adds wryly, 'there's not much money in thinking about thinking.'

Glorying in its own disutility, it seems, cultural studies has become the location of currently quite intense dialogue about the status and purpose of intellectual life and work as such. As the *New Statesman*'s associate editor John Lloyd put it in a column headlined 'Are intellectuals useless?':

The relationship between power and mind is fraught . . . Precisely because politicians are in thrall to focus groups and PR advice, they must have others think through issues which are more complex and time consuming. Whether or not intellectuals of the left [he has been discussing Stuart Hall, among others] are capable of this is another matter. Michael Ignatieff, one himself, wrote . . . that 'intellectuals have lost their monopoly of knowledge—which is a good thing; but they have also lost their independence, which is damaging to their moral authority'. (Lloyd, 1998: 12).

Indeed, intellectuals and journalists are now in direct competition for the ear of the powerful and of the public. And cultural studies has been a prime site where debate was conducted about the independence and authority (moral or otherwise) of academic writers skilled in 'complex and time-consuming' theorizations of the everyday world. A struggle has been taking place over who gets to represent 'knowledge' in public. Journalists, commercial researchers, academics, and independent intellectuals are all stakeholders in this field; they may even amount to a new internally competitive 'knowledge class'. Cultural studies has figured as one centre of the ensuing politics of knowledge in recent years; it is the chosen ground upon which different factions vie for the power of the idea.

The fit between cultural studies and media studies is not exact. To see how these 'kissing cousins' are in fact diverging as they mature, simply compare the best of the 'doorstopper' cultural studies anthologies (During, 1999) with the best of the media studies anthologies (Marris and Thornham, 1999). Institutionally you can find cultural studies in contexts where media studies is absent (e.g. some literature and postcolonial studies departments), and vice versa (e.g. in some technology, art, and industry contexts).

It is not insignificant that media studies began in large, non-vocational degree programmes at new, non-metropolitan universities. It was attractive to *students*. It has maintained its appeal despite the derogatory attention it periodically receives on the front page of the *Daily Express*, or acid editorializing from media professionals such as John Humphrys (presenter of the *Today* show on BBC Radio 4 in the UK). But still, as part of a more widespread attempt to move syllabuses from critique to utility, from theory to practice, from the world of ideas to the world of work, many media studies schemes have introduced or been merged with journalism education, and media studies has continued to grow.

Perhaps the material differences between journalism education and media studies are based on the fact that the former has focused almost exclusively in training media-*producers*, while the latter has invested most in educating media-*consumers*. Cultural studies, meanwhile, has become an *intellectual* or theoretical lingua franca, by means of which those who teach media and those who train journalists have begun to talk to (and to misunderstand) each other. An emerging picture suggests that 'cultural studies' is a *discourse of academics*, 'media studies' a *discourse of students*, and 'journalism' a *discourse of employers*. In some places these three figures—the intellectual, the teacher, and the trainer— are sharing the same tea-room kettle for the first time. Making tea together is a metaphor not for conspiracy, but free speech:

If there is a coven in the tea room bubbling up an urn-full of spells to trouble the world's moral order, they certainly haven't invited me to join them for a herbal Darjeeling. What I have noticed going on about the place is a debate about what kinds of protocols of speech might enable free speech to express a wider range of views on a wider range of topics than is currently the case in Australian public life. That project brought together people whose roots were in feminism, multiculturalism, Aboriginal cultural activism and much else besides. It was a vast and amorphous movement, part of which one can identify as Australian cultural studies. (Wark, 1997: 168)

Perhaps journalists and journalism educators have reacted to cultural studies so badly because it looks an unworthy and improbable David to their Goliath. It has been greeted not as a competitive 'warrior', so much as a virus, an infestation, unpleasant in its own appearance and habits and dangerous to the persons, haunts, and prospects of the journalistic community. But in fact, cultural studies and journalism are definite if unlikely bed-*fellows*, even if one of them appears to the other as more of a bed-*bug* (see Wark, 1997: 111, 179–85).

In terms of overall perspective, the cultural studies analyst is indeed like the journalist: both occupy professional positions that enable them to investigate and draw conclusions about *other people's lives*. They are both licensed to rove across the whole range of the social. One of journalism's key functions is to *generalize*; to explain to the general public the activities of industry, politics, the law, the economy, medicine; and in the leisure sphere, of the entertainment, sporting, and celebrity industries. Journalists 'translate' specialized knowledge into common knowledge; their credibility is largely based on their contacts, their access to people, places, and events of which their readers have no direct experience, and on their ability to produce convincing accounts of what they find there for non-specialists.

For its part, cultural studies has shown a systematic propensity to do the same. It has a history of 'generalizing' about different fields of social experience (from Hoggartian description of working-class life to audience ethnographies) and of trying to account for different forms of professional expertise, such as that of journalism itself. But cultural studies has also taken an even more 'generalizing' tendency upon itself, assuming a mantle last worn by philosophy: not content to survey its own patch with its own expertise, it roams across everybody else's fields of knowledge-production too, from science to sociology. In the words of Rita Felski, cultural studies is characterized by 'politically informed eclectic scholarship that includes both specific, empirical studies and broader, more speculative approaches'. Its *appeal*, she concludes, is 'the contradictory amalgam of concerns, the simultaneous and sometimes contradictory emphasis on both the particular and the universal' (Felski, 1998: 169). Furthermore, methodologically, it can even be argued that journalism and cultural studies use essentially the same means to explore the terrain. They both *textualize* an object of investigation in which they are not themselves expert, relying largely on documents, reports, interviews, and interpretations, which they then *communicate* to readers who are not directly involved.

The Service Industry of Truth

Cultural studies has been more interested in the cultural and textual form of 'news' than in the professional and industrial institution of 'journalism'. However, some attention has been paid to the historical significance of journalism as a whole. Here again, it is surprising perhaps how much overlap there is between the two fields. Journalism was founded as a modern project—it cannot be explained without reference to modernity, including the growth of democratic politics, popular sovereignty, mass citizenship, market economies, corporate and consumer culture. For most of its 200– to 400–year history, journalism has been a partisan in these developments, not just in the sense of being for or against a specific modernizing party or idea, but a partisan for modernity as such. It has been committed to the principles of the Enlightenment, preferring observation over authority, reason over obedience, the eyewitness over the catechism, and campaigning actively for science, technology, truth, and progress as commanding powers. Journalism represents (maybe *is*) the turn away from divine and royal 'warrants' for legitimacy towards rational and popular ones: it is part of the apparatus for 'governing in the name of truth', in Thomas Osborne's phrase (Osborne, 1998: 29–32).

If the Enlightenment was one parent of modernity, then journalism was certainly the other. James Donald says the idea that political modernity at least is a child of journalism can be traced back to Immanuel Kant. In answer to his own question 'Is the human race continually improving?' Kant 'looks around him for a sign that this might be the case' and, reports Donald:

the sign of progress is to be found in the feeling of *enthusiasm* provoked by the [French] Revolution. The important thing is the way that people 'in states and national groups' respond to the *drama* of the Revolution, the way it is generally perceived and judged by *spectators* who do not take part in it but observe it from a distance. (Donald, 1998: 218).

Donald concludes:

What is needed to make this new dynamic of modernity work? The answer, of course, is new forms of disseminating information; the medium of the press, which both represents the event and provides the forum for the articulation of public opinion. (Donald, 1998: 219).

This is also the argument of Hartley's *Popular Reality* (1996; and see Hartley, 1992: ch. 5). Political modernity is founded on popular sovereignty, a peculiar form of legitimacy because it belongs to people who are *sovereign but absent* from the everyday practice of exercising power in their name. Hence, in order to work, popular sovereignty requires a communication system able to represent their own sovereignty *to* the people (Kant's enthusiasm, drama, spectacle), and equally to represent *back* to their legislative and executive representatives the sovereign will of the people (public opinion).

Journalism is thus the textual system, the sense-making practice, of modernity (Hartley, 1996: 32–4). *Popular Reality* is not an 'attack' on or 'critique' of journalism, but an account of why it *matters* historically, written from the perspective of journalism's addressee by someone who would in a field like film studies be easily legible as a 'fan' of the form. More could hardly have been claimed for it. The argument was that modernity and journalism are so mutually dependent that each is inconceivable without the other. Journalism is a modernizing discourse, dedicated to the pursuit of the twin energies of modernity, which *Popular Reality* names as 'freedom' and 'comfort', but which can equally well be called 'democratic politics' and 'commercial-capitalist culture'.

However, it has been noticed by many critics that modernity is, to coin a phrase, an incomplete project. It never was quite as rational as its own rhetoric and aspirations made out. It always had another aspect, whether this is understood as irrational (Arendt), pseudo (Adorno), or feminine (Felski). Popular sovereignty was delayed, denied, begrudged, and hedged; reason was dogged by grotesque shadows—gothic, fascist, bureaucratic; comfort was unevenly distributed; universal brotherhood was ditched on the grounds of sexism and racism. Truth got a battering too, and reality was relativized. All this was happening in the modern period, but seemed anti-modern, or, latterly, post-modern.

Perhaps because of its investment in *modernist* 'technologies of truth', journalism has had a hard time dealing with the intellectual developments that underlie the critique of enlightenment. The 'postmodernist' questioning of what Toby Miller calls 'reason's dangers as well as its value' (Miller, 1998: 34) poses a challenge to journalism's historic place as the service-industry of truth, the communicator of reason, the popularizer of modernity.

Where cultural studies differs from Enlightenment philosophy and journalistic partisanship alike is that it is no longer confident about the emancipatory power of reason, or the educative possibilities of knowledge in an information age. It is much more reflexive about the grounds on which even its own truth-claims can be made. Not that it is alone in this doubt and scepticism: as Felski observes, even science has 'largely uncoupled itself from any foundational narrative of human progress', being 'no longer governed by the quest for Truth but by an unstable and often chaotic pragmatics of reception and use' (Felski, 1998: 160). In such a context, the status of journalism simply cannot survive unscathed, nor has it. Just as science, reason, and truth have attracted sustained criticism, and have had to take account of their own 'supplementary' anti-matter, so must journalism.

The necessary rethinking of the nature and function of journalism includes a need to move beyond pejorative comparisons between 'modern' and 'postmodern' forms; between the 'serious' and the 'sensational', investigative 'newspapers of record' and entertainment tabloids. Journalism may be modern but it has always also been a prime site for postmodernization. You can see it in the rise of tabloid papers, trash TV, supermarket weeklies, lad-mags, and lifestyle journalism from sex to gardening; in various stylistic innovations from the New Journalism to the *National Enquirer* and *Who Weekly* (with its marketing slogan of 'truth, integrity and a little gossip'); and in technical and economic developments associated with internationalization, inter-activity, and digitalization. However, while journalism has been 'postmodern' from the start, its own professional ideology has claimed the high moral ground against such forms.

Counter-intuitively perhaps, we would argue that 'popular' or 'postmodern' journalism has been present throughout modernity, and that from the days of the pauper press it has been doing the job for which journalism as a whole was first invented. It has done that job for people, groups, causes, and lifestyles that were—and are—ignored by the respectable modernist press (see Giddens, 1998: 46–53; McKay, 1998; Hartley, 1996: 72). Mainstream journalism has a history of neglecting new social movements. Evidence for this comes not from critical outsiders but, in this instance, from journalism-educators Laura Ashley and Beth Olson. They analysed the *New York Times*, *Time*, and *Newsweek* for coverage of the women's movement over two momentous decades, the 1960s to the 1980s:

Results show the women's movement was marginalized by the press. The coverage ... was sparse. The most astounding result of the research is the low number of articles it yielded. The women's movement was rarely covered, and when it was, it was treated with humor and puzzlement.... there is an obvious difference in the way the two groups were portrayed. In particular, the press delegitimized the feminists and legitimized the anti-feminists. (Ashley and Olson, 1998: 272).

Indeed, we would argue that the political domain itself has shifted beyond party and parliamentary politics, from the *discourse of power* (conflict, government and administration) and the decision-maker, towards the *discourse of identity* (privatized, feminized, suburbanized, juvenated, sexualized, and domestic) and the celebrity. Certainly, the two domains are now thoroughly merged (as witness the Monica Lewinsky and Princess Diana stories). Most of the important new social movements of the late twentieth century base their politics on culture and identity, not territory and power: feminism, environmentalism, the peace movement, youth, sexual, ethnic, and 'lifestyle' politics. None of these was initiated, nurtured, or popularized within the traditional public sphere, nor by the 'serious' news media. While they certainly attracted their own journalism, new social movements have also had to endure decades of scepticism, neglect, and travesty by mainstream newsmedia which could not 'place' them in the tradition of rationalist, universalist, progress-seeking, governmental modernity. The democratization of modern life, going hand in hand with its postmodernization, has begun to ripple through to parts of the social pond where it seems modernist journalism is ill-equipped to follow.

Journalism seems to remain most militantly (or nostalgically) modern in its professional ideology and pedagogy. Journalism education tends to promote the rational, public, civic, and informative aspects of journalism over the emotional, consumerist, private, and entertaining aspects. Journalists themselves don't always like the shift in their output from news to entertainment. Nor do they like their conversion into post-unionized workers who are more 'clerks' than 'crusaders', in Franklin's words, even as they hang on to that 'whiff of idealism and romanticism' that causes them still to see journalism as 'a central mechanism of accountability in a modern democracy' (Franklin, 1997: 66). If anyone has taken serious notice of the democratizing potential of postmodern forms of journalism, it seems to be those pests from cultural studies rather than journalism educators themselves. The latter are too busy holding the line between modernism (truth and power), and postmodernism (fantasy and identity).

But the 'high' modern system is itself peculiarly susceptible to fiction, as Benedict Anderson has famously argued: 'fiction seeps quietly and continuously into reality, creating that remarkable confidence of community in anonymity which is the hallmark of modern nations' (Anderson, 1991: 35–6). Modernity, in the end, is really like journalism—*a good story well told* (see Allen, 1998: 63). On this score it has to be admitted that cultural studies has been much more sensitive to such seepage than have political and social scientists on the one hand, or modernist journalists on the other. Even its critics admit that cultural studies is good at observing the seepage of fiction into reality; it is reputed by many to be an instance of it. But is this apparent disaster actually evidence that cultural studies is trying to pick up where journalism in the high modernist mould has faltered?

Cultural studies has adopted a 'social mission' that used to be understood as journalism's own, derived from the philosophy of the Enlightenment. In Felski's words, philosophy used to be the place where one might look for commitment to 'political emancipation through reason, and the cultivation of the human spirit through reflection and education' (Felski, 1998: 159–60). In one version of its historic function, this was and remains the 'social mission' of journalism too. While cultural studies has emerged as one of the most 'postmodern' of the new academic disciplines, for journalism a problem remains, despite the evident fact that a great deal of contemporary journalistic practice is not 'governed by the quest for Truth' either. Any 'uncoupling' of journalism from notions of science, progress, and truth must necessarily precipitate a crisis of legitimacy. If journalism is no longer 'the sense-making practice of modernity', then what is it?

Third Ways

That question leads well beyond the horizons of the present study. Here, it is enough to conclude with the suggestion that cultural studies, media studies, and journalism education all have something to offer each other in looking for the answer. None of them is so strong and self-confident that it can do without the support of the others, and all have limits to their explanatory power. They all share with the humanities at large, and more generally with universities, intellectuals, and even modern democracy itself, the same uncomfortable crisis of legitimacy that journalism is facing too. Doubts and uncertainties about the object and method of study lead to more profound questions about the conduct of public and private life, the place of intellectual and educational institutions, and the mechanisms for both government and participation. As the general cultural functions of government, media, and education converge, compete, and seep into one another, there is a great need to understand the media and the place of journalism within them.

The Key Centre for Cultural and Media Policy at Brisbane, under the influence of senior figures like Tony Bennett and Stuart Cunningham, responded to the convergence between government, education, and media by expanding the notion of 'government' to fill the analytical frame with 'governmentality' (a term derived from Michel Foucault). However, in *Popular Reality* and more recently in *Uses of Television*, John Hartley responded to the convergence by expanding the idea of 'media' into the 'mediasphere' (a term derived from Yuri Lotman). Hartley's stance, dubbed 'media republicanism' (by Mark Gibson), argued that concepts such as citizenship must be rethought in relation to media, and that democratic participation may continue in the era (and in the very form) of commercial, private, entertainment-oriented consumer communications. Indeed, he suggested that the period of 'democratainment' and 'D-I-Y citizenship' was already upon us; a prospect not equated with the deluge (Hartley, 1996, 1999). Doubtless many will want to disagree with this argument, but the purpose of the exercise is to take contemporary developments in journalism and media seriously, and to try to account for them within an explanatory framework that addresses current realities. It may then be possible to contribute to the development of academic and even journalistic initiatives.

In the context of mid-century Britain (empire, war, democratization, consumerism) magazines like *Picture Post* under Stephan Lorant and Tom Hopkinson, and newspapers like the *Daily Mirror* under Cecil King and Hugh Cudlipp, proved that positive, political outcomes were possible via a triangulation of *visual culture*, *popular journalism*, and *democratic politics*. Their work in promoting democratization, modernization, and style introduced the idea of the sovereignty of the ordinary. They played a role not only in securing the Labour election victory of 1945, but in educating the popular and governing classes alike in the new disciplines of citizenship—the need for welfare, employment, health, and social security. They showed how entertainment, media, and public affairs could be welded together and used to manage change. They made democracy sexy.

The challenge now is not all that different. The same combination of popular culture, democratic politics, and visual media can contribute to what Anthony Giddens in *The Third Way* calls 'democratizing democracy'. Giddens writes:

The appeal of democracy does not come wholly, or perhaps even primarily, from the triumph of liberal democratic institutions over others, but from the deeper forces that are reshaping the global society, including the demand for individual autonomy and the emergence of a more reflexive citizenry. Democratization is outflanking democracy, and the imbalance must be addressed. (Giddens, 1998: 70–1).

It seems to us that this exactly describes the context of media, and although it partly accounts for the crisis of legitimacy faced by media and education as well as by government, Giddens does not despair. He writes:

The crisis of democracy comes from its not being democratic enough. While . . . the proportion of people expressing trust in politicians has dipped over the past three decades, faith in democracy as such has not. (Giddens, 1998: 71–2; see also 46–53).

Because there remains a need for and a continuing function of government (Giddens, 1998: 47–8), it is Giddens's purpose to contribute to its renewal. He has nothing to say about media. But clearly there is a need to understand the place of the media in the developments he surveys, and their role in related changes. While the popular media are constantly criticized for their apparently anti-democratic tendencies (especially in the areas of ownership and control), there is less understanding of their role in decentralizing (i.e. 'generalizing') knowledge, or, via their cultural form, their role in stimulating, even teaching new forms of 'media citizenship'.

However, even if 'media citizenship' can be observed, it doesn't follow that the 'media republic' has been proclaimed. A big question for media research is how to bring modern democracy, with its now 200-year-old technology (including journalism) closer to the cultural/media citizenship that is already 'outflanking' government. One way to address that question is to bring the hard-won insights of media and cultural studies, which have themselves been tempered on the anvil of intellectual and educational crisis, into real dialogue with those who practise and teach journalism. It may even be that between us we may have something to teach those who practise government.

This isn't to choose between good, heroic (modern) journalism and bad, corrupt (postmodern) media studies, but to think about the *ethics of reading* for ourselves and our constituencies of students, readers, and audiences. Both academics and journalists can and do contribute to the extension of popular critical literacy among a democratizing reading public. They may disagree on the status of truth but agree on the need for truthfulness; some may prefer modernist realism to postmodern textualism, or 'public-service' journalism over commercial entertainment media. Professionals may wish to locate 'media ethics' in the journalist; we would prefer to locate them in the readership. But such differences should not keep the two apart.

All of 'us' need to return to what Thomas Osborne identifies as a post-ideological, ethically based practice of what might be called *speculative empiricism*: 'to reflect on the present status of freedoms in relation to the constitution of freedoms in the past' (Osborne, 1998: 167). He argues that such 'ethical realism' need not lead to the usual philosophical 'denunciations of present times', nor to the promotion of 'this or that project of enlightenment or reform', but simply be done 'in the interests of an exercise in judgement itself' (Osborne, 1998: 191). This is not only a task for social theory or historiography. It is that part of the 'democrat-ization of democracy' which citizens can and do perform for themselves, not least in conversation with intellectuals, teachers, and media com-municators. It is what Ken Wark declares in the Australian context to be not the 'third way' but the 'third moment of cultural studies': 'the positive attempt to imagine how Australian culture could be other-wise—what might free, open, diverse, creative culture be like?' (Wark, 1997: 169). We're up for that. But it's a task better accomplished over a beer than over a barricade.

2 | 'Intelligence is Always an Interlocutor': A Dialogue with the Literature

> Australians do not know and relate to Aboriginal people. They relate to stories told by former colonists.
>
> (Marcia Langton, 1993a: 33)

'The Content of their Character'

Discussing the question of 'who's got' something that might be identified as 'Aboriginal content' in the field of television provision, Eric Michaels felt constrained to make a statement:

I will begin by noting my own genetic lack of Aboriginal—or even Australian—content, and admitting that the topic excites me partly because it requires a reflexive posture if I intend to develop this any further at all. (Michaels, 1994: 22).

The same goes for the authors of the present work, both of whom are 'New Australian' migrants.

Not only genetically but also 'generically', as it were, our disciplinary background is not in Aboriginal studies, but in the interdisciplinary field of communication, media, film, and cultural studies. Michaels himself, Michael Meadows, Steve Mickler, and others are specialists in the analysis of Aboriginality and media. We are not even of that party; our interest is in *media*, and although both of us have published on Aboriginal issues during the 1990s, we both have research interests elsewhere in media studies. We are neither Aboriginal people nor Aboriginalists. Like Eric Michaels, we came to this project with no 'specialist background' in 'Aborigines per se'; like him, 'ultimately', we 'wanted to understand our, not their, media revolution' (Michaels, 1994: 22).

Our lack of Aboriginal 'content' both personal and disciplinary may of course be regarded as a weakness, but we are convinced that investigating Aboriginality from the perspective of the media can equally be a useful source of strength, given the economic, cultural, and political significance of contemporary media.

The formal topic of our study was 'the reporting and reception of Aboriginal issues in the Australian media' during the mid-to-late 1990s. We found it impossible *not* to think about wider questions:

- How and in what kind of 'public sphere' are community relations conducted?
- What is the relation between textuality and citizenship?
- What counts as a citizen and how is citizenship evolving to take account of 'identity'?
- How are 'audiences' or 'consumers' becoming 'authors' or 'producers' in the media?
- What would 'sovereignty' mean in the media context?

The media have become more important politically in the period since the Aboriginal citizenship referendum of 1967. The academic disciplines that have hitherto had most to say about Aboriginality, for instance anthropology, history, law, criminology, public administration, and politics, need to be joined by the interdisciplinary 'new humanities', specifically media studies. The perspectives, concepts, and methods elaborated in media studies in Australia and internationally since the 1970s can make a valuable contribution to understanding Aboriginal issues.

But equally—perhaps more than equally—we have found that media studies can learn much from an encounter with issues of Aboriginality. Issues that have preoccupied mainstream media studies are heightened and tested, sometimes to destruction, in the 'Aboriginal domain'. Equally, uses of media among Aboriginal and Islander communities may have much to teach mainstream media. Concepts of production, representation, regulation, audience, text, reception, and access take on new significance, or are put in question. Methods of research and analysis are tested both in principle and in practice. More fundamentally still, we found that the encounter between Indigenous and media studies required the rethinking of some very basic assumptions: specifically, what counts as 'knowledge', what counts as 'the media', what counts as 'Indigeneity', what counts as 'policy'. So from the outset this is a study of mutual teaching between Indigenous and media studies.

39

Mutual Unintelligibility the Precondition for Meaning

The process is exactly what Yuri Lotman describes in his discussion of the fundamental requirements for culture:

Human intelligence...cannot switch itself on by itself. For an intelligence to function there must be another intelligence. Vygotsky was the first to stress: 'Every higher function is divided between two people, is a mutual psychological process'. Intelligence is always an interlocutor. (Lotman, 1990: 2).

Lotman takes this insight to be fundamental—not in the sense that he pretends to address the 'as yet unsolved problem of the "beginning" of culture and the "beginning" of life', but in the sense that what he calls 'bipolar asymmetry of semiotic systems' is fundamental to meaning generation:

It has been established that a minimally functioning semiotic structure consists of not one artificially isolated language or text in that language, but of a parallel pair of mutually untranslatable languages which are, however, connected by a 'pulley', which is translation. A dual structure like this is the minimal nucleus for generating new messages, and it is also the minimal unit of a semiotic object such as culture. (Lotman, 1990: 2).

Media studies and Aboriginality may indeed be among those pairs of 'mutually untranslatable languages'. In our hands, an encounter between them may yield imperfect translation, but we believe with Yuri Lotman that such an interlocution is essential for 'generating new messages'.

The related questions of how new meaning is generated, how information is transmitted, and how it is stored and retrieved, which are the workaday questions of media practice (e.g. in the 'reporting' and 'reception' of Aboriginal affairs), are also fundamental questions about communication, creativity, and history (or memory). They are questions of culture. Thus a study based on translating between the 'asymmetric semiotic systems' of Indigenous and media studies is itself an instance of these elemental cultural functions and processes.

Lotman's great discovery was that '"thinking" semiotic structures need an initial impulse from another thinking structure and that text-generating mechanisms need a text from outside to set them going' (Lotman, 1990: 3). Meaning-generation is the result of 'mutual tension between...mutually untranslatable and at the same time mutually interprojected languages' (3). Lotman's model of meaning-generation operates at all levels of complexity (144). The most basic mutually untranslatable dialogic encounter is the 'language of smiles' between mother and newborn infant (144). At the other end of the scale, entire national languages both receive and transmit new meanings in their encounters with others (French and English; Russian and French; Nyungar and English, etc.), by borrowings, extension of existing terms, or new coinages.

Here's an example of how such translation between mutually unintelligible systems can work:

Sometimes the grammatical system of a language is employed to construct a new word denoting the introduced concept. This is how the word for 'policeman' is formed in a number of [Australian] languages. In Wunambal the word is *yirrkalngarri* from *yirrkal* 'rope, chain' plus the suffix *-ngarri* 'with, having': 'the one(s) with ropes or chains', recalling the not too distant past when the police chained up suspects and witnesses alike for transportation to the towns. Compare also the Kukatja and Jaru term *wayin-watji* ('chain-possessor'). The Gooniyandi term *mirnmirdgali* is formed in a similar way from *mird-* 'tie up' and *-gali* 'good at doing, habitually doing', as is the Kalkatungu term *ganimay-nyjirr* 'one who ties up (people)'. (Macquarie, 1994: xxvi).

In Wiraduri 'policeman' is *barramaldaayn*, 'one who grabs (people)'; in Eastern Arrernte it is *irrkwentye*, 'grabber'. Telling though this 'translation' may be, it is not the only model for Indigenizing the concept of 'policeman'. In Nyungar, for example, the word is *manatj*—a 'cockatoo'.

In the present context, it is useful to see the interdisciplinary encounters between differing academic disciplines in a similar way. Different genres of discourse within a language have produced the 'two cultures' of the arts and sciences. The mutual untranslatability of the social sciences and humanities, for instance, has 'generated' cultural studies. A dialogue between mutually unintelligible Indigenous and media studies is therefore a useful model for meaning-generation in the *means* of study.

It holds true also for the much larger and more important *object* of study, i.e. Indigeneity and 'the media' as such. These separate meaning-generating systems (semiotic structures) cannot function or come into being without others in parallel to 'set them going'. Hence, mutually untranslatable, asymmetric, and otherwise distinct systems, like 'media' and 'Aboriginality', nevertheless cannot function except as an 'indissoluble unit' with each other (among others).

For Lotman, semiotic (cultural, intellectual, thinking) structures are therefore 'binary' at the minimum (they cannot be less than binary though they can be more); they are 'asymmetrical'; and at the same time they are 'unitary'. Lotman calls the overall unit 'without which separate semiotic systems cannot function or come into being' the *semio-sphere*. It is the 'semiotic space or intellectual world in which humanity and human society are enfolded and which is in constant interaction with the individual intellectual world of human beings' (Lotman, 1990: 3).

Of course 'Australia' itself, as a semiotic (cultural) structure or system, is both distinct and simultaneously within the 'indissoluble unit' of a larger semiosphere which includes other countries, cultures, and semiotic structures. Thus, we would make two further points about the benefit of being outsiders, based on the two-way process of communicative dialogue:

- 'reception': Australian distinctiveness is only such within a larger 'semiosphere' that includes media and Indigenous systems in other countries and contexts, so an investigation of Australian media and Indigenous issues requires knowledge of how those others are received and transformed.

- 'transmission': Australia in its distinctiveness may 'speak to' other systems, not as an instance but as a generator of new meaning that restructures the whole unit or 'semiosphere'.

Task Forced to Death?

'Just what do you Indians want?' Alex Chasing Hawk replied, 'A leave-us-alone law!!'

(Vine Deloria, 1988: 27)

In order to orient our work to that which already maps the Aboriginalist field, we have undertaken a review of the existing literature. It is hard to resist the implication that the scholarly, critical, research, and academic literature is simply one more differentiated domain in an overall 'universe of Indigeneity', taking 'universe' here in Lotman's sense of that word—the 'universe of the mind' or 'semiosphere'. To the extent that this is so, this chapter and the next need to be seen as more than a theoretical and methodological 'introduction' to the 'findings' of our research into the media. Instead, they are part of those findings—an analysis of one end of the spectrum of 'media' within which Aboriginality is generated (created), reported (transmitted), and received (memorialized).

Academics are not used to thinking of their publications as being somewhere on a spectrum of knowledge-production whose other end features popular media figures like Rupert Murdoch or John Laws. But there are many among the Indigenous population in Australia and elsewhere who see research into Aboriginal issues as just one more technique designed to keep an over-governed population in its place. Here's Vine Deloria, Jr., of the Sioux nation, one-time Executive Director of the National Congress of American Indians, with a cautionary tale that brings government, news reporting, academic research, and the oppression of native peoples into a grim alignment:

The name of the game in the government sector is TASK FORCE REPORT. Every two years some reporter causes a great uproar about how Indians are treated by the Bureau of Indian Affairs. This, in turn, causes great consternation among Senators and Congressmen who have to answer mail from citizens concerned about Indians. So a TASK FORCE REPORT is demanded on Indian problems.

The conclusion of every TASK FORCE REPORT is that Congress is not appropriating enough money to do an adequate job of helping Indians. Additionally, these reports...advise that a consistent policy of self-help with adequate loan funds for reservation development be initiated.

Since Congress is not about to appropriate any more money than possible for Indian Affairs, the TASK FORCE REPORT is filed away for future reference. Rumor has it that there is a large government building set aside as a storage bin for TASK FORCE REPORTS. [...]

We are TASK FORCED to death.

Some years ago at a Congressional hearing someone asked Alex Chasing Hawk, a council member of the Cheyenne River Sioux for thirty years, 'Just what do you Indians want?' Alex replied, 'A leave-us-alone law!!'

The primary goal and need of Indians today is not for someone to feel sorry for us. [...] We need the public at large to drop the myths in which it has clothed us for so long. We need fewer and fewer 'experts' on Indians.

What we need is a cultural leave-us-alone agreement, in spirit and in fact. (Deloria, 1988: 13, 14, 27)

From such a perspective, the academic literature—the 'medium' of the 'expert'—can be politically as active, and potentially as destructive, as the 'mass' media upon which it reports. This goes not only for the literature we analyse below, but also for our own project. It is important, then, to recognize the possibility that here is just another TASK FORCE REPORT. Indeed, the present project results from work that was originally funded by the Australian Research Council, following the Report of the Royal Commission into Aboriginal Deaths in Custody, which had identified the media among the 'underlying issues' upon which it made recommendations (Recommendations 205–8; see Johnston, 1991: 77).

There's no way to get off the horns of this dilemma; nor any reason why one should try. For the writers of reports, Tim Rowse has identified a need for 'a combination of scepticism and generosity in the terms in which, for reasons of justice, Australia affirms indigenous traditions' (Rowse, 1993: 26). In that context, what many Indigenous people 'want' may include a 'cultural leave-us-alone agreement'. The homespun diction need not hide what amounts to a serious demand—another word for 'agreement' is 'treaty', and another word for 'leave-us-alone' is 'sovereignty'. Faced with that, we as authors of the present work have made simultaneously contradictory (mutually untranslatable) responses. Chasing Hawk's demand not to be TASK FORCED to death meets with immediate, almost intuitive assent—'Yes; point taken, message understood. "Treaty now!" for such an agreement!' But at the same time here we are, making one more REPORT.

Having expressed mutual respect and all that, there's still a question of what another TASK FORCE REPORT might be *for* (not that two academics make much of a 'force'). Here an insight of another outsider, Canadian writer Peter Jull, may prove helpful. Despite the plethora of research into Aboriginal people, making them sometimes complain that they are the most over-studied but least understood people in the world, the fact is that there is very little infrastructure for producing, storing, and exploiting knowledge for their own practical politics. Jull writes that 'we must renew international networks, attending more to their functional political value and practical information content and less to ceremony':

Unlike Australians and other predominantly European peoples, indigenous peoples have no textbooks, university programs, weekend training sessions, or journals to teach the political science or public administration of the radically new world they are creating. (Jull, 1994: 211).

This is certainly overstating the deficit (since there are indeed textbooks, university programmes, journals and the like in the 'Aboriginal domain' and under Indigenous control), but still Jull has a point when he says: 'Every indigenous organisation and region has areas urgently needing work. Each one needs experience and insights already gained by others' (211). He warns that negative practical outcomes follow from *not* putting knowledge to work in the realm of policy:

Despite computer technology, cheap international travel, and expertise, indigenous networks have not yet developed. Interested individuals engage in their own small circles, exchanging conference invitations and institutional visitorships, producing individually worthy talks and papers which vanish into the aether. This is an inefficient use of political resources, and enables Australian policy-makers to avoid reforms long accepted abroad. (Jull, 1994: 204).

Of course Indigenous knowledge is just that, but those who have access to some of the resources mentioned by Jull (including the present authors) can contribute to the 'heartening' 'renewal of indigenous policy debate' in the 1990s, so long as those who are helping are willing to respond to changes in political circumstances:

Previously, debate sometimes seemed to match dismissive one-liners by many Australians with patient truths from a 'righteous remnant' who had long defended indigenous causes. New times and new information are not always welcome, even to the second group. (Jull, 1994: 205).

These are wise words. 'Patient truths', 'righteous remnants', and 'long defense'—however true, however righteous, however long—can turn out not to be 'generous' to Indigenous practical politics at all if they continue in the defensive agenda when new opportunities arise to utilize the 'new times and new information'.

'Accommodating Difference' in the 'Universe of Indigeneity'

Analysts need not choose between the extremes of 'primordialism,' stressing ethnicity rooted in tradition, and 'construction,' stressing the political nature of identity.

(Marjorie M. Balzer, 1999: 203)

If, as Vine Deloria hopes, 'the public at large' is ever to 'drop the myths' and the 'experts' are to desist from making TASK FORCE REPORTS, there will inevitably be more dialogue between the Indigenous and non-Indigenous parts of the 'semiosphere', not less. But if Indigeneity is ever to achieve a status where it is not worth a TASK FORCE REPORT, then it has to be de-politicized, to be made mundane, banal (see Langton, 1993a: 41–3; McKee, 1997a). 'Expert' discourse and even TASK FORCE REPORTS themselves can contribute to and participate in the quotidian immediacy of everyday life; they don't *have* to be instruments of 'low intensity' warfare between Indigenous and settler traditions. The same applies to the media at large. They can be used for whatever is wanted. No medium is intrinsically or essentially negative or positive in its effects. The media and experts alike can report Aboriginality via its mundane rather than its 'fatal' aspects.

However, where this already happens, it is clear that problems remain. Neither expert nor media knowledge is exempt from 'governmentality'—ordinary citizens of whatever tradition or descent are universally the subjects of government, which works through the institutions, practices, and discourses of everyday life. A 'leave-us-alone law' would not magically remove its beneficiaries from the general and unceasing flux of population management, policymaking, administration, and research. Indeed, Steve Mickler has very helpfully identified a 'right to be ordinary' for Aboriginal people (1998: 283–4, 288–306). In the era of the knowledge economy this must include taking seriously their right to be sampled, surveyed, and statisticalized (if that's a word), as part of the 'public at large'—as 'rightful' members of the communities of consumers, audiences, voters, citizens.

But before such an outcome can be achieved, the question of the relationship between Aboriginal and non-Aboriginal populations has to be settled at a higher level of organization. The question is, whether Aboriginal people 'count' in governmental calculations as an autonomous 'national' population, or as a (demographically differentiated) segment of an Australian 'public at large'. The implication of taking seriously Indigenous peoples' 'right to be ordinary' *before* any such settlement is made clear in a recent and comprehensive study of the Australian population's 'everyday culture'; Aboriginal people all but disappear.

In *Accounting for Tastes: Australian Everyday Cultures* (1999), Tony Bennett, Michael Emmison, and John Frow apply Pierre Bourdieu's sociological model of culture to Australia. As 'Australia', they use 2,756 survey respondents (ruddered by a pilot survey and interviews); the categories into which they most frequently divided this population were those of gender, class, age, and region. As 'culture' they:

asked questions about everything we could think of as 'culture,' including home-based leisure activities, fashion, the ownership of cars and electronic equipment, eating habits, friendships, holidays, outdoor activities, gambling, sport, reading, artistic pursuits, watching television, cinema-going, and the use of libraries, museums and art galleries. (Bennett *et al.*, 1999: 1–2).

Among the questions they *didn't* 'think of as "culture"' was the extent to which 'being Aboriginal' might overdetermine some or all of these others. They were certainly not insensitive to the question of 'nation' in relation to culture:

One of our strongest reservations regarding Bourdieu's *Distinction* concerns its insularity in discussing French culture as a hermetically sealed closed system. (Bennett *et al.*, 1999: 5).

But they cash in this insight in relation to 'the degree to which, historically, Australian culture has been shaped by the cultural flows of different phases of European and Asian migration', such that 'boundaries between different national cultures are becoming more porous' (5). In other words, they presume *Australian* 'national culture' to be *nationally unitary*, whatever its openness or otherwise to international influences. Their model of *Australia* is as 'insular' as Bourdieu's in that sense. They don't imagine it as having *internal* 'boundaries between different national cultures'. As a result of this, Indigeneity is necessarily assimilated into the statistical model of Australian everyday culture at large, and given the small proportion of Aboriginal and Islander people within that population, they make an appearance as isolated, almost accidental variables:

- Aborigines prefer to **holiday** in their own state rather than overseas; such practices are 'conservative and restricted', rather than 'more active, more open to the unfamiliar, and more inclusive' (109).
- Aborigines 'score well above the mean' in identifying their '**diet** as "health-food" or "natural"'. This 'may indicate not so much that they consciously follow a healthy diet as that they consider their normal diet to be inherently healthy' (120–1).
- **Touch football** is 'the closest thing on our scales to a "popular" form of sporting activity. To be "popular," however, is not the same thing as to be inclusive: touch football is quite strongly exclusive of women, of middle-aged and old people, of migrants, and of Aborigines' (131).
- 'Participation [in **lawn bowls**] is negatively correlated with income.... Aborigines do not play it at all' (132).
- 'The poorer you are, the less likely you are to **play a sport**... migrants and Aborigines play less than the Australian-born and non-Aborigines' (133).
- 'Those classes like the professionals and para-professionals which had scored very highly on the playing of sport score very low on watching it, whereas manual workers, who play little sport, watch it a great deal.... Perhaps the most dramatic demonstration of this reversal between participation and **spectatorship** is given in the relative figures for Aborigines' (139–42).
- 'Aboriginality has few significant general effects [in the area of public/private culture], although **art galleries and museums** do register as being more important for Aboriginal than for non-Aboriginal Australians. This is also true for **public musical**

performances, opera, and, most especially, cultural festivals, where Aboriginal participation is just a little under twice that of non-Aboriginal participation (236).

That is the full extent of Aboriginality in *Accounting for Tastes*. Does this describe Indigenous everyday culture? Is it a map of the consequences of statistically granting the 'right to be ordinary'? Comparative data are certainly interesting—Aboriginal people's cultural tastes map onto social class categories as a peculiar amalgam of employer/managerial taste (arts, music, health-diet) and poor-people/manual-worker taste (holidays, sports participation/spectator rates). (see Bennett *et al.*, 1999: 251–3). Conversely, general Australian preferences may unexpectedly display 'Aboriginal' characteristics:

In considering the regimes governing outdoor leisure activities, we are concerned with a relation to the natural world other than that of work. . . . in the case of activities such as bush-walking, camping, fishing, and hunting, there is a clear difference between the two metropolitan locations (inner city and suburban) and the provincial and rural locations, where people engage more fully in these activities. (109).

However, such glimpses of everyday culture surely do not amount to an 'accounting for *Aboriginal* tastes'? Nor do they begin to address the relationship between Aboriginal and 'Australian' culture (but see Tom Griffiths's impressive *Hunters and Collectors: The Antiquarian Imagination in Australia*, 1996, especially the epilogue: 278–82). It seems indeed that the latter—the relation between Aboriginal and Australian cultures—needs to be settled before the 'ordinariness' of Indigeneity can be achieved and the TASK FORCES can return to base.

So it's not a matter of purifying the Indigenous 'semiosphere' of non-Indigenous influences by taking Wajala [white people's] research off the backs of epistemologically oppressed Indigenous people. What's needed was implicitly recognized by the Royal Commission into Aboriginal Deaths in Custody when it placed the *media-related* recommendations in a section of its final report entitled '*Accommodating difference: relations between Aboriginal and non-Aboriginal people*'—i.e. taking the *media* to be the *means* for that accommodation of difference. In fact formal academic work can join the media (if it is not already merely a differentiated part of the media) to help to perform that task, and thereby promote reconciliation. But such a procedure does have to be structured as dialogue (Lotman-style); there is a need for a communicative 'treaty', since 'difference' cannot be 'accommodated' unless it is 'recognized'. Such 'recognition' is normally accorded to *nations*.

Under such terms, it may be possible to side-step and to go beyond a by-now traditional 'failure of communication' that has, in Vine Deloria's words, 'created a void into which poured the white do-gooder, the missionary, the promoter, the scholar, and every conceivable type of person who believed he could help' (Deloria, 1988: 9–10). It is in that spirit that we continue. We are emboldened by the words of Marcia Langton, who recommends a category of 'Aboriginality' that is:

generated when Aboriginal and non-Aboriginal people engage in actual dialogue, be it at a supermarket check-out or in a film co-production. In these exchanges, as in any social interaction, the individuals involved will test imagined models of the other, repeatedly adjusting the models as the responses are processed, to find some satisfactory way of comprehending the other. It is in these dialogues . . . that working models of 'Aboriginality' are constructed as ways of seeing Aboriginal people, but both the Aboriginal subject and the non-Aboriginal subject are participating. (Langton, 1993a: 35).

Langton's 'working model' is derived from *social* dialogue between actual people; but her book extends that model to a dialogue via what Valentin Volosinov once called 'colloquy of large scale'—i.e. publishing, or the 'republic of letters'.

A 'universe of Indigeneity' has been invented or imagined or narrated in the 'republic of letters'. This republic is one to which Indigenous people have not always been granted entry visas. Its internal governing 'order of discourse' has been elaborated by persons and in circumstances that may have little to do with Indigenous people '*per se*' (in Michaels's phrase). There is no directly causal relation between the 'semiosphere'—the universe of culture, discourse, language, writing, sense-making in general—and the lived experience of Indigenous and non-Indigenous persons, whether in the supermarket or on the film set. The Aboriginal descent of any person does not determine the meaning of Aboriginality in sense-making systems. 'The literature' is by writers and is for readers who may include Indigenous and non-Indigenous persons.

The 'universe of Indigeneity' is not confined to persons of Aboriginal descent. Indeed, if proportionality is any guide, the major finding of our research into the reporting and reception of Indigenous issues in the Australian media is this: compared with the proportion of Aboriginal and Islander people in the Australian population in the 1990s, Indigenous stories were massively over-represented in the media. Thus, their 'reporting and reception' was an issue for *Australia*.

It would be going too far to say that actual living historical Indigenous people are irrelevant to their representation in the 'universe of Indigeneity', since what is imagined and represented there has material outcomes for actual Aboriginal people as well as for others. But the problems, desires, fears, policies, and politics being thought through in the 'universe of Indigeneity' may not originate, and should not be sited upon, the bodies, persons, cultures, histories, or 'reality' of Indigenous people. They may also originate in and be sited upon social and governmental histories, discourses, and practices at large. In short, Aboriginality may or may not be a problem for Aboriginal people, but *in the literature* it is mainly a problem for the non-Aboriginal sphere of life. It is that 'problem' that tends to be represented in media: Aboriginality as a problem for whites.

The compulsive attention to Aboriginal issues across all media says something very important about 'reporting', whether in TASK FORCE REPORTS or in journalism. In fact, it inverts the predominant liberal-democratic 'myth' of reporting as a practice, which is, crudely: 'something happens; someone reports it'. On the contrary. Reporting precedes, shapes, and even makes events, and necessarily so. The corporate, socio-industrial paraphernalia of news-making, for instance, could not be sustained by simply waiting for things to happen. News is manufactured—not only in the industrial sense, but also in the semiotic sense of creating meaning *for* events. Stories are generated not by 'something happening' but by a structure of narrative forms, generic conventions, political exigencies, economic imperatives, and cultural functions. They're written before the journalist arrives on the scene (or, more likely, phones a 'source'). This predictability of discursive outcome is indeed what journalistic training is designed to produce. So the fact that there are so many stories in the non-Aboriginal media about Aboriginal issues is saying something about the way that media work, about the intense but possibly disguised importance of Aboriginality in that context.

Just as 'reporting' is neither a reflection *of* nor a reflection *on* Aboriginal people, so, frequently, it has very little to do with the personal beliefs, understanding, goodwill, or otherwise of the individual reporter (academic or journalist). Its regular patterns, predictable content, and standardization over both time and space suggests that 'reporting' is a compulsive re-narration of stories that have their explanation in white history. It's not so much that 'White Australia has a Black History', as the old slogan has it (see Mickler, 1998: 163), but more a matter of 'Black History on White Paper'—a phrase attributed to Ngarrindjeri woman Doreen Kartinyeri (of Hindmarsh Island fame; see *Alternative Law Journal*, 21/1, 1996: 1). In short, while 'events' may not determine reporting, 'history' does. The over-representation of Aboriginality in the Australian media suggests that there are historic issues that are as yet unresolved; contemporary sense-making is gnawing and tugging and worrying at them because they are there, unhealed wounds in the body politic (see Mickler, 1998: 151–8).

'Race' – Pentagon, Diamond, Binary – or Blind Alley?

Today hunting is mostly done on Nintendo video games and they're talking like New York rappers.

(Joe Edgar, 1996: 112)

Why is Indigeneity understood as a matter of *race*? It looks to some observers very like a matter of *nation*. Why is Australia seen (and not only by a provocative political party of that name) as 'one nation'? It looks very like one *state*. And why is the Australian state commonly confused with the Australian continental *land-mass* (popular mapping often forgets even the state of Tasmania)? These are not rhetorical, but historical questions (see Griffiths, 1996: 229–30). At different times the 'obvious' answers to them have all been quite different.

The boundary of the Australian state is constantly evolving—most recently in the 1990s when its area was tripled by setting territorial limits further out to sea. Far-flung Australia includes various islands with ethnically distinct populations—Groote Eylandt, Bathurst, Melville (Aboriginal), Torres Strait (Islander), Christmas (Malay), Norfolk (Pitcairn), Macquarie (scientists), not to mention the immense tracts of the Australian Antarctic Territories. The Torres Strait Islands are under Australian jurisdiction and not that of Papua New Guinea, despite the fact that Islander people also live in PNG. But PNG was itself once an Australian colony, and might, had political circumstances been more propitious in 1976, have been proclaimed its seventh (and only 'black') state, instead of achieving what many saw at the time as premature independence. Reaching further back into colonial/imperial history, there were those who expected 'Australasia' ultimately to become the unitary state, with the North and South Islands of New Zealand federating alongside the six Australian colonies. There was, in short, nothing self-evident about the current boundary of the Australian Commonwealth, especially given that in 1933 the white electors of Western Australia voted by a thumping majority to secede from it (the Empire wouldn't have them back, however). The possibility that the Torres Strait Islands, which enjoy majority-Indigenous populations,

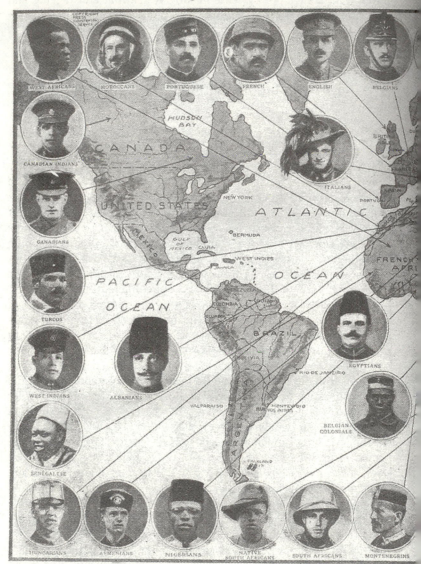

6. How many races are there? As the US entered World War One in 1917, an An
'Canadian Indians', 'Native South Africans', Belgian Colonials' and Maoris, among
Weekly (USA), 1917; *The War Budget (UK)*, *April 26, 1917.*

zine combined race, nation, and belligerence to arrive at an answer. It illustrated
enous people, but the Australian 'race' was already unequivocally white. *Source: Leslie's*

Research

might wish to experiment with similar ideas, perhaps to be followed by the majority-Aboriginal populations of Melville, Bathurst, and Groote Eylandt, need not be ruled out. Henry Reynolds has tried to resolve some of these historical issues by drawing a distinction between three Australian nations within one state (Reynolds, 1996: 177).

The same indeterminacy applies on a much greater scale to the question of race. How many races are there? During the twentieth century, the meaning of 'race' evolved from a usage that wobbled unpredictably between 'biological' definitions—'mongoloid, caucasian, and negro'—and much more elaborate distinctions between 'races' that would not now be recognized at all. An early example of the latter was an American journal's attempt to explain to its readers who the combatants were in the First World War just as the USA entered that conflict; presumably on the grounds that they would wish to know who was friend, who foe. A map of the world was printed under the headline 'Forty Races at War in the Mightiest Conflict of All Time' (*Leslie's Weekly*, reproduced in *The War Budget*, 26 Apr. 1917, 336–7). Around the edges of the world map, with arrows showing where they came from, were forty portraits of the racial types involved (all men, all hatted, most in military uniform). The 'races' pictured thus were:

Germans, Austrians, Russians, Poles, Cossacks, Kurds, Siberians, Kalmuks, Japanese, Tonkinese, Annamites, Australians, Maoris, Sikhs, Pathans, Ghurkas [*sic*], Sepoys, Arabs, Turks, Madagascans, Rumanians, Bulgars, Serbs, Montenegrins, South Africans, Native South Africans, Belgian Colonials, Egyptians, Nigerians, Armenians, Hungarians, Senegalese, West Indians, Albanians, Turkos, Canadians, Canadian Indians, West Africans, Moroccans, Portuguese, French, English, Italians, Belgians.

The caption listed whether each of these races was fighting with the Allies or the Central Powers (the Poles and Albanians were apparently to be found on both sides). The USA itself, and the 'South American republics', were not listed, nor were any Scandinavian countries, Persia, Spain, the Dutch East Indies, Siam, or China. American readers of *Leslie's Weekly* may not have known that among their enemies were now not only the German and Austrian 'races' but also Turks, Bulgars, and Hungarians. It may equally have surprised them to know that coming to the aid of Uncle Sam were the Kalmuk, Maori, Madagascan, Native South African, Belgian Colonial, and Canadian Indian 'races'.

This intriguing document shows the looseness of the distinctions between 'race', 'nation', and 'state'. Some 'racial' distinctions are clearly national (Germans and Austrians, for instance). But the map also preserves racial distinctions *within* nations or states: Canadians are differentiated from Canadian Indians; South Africans from Native South Africans; Australians (white) from Maoris; Belgian Colonials from Belgians; Sepoys, Gurkhas, Pathans, and Sikhs from each other in India, Cossacks, Kurds, Siberians, and Kalmuks from Russians. Neither scientific nor comprehensive, but practical and journalistic, the 'Forty Races at War' map shows that at the outset of the last century, racial difference was being popularized in America and Britain as a geo-political network with a tendency to pluralize races rather than reduce them. Although they certainly served in the War, Aboriginal people are not mentioned in this taxonomy—the Australian 'race' is taken to be white (while the New Zealand 'race' is Maori).

'Black History on White Paper' has continued to have this added dimension for Aboriginal people; the indeterminate and changing meaning of 'Black'. They have successively been subject to imported notions of what 'race' means, how it should be identified, differentiated, and managed. They were rarely if ever cast in the role of a *national* community. Even now that notion is not widely accepted. The *Australian nation* is routinely conflated with the *state*, allowing no space for several nations in one state. And because there was no unitary *Aboriginal* nation before colonization—there were several hundred different language groups—there is scepticism among Aboriginal people themselves about political organization at the national level. Without a 'nation', without a 'state', Aboriginal people are hemmed ever further in by 'race'.

The presumption that Aboriginal and Islander people are 'black' (which is not the case for Indigenous Americans) means that in Australia, compared with the USA, Indigenous people continue to carry a *structurally* greater burden of the available discourses on *race*, even as they are excluded from the available discourses on *nation*. Within the world economy (the 'econosphere', perhaps) the USA is often said to be the 'locomotive' providing major productive energy to the economies of other countries. The same 'locomotive' power can be observed in the 'semiosphere' during the current period. Meanings generated in the American context are transmitted around the world; the denizens of regional 'semiospheres' make sense of their own phenomena via American discursive frameworks. Discourses that in the American context apply to African American Blacks are applied in Australia to the only referent available: Indigenous 'Blacks'.

Because of differences within the two national cultures, Aboriginal people in Australia bear a burden of binarized raciality that does not apply in the same way to Native Americans. Thus, the coverage of Indigenous affairs in the Australian media is very much higher than the coverage of Native issues in the US media, despite the demographic

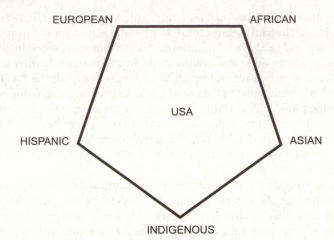

The *SBS World Guide*, 4th edn. (1995), gives the following population figures for the USA for 1993: 80.29% white; 12.06% Black; 2.92% Asian and Pacific Islander; 0.79% Indigenous (Indian, Eskimo, Aleut); 3.94% others. Hispanics 'of any race' were estimated at between 19.3 and 25.2m (between 7.6% and 9.9%). Note that in the USA, Pacific Islanders are grouped among the Asian 'bloc', whereas, in Australia, Islanders are grouped as Indigenous.

fact that Native Americans comprise a comparable proportion of the total population of the USA.

'A remarkable historical artifact, distinctive to the contemporary United States' is what David Hollinger calls the 'ethno-racial pentagon' (Hollinger, 2000: 199). Five 'unequally inhabited' ethnic 'blocs' are recognized in state bureaucratic information gathering: European, Asian, African, Hispanic, and Native Americans. These 'blocs' of the pentagon have, Hollinger says, 'come to replicate the popular color-consciousness of the past: black, white, red, yellow and brown'. Thus the architecture of the pentagon structure 'has its unmistakable origins in the most gross and invidious popular images of what makes human beings different from one another' (202). However, as he is quick to point out, it was 'enlightened antiracism that led to the manufacturing of today's ethno-racial pentagon out of old, racist materials' (202), the impetus to create the pentagon being anti-discrimination and affirmative action policies sponsored by the US federal government. To enforce such policies, it was necessary to know who was in which category. The blocs 'get their integrity not from biology, nor even from culture, but from the dynamics of prejudice and oppression in US history and from the need for political tools to overcome the legacy of that victimization' (204). In other words, these 'racial' categories are not only historical, but *American*. The politics of the pentagon is internal to American developments, necessarily organized around the relations, disjunctions, and contradictions between the five categories. For instance:

- the suppression of internal ethnic difference within blocs;
- the question of where to 'place' people of mixed-bloc descent or marriage;
- the emergence of 'Hispanic' as a *race* in this context;
- the ability of those in the 'European' category, unlike those in the African, to choose ethnicity (e.g. Irish, Italian) without commitment or cost;
- the 'one drop [of blood] rule', that makes a person of African ancestry 'black' even if they have a white mother, but holds that a black woman cannot give birth to a white child (Hollinger, 2000: 200, citing Barbara Fields).

Such matters are of continuing importance within US ethno-politics. But they may translate 'unintelligibly' to foreign contexts. There is no such 'ethno-racial pentagon' in Australia, either demographically or culturally. Differences of race, ethnicity, culture, and colour are organized around different historical fault-lines. One such is what used to be regarded until the 1950s as a distinction between 'British' and 'foreign' whites, where 'foreign' referred to postwar European immigrants, often 'DPs' [displaced persons]—Jewish, German, Scandinavian, Italian, Maltese, Greek, Albanian, and Yugoslav (see Feldmann, 1951: 16). This distinction has survived into the present era as 'Anglo-Celtic' and 'multicultural' Australia respectively. A more profound distinction exists between white, Asian, and Indigenous Australians. It is strong enough to smother internal differences in each category, including Indigenous people, who should, according to Henry Reynolds, be regarded as two separate *nations*—the Aboriginal nation and the Torres Strait Islander nation (Reynolds, 1996). 'Asian', as in other countries, makes little distinction between people from China, Japan, Korea, and South-East Asia. But equally important in the context of Australian history is a distinction within the 'British' white category that was once highly racialized but is not now regarded as 'racial' at all: that between 'Anglo' and 'Celtic'—English Protestant 'sterling', and Irish Catholic 'currency'.

In the USA, the 'pentagon' is by no means the only model of racial relation. Hollinger notes that a more binary distinction between 'white' and 'non-white' or 'people of color' competes with the pentagon. In the

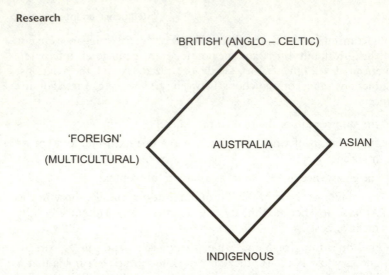

'BRITISH' (ANGLO – CELTIC)

'FOREIGN'
(MULTICULTURAL)

AUSTRALIA

ASIAN

INDIGENOUS

The *SBS World Guide*, 4th edn. (1994), gives the following population figures for Australia for 1994: 94.49% white; 2.1% Asian; 1.1% Indigenous (Aboriginal and Torres Strait Islander). 3.94m (22.7%) were 'foreign born': 1.2m came from the UK and Ireland, 1.5m from continental Europe, 558,400 from Asia and 287,500 from New Zealand.

'people of color' categorization, 'all distinctions between various "co-lored" peoples are less significant than the fact that they are non-white' (Hollinger, 2000: 199).

> WHITE : NON-WHITE (PEOPLE OF COLOR)

Hollinger points out, however, that this 'blueprint' (*sic*) is not the one favoured by administrative agencies, where the pentagon is used 'as guide to the cultural life' of the United States. 'The white-colored dichotomy does not have a strong cultural content, but the ethno-racial pentagon does, and increasingly so, especially for educational purposes' (199).

The pentagon is forceful politically as well as culturally in the USA, where Hispanic and Asian identity is increasingly significant. But the 'export market' in the politics of race, if we may put it that way, as internationalized via film and television, music, journalism, popular culture, and academic research, is organized around the white/non-white dichotomy more than through the pentagon. Ever since the Civil Rights movement of the 1950s and 1960s, the American political discourse of 'race' has been internationalized via concepts, positions, struggles, narratives, and rhetoric that were first forged in relation to Black America.

Vine Deloria has suggested that Black and Native Americans have responded historically in different ways to their colonization. Blacks engaged white society directly through the Civil Rights movement and its successors, while Indians sought to withdraw, to protect the internal structures of their traditional societies. There is an important implication of this variegated response in the Australian context. The two different responses— engagement and introversion—are clearly discernible, but among different segments of the *Aboriginal* population, not as differences between Native and Black ethnic 'blocs'. On the one hand, Indigenous communities living close to their traditional land in traditional ways may have issues in common with Native Americans living in reservations. Certainly their internal politics have been observed to be notably introspective (see Rowse, 1992: 34). And those common issues may in turn be developed into common cause, with transnational Indigenous organizations of the kind recommended by Peter Jull (1994: see below). On the other hand Indigenous people living in urban contexts may find that Black politics has more direct relevance. Again, it is clear that activists and analysts alike have learnt much from African America.

The influence of Black America on Indigenous Australia has been much commented upon in the cultural and consumer field, as well as in relation to political activism. Here there is no ready distinction between rural and urban Aboriginal cultures, since both may be affected, and indeed the importation of American Black cultural preferences may be especially strong among first-generation urban Aboriginal people (especially the children). Thus, Quentin Beresford and Paul Omaji, in their book *Rights of Passage: Aboriginal Youth, Crime and Justice* (1996), locate the 'rites of passage' of their title not in the traditional 'anthropological' domain of tribal initiation, but in anti-social and resistive behaviour. According to the authors and their sources in government, this is learnt—via TV, music, and subcultural style—from Black America. They cite unpublished comments by the WA State Government Advisory Committee on Young Offenders to the effect that:

The presence of graffiti in the suburbs and city showing the 'tags' of groups modelling themselves on Black American groups...illustrates that many-Aboriginal youth are shifting their identification in line with urban black cultures in other countries: the Noongar youth do not listen to country and western like their parents—they prefer Bob Marley. (Beresford and Omaji, 1996: 126).

The *use* made of their 'identification with urban black cultures from other countries' by 'Aboriginal youth' is to achieve personal sovereignty:

To Aboriginal youth, it is likely that car theft and high-speed chases partly serve the function of identity-formation.... Car theft and high-speed driving provide the means to the rite of passage from childhood to manhood central to traditional Aboriginal social custom. Mostly the youth involved are first-generation urban Aborigines. Their heroes are television 'bad guys'. 'They have more in common with Negroes in Harlem than with their Noongar ancestors.' (Beresford and Omaji, 1996: 143 [internal quotation from WA Legislative Assembly discussion paper on *Youth and the Law*, 1992: 44]).

Beresford and Omaji are content to dub this a passage into 'manhood', even though they say that it is just as true for girls: Aboriginal offenders 'seem to think, and especially the girls, that if they get into trouble it's a big thing...a status symbol' (127). Their overall thesis, then, is that the importation of African American identification now achieves for young Aboriginal people what traditional initiation rites may once have managed:

Cultural dislocation and dispossession have disrupted, and even removed, these traditional rites of passage into adulthood for many Aboriginal youth, and especially for those recently urbanised groups. The cultural vacuum has steadily been filled by Western influences of school, peer group and television. (125–6).

Beresford and Omaji may be over-interpreting relationship between the 'influences' and 'dispossession' here, since the same 'influences' apply to remote Aboriginal communities trying to maintain traditional culture. Joe Edgar, of the Broome Aboriginal Media Association's Radio Goolarri, has pointed to the very same forces working in the Kimberley:

What with the state and influence of the ever-impending tide of multi-media, the multi-nationals and commercialisation creeping ever so rapidly into the most remote parts of the Kimberley, certain important aspects of our culture have been and continue to be lost forever. For instance, there's a saying at home that sport is killing our culture. It's not just the influence of sport. It's the ability of the media to capitalise on its popularity here in Broome, and even in the most remote outback location in the Kimberley. Just about every school-child has at least one item of attire, perhaps a T-shirt, a pair of Reeboks or a baseball cap, depicting Michael Jordan or Chuck O'Neill or some other basketball superstar or team, and they're not even Australians. (Edgar, reproduced in Chapter 6, below).

Edgar goes on to indicate how the popularity of both African American and Australian sports requires a major investment of time by Aboriginal people, and how this has an effect on traditional pursuits:

Not many are the days of loading the truck and going fishing, hunting or looking for bush fruit, or gathering your spears and going for long walks, learning the skills and talking the language. Today hunting is mostly done on Nintendo video games and they're talking like New York rappers. (See Chapter 6, below).

Edgar says that among the questions that 'we as media, indigenous media, are faced with today', is this: 'Are we in a position, if not to stem the tide, at least to come to a compromise and still maintain our culture and identity in this very multi-racial community which is Australia?'

It is worth recalling that Joe Edgar speaks from the position of one who is actively involved in *increasing* the 'ever-impending tide of multi-media' in the north-west of Western Australia, through the work of the Indigenous radio station Radio Goolarri. In other words, both media themselves, from broadcasting to Nintendo, and the Black American 'influence', from basketball to 'New York rappers', may work both ways. They may be seen to be undermining or supporting local cultures. They may be seen as an influx, 'creeping ever so rapidly', or they may be seen as a point of identification for everyone, down to the last schoolchild in the most remote community. Black America is certainly alive and well in Indigenous Australia. How the ongoing dialogue between the two is managed is a matter for 'compromise'—Indigenous media activists wish to maintain their culture and identity while using the technological and cultural resources, from baseball caps to radio stations, associated with 'this very multi-racial community which is Australia'.

Race + Class = Indigenous Nation?

Everyone is cast either as Uncle Tom on the right or as Malcolm X on the left. Of course, Aboriginal youth definitely don't want to be on the Uncle Tom side.

(Noel Pearson, 1994: 184)

There is a class dimension to 'racial' categorization. The African American struggle, where it concerns urban Blacks (i.e. where it is Northern not Southern), is also clearly a translation into American and ethnic terms of what would in industrial Europe, especially Britain, have been understood in more purely *class* terms. American public debate about class is conducted by talking about race; not the administrative 'pentagon' but the binary difference (here understood as antagonism) between people of colour and whites.

Australia does not map neatly onto either American or British models in this context. Its 'lived experience' of class is unique. Aboriginal people don't map neatly into 'class' discourses either. Nevertheless, both remote (traditional) and town-dwelling or urban Aboriginal people have certainly been subjected to policies that were imported from the British way of dealing with the labouring classes. Remote policies were modelled on the treatment of British agricultural and livestock workers (most famously perhaps on the Vestey stations). Equally, town-dwelling Aboriginal people were subjected to policies designed originally for the nineteenth-century urban poor of London, Manchester, and Glasgow. Under the heading of 'Philosophy' in its discussion of Australian welfare systems, the authors of *Bringing Them Home*, the Report of the 'Stolen Generation' inquiry, are quite clear about the British class origins of Aboriginal policy in Australia (although these 'origins' are earlier than they say):

In Western terms, welfare as a form of child saving has its origins in late 19th century middle-class concerns about the 'dangerous' classes, single mothers and working class families in industrialised regions of England. (National Inquiry, 1997: 434).

They comment:

We have seen that Indigenous families were historically characterised by their Aboriginality as morally deficient. There is evidence that this attitude persists. A focus on child-saving facilitates blaming the family and viewing 'the problem' as a product of 'pathology' or 'dysfunction' among members rather than a product of structural circumstances.... Indigenous families face both race and class prejudice among many welfare officers. (National Inquiry, 1997:434).

But just as there is no politically significant African Australian population (no political tradition sited upon them), so Aboriginal people are not an industrial working class. On the contrary, the white colonists themselves were drawn from that class and colonial administrators were trained to deal with it. Between them, they developed the policies of *internal* (White Australia) egalitarianism and *external* (anti-Aboriginal) racism that filtered up to become the first truly independent 'identity' of the Australian colonies against the stated interests of the Imperial power in London, which was to protect all ethnicities under the Queen-Empress.

Latterly, many of the issues arising from *both* of the powerful semiotic and political 'locomotives' of *European class politics* and *Black American ethnic politics* have been imported to drive *Aboriginal* affairs in Australia. Aboriginal people have been overburdened with discourses, policies, and prejudices associated with class and race elsewhere. Whether these engines have taken Indigenous people to places where they want to go is a matter for them (notwithstanding the following case). What's important in the present context is that the *media* for generating meanings for Indigeneity in Australia out of 'dialogue' with the asymmetric, untranslatable discourses of European class and American Black politics, are the same media that form the object of study of this book.

A celebrated example of media coverage of a racially motivated murder in Australia in 1992 is very revealing of how the discourses of white egalitarianism mixed with anti-Aboriginal racism, together with the importation of class/race antagonism, in this case white racism, can work out in practice. Louis Johnson was of Aboriginal descent but was adopted by a wealthy white family (his adoptive father, Bill Johnson, was himself originally from England). Louis was murdered on his nineteenth birthday in a roadside attack by white youths. Bill Johnson later wrote of the class/race identity of the killers, two of whom were convicted of the murder; the other three people involved were never charged:

These kids went to beat up or to kill a black person. Louis was the one that they met and killed. That's admitted. And we're not talking about deprived white kids who have had a lack of education. One of the two girls in the car went to one of the most expensive schools in Perth. You're talking about the mortgage-belt in the northern suburbs where this racist murder occurred, committed by middle class kids. The other obscenity which really hurts me is that none of the kids had been in this country longer than November 1988 [just over three years at the time of the murder]. They're all English. (Quoted in Mickler, 1998: 312).

In other words, what looked like a classic example of *Australian* racism was itself *imported* from England, where unrepentant racist murderers were soon to become familiar figures in the British media, after the Stephen Lawrence killing (and subsequent Macpherson Inquiry) in London. Attitudes that had been hardened in the UK, where white racism was directed primarily against Afro-Caribbean people, were simply transferred to an Aboriginal Australian youth. It wasn't specifically anti-Aboriginal racism that motivated Louis Johnson's killers. He bore the burden of an imported binarization of racial antagonism.

The fact that his killers were middle class and English (as well as white) could not have been known immediately to those who found the injured Louis Johnson. But his own Aboriginal descent was immediately and lethally significant, despite his middle-class upbringing and affluent family life. He was treated stereotypically by the ambulance officers who came to the scene—they assumed he'd been petrol sniffing and took him home, where, after telling his sister he'd been attacked by 'nazis', he died (Mickler, 1998: 54–5).

His Aboriginality was also significant to the Perth media. In an instance of what Steve Mickler calls 'posthumous discrimination':

Although the Perth media had been preoccupied with youth and juvenile crime...its treatment of Louis'...murder...was subdued. His brutal murder was treated as a different kind of crime, one that did not fit the actual but unadmitted news agenda of innocent non-Aboriginal victims of Aboriginal lawlessness. *The Sattler File*'s [Perth's leading radio talkback show] lack of interest in the killing was particularly conspicuous and revealing—here we had a cowardly and unprovoked attack on a citizen by a group of youths and juveniles—seemingly tailor-made for the program's theme of uncontrolled 'feral' teenagers roving the streets. The program ignored it. (Mickler, 1998: 55–6).

It is hard not to conclude that there is a pattern of *internal* (white) *egalitarianism* and *external* (anti-Aborigninal) *racism* working here. 'Juvenile crime' was a news category that was routinely—almost 'traditionally'—filled by reporting instances of *Aboriginal* juvenile crime. Middle-class white English teenagers and youths from the mortgage belt, including a girl attending 'one of the most expensive schools in Perth', were too close to the 'we' community of readers and audiences to make convincing representatives of threats to it by a 'they' group. Equally, a 19-year-old Aboriginal boy was not a readily identifiable personification of the 'victim of juvenile crime' category. The actual circumstances of Aboriginality, class, and crime were of very little relevance in the way the events of the Louis Johnson case played themselves out, both at the time of the killing and in the media coverage of it afterwards. What was played out was a 'script' based upon imported racial stereotypes.

Australian media coverage itself, in common with intellectual and public-policy analysts, has imported frameworks of explanation from the USA and Europe to model Indigenous issues. Simultaneously Indigenous people too have imported concepts, political strategies, and cultural styles from African America in the course of elaborating their own positions within the Australian context. Indigenous people are the bearers of discourses of 'race' in Australia that in the USA do not apply to Native Americans. Within the overall Australian 'semiosphere', the

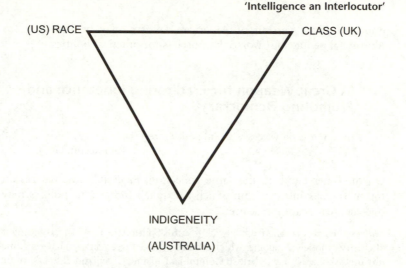

global politics of 'race' and 'class' find a 'local habitation and a name' in a demographically disproportionate attention to Indigeneity. There are political implications to this, not necessarily working to the advantage of Indigenous people in Australia. They have been spelt out very clearly in two contrasting contributions to a book on the 'Politics of Mabo' that was published soon after the Keating Government enacted its Native Title Legislation in 1993.

As one of the leading figures involved in the negotiations with the government, Noel Pearson, Executive Director of the Cape York Land Council, wrote:

A problem that pervades our politics is that people have a conviction that things could be better but cannot think in a hard-headed way about the steps that should be taken in order to get that result. We've internalised black American notions of political behaviour (and they're internalised by white people too). Everyone is cast either as Uncle Tom on the right or as Malcolm X on the left. Of course, Aboriginal youth definitely don't want to be on the Uncle Tom side. They want to be on the 'no compromise' side of politics. We've internalised those notions of radicalism and sell-out and this limits our capacity to negotiate our way through a very difficult situation in which our armoury is not great. (Pearson, 1994: 184).

In other words, being 'Black' *as well as* Indigenous can prove to be a double-edged sword for Aboriginal and Islander politics. It can be an added burden at just the moment when the heroic example of the American Civil Rights and Black Power movements seems most apposite—i.e. when 'Aboriginal youth' take pride in their Aboriginality. The imported Black version of American Leftism may be inspiring for Aboriginal people, but worse than useless for practical politics.

'A Great Weapon for Eradicating Ignorance and Promoting Democracy'

I will not say it was easy. Good policy rarely is.

(Paul Keating, 1993)

On the other hand, in the same collection, Peter Jull summarizes an international context within which Australia's Indigenous politics may make a great deal more sense:

Mabo switched Australia from a track towards South Africa or Ulster, sending it after better models. Analogies which seemed remote three years ago have become obvious. Alaska, Nunavut, British Columbia, Lapland, Greenland, Russia's Arctic coast are all working through the same issues facing Australia. Others have debated and tried many options already. We can learn from them at no cost. ... *Mabo* should remind governments that indigenous peoples want recognised rights and negotiated social outcomes, not privileges conceded or pats on the back. Other 'first world' countries have accepted this reality and are implementing reforms to make it workable in daily practice. The strengths and weaknesses of practical models abroad are a most valuable and under-utilised resource for Australians. (Jull, 1994: 212).

Interestingly, Jull is scathing about 'rather tawdry' bureaucratic programmes overseas (Canada) in the welfare, housing, or alcohol areas, and sceptical about the 'alleged' policy in Australia of 'self-determination' including ATSIC (the Aboriginal and Torres Strait Islander Commission). He argues, however, that Australia's unique contribution to international Indigenous politics has been the shift from 'failed bureaucratic moulds' to 'high level negotiations between governments and indigenous peoples'. Only this can 'break impasses' (Jull, 1994: 204–5). He cites three 'precedents':

1. Paul Keating as Prime Minister taking 'the lead role in indigenous affairs in Cabinet' (his 'leadership left political circles behind and often clucking disapproval');
2. Keating's 'face-to-face negotiations with indigenous representatives of the principal groups concerned with "native title" as defined by Mabo';
3. The appointment of the first national Aboriginal Social Justice Commissioner, Mick Dodson. (204–5).

What Paul Keating produced, in fact, was certainly a novelty in Aboriginal politics; a peak group, including Noel Pearson, whose members were deemed to 'represent' the *national* Aboriginal community (perhaps in advance of such an entity coming into existence). This group was organized *politically* in its dealings with the Labor government—in other words it was constituted not as a devolved arm of government (like ATSIC), but as a *political opposition* with whom Mr Keating could deal. An Aboriginal body emerged with equal status to state and territory governments and powerful interests such as miners and pastoralists (represented through their political associations). This body—known as the 'A-Team'—wasn't simply a consultative group designed to feed expert knowledge into a drafting process. It was a full participant in *negotiations*, and was therefore responsible for conducting the political 'art of the possible' on behalf of Aboriginal people at large when concessions, horse-trading, and compromise were needed in the run-up to the legislative deadlines. Mr Keating himself made the point in his Second Reading speech:

[We held] discussions with Aboriginal and industry representatives and with the states and territories. These were positive, detailed talks. They raised many important matters which have been taken up in the legislation I am presenting here today.

I will not say it was easy. Good policy rarely is. And the result will not—and could never—satisfy everyone. If it is to be good legislation it should not even try. This legislation is principled and workable, the product of a sustained and thorough policy process. (Keating, 1993).

Having achieved this high-level national attention to Indigenous policy-making, Jull argues that Australia's attention can turn from *programmes* to *politics*:

Australian public bodies must learn the truth which other 'first world' countries have reached through trial, error, and disappointment: that social and economic outcomes are not *the problem* to be solved, but are symptoms of powerlessness. Powerlessness is political, and not cured by ingenious socio-economic programs alone. (Jull, 1994: 205).

The 'powerlessness' described here has given rise to its own versions of urban (and 'urban' meaning 'Black' even in rural contexts) resistance and liberation politics, ranging from music, subculture, and civil disobedience (see Beresford and Omaji, 1996: 17, 79–80, 128–30, 142–4) to the Aboriginal Provisional Government (APG). But such inspirational politics, whether modelled on Bob Marley or Malcolm X, can prove to be a serious disadvantage in formulating 'principled and workable' legislation in negotiation with people from opposing positions. As Henry Reynolds has put it (in reference to the APG): 'While the destination is clearly determined the way to reach it is poorly articulated' (Reynolds, 1996: 139).

That is a crucial insight. The 'way to reach' such destinations can only be worked out in public discourse (i.e. in the media), and only by dialogue between different (and differing) parties. This is classically what a public sphere is for. But any Indigenous public sphere must necessarily be a strange-looking object—certainly not spherical. It precedes any state or nation whose 'public sphere' it may be, and it may have more affinity with developments in the farthest reaches of the northern hemisphere than with the 'Australian' public sphere as currently constituted.

An Indigenous public sphere requires a level of 'national' organization of the Indigenous 'polity' that has no precedent in Aboriginal and Islander history. However, 'ethno-nationalism' itself is fraught with dangers for Indigenous peoples, as events in Chechnya, former Yugoslavia, Rwanda/Burundi, and elsewhere attest. Writing of the Indigenous Khanty-Mansi groups of Western Siberia, Marjorie M. Balzer says:

Khanty leaders rarely act at the level of mass political identity by speaking for their whole people....Their activism is one variation in a broad range of potential nationalisms and attempts at cultural empowerment. More accurately, it is a form of nonchauvinist ethnonationalism, a politicized yet usually liberal ethnic consciousness born of the need to defend their cultural heritage and lands. It fits with membership in the wider community of Native-rights agitation. (Balzer, 1999: 221).

Like Jull, Balzer discusses the advantages to be had from Indigenous rights organizations working together across international boundaries (e.g. linking Siberian with Native American, Saami, and Inuit groups). One reason for this is that they share problems both *internally*, in the extent to which they can speak on behalf of 'their whole people'; and *externally*, in the degree and direction of activism needed to defend, survive, and adapt. She finds a variation of much-maligned 'liberal' politics preferable:

It is urgent to understand the dynamics of how mildly politicized ethnonationalism, oriented toward positive goals, can be maintained by the minorities... without turning into the polarized, embittered nationalisms of former Yugoslavia or Chechnya. Polarization stems far more often from the 'centre'...than from powerless peoples on the periphery, but their radicalized responses can spin out of control, creating a storm of mutually self-defeating hatred (222).

Comparing Siberian and American Indigenous experiences, she writes that 'I have come to understand the degree to which they can offer each other not only dialogue and advice, but also adaptable aspects of their own models, constructed and reconstructed from interactive histories with Russian/Slavic and Euro-American/Anglo others' (220). In this context, many Native American leaders have:

rejected full assimilation while accommodating themselves to living with dignity in the Anglo world. On both sides of the Bering Sea, multiple identities on multiple levels, activated situationally with flexible style, have become normal for indigenous leaders, if not for all their peoples (220).

Balzer concludes that 'Native consensus-style democracy (not necessarily United States majority-rule democracy) may be a means toward ensuring more liberal varieties of ethnonationalism' (223)—that, plus land and good lawyers.

In his autobiography *Long Walk to Freedom*, Nelson Mandela reports a world tour that he took soon after he was released from prison in 1990. He writes:

I went up to Harlem, an area that had assumed legendary proportions in my mind since the 1950s when I watched the young men in Soweto emulate the sharp fashions of Harlem dandies. Harlem, as my wife said, was the Soweto of America. I spoke to a great crowd in Yankee Stadium, telling them that an unbreakable umbilical cord connected black South Africans and black Americans... To us, Harlem symbolized the strength of resistance and the beauty of black pride. (Mandela, 1994: 698).

Mandela goes on immediately to include Aboriginal people in this sweeping 'north–south' dialogue. En route from North America to Europe, his plane took in a refuelling stop at Goose Bay on the Arctic Circle. Mandela writes:

As I was strolling on the tarmac I noticed some people standing at the airport fence. I asked a Canadian official who they were. 'Eskimos', he said.

In my 72 years on earth I had never met an Innuit and never imagined that I would. I headed over to that fence and found a dozen or so young people in their late teens who had come out to the airport because they'd heard our plane was going to stop there. As a boy I had read about the Innuit (the name 'Eskimo' was given to them by the colonists), and the impression I received from the racist, colonial texts was that they were a very backward people.

But in talking with these bright young people I learned that they had watched my release on television and were familiar with events in South Africa. 'Viva ANC', one of them said. The Innuit are an aboriginal people, historically mistreated by a white settler population. There were parallels between the plights of black South Africans and Innuit people. What struck me so forcefully was how small the planet had become during my decades in prison. It was amazing to me that a teenage Innuit, living at the roof of the world, could watch the release of a political prisoner at the southern tip of Africa. Television had shrunk the world and had, in the process, become a great weapon for eradicating ignorance and promoting democracy. (Mandela, 1994: 699–700).

Just as 'racist, colonial texts' can convey false impressions of Indigenous peoples, so television can be a force both for dialogue between Aboriginal and other colonized people around the world, and for promoting democratic change from one end of the planet to the other. This is the Indigenous public sphere, just as necessary to Aboriginal self-development as is more local debate about ways, means, and directions.

3 | 'Narrative Accrual' in the Australian Semiosphere

History will be kind to us. I intend to write it.'
(Attributed to Winston Churchill)

In the academic, government, and media coverage of Indigenous issues, a distinction operates between different discursive places within an overall 'universe of Indigeneity' created in the stories and by the narratives that comprise the coverage.

Two domains in the 'universe of Indigeneity'

- Indigeneity of **law-formation**. A sphere of and for *anthropology and administration*, emblematized by the work of Fred Myers (1991) and Tim Rowse (1992, 1993). It is centred on land, and interested in traditional forms of life, land rights, remote communities, ATSIC. It is dedicated to the reproduction of orderliness, and is conducted by academic discourses and discourses of governance. Its characteristic narrational form is cyclical myth.

- Indigeneity of **anomaly**. A sphere of and for *correction and protection*, emblematized by the work of the National Inquiry into the Separation of Aboriginal and Torres Strait Islander Children from Their Families (1997), and by that of Quentin Beresford and Paul Omaji (1996). It is centred on persons, and located in urban and suburban life, interested in the impact of the welfare and justice systems, of carers or fiduciaries of Aboriginal populations, and in Aboriginal people living a non-traditional life. It is dedicated to action discourses. Its characteristic media form is news.

The terms 'law formation' and 'anomaly' come from Lotman (1990: 151–3). He distinguishes between two types of structure within the 'semiosphere'. Social, cultural, and religious structures are 'fixtures in its space', while others 'have a higher degree of freedom of choice in their

71

LAW–FORMING TEXTS	ANOMALOUS TEXTS
Fixed in space	Mobile – 'able to cross the structural boundaries of cultural space' (infringement)
No new information (repetitious)	One-off occurrences (anomalies)
Narrative determined by nature (season, cosmos, land); story can begin at any point	Narrative determined by succession of deeds (plot)
Identity (e.g. night/winter/death are transformations of each other)	Difference (surprise, news, accidents)
Reduces diversity of world to 'invariant images'	Adds to knowledge of the world
About 'me' (the listener)	About the world
Cyclical time	Linear time
Functions to create a picture of the world	Records chance events, crimes, disasters, violations of some established order
Records principles	Records events
Gives rise to law–affirming texts both sacred and scientific	Gives rise to historical texts, chronicles, records
MYTH	NEWS

THE SEMIOSPHERE

Adapted from Lotman, 1990: 151–3

behaviour' (151). Two 'primordial types of texts' must be contrasted—'the central cyclical text engendering mechanism cannot typologically speaking exist on its own: it must have in opposition to it a text-producing mechanism organised according to linear time and which records not regularities but anomalies' (153). The two types may therefore be contrasted as in the diagram.

The modern 'plot-text', says Lotman, 'is the fruit of the interaction and mutual interference of these two primordial types of texts' (1990: 153). This applies to literary and cinematic texts alike—the novel and the movie. But it also applies very strongly to texts that may at first sight seem too ephemeral to require explanation of this kind, principally TV drama (especially soap opera, but also including mini-series and tele-movies) and news. And in our view it applies equally to texts on either side of the fact/fiction boundary. Thus, bearing in mind the 'interaction and mutual interference' of the two types, it might still be useful to posit that while journalism tends to conform to the 'anomalous' category, drama, including soap opera, tends to conform to the 'law-forming' type of narrative. Strong evidence for the latter comes from a detailed and intriguing analysis of the ABC-TV mini-series *Heartland* (broadcast in 1994) by John Morton (1996: 117–35). His argument is that in the sexualized relationship between an Aboriginal character (played by Ernie Dingo) and a white Australian woman (played by Cate Blanchett), *Heartland* is an 'allegory of reconciliation'. Its *method* is that of fictional story-telling, but its *effect* is, literally, law-forming:

I would suggest...that while an earlier racist ideology rendered Aboriginal people impotent, the clear intention of the sexualised images of reconciliation is to (re)assign power. This bestowal is surely the same as that which has occurred in the acknowledgement of Aboriginality in Australian history that determined the High Court's Mabo judgement—and nowhere has it been symbolically worked through more thoroughly than in *Heartland*. (Morton, 1996: 126).

In addition to its application to media texts themselves, we believe that the two-type categorization of the 'universe of Indigeneity' applies also to academic and 'long-form' truth-narratives like government reports, textbooks, and research. They may be organized around 'law formation' and 'anomaly' too. This typology seems useful in the present context for two reasons.

First, it is neither anthropological nor political in itself. It is a typology based on Lotman's attempt (a convincing attempt, in our view) to explain narration, the production of text, and the organization or structuring of different kinds of text, in the cultural universe of a given time and place. This makes it useful in a project such as this one, where the main focus is on media coverage of Indigenous issues—the *textualization of* Indigeneity in fact. It provides a perspective in which news coverage can be understood as part of a larger semiotic system that will in practice determine what form particular news stories take, and what they mean. It suggests that analysis needs to address the widest possible range of stories, and not simply to confine itself to one genre, least of all 'hard news' alone. And it supplies a comparative element for the analysis of Australian material. Yuri Lotman worked about as far away from Aboriginal Australia as it is possible to get (in Tartu, Estonia, in the former Soviet Union). His general model of the semiosphere is helpful in trying to understand what texts about Indigenous issues are doing.

Second, Lotman's typology of texts brings together kinds of story that are usually so strictly separated from each other that they seem to be unconnected: scientific enquiry and news, for instance, or traditional myths and contemporary soap opera, or fact and fiction, right down to micro-distinctions such as those that operate within a given form, such as 'hard' and 'soft' news, news journalism and feature journalism, the daily press and the magazine press, print journalism and broadcast journalism. In each case these are strongly felt distinctions that may indeed sustain entire industries, certainly specialist careers. But the stories produced within each specialism may share important characteristics with those from elsewhere. The separation of different story-telling institutions is confirmed by the organization of print and electronic media into generic categories, scheduled at different times and places, produced by different organizations or teams, for different cultural purposes.

Truth-seeking stories are produced by such great over-arching cultural institutions as 'science', 'education', and 'government', and are kept radically apart from stories produced by 'the media', that seem to deal only in ephemera, such as the news and entertainment. But the very effort made to keep different story-types separate is evidence that the different categories, organizations, and institutions are parts of a larger, common structure. Discourses of *action* need to be contrasted with discourses of *order*—neither can be understood without the contrasting co-presence of the other. News vies with myth, but in Lotman's typology myth shares the same aims as science (reducing the world to order to understand it), and uses the same techniques as soap opera. Meanwhile news is a species of history, using the same techniques as the action-hero plot. Narratives from apparently dissimilar contexts, like academic research, media information, and media entertainment, may turn out to occupy the same category in the overall scheme of things in the 'semiosphere'.

Using Lotman's typology, it is clear that 'the journalist', like the detective, functions as a latter-day transformation of a very ancient plot hero: one who 'can *act*'. The action hero, says Lotman, 'may be a noble robber or a *picaro*, a sorcerer, spy, detective, terrorist or superman—the point is that he is able to do what others cannot, namely to cross the structural boundaries of cultural space' (1990: 151). Detectives in fiction and journalists in fact are among the few occupational categories in modern associated life that are culturally licensed to ignore the usual 'prohibitions'. That is indeed their job. They must disobey interdictions (foot-in-the-door), infringe prohibited places (government or corporate secrecy), explore otherwise hidden domains (specialist areas of life, like 'the economy'), in order to bring to light (i.e. to narrate) their stories. They bring arcane knowledge to general readers. They are necessary to cross boundaries and bring back stories on behalf of the culture at large.

Despite their 'interaction and mutual interference' in modern texts, a sign that 'law formation' and 'anomaly' are still distinct is that in the literature about Aboriginality there is very limited cross-referencing between them (but see Rowse, 1993: chs. 2 and 4 especially). Using the typology of 'law formation' and 'anomaly' in this context may suggest that there is a neat division between traditional and modern, outback and urban, remote and settled, 'authentic' and Europeanized Aboriginal domains, but in fact it requires the reverse. The whole point is that both mechanisms require the other to exist at all—they cannot exist on their own. The typology brings them together, it does not separate them. There are issues that cut across both—questions of sovereignty, citizenship, and self-determination, for instance. There are also issues that are not commonly addressed at all in either domain; chiefly, in the present context, Indigeneity and the media.

On one side is law formation, fixed in space, where central narratives are concerned with identity, nature, reducing the world to order, and where stories are about the 'we' community, recording principles. On

The 'Universe of Indigeneity' and the 'Two Domains'

the other side is found mobility, infringement of boundaries, narratives about action, the world, difference, and anomalous occurrences, and where stories are about 'they' identities, recording not principles but violations, crimes, and events. In short: myth and news.

But, as we have emphasized, these opposing text-generating mechanisms are not capable of independent existence on their own; as Lotman says, each needs the other to exist at all. It is important to notice the implication. The 'anomalous' domain, which appears to be *the* one and only Aboriginal domain in much news coverage of Indigenous issues (because of the type and function of news), is merely one side of the narrative coin, needing to be understood in relation to law-forming narratives that exist elsewhere in the 'semiosphere'. In other words, this is only the half of it.

But it is *systematically* the half. Here our argument falls into step with that of Bain Attwood, who describes in a robust and serviceable phrase how a nation is constituted and becomes aware of itself, by a process of what he calls '*narrative accrual*':

In the late nineteenth and early twentieth centuries the Australian nation was created by 'narrative accrual'—a process whereby a corpus of connected and shared narratives constitute something which can be called either a myth, a history, or a tradition. Furthermore, it was only as the people came to comprehend and know this story that they came to realise and be conscious of themselves as Australians. (Attwood, 1996: 101).

Here is 'law-forming' narrative incarnate. But it will be noted that Attwood locates this 'semiosphere' at the level of the *Australian nation*. That is to say, the 'narrative accrual' he is describing created something semiotically much larger than the 'universe of Indigeneity' that we have been discussing, for it encompassed 'Australian' and 'British' as well as 'Aboriginal' components:

This history of the nation constituted the British, the Australians and the Aborigines as its principal protagonists, and discovery, settlement and pioneering as its principal events. And this narrative—which is also to say Australia—assumed a particular content only in terms of these constituents (101).

Attwood's purpose is to show how, if the relations between its British (imperial/colonizer/heritage), Aboriginal (Indigenous), and Australian (pioneer/settler) components change, then 'Australia' as a whole must change in meaning:

There was, consequently, a textual interdependence between each of the protagonists, 'the British', 'the Australians' and 'the Aborigines', as well as between these and the foundational events. This is to argue, then, that each category of the history, for example 'Australians', was and is profoundly dependent upon the maintenance of a particular relationship with the other [categories], for example 'Aborigines'.... Consequently, as these internal relationships change, the meanings of Australia are severely disrupted, and this is the case, I will argue, with Mabo (101).

For the purposes of the present study, the implication of Attwood's schema is that the 'universe of Indigeneity' we have identified is itself part of the process of 'narrative accrual' that constitutes Australia. Together, the 'anthropological/administrative' domain of 'law formation', and the 'anomalous' domain of 'correction and protection', make the 'Aboriginal' constituent of Attwood's schema. This in turn is a component within a larger 'semiosphere' in which Australia as a whole 'accrues' narratively.

Taking the long view of history, it can be argued that during the period when there was intense dialogic traffic between the 'British' and 'Australian' components of 'Australian' narrative there was less need and

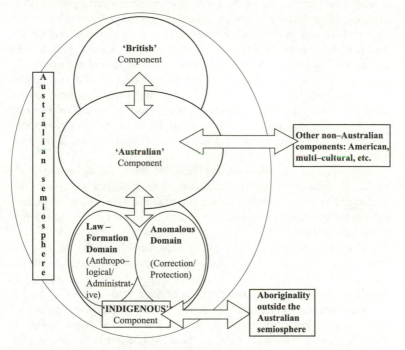

The 'Narrative Accrual' of the Australian Nation

Note: 'Components' adapted from Attwood, 1996.

room for dialogue between the 'Australian' and 'Aboriginal' components (and in any case that dialogue was conducted in the language of anthropology, not history, as Tom Griffiths has pointed out: Griffiths, 1996: 230). Indeed, as Australia was 'accruing' its nationhood in the late nineteenth century, right up to the creation of Australian citizenship as a separate category from British in 1949, the dominant 'narrative' of Aboriginality was that of the 'dying race', and the dominant policy assimilation. John Morton, borrowing W. E. H. Stanner's phrase, accurately describes this period as the 'great Australian silence' (1996: 135; and see Stanner, 1969: 13)—a time when dialogue was at a very low ebb. It was only after accounts had been more or less settled with Britain in the postwar period that the dialogue between Australia's 'Aboriginal' and 'Australian' components began to intensify. Emblematic dates were the UK's entry into the EEC in 1973, following closely upon Aboriginal people's entry into Australian citizenship in 1967; as the links with Britain receded, those with Indigenous Australia became increasingly insistent.

With the amendment of (British) common law by the Mabo and Wik decisions on Native Title in the early 1990s, all the internal relationships changed. Australia turned out to 'mean' something quite new. Its origin, *terra nullius*, was overturned. Its future turned on the outcome of new dialogue with Indigenous people. Aboriginal and Islander people were 'discovered' by history to be separate from the Australian nation, resulting in 'three nations encased within the Australian state' (Reynolds, 1996: 177). They became more important than the 'British' component of Australia (which, however, didn't 'go away'—as witness the referendum in November 1999, when a particular model of an Australian republic was rejected, with the result that the British Crown remained the Australian head of state).

These changes provoked an explosion of discourse right across the media, government, and the academy. The 1990s in Australia were characterized by unusually intense internal dialogue about what is at stake in the meaning of the new relationships, from Mabo to One Nation to the referendum.

Taking the 'synchronic' view of the 'semiosphere', it can be seen that although new meanings have been generated from new dialogue, the old ones don't disappear. Cultural evolution is not the same as biological; there's no such thing as extinction. Once generated, cultural texts and meanings remain in existence, available for later times to make use of. This is as true for national narratives as it is for re-runs and repeats on TV. Indeed, Bain Attwood discusses the persistence of a 'British' narrative of Australia that has brought into the current period the meanings of the past, provoking great political turbulence in the process. He posits a distinction between 'conservative' history and 'new Australian history' to describe the difference between narratives that promote the 'British' and 'Aboriginal' heritage in Australia respectively. Beyond the detail of the argument he is conducting with other historians (notably Geoffrey Blainey), with conservative politicians (the National Party), and with mining representatives, it is possible to see that the relations between the 'British', 'Aboriginal', and 'Australian' components of the Australian semiosphere have been engaged in dialogic turn-taking. For several decades around and after Federation in 1901, dialogue with the 'British' component predominated. Since 1967, and increasingly intensively into the 1990s, dialogue with the 'Aboriginal' component has come to the fore. These very large-scale shifts and changes in 'narrative accrual' must form part of (and the context for) any investigation of 'media coverage'.

It is most important to remember that the 'dialogue' under discussion here is between components in a semiosphere. It may or may not include dialogue with actual Aboriginal persons. The dialogue is between 'Australia', as 'narratively accrued', and the 'universe of Indigeneity', which is itself, as we describe below, internally organized into two contrasting 'Aboriginal domains' of 'law formation' and 'anomaly', both of which are determined by the structure of and dialogue between this larger set of components. What is it that 'Australia' needs to know about 'Aboriginality', especially during the long phase when it was concentrating on its relationship with Britain (a period of decolonization from the British Empire, while maintaining a 'British' cultural and legal identity)? During such a phase, dialogue with the 'Aboriginal' component was quiescent rather than creative. What better to keep things quiet than a set of stories, discourses, and narrative structures that distinguish between traditional Aboriginal life, to be investigated by anthropologists and reported in government documents, and (sub)urban Aboriginal persons, to be investigated by the forces of state correction and 'welfare', and reported in the newspapers? The 'universe of Indigeneity' *generated* stories about Indigeneity within the terms of the 'narrative accrual' of Australian nationhood as a whole, and the major 'narrators' of that nationhood, government and media, divided up between them the Indigenous universe they had created.

The whole structure would be neat and tidy if it wasn't for Aboriginal people and politics themselves, on the one hand, and the crisis of legitimacy precipitated by Mabo and Wik (i.e. literally 'rewriting Australian history'), on the other. The orderly generation of stories in government reports and the news media about Aboriginal life and crime was radically disrupted in the 1990s. To understand media coverage of Indigenous issues during this period, then, it is necessary to:

- contrast the two different 'Aboriginal domains' with each other,
- contrast the 'universe of Indigeneity' thus constituted with 'Australian' and 'British' components of the Australian national narrative over time,
- understand how Indigenous appropriations of the domains, of their component of the stories, and of the media themselves, are producing new patterns and relationships in the Australian 'semiosphere'.

The Law-Forming (Anthropological/Administrative) Domain

Culturally ambiguous Aboriginal organisations are historic necessities.

(Rowse, 1992: 35–6)

The first of the two 'Aboriginal domains' identifiable in the literature is the anthropological/administrative domain. It is from the anthropological study of existing Aboriginal societies that those who are interested in Aboriginal governance draw their models. What Aboriginal 'self-determination' might mean clearly depends at least in part on what Aboriginal people in various contexts have in the past defined or continue to understand as 'self'. Moves towards Aboriginal sovereignty require that the form and extent of the 'Aboriginal domain' needs to be explored and elaborated.

The term 'Aboriginal domain' itself seems to originate with the anthropologist John von Sturmer's consideration of a (literal) *topographical* domain (in fact, western Arnhem Land), 'in which the dominant social life and culture are Aboriginal, where the major language or languages are Aboriginal, where the system of knowledge is Aboriginal; in short, where the resident Aboriginal population constitutes the public' (1984: 219). Appropriately, this Aboriginal domain is founded on *land*. But it has not remained with land. In the passage just quoted von Sturmer identifies 'social life', 'culture', 'language', 'knowledge', and 'the public' as constituting the Aboriginal domain, rather than confining 'domain' to the land upon which these are sited. Indeed, and perhaps in keeping with traditional Aboriginal nomadism, all such matters are *portable*.

Taking his cue from that, Tim Rowse has extended the concept to include much smaller and more contingent (perhaps even 'virtual') 'places' than an entire region. Reviewing the work of other anthropologists in the field, including Stephen Harris, David Trigger, and Peter

Sutton, he cites examples where an Aboriginal domain may need to be understood not geographically but as something that operates alongside non-Aboriginal institutions in *time* rather than space. For instance, the whitefella domain of the cash economy, occupied by Aboriginal people during the working day, may alternate temporally with an Indigenous domain after hours and at weekends. The 'Aboriginal domain' may also be distinguished neither in place nor time but through *practices*. It may be concentrated in what non-Aboriginal tradition assigns to the private rather than the public sphere—cited in Rowse as entertainment, gambling, sport, religion, and ceremonies; styles of behaviour and modes of thought and communication (Rowse, 1992: 19–21).

Rowse discusses relations between these Aboriginal 'enclaves' and what he calls 'welfare colonialism', i.e. government subsidy, the administration of Aboriginal Affairs, and the imposition *by* Government *on* Aboriginal people of 'Aboriginal self-determination' policies. He concludes that the Aboriginal domain is 'enclosed' within Australian society, and therefore that 'self-determination' necessarily operates in a larger framework that is decidedly not determined by Aboriginal people. Thus he argues for policy 'sympathetically to manage the cultural dualities' inherent in such a situation: 'culturally ambiguous Aboriginal organisations are historic necessities' (1992: 35–6).

Although it is inevitable that considerations of 'Aboriginal self-determination' should be founded on existing Aboriginal society, there are well-known problems associated with finding a generalizable definition of what such a society might comprise. The very name of 'Aboriginal people' is not their own but an appellation conferred upon them by the invading power. They share this interesting fate with many other conquered nations, including England's first colony, which was named 'Wales', from the Saxon word for 'foreigner' (i.e. indigenous Briton, not a Saxon). The Welsh word for Wales is Cymru, derived from the Celtic word for 'compatriot' (MacKillop, 1998: 377). Within Aboriginal cultures, are there existing concepts of 'community', 'the general good', 'the public', or even 'Aboriginality' ('compatriot') upon which to build representative and governmental institutions? How do traditional familial and kinship structures relate to modern organizational ones? What weight should be given to the traditional authority of senior men and family heads? What is the status of knowledge, and how can traditional secrecy be accommodated into democratic processes? Should there be a 'bicameral' distinction between ceremonial and democratic representation among Aboriginal people? How can administrative, legal, and bureaucratic requirements for accountability be accommodated to Aboriginal realities? How do modernist ideologies of sexual and gender equality map on to traditional divisions of labour? Rowse cites Peter Sutton's point that 'Western society is built for speed in dealing with people you do not already know', and he comments that 'this impersonal facility can be odd and even abhorrent to Aboriginal people' (Rowse, 1992: 55). In short, an 'Aboriginal domain' founded upon Aboriginal principles is likely to find Western models of good government challenging, and vice versa.

However, in his attempt to derive administrative procedures from anthropological studies of 'self-determination', Rowse discusses the importance of speech acts in this context. He cites the work of the American anthropologist Fred Myers among the western desert Pintupi people, who emphasizes talk, consensus-reaching, and collective decision-making in *constituting* 'the Aboriginal domain'. Noting that the achievement of collective assent seems to be the purpose of meetings, even though nothing may come of the decisions reached, Myers concludes that meetings 'are an end in themselves: the meeting *is* the polity' (Myers, 1991: 271–2).

Myers argues that among the Pintupi, authority is not the organizing principle of the community. Instead, 'they sustain the community not by legislation or subordination of individuals to an institution that represents them collectively, but rather by continually renegotiating their relatedness in consensus' (1991: 270). He analyses the role of meetings in achieving this consensus, saying that the 'power of meetings to create binding determinations is limited'. Instead:

The actions of meetings (decisions, deliberations) do not have a status hierarchically superior to other forms of social action (that is, as principle to case or as rule to application). Meetings tend to deal with idiosyncratic threats to relatedness among those whose lives impinge on each other. Thus, the subjective, moral dimensions of shared identity are notable in speaking. (1991: 270).

Although it is likely that few things were further from Myers's mind when he wrote that passage sometime in the 1980s, in fact it contains an accurate and succinct definition of *the role of the media in constituting a public sphere*. The media do indeed 'tend to deal with idiosyncratic threats to relatedness among those whose lives impinge on each other'; and they are in fact notable for emphasizing 'the subjective, moral dimensions of shared identity'. And the status of the media, like that of the Pintupi meeting, is not 'hierarchically superior to other forms of social action'.

Myers's point is that 'political strategy in Pintupi meetings aims at sustaining the relationship among speakers rather than encouraging antagonistic debates about policy' (1991: 271). He argues that 'the formal features of speech reflect the meeting's function of constituting the polity':

Because the outcome—the consensus no one opposes—appears to come from outside, no one's autonomy is diminished. Indeed, the polity is established as those who accept it. This reflexive property of meetings makes 'consensus' as important in constituting a polity as it is in formulating a policy. (1991: 271).

'The polity' is constituted through dialogic speech as 'those who accept it'. This is a good working definition of 'the indigenous public sphere'. Indeed, it is a good working definition of any public sphere—certainly of the mediated public spheres of Australian and other national polities.

Myers's object in this analysis is not to show homologies between Pintupi and Australian public spheres, but to show how the

salient features of life in this 'egalitarian' society make it sociologically necessary to emphasize the individual and the self. The high value placed on individual autonomy and the work and strategies required to achieve a polity when dominance must appear muted pose a problem for the society's participants, not one imported from outside. Collectivity *is* a problem for the Pintupi. (1991: 23).

Is it only a trick of the rhetorical light that makes this description of Pintupi society appear so accurately to describe Western societies at large? Myers himself is in fact caught between universalistic and particularistic discourse. He declares his disciplinary goal thus:

This study is intended as a contribution to our understanding of the emotions and the mind as reflexive products of social action, and to our comprehension of the logic and content of 'politics' among hunter-gatherers as part of a larger totality of relations. (1991: 23).

Presumably 'our' (in 'contribution to our understanding') is universal; it refers to the anthropological subject, or even to Western knowledge in general. Similarly, 'the' (in 'the emotions and the mind') refers to 'the human'. But 'politics' is significantly distanced from 'our' universals by Myers's use of particularistic scare-quotes— ' "politics" '. Politics based on the meeting seems to be confined to 'hunter-gatherers'. But of course it is not; 'speaking' is the fundamental institution of *parlia*mentary democracy, as its name reminds us. A 'larger totality of relations'—a semiosphere—encompasses both Indigene and anthropologist, specifically in the 'domain' of politics.

The Anomalous (Correction/Protection) Domain

The political difficulty for us was that in most areas of the country people have got nothing to lose: they've lost the bloody lot.

(Noel Pearson, 1994: 184)

Politics seems paramount in the 'anomalous' Indigenous domain, but it is a long way from the polity of the Pintupi meeting; it also seems distant from the everyday realities of individual Aboriginal people caught up in 'correction and protection'. In the 'anomalous' domain, politics appears to come from another place entirely, to be perpetrated upon the lives and bodies of Aboriginal people. Inevitably, then, such politics cannot take the form of decision-making in a polity established by the dialogic speech of those who accept it. It is not administration *by*, but *of*, Aboriginal people. They appear in this domain as the objects of policy, and politics appears only as the bureaucratic and legal enforcement of (and compliance with, evasion of, or resistance to) policies agreed elsewhere.

To turn to the world of the 'stolen generations', as described in *Bringing Them Home* (National Inquiry, 1997), and to the world of the Aboriginal juvenile offender, as described in Beresford and Omaji's *Rites of Passage* (1996), is to turn from *law* to *persons*, and from land to urban and suburban life.

In contrast to Aboriginal people in the 'administrative/anthropological' domain, the people in the 'anomalous' domain are those for whom Native Title has least direct meaning—for them it has been 'extinguished'. Their connection is not with land—they are configured as persons. The opening paragraph of the 700–page *Bringing Them Home* Report signals the point: 'This is no ordinary report. Much of its subject matter is so personal and intimate that ordinarily it would not be discussed' (National Inquiry, 1997: 3). So far away from the Pintupi polity is this that speech itself is understood as abnormal. Such 'ordinariness' that cannot speak about the 'personal and intimate' is well known—it is the family.

Tim Rowse, perhaps the leading analyst of what we have called the 'anthropological/administrative' domain, has written that: 'To the literatures of history and anthropology we must now add what is emerging as the most characteristic genre of Aboriginal writing—autobiography' (Rowse, 1993: 26). Two important chapters of his book *After Mabo* ('Lives in custody' and 'Art and identity') are devoted to showing how this is so. His paradigm example of the 'emerging genre' is Ruby Langford's *Don't Take Your Love to Town* (Langford, 1988). He values her story not only for its incidents, but also for its 'positioning of the reader', who has to 'work hard' to see its 'coherence', but 'the effort delivers a more innovative and uncomfortable knowledge':

The subject whose life is narrated is frequently rendered in terms of its opacity to itself. We are invited to witness the frustration of her efforts to realise her inner life in autonomous statement and action. But if there is an obstruction to the emergence of 'Ruby Langford' as the subject and assured interpreter of her own destiny, it is neither non-Aboriginal hegemony, nor (as in [Sally Morgan's] *My Place*) the weight of colonial history. It is something more immediate: the contingencies of kinship, fractured by rural-urban migration and by the fickle vulnerabilities of men. (Rowse, 1993: 103).

'Something more immediate' than the accrued narratives of history and hegemony turns out to be that relationship between self and sexuality, identity and migration, destiny and family.

Rowse puts family, sexuality, and self at the centre of what he calls here, although not in other writings, 'Koori experience' (1993: 103)—the use of the south-east Australian (modern, urban, collective) term 'Koori'. This terminological shift from the 'Aboriginal domain' of *Remote Possibilities* (1992) to 'Koori experience' in *After Mabo* (1993), is a shift from anthropology and administration to politics and power. It signifies his own migration from the anthropological domain to that of 'protection and correction'.

Rowse is aware of how uncomfortably ideas of *self, sexuality, and family* sit with received notions, both official and popular, of what constitutes a political domain. In particular he understands how state policies directed at Aboriginal families make a nonsense of the familiar (European) distinction between 'public' and 'private' life. For Indigenous people, the European institution of 'the family' has been not a refuge but an offensive weapon:

Child removal, practised in all states and territories at some time, has been the most radical and coercive attempt to eclipse the adult authority which is essential to the social and cultural reproduction of Aboriginality. To understand this policy tradition it is not sufficient to know something of the conditions of such institutions as [various Homes for Aboriginal Boys and Girls around Australia]; it is also essential to suspend our favourable presumptions about white Australian family life. (Rowse, 1993: 44–5).

Although not everyone likely to read Rowse's book would necessarily share his 'presumptions' about family life, white or otherwise (many have no 'favourable presumptions' to suspend), this is a crucial insight. It is a Foucauldian conceptualization of the family as a product and

85

instrument of state policy, first elaborated by Jacques Donzelot (a student of Foucault) in *The Policing of Families* (1979). A landmark Australian 'study' of the pathological effect of child-removal in the context of Aboriginality is the film *Babakiueria* (1986)—a short tragi-comedy that dramatizes the relations between Aboriginal and non-Aboriginal Australia, and those between family life and state policy, by reversing the historical roles. Here, Aboriginal settlers invade and take over the Australian suburban backyard (borrowing the 'native' name 'barbecue-area' for their new country) and, for their own good, remove the children of the bemused and hyper-normal white family they find there. Throughout this process, opportunities are not neglected for commenting on possible reasons for demoralization, fight-back, juvenile delinquency, and poor relations with the agencies of correction (the police) and protection (the welfare), and are the more telling for being realized in a comic genre. The *normal* is political; everyday life is the product of policy. (*Babakiueria* was produced by Julian Pringle, directed by Don Featherstone, and written by Geoffrey Atherton. It was broadcast on ABC-TV in 1986).

Rowse warns against directing 'reforming concern' only to 'more spectacular forms of carceral oppression' (1993: 47), such as institutions of correction (prisons, detention centres) and protection (children's homes, hospital, welfare agencies). He argues that such a focus deflects attention away from 'the "normal", non-Aboriginal family as the consummate site of Aboriginal confinement' (47). He cites a series of autobiographical accounts of the 'family as prison' to demonstrate the damage done to Aboriginal adults by their own treatment as children. He quotes evidence given to the Royal Commission into Aboriginal Deaths in Custody to the effect that 'children have borne the full force of attempts to eradicate Aboriginal culture' (46) by removal to institutions, and by fostering or adoption into non-Aboriginal homes.

Rowse's method here, of relying on the testimony of individual Aboriginal witnesses, was taken up in a big way by the National Inquiry into the Separation of Aboriginal and Torres Strait Islander Children from Their Families. Some of the testimony is brutally direct in showing how institutional life and fostering or adoption into non-Aboriginal families impinged upon self, sexuality, and family, and thence on whole ways of lives (i.e. culture). In a section on 'Parenting', the Report argues that:

Most forcibly removed children were denied the experience of being parented or at least cared for by a person to whom they were attached. This is the very experience people rely on to become effective and successful parents themselves.

Experts told the Inquiry that this was the most significant of all the major consequences of the removal policies. (National Inquiry, 1997: 222).

The import of this estimation of 'the most significant of all the major consequences' can only be measured against the fact that the Report goes on to conclude that child removal amounted to genocide (NI, 218):

The policy of forcible removal of children from Indigenous Australians to other groups for the purpose of raising them separately from and ignorant of their culture and people could properly be labelled 'genocidal' in breach of binding international law from at least 11 December 1946.... The practice continued for almost another quarter of a century. (NI, 275).

From December 1946, when the UN General Assembly (including Australia) adopted a resolution declaring genocide to be a crime under international law, child removal 'constituted a crime against humanity' (NI, 275). It is a crime whose victims are damaged *as parents* later on:

'That's another thing that we find hard is giving our children love. Because we never had it. So we don't know how to tell our kids that we love them. All we do is protect them. I can't even cuddle my kids' cause I never ever got cuddled. The only time was when I was getting raped and that's not what you'd call a cuddle, is it?' [*Confidential evidence from a woman placed in Parramatta Girls' Home at 13 years in the 1960s.*] (NI, 225).

Childhood 'experience' of sexuality (rape), 'family' (a 'Home') and self ('that's not what you'd call a cuddle, is it?') could not be more personal. The love of children, parenting, intergenerational cuddling could not be more 'ordinary'. These ordinary personal experiences in the most private reaches of private life were, however, consequences of genocidal crimes against humanity—than which there is nothing more 'public' or 'political' for the culture involved.

The 'anomalous domain', then, with its emphasis on the personal, on autobiographical anecdote, and on 'correction and protection', turns out to be the very place where Indigenous culture was at its most 'public'. Much of what ends up in the news media about Aboriginal people is focused on individuals' encounters with the agencies of correction and protection. The 'anomalies' that are narrated for the benefit of the Australian (as opposed to Aboriginal) public are stories of infringement—crime, welfare, the justice system, personal breakdown. This is where public policy and public narration alike impinged most forcefully on the Indigenous nation. It was also where Aboriginal people constructed their own sense of themselves, where (as Peter Read has put it) they conducted a hundred-year-long 'war' of resistance (Read, 1988). A prime site for the conduct of that struggle has been the dispersed, apolitical, ordinary, normal, Australian family–the heart of 'Babakiueria'.

The 'anomalous' domain of 'correction and protection' stretched right into the heart of the Australian 'settler' family (a place of radical unsettlement for them), where Aboriginal children were fostered and adopted. It extended to the neighbourhoods, schools, and streets in which separated Aboriginal children had to grow up. In such circumstances, as Rowse points out, 'adoptive or fostering families did not have to be sexually pathological to inflict damage; they had merely to be normal' (Rowse, 1993: 45). The purpose of the removal policy was to separate Aboriginal children from their culture and their identity as Indigenous people. Perversely, then, the genuine parental love of non-Aboriginal people for institutionalized, fostered, and adopted children, where it occurred (see NI, 1997: 169–70), served not to protect the child but to implement the policy.

According to the 'stolen generations' Report:

> The impacts of the removal policies continue to resound through the generations of Indigenous families. The overwhelming evidence is that the impact does not stop with the children removed. It is inherited by their own children in complex and sometimes heightened ways. (NI, 1997: 222).

These 'inherited' impacts include effects on parenting; the children of 'stolen generation' children are more likely to lose their own children to care, welfare, or justice agencies. Those children in turn have experienced higher levels of behavioural problems, violence, substance abuse, the passing on of unresolved grief and trauma, and depression and mental illness (NI, 222–8; Beresford and Omaji, 1996: 32–51).

In such circumstances, Indigenous people are perhaps more in need of Chasing Hawk's 'leave-us-alone law' than ever. The National Inquiry goes to great lengths to Indigenize the procedures for dealing with Indigenous children in the 'correction and protection' systems, with separation a 'last resort', and then only done within the context of the involvement of Indigenous families, communities, and organizations (NI, Recommendations 44–54).

Rowse discusses the difficulties that follow when state agencies step in to deal with the damage that has already been done to Aboriginal adults' authority by these same agencies' policies in the past (1993: 47–51). The disaffection of young Aboriginal men and women, boys and girls, is directed not only against 'society' but also against the authority of their own parents and elders. 'Indigenous parents are now, as a result of many colonial changes, under challenge from their own children and youths' (Rowse, 1993: 51). Beresford and Omaji devote considerable space to an analysis of what they variously call a 'subculture' and an 'underclass' of Aboriginal youth in Western Australia that has grown up during the 1990s:

In the early 1990s then, the signs were clear that Aboriginal youth had been driven to the margins of society. . . . In the years since then . . . a sizeable pool of Aboriginal youth has been alienated by the interaction of family poverty and dysfunction, educational failure and labour market exclusion. Many have sought refuge in a subcultural lifestyle focused on crime and drug abuse. This lifestyle conforms with all that is understood about the presence of an underclass in industrial societies. Whatever the disputes about the use of this term, it evokes the lived experience of those excluded from the mainstream economic life of the community, who see no prospect of a future for themselves and who, eventually, live substantially in hostility to their society. (Beresford and Omaji, 1996: 121).

This 'marginalized subculture' that expresses 'hostility to society' is called by Beresford and Omaji a '*refuge*'—the very term that classically describes the social function of the family. But Aboriginal people's own families are not necessarily a refuge. Indeed, Beresford and Omaji conclude: 'Our investigations made it clear that this feeling of lack of authority and control over their own children is a necessary starting point for any exploration of the impact of family life on patterns of juvenile offending within the Aboriginal community' (1996: 33). Although their study was published before the 'stolen generations' National Inquiry, they anchor their analysis on the impact of forced removal:

The social environment commonly experienced by many of the parents whose children are today caught up in the juvenile justice system has involved cultural dispossession and forced institutionalisation. These experiences have had a marked bearing on three interrelated characteristics common to many Aboriginal families—difficulties in the role of parenting, a pattern of domestic violence and a lifestyle of material disadvantage—all of which are known to correlate with children's involvement in crime. (Beresford and Omaji, 1996: 33).

Sexuality, self, family: these aspects of identity, formed in the most private places of the private sphere, turn out to be the place where Aboriginal culture's most public difficulties are 'nurtured'. 'Correction and protection' has reached into this sphere so deeply that in places there's nothing left but a traumatised crater of 'anomaly':

The authoritarian way of missions typically remains a deeply embedded model of adult–child relations: 'they parent in the same authoritarian manner as the mission without meaning to be cruel. . . . They don't want their kids to go through what they went through and when their kids do wrong they physically punish them.' (Beresford and Omaji, 1996: 43).

Parenting Aboriginal children and teenagers has been made more difficult by the high rates of imprisonment of adult males...In our survey of Aboriginal youth, a staggering ninety-eight percent of those interviewed in detention had had a close family member in jail...(43–4).

In Aboriginal communities, the term family violence, as opposed to domestic violence, is preferred as it includes spouse abuse as well as violence between adult relatives, neglect and sexual abuse of children and elder abuse (44).

Young Aborigines interviewed by [the WA police's Motor Theft] Squad members expressed their strong disapproval of their family backgrounds: the widespread alcoholism, the disinterest [uninterest?] shown by parents in their children, the syndrome of absent parents, the physical and sexual abuse committed by parents and the substandard accommodation lived in by many of the children (46).

These terrible truths are not, for all the focus of this book, Aboriginal truths. What is unique to the present context is that policies, practices, and prejudices developed over a long period to deal with the industrial poor of England, which have left their mark on many a white person who was institutionalized as a child, often by the same organizations as those involved in forced removals of Aboriginal children, were—uniquely— applied to Aboriginal people only because of their Aboriginality. It is perfectly clear from the passages we have just quoted that what you are looking at here is the crater left by genocidal policies. But, equally clearly, the state policies responsible were never intended to produce these particular outcomes (although genocidal 'assimilation' was indeed official policy). But the policies themselves weren't unique. As is now well known, they were applied enthusiastically to the industrial poor of Liverpool, London, and Glasgow. They included forced separation of children who were told the same stories as Aboriginal children were (that their parents were dead, or didn't want them), and then shipped to missions in Western Australia and elsewhere, never to receive news of their family again.

For Aboriginal people, however, 'correction and protection' has turned out to be more than the usual sham, for there was neither a traditional Aboriginal nor a modern 'Australian' sphere of the 'normal' to which they could 'return' once they'd been 'corrected' and 'protected'. For them, anomaly was a permanent condition; 'normality' a place of confinement or worse. Children were the targets (not 'victims') of this set of social arrangements, and sexuality, family, and self, for them, were supposed to develop only when the child's Aboriginality had been denied or erased. The 'private' sphere of 'the family' was not a place of refuge, but of danger, requiring not the building of identity but its destruction.

Because forced removal into the 'anomalous' domain affected so many Aboriginal people at once (and still does), such a childhood is more than an individual 'experience'. Its dreadful legacy can permeate a whole Aboriginal community in a given place. The *damage* caused by a history that Aboriginal people share with quite a few non-Aboriginal people comes to look like a description of Aboriginality itself. And the list of adult behaviours familiar to anyone who has spent a few years in an orphanage comes to look like a description of Aboriginal culture. The 'personal' consequences of living in the *anomalous Indigenous domain* are transferred from individual persons to the collectivity—applied to 'the Aborigines' as a whole.

It is at exactly this point that the media step in; to report on personal, anomalous infringements of structural boundaries, and to contrast this domain with the law-forming domain.

The Politics of Kissing

> It's all part of a plan to breed you mob out.
> (Ernie Dingo's last line in ABC-TV's *Heartland*, 1994)

The two domains we have tried to describe, law-forming and anomalous respectively, together amount to a 'universe of Indigeneity' that is itself in dialogue with other components of the Australian semiosphere. That dialogue is both historical and mediated—it changes over time and it can be tracked through media 'texts' of various kinds. During the 1990s, an especially intense period of dialogue occurred between the 'Aboriginal' and 'Australian' components. It did not entirely take the form of law formation on the one hand (Mabo, Wik, Native Title), and anomaly (care, welfare, justice) on the other. There was something else: there was kissing.

Kissing is a long-serving device used in factual and fictional tales alike to signify reconciliation. In the 1990s, it has been used in the same way to promote reconciliation between the 'Aboriginal' and 'Australian' components of the Australian semiosphere. Two landmark examples have been identified.

The first, from the news media, was a cover of the *Age* newspaper's *Good Weekend Magazine* (21 August 1993). It showed an Aboriginal man and white woman kissing, and was captioned 'It's Time'—an allusion to a famous slogan used during the federal election of 1972 by Gough Whitlam, signalling the end of a long period of stagnation and heralding a new era of change and modernization. The story it illustrated was a feature headlined 'Aboriginal Reconciliation: Time to Get Serious'. Showing a white woman and Aboriginal man was as serious a semioticization of reconciliation as could be imagined. Indeed, John Morton suggests that it was unprecedented and revolutionary:

This explicitly sexualised public image of reconciliation, with its conjunction of black man and white woman, is quite new in terms of the history of Australian race relations and says something about the revolutionary nature of the Mabo era. (Morton, 1996: 124).

The second emblematic kiss was a much more sustained affair, from the ABC-TV drama series *Heartland*, first broadcast in 1994. It starred the Aboriginal actor and entertainer Ernie Dingo and Cate Blanchett (in her first leading role). The series has been discussed in detail by Morton, who concludes with an argument about how it symbolizes a new direction in politics, where adversarial antagonism may be forced for good practical reasons to give way to more cordial mutual accommodations:

In the absence of any foreseeable effective revolution by Aboriginal people, and any subsequent violent displacement of the Crown, it is clear that Aboriginal rights can only be secured through the liberal democratic process inherited from Britain. It follows that Aboriginal people's only prospect for getting what they want is in the Aboriginalisation of that process, which, in a liberal democracy, must partially entail an effective mobilisation of its discursive regimes of representation. *Heartland* is a case in point. (Morton, 1996: 132).

'Effective mobilisation of discursive regimes' means 'Aboriginalizing' the 'Australian' component of the Australian semiosphere; Cate Blanchett kissing Ernie Dingo is the sign that the dialogue has begun. Morton argues for a *politics* based not on white 'appropriations' of Aboriginality, but on a more cordial two-way exchange:

The [Australian] state is, in fact, an organised political community with government recognised by the people. As such, it must be responsive to the wishes, needs and will of the people, and not always in such a way as to coerce, repress and call forth resistance. In this sense, it is not surprising that a logic of salvation or redemption pervades the appropriation of Aboriginality in contemporary Australia, since, increasingly, through effective resistance, persuasion and accommodation, the will of the people and the rhetoric of the state have come to demand that something be done to make amends for past injustices. *Heartland*, being more than some simple romance of the primitive, demonstrates that this movement, including its expression in Mabo, is not based exclusively on 'imperialist nostalgia' for some 'Eternal Dreamtime'. (1996: 133).

In short, *Heartland* points to the future, not to the past, and to a politics where reconciliation is understood as exchange, with uncertainties, losses, but also gains, for both sides:

One does not necessarily judge exchange by considering only the advantages reaped by one side, thus relegating the other to an agentless subject position. *Heartland* could be taken as a model of this truth, as it moves its characters through a series of uncertain negotiations of identification between black and white. The recovery of native agency calls into question the whole logic of 'imperialist nostalgia' and indeed presents the possibility that imperialism might be transcended. (1996: 133–4).

Heartland was perhaps a 'nationalization' of the progress made towards the Aboriginalization of the Australian semiosphere during the period of the Keating government (1992–6). Its chosen metaphor for reconciliation, a sexualized relationship between Aboriginal and non-Aboriginal Australians, took the 'personal' and 'boundary-crossing' elements of the 'anomalous' domain and brought them into the 'law-forming' domain. Here the relationship between Dingo and Blanchett established a principle, reducing the world to a new orderliness, in which the 'universe of Indigeneity' joined with the 'Australian' component of the Australian semiosphere. The kiss was a promise.

Heartland made its promises in dramatic, fictional mode. Time was required to determine whether the worlds of politics and news would live up to that promise. The election of a conservative federal government in 1996, the rise and fall of the One Nation anti-Aboriginal party, and the intense media coverage of Native Title and land rights, may have suggested that this was a kiss that died on the lips. But the very intensity of the debate, the vicissitudes of a relationship between parties who feel mutually unintelligible, bespeak a 'mutual attraction' between the 'Aboriginal' and 'Australian' components of the Australian semiosphere that is evidence not of a one-night stand but a of dialogue leading to a long-term affair. The terms in which that dialogue is conducted are not via traditional 'public affairs' only—we have tried to show how the personal, sexual, and private are also key components of the Indigenous Public Sphere.

Part Two | **Reception**

4 'The Meeting is the Polity': The National Media Forum

> The central challenges the Council [for Aboriginal Reconciliation] have offered the public can be typified as: 'Are you prepared to look for the common ground with those you do not necessarily know or understand?'
>
> (Patrick Dodson, 1994: ix)

An immediate catalyst for the present research project was the Report of the Royal Commission into Aboriginal Deaths in Custody in 1991. The Report made a number of recommendations relating to what it saw as 'underlying issues', and among these were four relating to the media (see Introduction), of which the last (208) is this:

In view of the fact that many Aboriginal people throughout Australia express disappointment in the portrayal of Aboriginal people by the media, the media industry and media unions should encourage formal and informal contact with Aboriginal organisations, including Aboriginal media organisations where available. The purpose of such contact should be the creation, on all sides, of a better understanding of issues relating to media treatment of Aboriginal affairs.

The idea was simply to get journalists and Indigenous people into better contact with each other, to promote excellence in the reporting of Indigenous issues, and to promote Aboriginal media organizations themselves. This seemed like something media academics might properly take on, since of course neither state nor federal governments could directly implement Royal Commission recommendations relating to private and editorially independent media. Thus, in conjunction with other interested parties from the media and from Aboriginal-led organizations like the Deaths in Custody Watch Committee and the Aboriginal Legal Service locally, and the Council for Aboriginal Reconciliation nationally, we (Hartley in 1992 and 1994, Hartley and McKee in 1996, and McKee in 1998) convened a series of 'Media Forums' in Western Australia. They were designed to bring media organizations, journalists, journalism trainers and regulators into direct contact with Aboriginal people and organizations, with a view to implementing the Royal Commission's recommendations.

The Media Forum series was particularly important to the present research project, which was itself sparked off by the same recommendations. The Forum provided a new model for 'reception studies' in 'audience research'. The reception of Aboriginal issues in the Australian media is a matter for Indigenous people themselves, of course, but it is also a matter of importance for media professionals, government policy-makers and regulators, and for the public at large. Inviting representatives of these different 'audience constituencies' to talk through the issues in public struck us as the best possible way to conduct 'audience research' in the area. It is a parliamentary 'method'.

This 'audience research' did not confine the conceptualization of media readerships to individuated consumers. On the contrary, people were invited from both Aboriginal and other communities who were *also*, for instance, academic researchers, political activists, media professionals, or people who had a experience of media coverage of *their* stories. In short, this was the ultimate 'active' audience, and one moreover which had a collective and not an individual stance in relation to media coverage. We were seeking to understand the reception of media coverage by a collective readership, 'a people' if you like.

We did not want to sample the untutored and uninterested responses of randomly selected members of the general population, for we believed first of all that such an approach is too individualistic, relying on an outmoded consumerist model of media reception, and secondly that what it does measure is historic, the past—it samples the efficacy of previously conducted campaigns. It also prejudges what 'the general population' encompasses, which is unwise in the present context where Aboriginal people do not universally agree that they 'belong' to the Australian general population at all. We wanted to gauge the reception of Aboriginal issues by a collective readership, made up largely of Aboriginal people themselves, but also including rehearsed and interested responses by non-Aboriginal parties, whose reactions might be taken as *dialogic* with that coverage, leading to changes on both sides. This approach to audience research has affinities with both feminist and Indigenous models, positing the audience as organized, with a voice, not as individuals with behaviour (Felski, 1989; Langton, 1993a; McKee, 1999). It has the further advantage of breaking down the idea that 'the media' or 'the researcher' are always 'the writer' while 'the audience' is always 'the reader'. In our approach, audiences are writers, and media professionals readers, or at least listeners, for a while.

During the conduct of the ARC project's research, and while organizing the Media Forums, it became clear that no-one else was doing exactly this work on a national basis, although like ourselves there were local centres of academic research and political activism in different states, especially Queensland. The Aboriginal and Torres Strait Islander Commission (ATSIC) also held a national conference on Indigenous people and the media in Brisbane in 1993. But there was no nationally organized and sustained attempt to implement the recommendations of the Royal Commission. At the same time, however, it also became clear that simply holding a reactive media forum every year or two, where the usual round-up of complaint and mutual misunderstanding was reiterated by the usual suspects, was not only chipping away at the problem too slowly, but was also likely to lose the interest of the very people most important to the process, namely media professionals on the one hand, and Indigenous leaders on the other.

This is why we decided for the 1996 Media Forum not only to go national, but to try to set rather than react to the media agenda. As Rupert Murdoch himself has famously advised, where there's a problem in getting your policies across, then 'change the culture'. Indigenous people are among the least represented in the institutions of parliament, government, and public administration, even allowing the bi-partisan policy of 'self-determination' for Aboriginal and Islander people in their own affairs. It seemed timely therefore to move beyond a model of *administrative* 'self-determination' towards some notion of *national* self-representation. However valuable ATSIC may be, it confines self-determination to administrative processes within a body that remains an arm of a government which is decidedly not under Aboriginal control. As the new Coalition government demonstrated within a month of taking office in 1996, ATSIC is subject to the will and whim of a Minister who is responsible not to the Indigenous community but to the Federal Cabinet.

Given the absence of any national forum for the expression of Indigenous political and governmental aspirations, and given the importance of the media in communicating such matters to the community both Indigenous and non-Indigenous, the idea was hatched to bring national Indigenous leaders together, and ask what needed to be said to both Indigenous citizens and those of Australia as a whole. 'The Aboriginal Public Sphere' was intended to be just that—a forum for Indigenous leaders to speak on the full range of governmental and political responsibilities, not just on the well-worn 'Aboriginal issues' to which they were often confined. It was expected that such an event would attract media interest, and thence act as a catalyst for wider community discussion of these issues. This was the rationale for holding 'The Aboriginal Public Sphere' as part of a *Media* Forum; on the argument the media are, for most citizens, the place of participation in politics and government.

We sent invitations to John Ah Kit, Tiga Bayles, Mick Dodson, Patrick Dodson, Gary Foley, Simon Forrest, Mary Graham, Olga Havnen, Colleen Hayward, Jackie Huggins, Marcia Langton, Michael Mansell, Lois (Lowitja) O'Donohue, Pat O'Shane, Noel Pearson, Charles Perkins, Rob Riley, David Ross, Peter Yu, Galarrwuy Yunupingu, and Mandawuy Yunupingu (who we thought might include a fair proportion of any national leadership in those far-off days of Labor hegemony) to address the 'Aboriginal Public Sphere' as the opening event of the 1996 National Media Forum. As it turned out, only about half of our 'virtual Cabinet' was able to attend (see also Yunupingu (ed.), 1997, which contains papers by Galarrwuy Yunupingu, Lois O'Donoghue, Mick Dodson, Pat Dodson, John Ah Kit, Marcia Langton, Noel Pearson, David Ross, Peter Yu, Michael Mansell, and others). The session was introduced and chaired by the late Rob Riley in one of his last public acts before his untimely death in May 1996, and an edited transcript of it appears below. In the context of this book, the speakers' comments represent a public form of 'reception' studies: dialogue and discussion about the role of Australian media, and the place of Indigeneity within it—as seen from the point of view of those closest to the issues.

The Aboriginal Public Sphere

ROB RILEY
Former Chief Executive Officer of the Aboriginal Legal Service, Perth, WA
Can I ask people to take their seats and get ready, because it's time to bounce the ball down to get started. I'd like to introduce Mr Fred Collard. Fred is an elder from the metropolitan area—has family background all over the South-West—and is involved with the Council for Aboriginal Reconciliation in WA. Fred's going to provide an official welcome. Thank you.

FRED COLLARD
Nyungar Elder, and Co-ordinator of the WA Council for Aboriginal Reconciliation
Thank you, Mr Riley and I'd just like to say a few words in Nyungar to welcome you here, then I'll interpret it back in English.

Kayu ngunyu jukian ngunyu kurduis ngullu Nyungar, Wajala, djurupin nunuk kuliny nitchu ngullu budju warnkiny

What I've just said is 'Yes, my sisters and brothers, the Aboriginal and white people here are happy you have come to our ground, our land, to talk.' I'd like to say welcome my brothers and sisters and enjoy your stay here and exchange of communications that's going on around Australia in the Aboriginal arena.

ROB RILEY

The next person may need some introduction to those of you from those eastern states where they play a funny kind of football [rugby], but Chris Lewis is very high profile in Western Australia, and across into the Northern Territory, South Australia and Victoria. He's a very active sportsman as a star player for the West Coast Eagles. It's very good that Aboriginal sportsmen are getting involved in Australian Rules football. Chris has proved himself in that area.

A very significant event happened yesterday with the launch at the Fremantle Arts Centre Press of a book called *Rites of Passage*, by Quentin Beresford and Paul Omaji. Chris Lewis was involved in the book as one of the researchers; going out and talking to young Aboriginal people who have been caught up in the criminal justice system. One of the issues taken up in that book, which is also the subject of this Forum, is the very negativity of the media in terms of how it reports juvenile justice. But, not wanting to steal too much of his thunder, I'll introduce Chris Lewis to you.

CHRIS LEWIS
West Coast Eagles
Thanks Rob. First of all, it's good to be here to talk to you people and give you my views on media. So thanks for having me here today. It's good to see a few familiar faces around the place; Mr Mansell, the media reports I've heard about you are lies, I suppose, as you're a pretty nice bloke. It's good to finally get to meet you mate.

Playing football for one of the top AFL sides in the West Coast Eagles, we are always in the media spotlight. When I first started playing footy I was always pretty shy of the camera, because I didn't really know what to say. Over the years I've learned by trial and error on how the media operate. Sometimes it's been good, but I suppose 70 per cent of the coverage from my point of view has been bad. Through my football actions, I've been judged—you know, before people have actually met me—and I suppose that judgement has been carried to people through the media, through newspapers or TV.

Even though I've never studied media, I think I've had a crash course in what goes on and so now, my example can help people who are going to be in my position in the future, not only to get to know the media but also to handle them, and use them in a way so that they can gain from it. I suppose in these days Aboriginal issues and Aboriginal people are pretty close to the top of the news agenda, and I think the way that the media portray those people is very important to the way that we move forward as a nation—not only black and white Australia, but as one Australia.

I know that (how can I put this?) a lot of media see Aboriginal people as just one type of person, but there are different types of people. For example, I myself am a city person, who grew up in a city. I wouldn't really know how to live in the bush or anything like that—hunt a kangaroo or go fishing. But there are other people in this room who have a more traditional life. Aboriginal people come in different groups—old, young, traditional, non-traditional—and the media ought to recognize these groups, whereas I think a lot of people these days just put us under one umbrella. Even though we are all Aboriginal, I think in different areas we change by the way we live.

So, now I'd like officially to open the National Media Forum. Over the next couple of days hopefully the issues that are important to you and to me and the rest of Australia might get thrashed out a bit and brought out into the open. Once again, thanks for having me here to open the Forum and to meet some of the people that I grew up looking at and reading about in the newspaper who are here on the platform; it's very good finally to get to meet those people.

ROB RILEY

I think Chris was alerting us to some of the keynote speakers here, and alerting us to the whole purpose of the Forum in bringing Aboriginal people together who have a national profile. That is, collectively thinking about the big picture as Aboriginal people, and thinking about where this country is going in the next few years as it heads towards the Centenary of Federation. We hope that the National Media Forum will serve the purpose of being able to generate discussion and understanding on a number of issues.

For those who don't know me, my name is Rob Riley. I've been asked to chair this first part of the Forum and if I can, before I introduce the speakers to you, I'd like just to give you an overview of what I believe this exercise is about. The purpose of talking about 'The Aboriginal Public Sphere', in a Forum which is about the involvement of Aboriginal people in the media, is very much to try, with the assistance of the people who are working in the mainstream media particularly, to understand and accept the fact that Aboriginal people right around the country have been working in the public life of Australia. They have been trying to articulate a range of views that Australia as a country has to recognize.

Australia is heading towards the twenty-first century, and there's a lot of discussion happening in respect to constitutional reform and the role that Indigenous people have to play in the make-up of Australian society. One of the crucial messages here is that the media play a very crucial role. But quite often our experience has been that the media have been very lazy. They're lazy in the way that they've reported stories, or that they've taken the easy way out when it comes to researching and making sure that they put a balance on the issues that affect Indigenous people around this country. I would anticipate that this is one of the clear messages that a lot of the speakers this afternoon will focus on in some degree.

Another area that I think they will talk about is the experience of their own work, and what they've been doing, and how the media have affected that performance. So you're going to be given an opportunity to hear a fairly broad range of views from people who have a very varied work experience in Aboriginal Affairs. I don't think we should under-estimate the extent to which that work can be enhanced or diminished by the reaction of the media.

The other thing that I feel is very important and that we have to take some responsibility for, is to promote the vision and views of Indigenous people, because if we don't do it, we can't rely on non-Aboriginal people to do it for us. There are two significant political opportunities coming up for Indigenous people in Australia. They are, obviously, the Olympic Games in the year 2000, and the Centenary of Federation in the year 2001. If Indigenous people don't grasp these opportunities to drag the rest of Australia up to speed into seeing the reality of what Aboriginal people experience in this country, then we will have nobody else to blame but ourselves. So I say to all Indigenous people that we've got a collective responsibility to promote the issues that we see as important for this country to address.

For instance, I'm mindful of the discussion that has been focused on the need for changes in the Constitution, and for an Indigenous Bill of Rights, to address the issues that affect us on a daily basis, whether it's in the area of education, health, employment, politics—or whatever else. These are issues that we have a collective responsibility to try to get across to the general public. But here the media have a crucial role to play, in making sure that they report accurately and fairly.

Sometimes, on the contrary, the media exercise sensationalism, or they're only interested in selling newspapers or making big bucks for the Howard Sattlers, the John Lawses, and the Alan Joneses of this world; those who deliberately provoke a very negative reaction against Indigenous people. If we don't challenge those sorts of views and if we can't convince the media that there's a different way of reporting issues and getting fair-minded Australians to think about them, then, as I said, we've only got ourselves to blame, and we've only got a very short time in which we can make the most of the opportunities coming up.

One of the things that I am regretful about, as some people have mentioned this afternoon, is the lack of young people on the panel. Where are they, and when are they going to get an opportunity to speak at these sorts of Forums? When organizing this panel, I was asked to try and attract people who have a national reputation, and who have developed a profile in Aboriginal Affairs by working at the hard slog for at least fifteen or twenty years. Such people do have a vision about the Indigenous issues that need to be addressed by society.

Hopefully the Forum sessions tomorrow will involve a lot more younger people, because another responsibility that we have, if we accept the role of leadership, is to encourage young people to get involved in the movement. One of the biggest fears that I have is that there aren't too many young people who are prepared to take up the mantle and start moving into the area of Aboriginal politics. People shy away from it simply because it's a very daunting exercise at the best of times. You've got to run the gauntlet as far as credibility within your own community goes, and then you've got to establish some sort of recognition and acceptance in the wider community. Somehow we've got to encourage young people to take up their responsibilities, and share our wisdom and experience with them so that they feel comfortable about the role that they're being asked to take on in the future.

PATRICK DODSON
Chair of the Council for Aboriginal Reconciliation; former Royal Commissioner for WA, Royal Commission into Aboriginal Deaths in Custody
Thank you, Mr Riley, and thank you to Fred Collard and Chris Lewis for the welcome to this part of the country, to the Nyungar part of the world.

Let me first of all talk about the responsibilities that I have as a member of the Council for Aboriginal Reconciliation, and what we're trying to do in the media area. Secondly, let me talk about some of those matters that are more of a personal reflection based on the experiences of one or other of the fields of endeavour that I've had the privilege to work in. The Council has a responsibility under federal legislation to promote a process of reconciliation, and that in itself is a fairly difficult concept for a lot of people to grasp; that it is a process. A process means that there are no preconceived outcomes that you're likely to achieve. You presume from the very beginning that there are many unresolved and unthought-through issues that have given rise to the lack of justice and destabilization, the poor relationship, the theft of the land, the taking away of kids. All those matters that are crucial to the very fabric and psyche of this country are based in fact, but they are also based in theoretical and intellectual argument; argument about who owns the country, arguments about sovereignty, about the Constitution as it exists, and the interaction of States and Commonwealth. All these arguments are very important to Aboriginal and Islander peoples throughout this country, as well as to non-Aboriginal people.

So there is a process that is within this context and to one side of it, to some extent. The Council is trying to promote information about some of the key issues that are at the source of the divergence of views, or the opposition to or rejection of views, whatever they might be, that we sometimes glean from the media. This *process* of reconciliation has been going now for about five years, and people still say we don't know what reconciliation is. But that is fine because it is an evolving concept in terms of its practical expression.

So long as there continues to be social disparity, social discord, social injustice, the concept of what reconciliation is will remain elusive. As I said when launching the *Rites of Passage* book, so long as we continue to happily lock up the young Aboriginal kids of this country, put them into institutions, ignore the research and the databases that have been compiled in relation to these matters, and so long as the broad community turn a blind eye, then the process of reconciliation is really about another light year away from where we're going to be by the year 2001. And that's just one area.

The Council has to deal with how to penetrate this environment; how can you have any impact that might lead to the appreciation and valuing of the Aboriginal and Torres Strait Islander culture and position within this country and this nation? And then how do you get that intellectual or emotional appreciation translated into political reality that will empower people to exercise and enjoy their rights if they so wish? That's what the process of reconciliation is about. It's about really hard issues. It's about real people. It's about people who oppose us on a daily basis and people who want to smother you to death like a labrador dog because they think they know everything that's best for you. So it's a really challenging endeavour and it's a snapshot in the history of denial and refusal and rejection and frustration and hurt that has been caused in this country. It's a snapshot within that process of two hundred years.

The parties in the parliament say—we'll give you a ten-year opportunity to put twenty-five people together, whoever they are, it really doesn't matter, and we'll ask them to set up some sort of strategy, over a number of areas, with outcomes that can be assessed according to public service criteria, and we'll give you a full million dollars, and hope that this is able to turn around entrenched and embedded attitudes that have been built up from the days people learned in the schools that Captain Cook discovered the country and that the natives have protruding foreheads and elongated calves, as well as that perception of the treacherous natives who were there to kill the sheep and kill the settlers, and whatever else. Deal with that bank of negative, stereotypical perception and inculcation.

So, the Council in trying to deal with this obviously can't do it on its own. It has sought to do it in a systemic way. What for instance can you produce that might have an impact on those who come into contact with Indigenous people as they go about producing their copy or their stories, etc? What are the sorts of things that they need to be aware of? We've produced a video, not just to train people in the media, but we've also done it with the legal profession, because they're the people at the other end, who represent most of our mob when they go to court, and though it doesn't cover everything, it's a beginning—what they need to become aware of. We're encouraging institutions like the law and the media to take this matter on, and bring it into part of their normal processes, so that awareness of Indigenous issues is not something new, or done because someone's got a bit of money to inject into it this financial year. It's something that's actually built into the fabric of how you go about training young journalists in the future. How you go about training young lawyers in the future and hopefully around a number of other professions like the educators, etc.

We've also produced articles and magazines and put things into publications such as the *Australian Women's Weekly* ('Together We Can't Lose', February 1995), so that there's a general airing of views. There's no one in Australia who can say today that they've not heard about a process of reconciliation. They mightn't agree with it, but they can't say they've never heard about it, or that they don't know what the issues are. There are in fact key issues that have been identified starting from land and sea, to custody to empowerment, and they are required to be debated and discussed in regional local forums so that people can begin to come to an understanding of many of the things that the leaders here and other leaders out there and in other places daily try to get across. The Council doesn't take the lead position on that.

Doing these things places the Council in an interesting position. It places me in an interesting position. First because it is a multi-party Council; it includes members from each of the major parties—the Liberals, the Labor Party, and the Democrats. Second, because it is multi-cultural: Torres Strait Islanders, Aborigines from various parts of the country, non-Indigenous people. Third, because the legislation has the unanimous support of the parties in parliament; we are seeking to maintain a political commitment to whatever the outcomes are of the work that people such as those on the platform here today are doing. And how difficult that is you'll hear from them no doubt; that people have racist perspectives in all their dealings with our culture, and all their dealings with particular land claims, or whatever it is that we are exposed to on a day-to-day basis.

What we are trying to do is maintain the challenge to the non-Aboriginal people to go beyond the immediate perceptions that they have about us—to go beyond the glib phrase that 'blacks are lazy', 'they won't work', 'they only want the dole', etc. Go beyond that sort of rubbish, particularly among the upper echelons of leaders—it might be a bit hard for the taxi-drivers to get beyond the perspective—but the people who are supposed to run the country are meant to have some intellectual capacity, and one would wonder at times! But not to worry. The challenge is for those people who legislate not only in the political arena but in all the decision-making areas: the judiciary, the captains of business, the people who are involved in social clubs and Rotaries and so on—very important.

I've spent a fair bit of my life, in recent days, talking to those sorts of people and if ever you're feeling a bit bored in life I can suggest you try and get on that circuit because the challenge to what you think is sacrosanct, the challenge to what you think is starkly obvious—that blacks require justice in this country, that you own the land—you find very clearly that someone else has a different view to that, and not necessarily a racist view, just an oppositional view out of the darkness of time when man first lived in the caves—these blokes walked in when we walked out! So, it's really a challenge to us and that's what the process of reconciliation is about. It's taking along what you are wanting and you can think about. It's taking along your challenge, the arsenal of experience and knowledge from out there where our people are, taking that along to those forums and challenging those people. The media are part of that as well.

Being in the forums that are going to extend, hopefully, the understanding of the issues that are crucial to the delivery of justice for people in this country—that's what the process of reconciliation is about. But it can be difficult when you try to work on a consensual basis—that is, trying to balance the interests of the various parties that sit on that Council, plus the interests of the Aboriginal people in general and the non-Aboriginal people in general, if you consider those as two general blocks.

So, that in the main is what we've done. I think Galarrwuy will talk about some of the other practical examples, where we've taken journalists out in co-operation with local communities, for them to be the bosses while the journalists have been placed under strict rules—like don't ask any questions for the first day, you can only ask questions when these people give you permission. Imagine the Canberra Press Gallery having to do that for a full day! Which they did do, to their credit. They did it when we took them up to Mount Anderson out near Derby. We took them over to Galarrwuy's country but he'll tell you a bit more about that I would hope.

Let me just finish on two last points. The first point is trying to find language that includes others; an inclusive approach to life. Trying to find language that includes other people in order to reduce and diminish fear and opposition. The risk that is involved in that is that people say, 'Well he's only an Uncle Tom, don't worry about him'. You know. He doesn't have the strong, strident language that you used to use when you were a young fella in the streets. If you look at some of the earlier press releases when I was a young fella you'd probably see those things. But now you see some more mellow language—well maybe it's mellow, I don't know. But language is an important tool, an important tool in the process of achieving the outcomes you desire. If someone calls you a 'black C' or you call someone a 'white C' or something, immediately it sends off the antennas—and it sets up the barriers to any worthwhile dialogue and communication about the issues of substance. And you don't have to use abusive words. All you have to say is, 'Well I'm thinking about a treaty.' And they say, 'Well hang on, it's not the same treaty that I'm talking about, well hang on...' So language is a very important thing. It's very important to understand its role in the process of the struggle. And not only your own language, but the language that the other people are using, which is more difficult for us, Indigenous people, because we don't all have the high words and the smart education or the fine nuances within which the language is used.

Journalism is a very important thing too because journalists popularize difficult and complex issues, and how they popularize them is communicated to the majority of people. But they haven't found ways of dealing with some of these more challenging matters, and not just the matters that we put forward like sovereignty or treaty, or constitutional change or amendments to Acts or whatever. Nor have they found ways to deal with the challenge of the language that the *non-Aboriginal people* use; language that underpins the educational systems, that underpins the philosophical frameworks, the intellectual ways. They conveniently side-step and push away the fundamental challenge for justice and equality because it doesn't fit in the programme or some other jazzy word that's used. For fundamentally not facing up to their own lack of integrity— that's at the guts of these things. How do you get that across and how can the journalists get that across?

How do you get journalists not just to train their investigative guns on the integrity of the leaders and other people from the Aboriginal and Islander side, but also on the integrity of certain other people? It's assumed that when someone's a Minister they have integrity unless there's some scandal that journalists are able to dig up. But half of these ministers have probably not sat down and talked to the Aboriginal people on any matter. Meanwhile the onus is placed on the Aboriginal people to produce; they bear the burden of the accountability structures—nowhere else is the same measure applied in the reporting and in the investigation. It's a fine way that lets these people who have responsibility off the hook, who have a duty of care in the way that they carry out their responsibilities.

I'll stop at this stage and no doubt you'll learn many other things from these very learned people in respect to people in the community. I'm very proud to share the stage with them.

ROB RILEY

The next speaker is a person with a very long involvement in a very specific struggle about land. The protection of the very essence of Aboriginal culture, identity, and spirituality has been the hallmark of the work that Galarrwuy Yunupingu has been involved in for too many years to remember now. Certainly the Gumatj people and their Bark Petition to the Government in the early seventies put the issue very clearly about Land Rights. I know that Galarrwuy particularly wants to talk about the way in which the media operate in how they report those sorts of issues. Galarrwuy has received recognition for his work in this area. In fact he has been recognized as Australian of the Year; that underpins the recognition of the importance of the role that both Galarrwuy personally and the Northern Land Council, the organization that he's headed up for a long time, have played.

GALARRWUY YUNUPINGU
Gumatj Association, Inc., Chair of the Northern Land Council, former Australian of the Year
[Opening in Gumatj language.] I'm glad that I am sharing this Forum with you and have been asked particularly what I can offer in the way of comments on media. I simply spoke in Gumatj saying that media are an old custom to Aboriginal people. The word 'djerma' in our society—particularly in the tribal areas—'djerma' is well and truly alive. From where we sit as Aboriginal people, 'djerma' is still well and alive from our way of delivery.

And I'd like to speak about that briefly because I think we are all excited coming out here to talk about the media and how best we will attack them. The media are a powerful thing, with their own ethics, their own beliefs. The media have their own guidelines to operate by and everybody who's involved in media must stand by them or else get out of it. And Australia has become accustomed to that. But it is simply a white, Europeanized belief, created in England where they originally came from. They came with everything, including their journalism and their ethics. They arrived here and formed a society or association, and called it journalism, and these are the kind of people who write stories. In fact the Aboriginal people were left out of it when the stories were first developed in newspapers in the early days, and later in radio and on television. Aboriginal people were left out of it all because we weren't part of it until the late sixties.

The Land Rights issues, I suppose, were the touching point because everybody else in the media, other than Aboriginal people, would talk about it. If there was a mention of Aboriginal people and what they do, this was a secondary thing. Nobody wanted to hear it or even talk about it from our point of view. We weren't on the agenda of the community, we weren't even a part of the society, we weren't even a citizen. We weren't even enough to be a headline. So Land Rights started when we simply wrote our story on a bark painting. Rob Riley has just mentioned that briefly to you—that our way of communicating was a bark painting. All these paintings up on the wall that you see here today—that's how we expressed our feelings. That's our simple message—a story that can be seen and interpreted. It's a story of that particular society or that language group. But the painting—on it is a message—was the same thing that you would write on a headline in today's news, except that today's news may come and go, in white man's society. . . . But we are telling the same story as our ancestors did. It's the same story, the same concept, and we want to walk on that—that's our belief. We want to continue to tell the white society— mainstream Australia—that we do come from that. We do come from that and we are with that, carrying it towards the future and what is going to be our future in the way of story-telling.

So—the cry of Land Rights; the Tent Embassy in Canberra; the walk-out in Wave Hill by the Gurintjis; and all these whitefellas in the media all jumped up and said 'Good news but bad news.' They all came running to Wave Hill. They all came running to gold. They all came running with their cameras sticking out, you know, tapes going, camera hanging down. It's supposed to be 'bad' news because we are just about to call a riot or cause big trouble for the Australian community, particularly among the white people. We're breaking their rules. We're breaking their belief system. So these people ran around with cameras and papers and pens, trying to tell people that we're just about trouble. But nobody realized, nobody realized. They shouldn't have done that. We were just instigating the time of the Aboriginal stories. We were just opening up the question of how to get into society. Because since the Tent Embassy, and Wave Hill, and other such events, we got in there all right, and we've never come out of it. The Aboriginal people had seen the sense of being in there, because otherwise we would have been outside—and still today if we don't do things like that. So, to win these people who were paternalist—who had the feeling towards the Aboriginal people that we were not part of the community—to win them we had to play their own games. And Aboriginal people knew that. They weren't dumb. All our leaders back in the sixties did all that. We need to pick up that kind of courage today to do it in a different manner.

Pat Dodson has already talked today about a different direction; a direction of changes. Because with Reconciliation we are trying to win the people within the media; the people who are behind the media, the power-brokers. People who tell the little people running in and out collecting stories what to do. They are the people we are to convince—that they must come to our side, if there are going to be stories about Aboriginal people. Aboriginal people are very strong cultural people. The way we deliver stories is in a way that we have feeling for it. That 'djerma' I talked about. Our stories are all broken up into categories. Different people come from different cultures; there are different sub-texts. We deliver the story in a different manner, relating our way of speech to our sister, to our mother, to different members of our family. There's a different way of behaving for each circumstance. That's the way to communicate. And these differences are there for a reason. They are to maintain a social structure and the culture in place.

But the modern media come in and they want to stick their nose in everything, but they pronounce your name really badly. And I get really annoyed with it, you know. They try so hard with foreign names; you listen to the radio and they try so hard—if it's not an Aboriginal name— to make it perfect. You want to ask why. Why don't they care about Aboriginal names, and why do they really care about other people's names, including their own? When they say, 'What's your name?' and you say, 'Mr Yunupingu.' 'Who?' 'Mr Yunupingu.' 'Who?' 'How do you spell it?' That's irritating, you know. That's annoying. You don't have to go through that. You don't have to put up with that. These are the obstacles we need to break down. These are the things that you want to communicate with. My name is as important as yours is. So you respect my name and I'll respect your name. And that's simple word to word. But say you're talking to a media person. They get upset. They get all boiled up and they throw your bloody stories out the window. They don't even print it. That is an attitude problem, which has been around for a long, long time. How they feel towards Aboriginal people in this country.

Perhaps now I'll mention the workshop we ran through the Reconciliation Council. Every member of the Council, Aboriginal members particularly, has to take the chance to take a group of people to their homeland, or to their communities, and involve Aboriginal leaders and Aboriginal people in communicating. [A group of mainstream media journalists went to a remote bush location at Dhanaya, as guests of the Northern Land Council, to 'listen and learn']. And we saw the media people come out to my place. Sat them down on the ground. Made a fire and gave them a few guidelines. One of the things—they don't ask questions. For twenty-four hours these journalists were told not to ask any questions. And you should have seen the faces of those people, you know. Nobody had told them that before. But the second thing was the worst thing for them—to take off their watches and put them away. They just didn't like that. There was to be no communication until twenty-four hours after that, and then they were allowed to talk openly. But by that time they were finding themselves more relaxed. And some of them wrote back to us to say how well they appreciated being told to take their watches off, and being told not to ask questions and so on. They wrote to us saying that they had gone back to their organizations throughout the nation as a different person. The journalists were saying how well they appreciated us taking them to our country. But this is the response to a simple way of doing things—how to communicate with people. And these are very important people. But they have had very little to do with Aboriginal people, until we took them out to make them sit down to share that experience person to person. It is only then that people will change their attitudes and it goes further than that person. It goes to their family and their community, to their media, and so on. So that person must be very, very important. And we've done that. And I'm glad we've done that.

There are a lot of important things that the land councils are involved in doing. We've gone ahead with making videos and newspapers of our own. The Northern Land Council and the Central Land Council work together to produce a quarterly newsletter which is called *Land Rights News*. We've done that for a reason—because a certain Northern Territory newspaper is so radically racist, and we can say that because we've had to live with it all the time. If there's a mention of Aboriginal people doing things, they report it so badly. Continuously. And therefore we had to create our own newspaper to tell Aboriginal people—our constituents in the Northern Territory—the news as it's being delivered; whether we are receiving land back through our land claims. Because as soon as you give Yolngu stories to a journalist, they twist and change it and at the end of it, it comes out no good. Not acceptable to you. Whether it is truly reflecting your image or not is up to the reporter.

I think throughout this Forum, a lot of people will be sharing about these kind of things. I thought I'd just mention those things. I've got a paper here but I didn't speak to the paper because I may have stuffed it up, you know. Nobody would have liked to hear it. So I'm standing here just talking to you—and that's the Aboriginal way of doing it. Written papers are whitefella stuff, you know. Mind you, it's a whitefella journalist who works for me in the Land Council who wrote some of the points in that paper and they are really strong points. I wouldn't mind sharing them with you. Thank you.

Rob Riley

Our next speaker is a person who has been involved in the Union movement for some time, and very much involved in education. I think it's time we introduced a woman on to the panel and this is Colleen Hayward. She's been a National Executive member of the Australian Council of Trade Unions, and a senior officer of the State Schoolteachers' Union. She also worked with the Royal Commission into Aboriginal Deaths in Custody as the assistant head of the Aboriginal Issues Unit.

Colleen Hayward
Former member of the ACTU [Australian Council of Trade Unions] Executive and WA State Schoolteachers' Union
Thanks Rob and thanks everyone. A lot of you are known to me and a lot of others aren't but I hope that will be rectified over the next couple of days. Can I start by telling a couple of brief stories. I worked for about

twelve months with Mandawuy Yunupingu on the national review of the Aboriginal education policy. At one time, all of the Aboriginal and Torres Strait Islander people on that mixed review were meeting; essentially having a black caucus prior to a meeting, not something that we had to do on a regular basis. We met at Mandawuy's hotel. We had previously left a couple of messages for him which he didn't get, and it was only as we were leaving that we managed to see him and grab him and the meeting was able to proceed. When he checked at reception, this particular five-star hotel in Canberra (which caters to Japanese tourists and I'm sure it never gets their names wrong) had failed to recognize the name and that's why the message didn't get passed on. This relates back to Galarrwuy Yunupingu's comment just now, of how the media and others are not really very careful about how they treat us and our names. But we did have to tell Mandawuy that perhaps he wasn't well enough known yet. . . .

Another thing mentioned by Galarrwuy is also worth saying—because I do have some notes that I want to follow. Whether something is in the media or whether it's in schoolbook texts, there's an assumption that if it's written, it must be true. And therefore the way that we Aboriginal people have told our stories in pictures, in dance, through oral histories, has never been given the credibility that it deserved because it wasn't written on paper—the whiteman's way. And if it wasn't then clearly it couldn't be true, whereas everything that gets written must be. So, my notes are written and I hope therefore that they're taken to be true.

Rob's already outlined some of my history in regard to the Trade Union movement, and that will be the focus of the comments I make today. I must admit, though, that one of the areas that has been most disheartening is that even within the Union movement, in holding the positions that I have over a period of about eleven years, that still when there are Union-type comments sought by journalists on Aboriginal issues, it's white officials that are approached, and who comment. Certainly many of the things that Unions have done in regard to Indigenous issues have led Aboriginal people and Torres Strait Islanders to being marginalized from the Union movement. My view is that it's often easier to instigate change from within the structure rather than from outside. And that's what's led to me being in the sorts of roles that I have been. A lot of positive changes are occurring but we've still got a considerable way to go.

Some of the things that have already been outlined and I'm sure will be further by speakers that follow is that we have a history of discrimination. Now that's nothing new to us but perhaps the depth of it is, in the context of the Union movement where we're told there's a group of people who support us and will essentially go the distance with us, if it's needed. (I'd like to think, by the way, that the negative that I'm about to outline will be counter-balanced by some of the other comments that I will also make). Legislation has historically operated to deprive Aboriginal people of reasonable prospects of work. Under so-called protection policies such as the 1905 Act in Western Australia, the States made agreements with pastoralists. These resulted in a serfdom for Aboriginal people. The land was not Aboriginal land, it was station and property owned by people who also owned us. We came with the land, like chattels. Discrimination was by the specific exclusion of Aboriginal people from designated employment, whether as a mandatory or discretionary measure. Some of it was implied exclusion by requiring the employment of non-Aboriginal, or white only, labour. Many examples of legislation dating back to the turn of this century could be quoted. But just one example is the Sugar Bounty Act of 1910 when people associated with that industry were actually paid a bounty if they could demonstrate that they had used no Aboriginal or Torres Strait Islander workers in the production of their product. That sort of legislation was enshrined and encouraged and protected within Union Awards and the way that Unions throughout Australian history have operated. Legislation, supported by Industrial Awards, also offered specific exclusion of Aboriginal workers by general omission. This is one of the things that is a common link with the way media portrays us; where it is 'out of sight, out of mind', and if no comment is made, we can't be there, we can't be an issue.

The most significant Aboriginal workers' action to secure wage justice was the 1966 Wave Hill action. I'm not going to go into the detail of that. I'm sure that most of you, at least, will already have some degree of background there. One of the things that was important in that particular dispute though was Aboriginal people standing up and saying, 'We've had enough of working under unjust conditions. We've had enough of working to fill somebody else's pocket. We've had enough of working for no recognition and no adequate housing and living conditions. We've had enough.' One of the things that came from that Wave Hill action, although it's a bit of a theory as to the exact extent, is the degree to which that dispute actually influenced the Australian electorate in terms of the lead-up to the 1967 referendum which, of course, was the first time that we were recognized as citizens in this country.

I was 13 then. But because the rest of my background is in education and in teaching directly, I need to say that even after that, it was actually up to the early to mid seventies before we moved away from the situation where you only needed one non-Aboriginal parent in a school community to complain, and the necessary impact was the removal of Aboriginal students from those schools. So we've come a long way, I guess, but all in degrees. Unions certainly have been perceived to be as racist as the rest of Australia, seeing Aboriginal people not as fellow oppressed but as competitors in the labour market, and as a resource of management exploitation designed to keep wages down. Unions' support for wage equality was not support for wage justice. Far from it. It was clearly designed to price cheap Aboriginal labour out of the workforce and make jobs and wage justice a non-Aboriginal preserve. Now, of course, we're still targeted in a range of spheres, and certainly in the media, where people are quite happy to blame the victims.

While Unions may claim a proud history, such pride cannot be equally applied to their work on behalf of Indigenous people in Australia. Following the 1967 referendum that recognized citizenship, if not prior occupancy, all of a sudden there was a deafening silence in the media, from Unions and from other so-called support groups. It was almost as though the successful completion of the referendum was somehow enough; that somehow with us being recognized as citizens in our own country that all the woes would be gone. Clearly this was not the case. While most people in Australia, including those who are officials within the Union movement, remain unaware that South Africa's apartheid system was largely borrowed from Queensland and Western Australian legislation, they nevertheless found apartheid appalling. It's one of the things that we've been able to grab on to in the international forum, the international stage, to help us where we should have been able to get the support from within our own country. Those sort of comparisons, however, are also pretty well generally ignored by the media.

There have been many questions about the position that Unions have taken towards Aboriginal workers in a historical context. The fact remains, however, that much has been done. Certainly the Reconciliation Council that Patrick has spoken about, in its work with Unions, has come up with a range of strategies to suggest to Unions ways that they might interact with Aboriginal people as individuals, organizations, and community groups. Those sort of publications came out when? Two years ago, Patrick? Three? I'm uncertain because I've not seen any documentation but that's not to say that there's not some around as to how much that's actually been taken up or whether or not people just received it all, gathered it, left it on the coffee table or wherever, and once again, that was the end of it.

I do have to say, and I know that some people, including those on the panel, may have a different view to this, but because of my involvement in Unions and my belief that they can do much to support us, I've got to say that it's pretty disheartening to find that Unions have supported the necessity for one group of people to have to work for unemployment benefits. We all know that every now and again the idea rears its ugly head, about being applied more widely—interestingly it hasn't that I'm aware of in this forthcoming Federal election—but in Australia an increasing number of Aboriginal and Torres Strait Islander people have to work for their unemployment benefit through the Community Development Employment Program. It's a programme that in too many communities, even though it needs community endorsement, sees Aboriginal people being paid at under Award rates. If we were any colour but black, no Union and no Union movement would tolerate that and certainly there are steps that are being put in place to challenge it, and to introduce over time proper Award rates but we still have a long way to go.

Even though I worked within it for a period of eleven years, that doesn't exempt the Union movement from racism. Some of it's direct, some of it's indirect. I've been to national meetings, for instance, where I've heard side comments—funny that, nobody's ever quite game to approach you directly—and I've been referred to as 'Miss Aboriginal Issues from WA'. Within the political structure of the Union movement in Western Australia political opponents of mine have referred to me as a 'Black Witch' and a 'Black C.' So we're not exempt from racism, even when you're not facing that kind of more obvious slur. I can recall a Trades and Labour Council debate on, of all things, the refurbishing of the Swan Brewery (and many of you will have been involved in the history of that). I was speaking, trying to convince people that if it was jobs that the TLC wanted then there'd be a hell of a lot more of them if they relocated the structure and refurbished it somewhere else, and then everybody would be happy. Whereupon one of the other delegates— non-Aboriginal (but that's no surprise given that there weren't any other Aboriginal delegates anyway)—said that she was sick and tired of Aboriginals trying to tell her what her position ought to be on Aboriginal issues when she was quite capable of making up her own mind.

So sometimes it's not direct racism. Sometimes it's indirect like that and certainly it continues to be a battle that we all have to undertake regardless of our areas of work. The outcome of that Brewery dispute, by the way, was assisted by the media. Their focus was not on the diversity inherent in Aboriginal cultures but rather that these people can't get their act together, look there are still differences between them. It's one of my continuing disappointments with the media that on any other issue, for example, environment, they don't ever quote just one expert. They actively seek a diversity of view—but we're all supposed to think exactly the same.

Among the challenges that Unions are now facing in terms of Awards and federal Industrial Relations policies, regardless of the government's political persuasion, are things like whether or not Unions will finally take up the challenge and have through Award variations such things as recognition and access to cultural leave. Leave for law business. Extended bereavement leave and recognition that family responsibilities, especially in regard to bereavement, apply to the whole Aboriginal community in recognition of the deceased person in their family. Let's see, when we get our first one of those award amendments through, how the media reports it.

And can I just close by saying that perhaps one of the greatest challenges facing Unions is not so much in their formal structures, although that's true, and not so much in their formal documentation, like awards and agreements, although that's certainly true too, but rather in their whole attitude and philosophy. Why aren't they, for instance, challenging the very definition of what is work. Why shouldn't our elders, for instance, be recognized for the work that they do in the area of cultural maintenance? This area, of course, is one which really challenges mainstream thinking but after all, that's why we're here today and tomorrow. And only then will we see that move 'from dreamtime to overtime' without our culture being a casualty and without us being crucified in the media. Thank you.

SIMON FORREST
Associate Professor, Kurongkurl Katitjin Unit, Edith Cowan University
Thanks Rob. The title I've given this yarn is:
'Aboriginal Knowledge, Intellectual Property, Aboriginal Land, an Indigenous Australian University'.

Historically, universities are a place where knowledge is held. A university is also a place where knowledge is created, and where the dissemination of both old and new knowledge takes place. There's been much discussion recently, mainly in the academic arena, about the development of an Indigenous Australian university which would carry out all three of the roles as mentioned before, as expected of a university. Just as important, an Indigenous university would have to be controlled by Indigenous people. Currently much of the Indigenous knowledge or intellectual property held by universities, and the dissemination of that knowledge, is carried out by non-Indigenous people. This sort of perceived ownership of our knowledge or intellectual property by non-Indigenous Australians has, I believe, a link with perceived owner-ship of our land by non-Indigenous Australians.

My colleague from James Cook University, Professor Errol West, has stated it is 'terra nullius of the mind'. I believe the treatment of our Indigenous knowledge has parallels with the treatment of our land by non-Indigenous peoples; the main aspect being that both our knowledge and our land has been colonized by non-Indigenous people for their own purposes with little regard to our views on ownership of that land or knowledge. When you analyse Professor West's comment about the treatment of our knowledge by non-Indigenous people, it sets the scene for the parallels in relation to Indigenous knowledge and the land to continue.

Under the guise of 'terra nullius' land was taken, as it was seen to be empty and not being used in the way non-Indigenous people thought it should be. 'Terra nullius of the mind' or knowledge or intellectual property has followed the same process. Indigenous knowledge is not open. Not everyone is exposed or allowed access to certain aspects of information or knowledge. In a Western culture, knowledge is open for everyone to know. So when non-Indigenous people saw us not using our knowledge and our intellectual property in the way in which they believed it should be used, just as with land, they took our knowledge and used it the way they thought it should be used.

Non-Indigenous ownership of the land was legitimized by non-In-digenous people themselves under their own rules and by giving the land they had stolen legality and status in their own terms and giving the land titles, such as freehold title, this method of self-legitimizing stolen land continued until the High Court decision regarding Native Title. I've written out in lay-person's terms what I thought the High Court decision said. Hold on a second:

Maybe Indigenous people had or have a right to their land and our process of taking their land and calling it our own may not have been right. We cannot change the past so we'll keep the land that we've already legitimized as our own. For the land that we have not legitimized as our own, we will let Indigenous Australians apply to have it back and only when they have met certain conditions and criteria that we lay down.

It's sort of a Clayton's giving back of land to Indigenous Australians.

I believe Indigenous knowledge and intellectual property has been treated somewhat the same. Throughout the last two hundred years or so, non-Indigenous people have researched aspects of our Indigenous knowledge and claimed it as their own. Non-Indigenous people went off into the bush and found all this stuff about us which we will call knowledge and intellectual property. Once that knowledge was gained from Indigenous people it was legitimized the same way land was and it was legitimized under the non-Indigenous rules and systems. It's still the same today. Non-Indigenous people will go off and do various studies and research. They gain the information or knowledge and then have it legitimized.

How is it legitimized? New Indigenous knowledge is legitimized by non-Indigenous people by writing a big document to report on the research they've carried out in order to find out that new knowledge, and then they call that document a Doctor of Philosophy or a Ph.D. And who legitimizes that knowledge, that new knowledge? Other non-Indigenous people who have been through the same process. The new knowledge about Indigenous Australians is in no way and never legitimized by Indigenous people. Once the new knowledge is legitimized, the people who did the research are then considered the experts. The Indigenous people who gave them that information or new knowledge in the first place are seldom recognized and certainly not considered the experts.

In universities around Australia, including the university where I am employed, Edith Cowan University, there is a battle going on about the rightful ownership of Indigenous knowledge and who has the right to disseminate that knowledge. The battle is similar in regard to the High Court decision with land. You see, universities endorsed the non-Indigenous so-called experts' perceived right to own the knowledge they have gained from us based on their own legitimization process as I've mentioned previously. The universities say that we Indigenous Australians can develop courses and areas of knowledge of our culture that are not already held and owned and legitimized by them as non-Indigenous Australians. Again, in lay-person's terms . . . hold on a second:

Maybe Indigenous people have a right to their knowledge and our process of taking their knowledge and making ourselves the experts may not have been right. We cannot change the past so we'll keep that knowledge that we have legitimized and we remain the experts. For any new, Indigenous knowledge that we have not already legitimized as our own, we will let Indigenous Australians to develop as they wish.

Really, it's not even a Clayton's giving-back like the Native Title. There is no recognition by non-Indigenous people that anything such as knowledge can be taken away. So there is no need to give anything back, or set up a procedure where knowledge and intellectual property can be returned. All that's being said by non-Indigenous academics is 'We keep whatever we have and you go ahead and do what you like, but don't do anything that is related to what we already have.'

I believe the establishment of an Indigenous Australian university should not only be used to carry out the three main functions that any university does (holding, creating, and disseminating knowledge). But there should also be a time when there is a handing-back of Indigenous knowledge, a bit like the handing-back of Uluru, which represented the handing-back of land. Both a symbolic and real event can be recognized in terms of the self-determination of Indigenous knowledge.

It is said that Knowledge is Power. Non-Indigenous Australians took our knowledge for their own purposes which, combined with many other things, resulted in a disempowering of us as a culture and a people. A giving-back or reclaiming control of our knowledge or intellectual property will reverse that process and will add to the empowerment of Indigenous Australians that is currently taking place in Australia today. Thank you.

MICHAEL MANSELL
Aboriginal Provisional Government, Tasmanian Aboriginal Legal Service
Thanks, Rob, for inviting me here and thanks to Fred Collard for allowing me to speak in his and his people's country. It's an interesting topic for the weekend; that is the relationship between Indigenous people in Australia and the media. From my experiences I can say that up until perhaps the mid to late 1980s, I'd enjoyed a fairly reasonable relationship with the media in Tasmania and when I came to the mainland. But after I went to a certain country overseas [Libya], the relationship seemed to change to the extent that if I'd have put out a media statement that 'tomorrow the sun will rise', the news that night would have been that 'Mansell says the world is doomed.' So by now I've given up any hope of getting the media to report accurately most of the things that I say, so I'll leave that to other people to discuss.

I want to go straight to the question of what is it that Aboriginal people in this country believe is in our best interests. Now, of course, I don't speak for all Aboriginal people and there are many Aboriginal people in this room that I'm sure I don't speak for but I speak for those who, in my travels around Australia, are looking for some form of vision and I believe it's essential that while we do criticize the problems that we have to suffer as Aboriginal people in this country, it's also important that we, and not white people, not the politicians, determine what is the answer to the problems that we face and so I'm going to do that in just a few minutes.

If this Forum had been held twenty years ago, I think it would have been unanimous that we would have believed the answer to our problems would have been to open up Australian society to allow greater access to all the goods and services that Aboriginal people had been denied in the 1970s. We were denied access to the law, we were denied access to education, housing, health, to land and a range of other things that white people always took for granted. And I believe that most of the programmes that came from the Whitlam Government were based on the notion of developing schemes that would hasten the opening up of access to the goods and services of Australian society for Indigenous people. And, to a large extent, they did.

Perhaps ten years later in the 1980s we would have said that the whole scheme of where our future lay again was in getting a better deal within the Australian political and legal system. We would have complained in the 1980s that not enough was being done but not many of us would have complained that the direction in which we were going was wrong. But we are now four years away from the turn of a new century, and we're still saying the best hope for Aboriginal people in this country, as a matter of policy, is to get greater access to the goods and services that white people take for granted. Underlying that policy, I believe, is this notion that the measure of success for Aboriginal people under the Aboriginal Affairs policy is the extent to which we are able to imitate the behaviour of white people.

Jack [John Ah Kit] sits over there, as a representative of his people. He's represented his people for a long time but if he wants to represent his people in the 'real' way, he has to join up the white man's parliament in the Northern Territory Legislative Assembly. In other words, he has to imitate the behaviour of white people who hold the power. If Michael Mansell or the other Aboriginal lawyers in this country wish to represent the legal interests of our people in whatever jurisdiction that we operate, we have to have a white man's law degree and we have to imitate the behaviour of white lawyers in white man's courts. If we want to be successful as teachers or leaders of our communities, we have to imitate the behaviour of white people. Now, if that's the basis of the policy to lead us into the next century, then heaven help us because there has to come a time when we question whether everything that the white man does is the only way to do it.

I was very interested in a number of speakers who were on this platform before me, indicating how on a range of things Aboriginal people need to imitate the structure set up by white people, our need to play by the rules set up by white people; and where we don't play by those rules, then we're on the outer. Now I'd be the first to concede that there are many Aboriginal people in Australia, and perhaps I'm one of them, who have been able successfully to imitate the behaviour of white people, and as a result we get employment, we get some of the riches of white society and we get access and recognition. But, let's face it, the bulk of our people cannot and need not imitate the behaviour of white people to be successful. Why should they?

If the answer is that they need not imitate the behaviour of white people to be successful, then we have to look at changing the underlying policy of Aboriginal Affairs in Australia. If the answer is that we don't want more and more Aboriginal people going into the white system and imitating the behaviour of white people, then what is to be done?

In the short time that's available to me, let me state it succinctly: the clear answer is that we must have land. There's no reason why the Crown Lands in Australia cannot be returned, without strings attached, to the Aboriginal community. I'm not talking about Native Title. I'm not talking to self-government. I'm talking about the land being returned to the original owners without strings attached. On those lands, Aboriginal people ought to be able to run their own affairs as they see fit, which means that the State Governments, the Federal Governments, the white man's courts and the police have no basis for having jurisdiction over us. We have got to be given the opportunity to build up our own structures, our own authority, within our Aboriginal communities on our own land.

This won't happen overnight, but over a period of time. Maybe in another twenty years, if this Forum is held here again, we can say we have advanced and we have developed the ability of Aboriginal people on the so-called Crown Lands to be able to run their own communities in a way that they see fit. I see no reason why Aboriginal people should not be able to raise all the revenue that's required to look after the interests of Aboriginal people in this country from the lands that we get returned. In 1991 the Australian Government's figures show that over $6 billion was raised in royalties and other revenue and taxation from the lands that are known as Crown Lands. Yet it only cost a bit over $2 billion to look after all of our costs, which means that we would be three times financially better off under our own system than we would be under the white man. So who's ripping off who?

Aboriginal people are continually complaining about the number of Aborigines going to prison, dying in custody, and, in Western Australia here, which is the worst state in Australia, of the number of Aboriginal children who are incarcerated for a range of petty offences. And people ask, well what is the answer to that? Again, I can't supply any easy solution. But in my view, one of the things that we need is our own legal system. We must offer an alternative to those kids and to other Aboriginal people whose conduct is declared to be illegal by a white parliament—which says, 'Well that conduct is now illegal and criminal and we will punish those who do it.' Aborigines then do something else. But now, 'We'll expand the law and make that behaviour criminal as well.'

And as a result of that, the white man determines what behaviour is acceptable and what behaviour is not acceptable, whereas if we were running our own legal systems, I am pretty sure that we would not criminalize the conduct that some of our older people, who have a social problem of drinking, are gaoled for. I don't think we would incarcerate kids and take them away from their families the way the white man does and is so ready to do. So we need the opportunity to be able to develop our own legal systems, not subject to the white man's overriding legal system, subject only to the rights of Aboriginal people in those communities.

And so what I'm talking about—yes—is Aboriginal sovereignty. No, it won't come overnight but at some stage we have to start discussing how it is that we are going to begin the process of building up, in our Aboriginal communities around Australia, the ability and the opportunity for Aboriginal people to run their own affairs. Things don't happen overnight but we have to initiate the discussion. But it's not just a matter of discussion. We can take the initiative on a range of things to provoke the discussion, as Rob would say, that I am always keen to do.

I hold up the Aboriginal passport as an example. Many of us who have travelled overseas campaigning for the cause, have had to travel on the Australian passport. Back in the 1980s when I filled in the form which said 'What is your nationality?' and wrote 'Aboriginal', and it came back with a pen crossed over it, and 'Australian' written in, it occurred to me that they were telling me that I was so unintelligent that I didn't quite know what my nationality was.

Now, I felt insulted that I had to travel on a passport that deemed me to be an Australian, even though no one could tell me where my parents, my grandparents, my great-grandparents, or the Aboriginal people when the white man first came here, had agreed that I was an Australian or that Aborigines were going to be Australians. At the time of the Constitution being enacted in 1901 we were excluded, so we weren't Australians then. And in the 1967 Referendum, we were simply allowed to become Australians, but we didn't vote to become Australians, so who decided that we were Australians? I think it's an unanswered question. So, at any rate, the Aboriginal Provisional Government drew up the Aboriginal passport.

Let me take a brief moment to explain to you how it works when you're coming back into Australia, because I've had no problems with travel around Italy, Germany, Austria, a range of other places. But when I've come back into Australia, you can imagine what it's like. Three hundred people have come from Europe and they're absolutely tired and the Greeks and Italians on these aircraft just want to get out of that door. And all of a sudden they see this little Aboriginal fella up the front of the line holding an Aboriginal passport. And the way it usually goes is this. The authorities will run across this one, two, three, four aisles and as I'm walking up there's a bunch of them waiting to see which one I'll go to; duck this way or duck that way. I eventually get called up and they say, 'Your passport?' I lift up the Aboriginal passport and the general line is 'Oh we don't recognize that passport.' 'Fair enough,' I say. And they say, 'Will you step aside because a lot of other people are waiting to go through?' 'No, I won't.' 'Mr Mansell, will you please come over here and co-operate?' 'No, are you detaining me? Are you placing me under arrest? If you're not, you're going to have to deal with me.' The officials usually confer, go round the back door. Back they come. And I allow them a few minutes because under Australian law what they're really trying to do is to determine your identity. And so, having studied a bit of this law, they usually send back a delegate who says, 'Mr Mansell, we can't allow you in on that passport, because we have to know who you are.' And I will say, 'You're telling me you don't know who I am?' So that line's usually gone and as I've said to them, 'Under Australian law and International law, if you don't allow me into Australia under the Aboriginal passport, it means that you are treating me as an illegal immigrant, and under Australian and International law, you have to deport an illegal immigrant to their country of origin.' So there's more than one way to skin a cat.

I do believe and the other members of the Aboriginal Provisional Government believe that it's time for us seriously to consider the underlying policy which leaves most of our people out in the cold, and which, let's be frank about it, is never going to give most Aboriginal people in this country access to the goods and services that other people take for granted. We must change this policy, I think, for just two reasons that immediately spring to mind.

The first one is that in my study of peoples elsewhere in the world, I have never seen a circumstance where one people can dominate another people and that arrangement be successful. I can think of a number of illustrations where it doesn't work. It didn't work in South Africa, where the Afrikaaners dominated the blacks. It hasn't worked in New Caledonia, where the French are dominating the Kanaks, and I can think of an even better example. It has never worked in this country and it never will.

The second one is this. If we are to give some hope to the next generations of Aboriginal kids coming on, we have to look at one important issue that goes with raising kids. When most white kids grow up, they believe that they have a reasonable chance of becoming a prime minister, a member of parliament, a member of the judiciary, a member of the business classes, a teacher, a doctor, a lawyer, a trades-man, or a range of other things. Why? Because this is their nation. It's designed to give those kids that opportunity.

What about our kids? How many of our kids grow up feeling that? I think you know the answer as much as I do. Most Aboriginal kids grow up knowing full well that they will be unemployed, they'll get into strife, they'll put in gaol, or they'll taken to an institution. Only a few of us will ever get through the net and be successful in white society. We have an obligation and a duty to change the policy so that more Aboriginal people get access to the things that they want, instead of the few.

In my view, this Forum offers us an enormous opportunity to begin the process. Let's not hide from the discussion, let's not close our ears to the thoughts that have been expressed by other speakers, or to what I'm saying and what other people following me will say. Let's really try to build a policy that's designed to give Aboriginal people a decent go in this country. Thank you.

DAVID ROSS
Chair of the Indigenous Land Corporation, former director of the South Australia Central Land Council
I want to thank the organizers for the opportunity to come and talk to you today and, more importantly, I'd like to thank the Nyungar people for the welcome. I've been to Perth many times over the years and it's the first time I've had such a welcome. Also very nice to see that people in this part of the country can still practise their language. It's a very good thing to see.

I do have a paper which I will read to you. There are points that I want to make that I think are very important, that Patrick raised earlier (I'm talking about reconciliation); some fundamentals that we all need to deal with and it's a couple of those fundamentals that I want to raise. In my view, 1995 would not be seen as a year in which images of Indigenous people were very well presented by the media. The coverage of the organization of which I am the Chairman, and that of the shameful Hindmarsh Bridge Royal Commission in South Australia, do not rate as examples that progress is being made in ensuring that the Australian public develops an understanding of Indigenous culture. On the contrary, it has to be stated that the media coverage and the subsequent public perceptions can only be seen as actively undermining our laws and our cultures.

Over the years, we've had to struggle to ensure that our lands and our cultures are protected. This has been a long and very difficult struggle and we have not been able to achieve all of what we wish. We have been able, in the face of some really incredible circumstances, to maintain a lot of our culture, language, and laws. Every land claim that has been won in the Northern Territory, the New South Wales Land Rights Act, the return of the Pitjantjatjara and Maralinga lands in South Australia, the return of land in Jervis Bay in New South Wales to its owners last year, the Mabo decision, the Native Title Act, and the Indigenous Land Fund were all founded on ownership of land through ongoing cultural and spiritual links with our country, regardless of the type of non-Aboriginal title under which it may be held.

These basic rights to land and culture are ones which separate us as Indigenous peoples and which we are entitled to and which have been denied to us for a very long time in the past. Yet, as Aboriginal peoples are still being subjected to the attempts to destroy and discredit these rights, we are now in a position where we have to fight to ensure that those rights we have struggled to maintain and assert are respected and protected into the future.

This is a struggle taking place in an era when we are supposed to be talking about furthering the reconciliation process. This is an era when there is hope that finally, as Indigenous peoples, prior ownership and occupation, not to mention sovereignty of this land, will be recognized in the Constitution. The aim of the reconciliation process is to promote, and I quote: 'a united Australia which respects this land of ours, values the Aboriginal and Torres Strait Islander heritage and provides justice and equity for all.'

We're now halfway through the debate of reconciliation. Yet only last year, the Ngarrindjeri people in South Australia were exposed to a very extreme witch-hunt. The South Australian Government established a Royal Commission whose sole objective was to determine the so-called truth of the Ngarrindjeri people's beliefs. This Royal Commission began as a consequence of media stories claiming that the women's beliefs and business near Hindmarsh Island Bridge were a fabrication and that this claim, in turn, became the primary term of reference for that Royal Commission. The Royal Commission was, in effect, an inquiry into the spiritual beliefs of our people. It amounted to a view that our beliefs are meaningless unless they are verified and endorsed by non-Indigenous people. In very simple language, if it wasn't written down by white people fifty or a hundred, a hundred and fifty years ago, whenever, then simply these things don't exist.

The reconciliation process will not be furthered until such campaigns to discredit and undermine our beliefs are themselves discredited and discarded. It is not up to non-Aboriginal people to determine the truth of any of our beliefs. Much of our tradition and culture has already been lost through the lack of understanding of Aboriginal cultures. It is not acceptable that this lack of understanding continues.

Unfortunately, the media, in this instance, can only be seen as one of the major players in the campaign designed not merely to divide and undermine the Aboriginal community, but more importantly, to discredit our spiritual and cultural beliefs throughout the wider community. Such campaigns, however, certainly aren't new. There are many similarities to that waged against the Jawoyn in the Northern Territory when their spiritual beliefs were questioned and challenged as sites of significance lay in the way of the proposal to mine Coronation Hill. Someone mentioned earlier the Alice Springs Dam. In that instance, the Commonwealth Government upheld the rights of the Jawoyn and the then Prime Minister, Bob Hawke, called for the respect for all spiritual beliefs.

The Mabo decision gave recognition to the fact that 'terra nullius' was a myth. It acknowledged the prior occupation and ownership of this land by Indigenous peoples. We all appreciate that recognition yet it is meaningless if, in the process of regaining some access and ownership to our land, through the operations of either the Native Title Act, Land Rights Acts, or the Indigenous Land Fund, that our rights to practise and pass down our laws and our cultural beliefs are forever attacked and discredited. We have to stand up to such campaigns as the Hindmarsh Island case. Not to stand up against such campaigns is to deny our culture, which will ultimately lead to the loss of all our culture.

The sentiments expressed by the Social Justice Commissioner, Mick Dodson, regarding the Hindmarsh Island affair and I quote:

We can freely sing our songs and tell stories, especially if those songs and stories can be marketed for a tidy profit, but the moment that the protection of those songs and stories may come into conflict with the economic interests of Indigenous society, we are told that they no longer have a place or, in this case, a Royal Commission is set up to prove that they don't even exist.

Our culture is alive. Our culture, or should I say our cultures, are very complex, and they are certainly under threat. It is time that the non-Indigenous people of this country recognized the realities that face

Aboriginal people and Torres Strait Islanders. If not, then talk of reconciliation, talk of Constitutional rights and us being a part of that, are
very shallow exercises if they are premised on a denial of our basic rights
to land and our cultures. Thank you.

OLGA HAVNEN
Central Land Council, South Australia
First of all, many thanks to Rob and to the Forum organizers and in
particular to the Nyungar people for your welcome to this country.

I've titled my paper: 'Push-polling for the Master Race: A Challenge to
Journalists'. During election campaigns in Australia there's been criticism of an electoral tactic called 'push-polling'. Put simply, the tactic
involves opinion-poll companies ringing electors, and after putting a
series of negative or untruthful statements about a particular candidate,
asking them which way they would vote. It's a strategy designed to
influence voters by planting false and misleading ideas in the electorate
about political enemies, and having those negative sentiments spread
throughout the electorate and by the media. It is said to have been highly
effective and to have cost at least two people their seats in parliament in
Australia.

It has been condemned by many commentators as a grossly unfair and
unscrupulous tactic and much has been made of this use of such
dishonest and un-Australian electioneering methods recently imported,
so it is alleged, from the United States, the home of dirty tricks in
politics. But there is nothing new about this, and this country certainly
didn't need the Americans to teach us how to bowl underarm.

The Australian media have been push-polling against Indigenous
Australians for at least the last hundred years. Since the white suprem-
acist *Bulletin* magazine of the turn of the century, which regularly
referred to us as 'Abos', 'Niggers', and 'Coons', there has been a consistent
tendency over the years for much of the media to propagate negative or
untruthful statements about our peoples, by planting false and misleading ideas in the mind of the public about Aboriginal and Torres Strait
Islander people. The tactic has been to approach Aboriginal issues using
trivialization, distortion, mistruth, and calculated ignorance and disre-
spect. Don't take my word for it, let's look at some of the evidence.

As part of research carried out for the Royal Commission into Aboriginal Deaths in Custody, the Murdoch monopoly in Darwin, the *Northern Territory News* and *Sunday Territorian* were surveyed over a six-
month period in the first half of 1990. Over that period, 110 stories, 6
pictorial stories, 3 cartoons, and 5 editorials dealt with Aboriginal matters. Of these stories, only 13 could in any way be described as positive or

mere matters of record. The rest, 88 per cent, were negative. Twenty-four were about grog. Eight attacked Land Councils and other Aboriginal organizations. The editorials dealt with poverty, land claims, Aboriginal drinking clubs, an attack on Galarrwuy Yunupingu for a 'sexist' attack on a conservative political candidate, and one attacked the Labor Party for collaborating with an Aboriginal person to stand for election. Of the six stand-alone pictorial items, three concerned Aboriginal art, two were of dancers, and the last was of a sporting event. As far as the *Northern Territory News* was concerned, Aboriginal people are an impediment to sensible social and economic development or of little use or interest unless we paint, dance, or kick a footy. Just as well some of us have colour, movement, and rhythm. It did well in the trivialization stuff but the news was really in its element when it came to lies and distortions.

In January 1990, a news journalist, a long vociferous opponent of Aboriginal Land Rights, ran a shock-horror story claiming the Yuendumu Council was avoiding paying court debts through a disturbing new strategy in Aboriginal Affairs, designed to stop debt-collection by refusing a bailiff permission to enter Yuendumu to enforce the court order. The story was based on the claims of a company director said to be owed the money. The story also carried an inflammatory quotation that did not appear in the article, so the author remained unknown, and left the impression that Aboriginal organizations were being obstructive, without any evidence. It turned out that the company director was the Yuendumu Town Clerk and his company owned a vehicle enabling him to minimize his tax. It also turned out that permission for the bailiff to enter Yuendumu could not and was not refused and in fact a bailiff later did go to Yuendumu to seize another organization's assets.

Later that year, the same journalist excelled himself in dealing with a matter of Aboriginal culture. When a senior Jawoyn man, prominent in his people's struggles for Land Rights and against mining on Sacred Sites, died in 1990, all media outlets in the Northern Territory were contacted by fax on the night of his death requesting that traditional practice be followed, not to use his name or image in any story about his death. In the guise of an obituary, however, the journalist used the dead man's name on a number of occasions, claimed he knew the deceased man well (erroneously according to his friends and family), and used the piece to attack the Northern Land Council and Land Rights legislation.

There are two obvious effects of this approach to reporting. First, as with push-polling, false and distorted ideas, if not downright lies, are implanted in the minds of the non-Aboriginal public. Old prejudices are confirmed and progressive and enlightened ideas are rejected in favour of a 'good' story. Second, the subjects of this approach, Aboriginal people, are transformed into clichés and caricatures.

The monopolistic nature of the media seems to leave little opportunity for these to be redressed. Of course, journalists and the media claim special privilege in their endeavour to bring us the news that they deem fit to print. 'Freedom of speech' and 'the right to know' are defended from those who would criticize them by citing some sort of 'holy relics': philosophers such as Voltaire are called on with the often-quoted 'I disapprove of what you say, but I will defend to the death your right to say it.' But what Voltaire may not have foreseen and certainly did not discuss was the way lies, distortion, and deceit abused that freedom of speech by the majority to attack the rights of minorities.

There is a basic inconsistency in the approach of those who would argue that freedom of speech is an inviolable right and then claim that racist statements do not damage, or that biased news policies do not harm other freedoms and rights. The reality is that rights, such as the so-called freedom of speech, are generally monopolized by those who own and control media outlets, while rights to live with dignity, free from fear of racist hatred, don't get much of a run. This is recognized by the International Covenant on Civil and Political Rights which explicitly says that the right to freedom of expression carries with it special duties and responsibilities. Among other things, the Covenant says that 'any advocacy of national, racial or religious hatred that constitutes incitement to discrimination, hostility or violence shall be prohibited by law'.

As I mentioned, racism in the Australian media has had a long history. In this, perhaps, has been reflected the majoritarian attitudes to Indigenous Australians and their rights. Not too many Indigenous Australians own shares in the nation's newspapers and broadcasters. So there has been little reason for media owners to show any concern for the rights of Aboriginal and Torres Strait Islanders. And where Indigenous Australians own a stake in the media, such as with the Aboriginal-owned Imparja Television Station in Alice Springs, we face prejudice through economic sanctions.

In 1990 again, when the Alice Springs Combined Organizations put two paid election advertisements to air, one about Aboriginal land and its importance to the economy, and one critical of the Country-Liberal Party Government, a $10,000-a-year non-Aboriginal advertiser withdrew advertising until the Combined Organizations had ceased. Five other advertisers, ironically tenants of the Aboriginal-owned Yipirinya Shopping Centre, threatened also to withdraw their advertising. Predictably the local Murdoch monopoly paper, the *Centralian Advocate*, did not name the advertiser who withdrew, nor indeed did any other media outlet in the Territory. So much for the right to know. That was left to the *Sydney Morning Herald*, which is not widely circulated in the Northern Territory.

For a partisan approach to freedom of expression one doesn't need to go much further than the hysterical response of much of the print media over Mabo and the Native Title legislation that followed that decision. Apart from a handful of thoughtful comment pieces, and with the honourable exception of editorial pieces by the *Australian*'s Paul Kelly [and in the *West Australian*, for which two leader-writers won the inaugural Louis Johnson Media Award in 1992], the majority of media outlets and journalists who worked for them slavishly and uncritically ran with the loony views of troglodytes such as Richard Court. Hundreds of 'names and addresses withheld' letters to the editor were printed expressing ideas which would have been welcome in the turn-of-the-century editions of the *Bulletin*. The unutterable shame of Australia's history identified by the High Court Mabo case was ignored in favour of beat-ups about Australians losing their backyards.

In this process, it is the role of journalists and media owners which should be examined. While a number may have an understanding of where Aboriginal Affairs fits into the big picture politics in Canberra, only a handful of non-Aboriginal journalists in this country have more than a rudimentary knowledge of Aboriginal culture and society, let alone language or law. While media operations place great value on knowledge of, say, foreign languages or experience of being a member of an ethnic community, none of them, to my knowledge, places a premium on extensive experience with Aboriginal people. When was the last time that you saw an advertisement for a journalist that stated 'Aboriginal studies or experience desirable', unless it was for a Land Council, or perhaps ATSIC. Indeed, ignorance of Aboriginal Affairs almost seems to be a virtue.

The television journalist who carried out the dawn raid on an Aboriginal community at Uluru back in 1985 has since gone on to be one of the nation's highest-paid current affairs journalists. When the Northern Land Council ran an educational workshop for journalists a couple of years ago, none of the junior or middle-level journalists from the *Northern Territory News* was cleared to attend. The only one who came was the same dyed-in-the-wool land rights opponent I spoke of before. Journalists, we're told, have the highest standards about seeking and printing the truth, but it is difficult for Aboriginal and Islander people to believe this. By and large journalists themselves are silent on the issue, and reluctant to take time out fully to understand Aboriginal matters, let alone to challenge the editorial policies which allow Aboriginal Affairs to be so badly distorted. They acquiesce in the push-polling we have experienced in the media for so many years.

Ironically, Indigenous Australians may have to look to foreign journalists in the coming years to get something of a better deal. In the years remaining till the end of the century, Australia will be discussing and debating the Constitution and Republicanism, a Bill of Rights, Federal/State relations, the internationalization of the Australian economy, and the further ratification of International Human Rights Conventions. Over that same period, the nation will also be preparing for the Sydney Olympics. In more ways than one, the eyes of the world media will be on us.

Given the woeful reportage of Aboriginal Affairs throughout most of the Australian media it seems likely that international reporters may look to the 'right to know' principle of journalists as an invitation to do some investigations into the position of Indigenous Australians. At the rate things are going, they won't find much to praise and a great deal to condemn. At the rate things are going, Aboriginal people and Islanders will be forced to use the Olympics to publicize our situation to the international media. It is sad, but I think I can predict at least some of the responses.

Australian politicians and editorials are likely to condemn these foreign commentators. They will say, 'They don't understand the full story.' 'They don't have the full facts.' 'They're only looking at one side of the story' and 'They don't have the right to say these things about Australia.' It will indeed be a test of free speech in this case to tell the truth about Aboriginal and Islander peoples. Those who attack free speech of such overseas journalists will do well to consider the words of Voltaire. Better still, they should reassess the impact of the historical weight of an Australian media that have, by and large, refused to seek and to tell the truth themselves. Thank you.

CHARLES PERKINS
Deputy Chair of the Aboriginal and Torres Strait Islander Commission (ATSIC)
Well thanks, Rob. Thanks everybody for inviting me and thank you, Mr Collard, for inviting me to come to your country. We've heard some brilliant speakers here today. It's just amazing that we have such a collection of intellect in the Aboriginal world who are prepared to come to Perth and gather together to say things on an opportune occasion like this.

We are on the edge of an apocalypse. I think we're literally on the verge of being finished as a nation of people. I say this after thirty, thirty-five years' experience of Aboriginal Affairs. I've never said it before and I say it now. You look around and you see what's happening to us. The high infant mortality rates are still being sustained. The amount of money that's going to housing, education, employment. The deceit on the part of some of our people, for example, black academics who've put the means test on 'Abstudy' in 1988. All of these are having a cumulative effect in Aboriginal Affairs where I paint that sort of a picture. It's not a nice one to paint. But that's how I see the reality of it.

I say, at this time, this year, we can possibly try and do something about it. We've got five years—just taking the end of the century, regardless of the Olympic Games—to do something about it. If we don't, then the next century is not going to be as bad as it is now, it's going to be much worse. It'll be much worse in the psychological sense; not so much in the literal, physical sense. There's a great deal of disintegration in the morale of Aboriginal communities right throughout Australia. It's a bit dispiriting for me to say that to anybody, but that's as I see it.

We can change it if we wanted to, but there's only one person in the world who can do that for us, and that's each one of us ourselves; the people sitting here today, the Aboriginal people sitting out in the back-blocks and the mission settlements, the ghettos around Australia. As I've said before on a number of occasions, when we wake up in the morning and look in the mirror, that's the person who's going to do it, nobody else.

You can depend on all the bullshit and politicians you like. For me the parties—one is as bad as the other. They're professional liars most of them. They wouldn't have a brain in their head, Labor or Liberal. You don't see any Aboriginal people working in places like Woolworth's, Coles, Myers, and so on but they've had more training programmes for Aboriginal people than they've had for racehorses. Every year there's another $100 million for training. Every bastard's training. But nobody gets anything. We're the most over-trained people in the world for no jobs.

So what we've done is we've locked ourselves into the Aboriginal industry. You look around. Where are all the entrepreneurs? Where are the business people? Where are the other people breaking out of Aboriginal Affairs? I'm a captive of it myself. Where do I go? I've got nowhere else to go. So if they turn me out in the paddock, I'm like a mongrel dog, I turn round and come back again. I'm lost. And that shouldn't be the way for our children. Our children should just be able to walk out into the street and say, 'Right, I'm going to England now. I'll just buy a ticket and go to England. I'll live in London for a while. I'll probably land in

Kangaroo Valley with all the other Australian lunatics and then get a job there and do this and do that and then go over to Sweden.' No, we're not in that sort of a game. We're not getting enough university graduates. We haven't got enough people in the professional fields. We haven't got that sort of independence of mind. We're not creative enough. We're locked into this Aboriginal industry; and people have done that deliberately on us and that's why I'm going to talk about the economy in a minute.

But just taking the media, that being the main theme today, there's a number of things I'd like to say about that. For example—how many Aboriginal people have you seen in the TV ads? You see black Americans, Asians, everybody else, Greeks, Italians, but you never see too many Aborigines. You might get one now and then but you really have to look hard because they put them up quick and they shoot them off fast. As for the newspapers, take, for example, the *Australian* article on Emily from Utopia the other day. I read that article and I nearly cried. The poor lady's up there, she's 80 years old. She's one of the greatest painters in the world. Her paintings are hung in every gallery in the world: places in France and Italy like the Louvre. But you've got some idiot here in Australia, some two-bit journalist from some fringe newspaper in Australia here, who writes an article that denigrates this lady. Some white people up there have used and abused her over the years in terms of getting her art off her and making derogatory comments about her. She can't respond. She can't read. They put two big articles out on this—and I said to the newspaper editor, 'Can I respond to that?' That was three months ago. My daughter Rachel Perkins asked if she could respond too. They didn't even print her letter to the editor, and there was no response to her request for right of reply. So that's our great newspaper, the *Australian*.

Apart from that, you've got all the other ones; like that newspaper in Sydney. If it gets any more conservative it will turn round and go back up its own arse. And you've got people like Piers Ackerman. Now there's a man who doesn't belong here. He should be in Iraq. He's writing on Aboriginal Affairs, which he knows nothing about. But he's influential to everybody around him; lots of people listen to him and read him. That's why he got that person from Brisbane saying those ludicrous things the other day about Aboriginal people—that we've got too much; we're living off the fat of the land; it's not equal in Australian society because Aborigines are getting everything. That's where they get it from, from these sorts of people.

Then of course we turn to the talkback radio people. Now we've got some prime examples of lunacy here. People who are being paid to cause race hatred in this country. Mega-bucks. They love it. They get big

135

money to do that, and we let them in this country. Why the Australians say, 'Yeah, we're fair people here, we really give everybody a fair go.' Bullshit. They allow these people to circulate in the community, make those comments, and pay them money for it. Then they turn around and say, 'Yeah, but we're your friend.' It's very difficult to find out who your friends are when you've got your enemy as your friend at the same time.

Then you've got the Press Council who's supposed to be protecting us all. Who's on the Press Council? The Press Council's run by the media barons. They make judgement on themselves like the police investigating the police. 'Sorry, nobody was murdered here, it just happened to be a body that rolled off the back of a truck. We don't know where it came from.' And it's the same with the Press Council. You appeal to them. What do they say? They take months to reply and they say, 'Oh sorry, it wasn't really an article that discriminated or defamed anybody at all. Next.' So that's the sort of people they are. And you know, these are the people we have to put up with here in Australia.

But the media in this country take every opportunity—not all of them, but most of them when it suits them—to come down hard on us, on Aboriginal leaders. And you've got some of them sitting here who've copped it. Right? One of them copped it in the Senate and in the newspapers—John [Ah Kit] over here. Michael [Mansell]—he's had his share. Paddy [Dodson]—he's bounced up and down all over the place and Galarrwuy [Yunupingu]'s had his—he's been punched all over the block, till he's punch-drunk. And they just give it to us because we're easy prey. There's not many of us around and so what do they do? They say, 'We'll give them a bit of a kicking this week because there's nothing else we can write about.' This press is very malicious and very criminal. And so is the radio because as a consequence of their stupidity and their racism, kids are going to their graves because they're black.

You're going to the grave because you're black. Because if the infant mortality rate that we've got pertained to white people, it would be a national scandal, wouldn't it? It's only black kids. Bury the bastards, you know. Show the statistics about it. Someone will mention it in parliament next week, but something else is going to happen—Carmen Lawrence will get into trouble or John Howard will say something stupid—and so that will take the pressure off everybody else. So that's the way we are in this country. And I tell you, the media in all of their forms are acting in a very criminal way because they're killing people.

And what are we going to do about it? We've done something about it. NIMA—the National Indigenous Media Association—has established a national body and that's a very powerful voice. We have the president of

NIMA here today [Jim Remedio]. So we have the president here today and they go right throughout Australia. We've got to be energetic, active, and creative and get on to the media and get the message across. We've got to battle them on their own ground, but let's also do a little bit of dragging to our swamp too, not to their swamp. We have to fight them in our swamp.

We've got to get more information out for people. We've got to put the facts on the table for everybody to see. We've got to get it to the United Nations and all these other places. ATSIC has got to play a big role in this. ATSIC is our elected representative. Well, let them say something—to the media, to business, to the politicians. We're not doing that well enough. We should be doing it stronger. We do the best we can, I suppose and there's all sorts of reasons for that, but we've got to do it a bit more strongly in 1996 and from then on.

Now the name—'black'. Every time the market goes down it's a 'Black Day in Australia for the Economy'. If there's a big crash on the road it's a 'Black spot on the road'. If there's a big strike at the wharf, they're 'Blacklegs'. Everything you associate with bad is black. The psychology of all of that is very important. I remember a long time ago when I was running round in Redfern there—it was only a couple of years ago! Well two or three—and they still sold that 'Nigger Boy' Liquorice. And I said 'Nigger Boy Liquorice? Gee, that's not nice, is it?' So I rang up the bloke and I wasn't too strong, I said, 'Excuse me, why do you put "Nigger Boy" Liquorice out? That's a bad term to use for anybody.' 'Oh, we've had it for years, and why not? It's the same with the boot polish and all that.' They thought it was just normal. I said, 'I tell you, I'll give you two weeks to get it off.' I didn't know what I was talking about. I mean two weeks— what am I going to do in two weeks? I thought I'd go up there and demonstrate or something like that. But he took it off. He didn't take it off in two weeks: he took it off in six months. But at least it had come off. There were other people, not only me, who protested about the same thing, and hence the pressure. So we've got to get people to realize that when things go bad, it's not 'black'.

They won't get away with these sorts of things on the women's side again—the women are too strong. They tell them off, like they did with the cyclones. Every time there was a cyclone around Australia they called it Elsie or June—do you remember that? It was all women's fault that there was a cyclone. Then they changed it: they call it Mick or Jim or Fred or something. And that's why they pick on us. We're not as well organized as other ethnic groups; they don't pick on the Jews, or the Italians or Greeks. They pick on us. They like kicking us. They think we're mongrel dogs—'Kick him again, you know.' And he can howl and scream but he's good for the news—a nice demonstration down the street, or a bit of a sit-in. Coverage for the papers.

So I'll come to something a little more constructive. I agree with what everybody else has said; Micky and Paddy and Rossy and them ... but I also wanted to say that one of the things that we're missing out on in this country is power. I'm not trying to say that we shouldn't look at the long-term questions and the principles and the concepts. What I'm saying is I want you to look at power. Who holds the power in this country? Well obviously white people do. And they're going to hang on to it. They've taken the country from Aboriginal people two hundred years ago. They only came the day before yesterday really, when you look at it. They're celebrating a hundred years after sixty thousand, for crying out aloud. You know, it's only like the day before yesterday. And they're putting plaques up and politicians are all running around themselves and what we ought to do is to say, let's look at the power structure in this country; and it's based on money. And that's what they've got and we haven't.

But the richest people in this world are Aboriginal people. We've got more assets than just about anybody. And what do we do with it? ... I don't know whether I should put all this on tape. ... Well, you know what they'll be saying. 'Ah yeah look, I told you those blacks are all rich bastards, they've got everything.' But yet we're the most poverty stricken at the same time. We're rich but we're poverty stricken. You know why? We don't know how to use our resources. We squander them. We've got millions and hundreds of millions of dollars' worth of assets. We've got $450–600 million in the New South Wales banks from the New South Wales Land Councils, who've got all those assets—lands, buildings—everywhere, all over the place. The same in the Northern Territory. The same in Western Australia and other places. If we put together all the fixed assets, the financial assets and the personal assets, we could do something in this country. We could revolutionize the place.

There's only one time when people would really respect you. You can tell them, 'Brother respect me, will you, please respect me.' But there's only one thing that people respect in this world and I hate to say it, but in my opinion it's the truth 99 per cent of the time, and that's money. If you've got assets and money, they look you in the eye and they'll think you're not a bad fella at all or you're not a bad lady at all—in fact you're pretty smart. Money generates respect from other people. If you go past in a big Mercedes Benz here with a flash suit on, they take notice of you. If you drove past in a push-bike and a pair of shorts, they say, 'Who's that bloody vagabond?' Now I'm being a bit hard here but I'm trying to make the point.

We've got to get all these assets together; we should combine them all for our communities at the local, at the regional, the state, the national level, and try to utilize our wealth in a better way. Don't put it in the bank that's going to give you a one per cent return or a five per cent return. Go for a bank that's going to give you nine percent. Don't give your money to somebody who goes and squanders it and then pisses off to Fiji or Europe with your money. Give it somebody who knows how to invest it, to get the best returns. Don't go into deals where you're going to get no equity from it. If you go into a mining deal, get a five per cent or a ten per cent equity, carrying interest. If you're going to go into a pastoral company don't go in just below 50 per cent, go for over 50 per cent. And so on.

Don't be satisfied with driving trucks around and looking black, or just trying to be a service industry. Go for more. Everybody else does. When you're doing business with other people they go for the throat. We don't. We say, 'Well look, what do you reckon, it's not a bad deal?' They say: 'Got this bloke. I'll rip him off.' And they go ahead and rip us off. We're too kind. We're the kindest people in the world. If we weren't the kindest and most tolerant people in the world there'd be wars ranging over this country all the time. We forgive and forget too easily.

We're very nice people, apart from aggressive people like me and a few of the fellas down there. We're really very nice people, and we put up with a lot in this country. And we've taken a lot as well, you know, from other people, and that's not necessary. We don't have to do that any more and that's why I say we've got five years to get it right. I've only mentioned economics but obviously there are other areas as well.

This is my closing remark. We've got a long way to go, but there are two things that are going to win it for us, and in my opinion we can win it basically within five years if we do these two things. One of them is: We've got to get unity. We've got to stop blueing among ourselves. Every time there are three Aborigines in a room, you're going to get four political parties. Every bastard wants to go their own way. So what we've got to do is to say, 'Let's stick together, try to work it out, even if I don't like you and things that you say and I reckon you're a bit of a mongrel, but look, I'm going to co-operate with you.' The Jewish people do it. The Italians do it. The Greeks do it. We're the only ones who don't do it. As a result we're being marginalized. You don't see many Aboriginal kids going to the big schools around Australia. The public schools like Scotch College and all of these sorts of places: we're not in there. But the Italians and Greeks are in there. They're getting their kids educated enough, and the educated people stick together and they work it out with each other. We've got to get it together too; so that one thing, unity.

The second thing is: within ourselves is the answer to everything, whoever you may be, wherever you may be, or what tribe you belong to—you can work it out within yourself. If you can get up in the morning and say, 'I'm going to do it' and give it a good go and give it your best shot, most of it will happen. Thank you.

JOHN AH KIT, MLA
Member of Parliament, Northern Territory Legislative Assembly
I think the speakers we've had today were excellent and I'm thankful to the Forum organizers for inviting me down here today to talk and to participate in the workshops. Thanks to Fred Collard and Chris Lewis and the Nyungar people here. I'd first like to pay my respects to the Nyungar traditional owners whose country we are standing on and thank them for welcoming me here today.

It gives me much pleasure to be here and present my paper which is called 'Can the Media Avoid Racial Stereotypes?'

Ladies and gentleman, I would like you to imagine the scene where a newspaper reporter goes back to the newsroom to write the story about President Nelson Mandela's arrival in Australia. The reporter sits down at the computer terminal and begins.

Prominent kaffir and President of the South African Republic, Nelson Mandela, arrived in Perth today.

Perhaps the same reporter was at there at the arrival of former Singaporean Prime Minister Lee Kuan Yew and that story begins:

The former Prime Minister of Singapore, Lee Kwan Yew, today told a group of Perth real estate developers that Singaporeans wanted to invest in Australia but were concerned about racial attitudes. Mr Lee, a chink by birth, was Prime Minister of Singapore from 1959 until 1989.

Of course, neither of the above examples would happen. Journalists wouldn't call people:

gooks, kikes, wops, wogs, dagos, slopes, jungle bunnies, poms, nips, limeys, eyties, huns, sheep-shaggers, camel-jockeys, shylocks, slant-eyes, dings, yids, tail-heads, fuzzy-wuzzies, sambos, nig-nogs, darkies, refos, gringos, gyppos, mex-honkies, pakkies, jiggaboos, niggers, spades, spicks, rock-apes, wet-backs, krauts, frogs, or septic tanks.

It's not just that they wouldn't get away with it, it's because journalists, among others, realize that these terms are more than just terms of racial abuse. They are also meaningless terms that stereotype people from a vast range of cultural and racial backgrounds. They know they are false stereotypes. Journalists are more enlightened than this. But are they?

All too often in reporting on Aboriginal people in Australia the issue becomes quickly blurred. The media seem to be trapped in this wish to describe people through stereotypes. Sure, Australian journalists don't refer to Aboriginal people these days as 'abos', 'gins', 'coons', and 'boongs', though all of these words were common up until the 1970s. But there are more ways of stereotyping than mere terms of racial abuse.

Before I get too much further into this speech, let me make it clear this is not a lecture about how you have to be politically correct to report things. It is a plea to make an effort to address the imbalance that occurs in the media when reporting on Aboriginal people and the issues that affect us.

During the 1995 election campaign, in which I ran for and won election to the Northern Territories Legislative Assembly, my political opponents campaigned in the bush against me by telling Aboriginal people that they shouldn't vote for me because I was a 'yella-fella'. Instead they were urged to vote for the 'full-bloods'—the Country Liberal Party's so-called 'real Aboriginal people'. Two of them, curiously enough, were running for the Country Liberal Party. This was supposed to turn people against me, but the tactic failed, as it had in the previous by-election with another Aboriginal candidate standing against the government.

Like all of the racially based campaigns that the Country Liberal Party runs in the Northern Territory elections, they are aimed at the largely ignorant non-Aboriginal population. While these tactics fail in the bush, they largely succeed in the major population centres of Darwin and Alice Springs. The CLP, aided by a largely compliant print media, adopts a pretty consistent campaign of fear and loathing of Aboriginal people, especially over issues such as land rights and sacred sites, and the threat these issues are alleged to pose to the comfortable, suburban lifestyle of most Territorians. It's an us and them campaign. There are 'real Territorians' whose future is under threat from Aboriginal people—who presumably are not Territorians at all.

There are also 'real' Aborigines: those who live out bush who are somehow more real than those who live in towns. If the 'unreal' Aborigines are not 'trouble-makers' and 'stirrers', manipulating people out bush, they are dismissed as lazy, drunken long-grassers who give the place a bad name with the tourists.

The notion of threat predominates in all these stereotypes. If such classifications were limited to the views of a few ratbags, it would be regrettable, but no great worry. However, they do in fact represent the views of a Party which has ruled the Territory for over twenty years. At times, this CLP Government goes further than inculcating fears among the non-Aboriginal population; it also doesn't mind the odd bit of racial abuse. The current Chief Minister of the Territory, an apparently educated man with legal training, recently said that it was quite acceptable to use the term 'coon' to refer to Aboriginal people. Presumably he would be happy to describe Nelson Mandela as 'kaffir' or Lee Kuan Yew as a 'chink', even if our mythical Perth journalist wouldn't.

Unfortunately, most of the media do little to dispel negative images of Aboriginal people, and much to condone them. They do this not by sanctioning the use of the words of racial abuse but by the unquestioning acceptance of stereotypes about Aboriginal people as 'objective reality'. Perhaps the best example of this, given your Premier Richard Court's obvious fear and hatred of Aboriginal rights to land, is on the issue of Aboriginal attitudes to development.

Between 1986 and 1991, first as Director of the Northern Land Council and then as the Executive Officer of the Jawoyn Association, I was closely involved with the defence of the area known as the Sickness Country in Kakadu National Park. The mining companies were out to destroy important sacred sites, such as Guratba, known in English as Coronation Hill. The miners, led by BHP, mounted a sustained attack on the beliefs of the Jawoyn people who were opposed to exploration and mining at Guratba. Three old Jawoyn men, living in very poor circumstances, were opposed by Australia's largest and richest company. I won't go into the details of the immense pressures these old men faced. Suffice to say they were considerable. But what was striking about the sequence of events was one simple thing. In virtually all of the endless media releases, background briefings, and public statements from the Jawoyn as well as evidence presented to inquiries by the Jawoyn, the following point was consistently made: *The Jawoyn people were not opposed to mining and development on their lands so long as sacred sites were respected and protected where necessary.* Almost invariably the media failed to pick up, let alone publicize, this point of view.

Instead, huge media coverage was given to Hugh Morgan when he attacked Aboriginal religious views and beliefs as being 'anti-Christian' and 'pagan'. Likewise, the media carried endless assertions that the Jawoyn had 'made up' their religious beliefs. The media unquestioningly carried statements by the miners—which were completely fabricated by them— to the effect that the custodians of the land were being manipulated, tricked, and cajoled by 'anti-development' advisers into opposing the mine. And the media completely swallowed the miners' assertions about the crucial value of the mine to the Australian economy. Virtually no one in the media looked behind what the miners were saying while they simultaneously marginalized Aboriginal religious beliefs and their economic development aspirations. The Jawoyn people were found guilty by the media of having a false, if not an invented, religion. They were being blamed for threatening the future of Australia's economy. They were seen as mere pawns in some wider game being played by advisers.

History proved the miners—and the media—wrong. A full-scale inquiry led by a judge with the Resource Assessment Commission found that the Jawoyn beliefs were genuine. It accepted that Jawoyn people were not opposed to development per se, and it found that the miners had grossly exaggerated the value of the project to the Australian economy. Since that time the Jawoyn have been at the forefront of pioneering minerals and tourist developments on their lands with active projects at Nitmiluk National Park and the Mount Todd gold mine among others. The Jawoyn people have taken a stake in these development and not a single job has been 'lost' to non-Aboriginal people of the region. In short, the Jawoyn have demonstrated that they are pro-development so long as their sacred places are not destroyed.

To those more alert among the media practitioners, the logical conclusion should have been that the lies that have been peddled about Aboriginal people just don't stack up, and those who have opposed Aboriginal rights have an agenda which should be investigated, rather than accepted at face value. Sadly, this has not proved to be the case. It seems that 'good news' stories about Aboriginal participation in the economy weigh less importantly in journalists' minds than the stereotypes of an alternatively lazy and shiftless mob of blackfellas, or a dangerous threat to the great Australian way of life.

What other conclusion can be drawn, when the media consistently give space and time to Richard Court telling lies about alleged Native Title threats to people's backyards, when time and again he has been demonstrated to hold deliberate and malicious false views? What other conclusion can be drawn when the media acquiesce in the holding of public inquiries into Aboriginal religious beliefs—yet quite happily accept non-Aboriginal beliefs as legitimate, acceptable, and beyond investigation? I don't remember any members of the media suggesting that there be a public inquiry into the beliefs of Catholics and their faith surrounding the canonization of Mary McKillop, though there was ready acceptance of the holding of public investigations into the spiritual beliefs surrounding the site for the proposed Alice Springs Dam or Guratba.

As I said, this is not about adopting some sort of unquestioning and censorious 'politically correct' attitude by journalists. Quite the opposite. It is however a call to media workers, not just here in Perth but around the nation, to go back to the basics and question the stereotypes that vested interests would have us believe about Aboriginal people. Look at our side of the story as well as the press releases from the boardrooms and party machines. Talk to us as well as to the smooth-talking spin-doctors employed by the powers that be. Instead of condoning the censorship of Aboriginal ideas, attitudes, and activities, as has been the case most of this century—look at them. Learn about them. Investigate them. Listen to us. Balance other ideas and attitudes against ours.

If you in the non-Aboriginal media are not prepared to abandon the old stereotypes about our people, you should not be surprised if we find it increasingly difficult to believe the media are anything other than a force designed to continue to repress Aboriginal interests and rights. If you are not prepared to abandon the old stereotypes, you might as well, when you are filing your story tonight, begin your opening par with the words:

Northern Territory coon politician and well-known yella-fella with a dash of chink, John Ah Kit, yesterday called on journalists to report Abo issues fairly.

But you wouldn't do that, would you? Thank you.

5 | Watching the Watchdogs: Community Reception and Discussion of Media

> Meanwhile, cultural studies continued on its merry way. Asking questions . . . Working particularly on the most intractable problem in Australian culture—finding ways to have a dialogue with Aboriginal people and to recognise their entitlement to speak; *on their own terms*.
>
> (McKenzie Wark, 1997: 174)

The 'Intelligentsia' Mode of Media Reception

At around the time of the National Media Forum, a conversation occurred between Alan McKee and an Indigenous lecturer attached to the Kurongkurl Katitjin unit at Edith Cowan University in Perth, Western Australia, where the state newspaper is the *West Australian*. 'The *West*' is the only daily paper indigenous to that state, and it enjoys one of the highest penetrations (proportion of population who read it) in the world. The paper has a strong investment in its inclusive embrace of all WA citizens. In 1996, the *West Australian* won the 'Best print entry' category in the Louis Johnson Media Awards. The award went to the paper's Aboriginal Affairs journalist Karen Brown, in recognition of several years' worth of sensitive and thoughtful work on Aboriginal issues.

Against this background, Alan McKee was talking to the Indigenous lecturer, who said: 'I see that paper [the *West*] in the shop, and I can't even pick it up, it's so racist'. He refused to 'engage with the text'. He took it as meaningful as a whole (i.e. it stood for white racism). Karen Brown's work was literally meaningless to him; the fact of her winning the award said very little about the representation of Aboriginality in that context. This example describes a certain kind of audience position: one where the 'state' paper does not comprise the words, images, and narratives on the page, but the history of hostility between Aboriginal and non-Aboriginal Australia. In such a way, the *West Australian* can plausibly be 'read' as a racist text in general, even when it publishes stories about Aboriginal affairs that win awards for excellence from Indigenous judges.

Around the same period, in May 1996, a press release detailed an Aboriginal march against media representation of Indigenous issues:

Wednesday 15 May 1996 at 12.15pm

The media has to stop its biased reporting about Aboriginal people, printing and sensationalising half truths instead of printing full truths. The media is causing racism in our society. Some people in our society are ignorant about our cause and what really happens in our communities. These people are stereotyping every Aboriginal and Torres Strait Islander they meet...the commercial TV stations and newspapers wake up and look at what you are doing. You give our society no real chance of true reconciliation. (Della Bona, 1996).

Joanne Della Bona, the organizer of the march, called it in response to two events that had occurred in the previous week. In the first, a friend of Della Bona's was refused service in a bottle shop. In the second, another friend was refused service at a ticketing service. In neither event were the media directly involved. Sufficient evidence of their racism was understood to have been found in the attitude of the persons responsible for refusing retail services to Indigenous citizens.

These two examples suggest one type of Indigenous 'readership position' in relation to media. It might be characterized as an intense engagement, an insistent circulation of meaning about them, but one that relies minimally if at all on individual texts, or on the meanings which might be made of them. This is a profoundly resistant 'audience', seeing the media as a source of racism, and willing to speak out in public against 'the media' as a whole. Some of the contributions to the National Media Forum display similar characteristics (see Di Potter, below, for instance).

But these examples do not suggest that the Aboriginal people in question have somehow got media analysis wrong. Instead, they point to a 'tactical response' to media as a whole on behalf of Indigenous people as a whole. The 'reception' of media texts includes a refusal to consume them. Such a tactic has a strangely familiar ring about it. The combination of strongly held negative opinion about the media with an equally strongly expressed refusal to engage with them is exactly the one that characterizes a certain 'top-table' kind of intellectual discourse:

Dr Jocelynne Scutt, a prominent Australian feminist barrister and an opponent of degrading images of women in the media...has spoken and written so frequently on the subject of sexism in the media [that] she is often invoked as an expert on the media by the media. It came as something of a shock to learn she didn't own a television set. (Lumby, 1997: ix).

The Aboriginal people cited above are using the same model of engaging with—of 'watching'—the media, in which intensely important meanings are made, and relations to the medium sustained, without the need to refer to the content of the medium in question. In honour of Dr Scutt, we can call this the 'intelligentsia' mode of media reception.

Watching the Watchdogs

We return now to the collective 'reception' of media undertaken by members of the public at the National Media Forum. The session following the national leaders' speeches brought together Indigenous and non-Indigenous people from the general community. It was chaired by Glen Shaw. There were no panel speakers, and no previously organized agenda. However, Robert Bropho, veteran leader of the Swan Valley Fringe Dwellers, had been invited to speak. In prior discussions with the organizers, Mr Bropho had expressed a wish to speak about police harassment of his community, and the neglect of that issue by the local media. Similarly, local activist Clarrie Isaacs had been invited to attend, but had instead arranged an alternative press conference to be held at the same time as this session, at a different venue. Glen Shaw opened the session by reading out the media release from Clarrie Isaacs in order to inform Forum participants of the alternative news conference. It was this notice that prompted the first question from the floor, which itself gave rise to the first substantial contribution from Mr Bropho.

GLEN SHAW
Chair of the WA Deaths in Custody Watch Committee, and Aboriginal Education Development Officer with the Trades and Labour Council
This session basically is for the local Aboriginal community to make comment on the media and we have a roving microphone here. So what I'll do is—I won't slow things down by making long-winded speeches—we'll get it under way and try and get some good comments from the local community.

DARRYL KICKETT
Consultant with Nyungar Land Council, Perth

Reception

I'd just like to seek clarification on this alternative media meeting. What's it about and what is actually meant by an alternative media meeting? Is it an attack on the meeting that's being held here? Is it an attack on the Louis Johnson Trust? Is it an attack on the boy who's been killed, murdered, by two white boys out at Scarborough, and out of that, led to these Media Awards, and this Forum that's being held here? So I'd like to seek some clarification on it, if anyone here is able to provide that.

ROBERT BROPHO
Elder, Swan Valley Fringe Dwellers
I think the meeting Clarrie [Isaacs] organized is on behalf of a lot of Aboriginal people who live on a daily basis, day in and day out, where racism is building up very fast in the way of police brutality. This meeting that I see here today, it's been going two days now, but I'll say this here and now—I'll give permission to all Aboriginal people visiting into the Perth area for this meeting, on behalf of the Swan Coastal Plains Nyungar people. My community has been in the Swan Valley for a lifetime. We were the last of the river people. I came here yesterday into the front office there. A lot of visiting Aboriginal people from other parts of the country had seen me there. Not one of them said g'day.

Now what I want to say about Clarrie Isaacs's meeting is that there's two sides to letting the media know. This is one, but it was set up in the wrong way. The other side is where the problems start—at grassroots level. All up in the north of this State, the east and the south, and all around the metropolitan area; the news is out there, every day. But the local media is not concerned with it. The local media becomes interested in imported news.

When I went to Los Angeles about the Marlo Morgan thing, the media in Australia, to a large extent, wasn't interested in the Aboriginal issues—of our religion and culture being completely destroyed by this white woman. But the moment we landed in Los Angeles, the media there was like vultures, it was news and it went from there in all directions to all parts of the world. I and another seven Aboriginal people journeyed over there to take out of this country the news of how we had been exploited and destroyed.

Now Darryl stood up and asked a question about why this alternative media meeting has been called down there. It is not what you thought in your mind, Darryl. It's the other side singing out, 'Hey, what about us? Can we be heard?' That's what it means. Yesterday, when all the visiting people came and started your talks here, we were burying a founder of the Aboriginal Legal Service, who helped build the Legal Service to where it is now, along with a lot of other Aboriginal people.

148

I can honestly say this now to each and every one of you here visiting today, no matter where you come from. Racism is building up to total destruction of us, the Aboriginal people, out there. Our children can't sit at the bus-stop without being questioned by the police. Our children cannot come to the streets of Perth with father and mother without being pulled aside and asked their names, and when Mum or Father intervenes, they're told to shut their mouths. It's a police blitz on all Aboriginal communities and mine in particular.

The latest incident was when I left to go to Los Angeles. I rang Vince Cuttage who's working with the police and asked him to help protect my community whilst I was away. While I was away it was attacked. A police raid. Looking for stolen property. Found a wheelbarrow, not on my property, or on my community's property. So these are the things that are taking place. I'd like each and every one of you visiting here today if you're coming from the north, the east, the south, or out of this country, you take back what was said here and turn it over in your minds because this is what's happening in this area; believe you me, we speak because we know it's happening to us.

Before I close, I want to comment a little bit more on deaths in custody. I've been to so many of these meetings and I think it's time that we stamped out where the deaths in custody begins; and you know where it begins? In your home. It's neglect of the growth, where this deaths in custody starts. I'll speak with a level mind because one of my friends was found hung in the Fremantle Lockup. I went to the court that day and a lot of lies was told. I know because he and I knew exactly who we was and how we felt but Deaths in Custody starts at home.

We can all sit down and say, 'These are the recommendations that should be taken notice of'. We've said it so many times. We can go away from here, and we can say, 'These are the recommendations of today'. Two or three years up the track we'll still be saying it. Ten to twelve, maybe thirteen people can be laying in their graves between now and then. But we've got to stamp it out where it begins. The police charges. Arrested, taken to court, sentenced to prison, and you undergo all the prison treatments and you end up hanging yourself. So it is said.

The alternative meeting down there is only just to say that type of thing, as I've just said, just to outline to you, the visiting media, because the local media here in Western Australia is not interested in what's going on here. The local media in Western Australia only listens to what they want to listen to and what they've been told to listen to. But the real truth out there where things does happen, they don't print it and you people visiting here don't know about it.

Reception

G L E N   S H A W

Thank you Robert. I'd just like to reinforce Robert's comments on that. The Watch Committee does a lot of media releases on different issues at different times, and the media apathy here in Western Australia is at a stage where those reports tend not to get picked up.

We have cases where young Aboriginal people are manacled in the prisons for months at a time. Manacled twenty-four hours a day, and it's not reported, even when press releases go out, it's not reported. The raids on the community, Robert's community, are never reported, so the wider community doesn't know about it.

The underlying racism within the police department here in West Australia is never recorded. The way young people are abused and assaulted by police, on an hourly basis, not a daily basis—on an hourly basis—is never recorded.

The attitude and the underlying racism within the policy-makers in this state is never reported accurately. The media are more than happy to report about the wonderful new boot-camp that they're building out in the desert. How wonderful it is—how it is going to assist in the controlling of problem youth within Western Australia. They didn't report that it's going to be a para-military style camp, where it's jackboots and people are forced to go into it, under rigorous, intensive mind-control training to try and realign their thinking. That is never reported. All that's reported is how good it's going to be for the community as a whole. Not how it's going to affect minority groups within this state. That's the type of reporting we have in Western Australia.

You look at the processes of eviction of Aboriginal people from their homes within this state. Before January this year we had a minister who was a Minister for Housing as well as a Minister for Aboriginal Affairs. On one hand he was saying, 'Oh it's terrible how families are broken up and dispersed', but on the other hand he's reinforcing the policy of evictions to throw Aboriginal people out of their homes and the families were being broken up and dispersed. But in the eyes of the Minister and in the eyes of the media, there was no conflict of interest in that. It's just a minister with two portfolios. It doesn't matter that he's being hypocritical. That's irrelevant as far as the media in Western Australia is concerned, particularly the print media.

These are the sorts of attitudes and the thinking of the majority of red-necked small 'l' liberal people within this state. And in *this* state [Western Australia]—you've seen the air, you've seen the sun—there must be a lot of people walking around here with red necks, because nobody seems to know what's going on. I could go on and on and on and probably fill in the full hour. Well I think this is for the local community to have their say, so let's open it back up again. We've got Jan Mayman. Well done Jan.

JAN MAYMAN
Freelance journalist; winner of Australia's highest journalism award, a Gold Walkely, for her reporting of Aboriginal issues in Western Australia

Sorry—I'm not a local Aborigine. I'm a journalist with a lot of experience in reporting Aboriginal Affairs. I used to work at Channel Seven. My job was to find news for them. Robert knows about this story. There was a raid on his camp. Children were bailed up with each other. Girls were bailed up. There were thirty police cars that raided your community, Robert. Do you remember that time? Was it thirty police cars?

Anyway, I told the Channel Seven News people about it. It was a terrible situation. It was worthy of South Africa at its worst. Channel Seven were very interested in the story, so they said. The next day was my day off. I only worked there part-time. Robert had his people at the camp, everyone dressed in their best clothes for the camera. All the children had their hair done up. They were all waiting to tell their story at last to the media. So what did Channel Seven do? They didn't bother to go out to the camp, they just went to the nearest park and they found a lot of Aboriginal mourners who'd been to a funeral. And like white people after a funeral, they sometimes have a drink or two—a wake. So these people weren't really in full control of themselves, and they got a very inflammatory interview reacting to the police. It was very bad for race relations but that's what one channel did in Perth. It was extremely dangerous. The effect of those images of those angry Aboriginals threatening violence against the police—it was incredible and it was disgraceful—the betrayal of Robert and his people.

I don't know whether you ever got an interview on Channel Seven, Robert, but I just want to say this as an insider. What you might hear might seem extreme if you haven't been involved in it, but it really goes on. I stopped working at Channel Seven over that incident. I found that it was really difficult to get any Aboriginal issues up. I remember there was one case—the prisoners at Fremantle had actually burnt down the prison. There was a prisoner doing a year in solitary confinement because he had the temerity to stand on the roof with a banner saying, 'We want a public inquiry'. His name was Morrish. Anyone remember the case? The people at Channel Seven were very interested in the story until they discovered he was an Aboriginal man and then they didn't want to know about it.

This is the sort of thing they're up against all the time. Whenever the word 'Aboriginal' was mentioned on air, the phones would just explode for a fortnight—I had to deal with the phone calls. I'd begin to recognize their voices—the phones would just explode with their complaints that we had the temerity even to have an Aboriginal story on air. I remember once Germaine Greer was being interviewed and she said something about Aboriginal issues. She hadn't even finished her sentence before the phones lit up. And the people used to say things like, 'Listen you, we know how far you have to walk to the carpark at night through the bush'. (And it's true, you had to walk.)

That's the sort of stuff that went on. I was continually told that the viewers didn't want to hear about Aboriginal issues on air. So what I want to urge you to do as Aboriginal and non-Aboriginal people—please ring in the same way. Target television stations, target radio stations. Don't let these people get away with it because I'm sure it's an organized band of people who rang in. I began to recognize their voices. And you've got just as much power too. You're consumers. You buy the products they advertise. Tell the people to call the television stations—get on to the news directors—really tell them something because that's the only way you'll get your message across on air. I hope I haven't taken up too much time. Thanks for listening.

GLEN SHAW
Perhaps you could try and, I don't know, legitimize is probably the wrong word but to try and understand why the media is the way it is when you look at the history of the State of Western Australia. You look at the infamous 1905 Act and the flow-ons from that. It was the first piece of legislation that classified Aboriginal people into three groups. Full-blood, half-caste, and quadroon.

If a person was deemed to be a 'quadroon', then the authorities in Western Australia had the power to remove their children. If the parents tried to stop the removal of those children, they were arrested for a breach of the Act. If an Aboriginal female was seen between dusk and daylight within two miles of a creek, an inlet, or an area where pearl boats were, that was a breach of an Act. If you got a job that the government didn't agree with and you went to work for that person, it was a breach under the Act. It was total control. Some parts of the Act was repealed in 1943 but most of it wasn't repealed until the 1960s.

Now the people who were enforcing that Act in the 1960s are still here today. They are still the people who are behind the policy-makers, the decision-makers of Western Australia. You've only got to look at the current Premier. His father was one of the oppressors of Aboriginal people and, like father like son. No problem with that. They tried to clean up the police force here in Western Australia. So they thought they'd bring in a Commissioner [Falconer] from Victoria. Now we all know how Victorian police react. Shoot them first. If they're still alive, ask them questions. Where's the logic behind that? We all know of the arrest rate of Aboriginal people and they bring in people with the mentality of 'shoot first, ask questions later'. Who's it going to affect? Logically it's going to affect the Aboriginal community.

They're looking at drafting legislation to give the Tactical Response Group the authority to detain without arrest. Now they don't put specific time-frames on it. So Aboriginal people can be walking down the street, and get dragged straight into a paddy-wagon and taken away. People don't seem to understand. We live in Perth, not in Pretoria. But it all comes back to the same thing, it reverts back to the mentality of the 1905 Act.

Now Aboriginal people live with the hatred. They live with the violence from the non-Aboriginal community. They live with the attitude. They live with the red-necks, they live with the conservatives on a daily basis. But when we try and get our story across to let level-headed people with common sense understand what the problems are, the people who have the greatest voice and the greatest power in this country, the media, turn a blind eye to it. They say, 'If we can't sensationalize it, we're not going to print it'. Now they're more than happy to print or tell of those things where there's some sort of reactionary story in it—you know, where it's confrontational or whatever. But when it's a clear attack on the Aboriginal community by the authorities of this state, it's given some sort of 'Oh well, we won't worry about that because it's okay for the state to do as they like so we won't bother printing it'.

So there are two societies in Western Australia. There's the Aboriginal community who fight hard on a daily basis and there are the policy-makers within this State who basically don't give a toss. They just don't care about Aboriginal people. It's clear that the policy of this State Government, and the people who support this State Government including small 'l' liberals within certain media organizations, towards Aboriginal people is that you either assimilate or you're marginalized. You have no choice. You either come and live in our towns, under our terms, and do as you're told, or you go out bush and we forget about you. It's as simple as that.

ROBERT BROPHO
I just want to comment a bit more on this. I want to come back a little bit more to the Lockridge Raid in '89 that Jan Mayman mentioned. A naked

12-year-old girl was ordered out of the shower on that day to walk out into the field with the rest of the Aboriginal people. That young girl is still living today. She's a young mother now with two children. To this day even she's ringing me and asking me whether there's anything coming out of that raid on that day.

Now it's important to explain to the visiting media people here how that raid came about. It just takes a phone call to the local police. No names and all you've got to say is, 'Guns have been sold at Lockridge Campsite—cool stuff'—believe you me, you'll get a raid. You can use it anywhere in Western Australia if you hate Aboriginal people. The latest incident was the one I told you of, was when I was over in Los Angeles. We got a complaint that a wheelbarrow was taken. With that they built up all the planning and plotting for an attack. They came on to the premises in full force. They were hoping that the Aboriginal community would retaliate and start smashing cars and whatever but they fell in a lot of mud because people just closed their doors and took no part in it.

So it's been growing from '89 right up until now. This is why we keep talking about it. And it's spreading. Now I'm studying it and so are a lot of other Aboriginal people. You're getting police cadets trained and all the old top-notch inspectors are being pushed out of the Force. Believe you me, I can foresee that violence is coming to the streets of Perth. It's going to come from those youth who sit in their homes and experience the brutality when there's a knock on the door: 'Get out of the road you black bitch'. 'Where's your warrant?' 'Oh we don't need it'. Now that's what's going on. And before I close I want to leave an open invitation to any visiting media people who want to go down to where Clarrie Isaacs and the other Aboriginal people are. It's not only you I'm asking whether you want to go down there. To the local media the invitation's still open there for you, including Aboriginal people too who are visiting here today, and you'll hear the other part of it. I've just come here to interpret some of it.

I've been at it for a lifetime now; something like sixty-six years, and I've studied it, and I class myself as Dalai Lama or Martin Luther King or Gandhi because I study the white people the same as they study us. I study the Aboriginal people who claim to speak for Aboriginal people and they're not. And this is what is going on today. There's a lot of divisions being created. Now we wrote strong letters, time and again, to Robert Tickner [Federal Minister for Aboriginal and Islander Affairs], asking for a Federal Police inquiry into the police treatment of Aboriginal people here. We've asked twice now and we've got nothing. What we can foresee at Lockridge, where we live, is someone's going to be killed. It's either going to be one of our children or one of their young men or women and then the retaliation will come on the day. A white police could be killed and a lot of blacks could be killed. Now they're even coming in vans with Alsatian dogs. And when I saw that I thought well I'm Nelson Mandela, we're in Africa. And that's what's going on. The local media, they'll do nothing for us. The invitation's still down there and now I'm leaving this room. What you say after I've left you can bloody well say. I couldn't care less.

GLEN SHAW
Thank you Robert. Any other comments from the floor?

ANN ANNEAR
Anglican Council for Social Responsibility, Perth
My name is Ann Annear and I've been an activist with Aboriginal people, especially with Robert's people, since 1980. In that time, with the struggle for land rights and the black deaths in custody issue, I and other people like myself were writing letters constantly to the *West Australian* about these sorts of issues, to try to get non-Aboriginal people to see the Aboriginal point of view. And our letters used to be printed.

But in the last four or five years I have written so many letters and these same friends of mine have written letters about the same sorts of issues coming up that Robert's talking about now. Never, never, do our letters get printed. And I want to know why?

GLEN SHAW
I think we'd all like to know why.

MAUD WALSH
WA Law Society, formerly WA Aboriginal Legal Service
I just want to say something very briefly and I want to reinforce what Robert has been saying since he's been here all morning. My name's Maud Walsh and I worked for the Aboriginal Legal Service in Western Australia for approximately fourteen years. Since my commencement with them down in the country I've heard about how the raids used to be on—in those days it used to be Cullacabardee—and the police used to chase out and you'd see the media following in the helicopter. The police chasing the cars out to the Cullacabardee camps, and there'd be the TRG going out there with shotguns and sticking them in people's necks and all that sort of stuff.

There was no media coverage on why the Aboriginal people were in those situations they were in, why they were in those cars. It was all—the highlight was on the police. The car chase. The burning of the car. The ultimate end of the chase. There was nothing at all stated about why that person was there, why he was being chased.

That was about twenty years ago. It's still happening. The reasons for the boot-camp (as Glen [Shaw] pointed out) being put way out in the bush Leonora-way was the same thing. Car chases and police being involved in car chases. The police, in my view, instigated all those car chases for the fun of it. They'd go out and they would pick on someone. They'd see some young fellas driving along in a car and just for the hell of it, they'd provoke them. In lots of instances. There are car chases all over the place. The media never ever reported on the police being involved in it in a positive sort of way, it was always the blackfellas that were being put in the bad light. That was the blacks' fault. The Aboriginals. They're the criminals. They need to be locked away.

And then unfortunately, very sadly there was some people killed and one of those people was a young woman and baby by the name of Blurton. And since that time [Peter] Blurton [the widower] has been in the papers. He's been the media man provoking and talking and acting as a politician saying blacks should be locked up they shouldn't be let out. It's not right that he be allowed to take the position that he's taken and provoke all this media coverage and hatred towards Aboriginal people. Where was the media coverage when that was occurring? There was not one thing said that this man shouldn't be there speaking out the way he was speaking. There was not one thing said about the police harassing and tormenting and torturing Aboriginal people in prisons and on the streets, as Robert said.

I've seen it with my own eyes. I've experienced being sworn at myself as an advocate for Aboriginal people in the courts. You're not supposed to be here. Who are you? Who do you think you are? And being shouted at, so it does happen. And there's nothing being done about it. They need an independent inquiry to investigate the police. The police investigate themselves and nothing happens. No one gets to hear about why the police acted in the manner do. Certainly the Aboriginal people don't get to hear about what's happening.

Since I've been with the Legal Service (I'm no longer with them now) but my time with them, I instigated many reports against bad behaviour by the police towards Aboriginal people both inside and outside custody. Those reports were eventually put up to the Commissioner and they were probably screwed up and thrown in the bin. No one ever heard anything more from them. And that's been going on ever since I can remember and it's still happening. Nothing's changed. Nothing's changed at all. What Robert has said here this morning is the truth and it's happening. It's going to continue to happen and I feel the same way that he feels that something very bad is going to happen unless something is done about it.

The media have a lot to answer for what is happening around the place. And I think the media should look into their consciences and find out and see what they're doing to other people before you put your pen to paper and wreck someone's lives or have someone killed.

DI POTTER
Indigenous business woman, In Touch Training, WA
Good morning everyone, my name is Di Potter and I'm a funny sort of a lady; I'm a black woman and I run my own business. But I have a passionate hate for media and I think that most Aboriginal people are very sceptical about speaking and saying what they really feel within their hearts and telling the truth because media do sensationalize the types of truths that are really happening.

I recall an instance back on New Year's Eve 1979. I went to my home town, Pingelly, which is a very racist town. I went down there and my son went with me and we went to the local hairdresser and I asked if I could have my son's hair cut and she said, 'No, I can't have you people in here because I would lose all my customers'. I thought, my God, you know, I can't get my son's hair cut. So I thought this was not right and I went home I said to Dad: 'Dad, this woman down here won't cut Nat's hair', and he said, 'Oh, look don't worry about it'. And I said: 'No, I'm not going to let this go because this happens too often in this particular country town'. I proceeded to call the Human Rights Commission who said, 'Oh look, we'll get on to the press'. So they got on to the press. It was the *Daily News* at the time. A couple of days later they came down and interviewed me and I told them what had happened. But when the story was actually printed it said that I had put my 5-year-old son up as a political thing against race relations in the town. That wasn't true. All I did was went in to ask for a hair-cut for my son. There was nothing political in going in and asking for a hair-cut, surely? So that type of reporting goes on all the time and you often hear Aboriginal people say, 'I made these comments but this is not exactly what I have said'.

So, just today, those people who are in the media here, in particular the white people, how you write things—please get it into context because it has a detrimental effect on us. I mean, my whole psyche was completely damaged because of that particular reporting because that's not really what I wanted to say. For God's sake, we do go out and have hair-dos and that type of thing! We don't just sit there and let our presentation dwindle, and to have that type of thing happening is just dreadful. I just want to let you know that I have a particular hate for media reporting and if I have anything that happens in the media then I get other people to do it for me simply because I don't want to talk to the media.

KATH MALLOTT
Deaths in Custody Watch Committee, Western Australia
I'm Kath Mallott, a [non-Aboriginal] member of the WA Deaths in Custody Watch Committee. I'd like to talk about a particular article which appeared in the *West Australian* on Tuesday December 5, 1995.

The headline is: 'Aboriginal Death First Since Probe' and it relates to a Coroner's inquest which started on this particular day into the death of a young Aboriginal man in prison. The reporter who wrote the headline—that this was the '*first*' death since the Royal Commission in Western Australia—had, only a couple of months before this inquest, attended another inquest into an Aboriginal man who had died in prison. So this later report is blatantly inaccurate. The headline is wrong. The reporter attended an inquest into a death in custody only months before he wrote that. The reason he wrote it was because the Council assisting the Coroner in his opening statement said: 'This is the first death in custody since the Royal Commission'. So that reporter denied his own knowledge of the situation and just wrote what Council assisting the Coroner said, even though he knew he had attended another inquest, months before, into an Aboriginal man who had died in prison and had actually reported on it.

On this same opening day Dr Sandra Eades from the Aboriginal Medical Service was called by Council representing the family. I was there at the time that Sandra gave evidence, and I've got a bundle of papers here which are my notes on Sandra's evidence (it was very harrowing evidence) relating to the social issues and the underlying causes that led to this man being homeless, alcohol-dependent, dispossessed from his community; being arrested in Wells Square and dying at the East Perth lockup the following day. Dr Eades' evidence took two hours.

Under cross-examination by Council representing the police, she admitted that the man had told her that he had drunk a cask of wine every day for the last twenty years, and that was the only statement that she made under cross-examination by the police. What did the *West* report in this grossly inaccurate article? Did they report the two hours that she'd given of the social issues, the underlying causes? No. They reported the alcohol consumption. And they reported it in a way that makes it look like Sandra Eades had walked into that court, got up on the stand, and said: 'This man told me that he drank a cask of wine every day for the last twenty years', and then got down off that stand and walked out. If you read the article, that's the way it presents.

Not only to the non-Aboriginal community; it presents that way to the Aboriginal community. To Aboriginal people who go to Sandra Eades because they want to relate to her as another Aboriginal person in having their health and illnesses treated. So what does it do for the trust that Sandra Eades has built up with her Aboriginal patients, if it's portrayed in the manner that she just walks into the court and says this? She actually gave two hours of very harrowing evidence that led to that man being arrested in Wells Square.

Now when I read that on the second day of the inquest I was incredibly angry and I challenged the journalist at the inquest and I said: 'Did you not attend the Coroner's inquest into another man that died in custody three months ago?' And he said: 'Oh yes, yeah'. And I said: 'Well, doesn't that make a lie of your headline?' And he said: 'Oh yeah, yeah. It's just that Council for the Coroner said that in his opening statement'. Anyway, I told him what I felt about the article.

That morning, the police had been giving evidence and, under cross-examination by the Aboriginal Legal Service who were representing the family, they were forced to admit what was really harassment of Aboriginal people meeting in Wells Square. What it amounted to was this: there are three shifts a day for police. The police admitted that one patrol car on each of the three shifts would visit Wells Square five or six times, and would name-check people. That meant that one person in Wells Square could be name-checked up to *eighteen times* in one day. And that amounts to police harassment in anyone's language. While the police were giving this evidence, I turned and looked at the journalist and he was sitting reading a magazine and not making any notes and then it was at lunchtime that I challenged him about his article and he said: 'Well look, there's not much happening today, I'll go back to the office and see if I can fix it and get them to print something else tomorrow'. I said, 'Well how can you say there's not much happening today when we've just had, you know, eight policemen...'

This is lazy, irresponsible, sloppy journalism. And it's because, I think, the journalist was too young to know any better. He was too young to challenge the sub-editor who cut his article down and paraphrased it to the point where it was not true. That's why we need senior journalists, who know what they're doing, who know the community and who understand and have thorough knowledge of the issues. Thank you.

GLEN SHAW

Thank you Kath. Does anybody else want to make comments from the floor? We're running out of time, ladies and gentlemen; does anybody here have anything positive about the media in Western Australia? That would be interesting. Hang on. Yep, we got one. There's got to be one in every crowd, doesn't there?

PHIL MONCRIEFF

ATSIC Regional Councillor for Carnarvon, member of NIMA, Yamatji Aboriginal Media Corporation, Western Australia

Hi, my name's Phil Moncrieff. I'm a Yamatji person. I'm from Carnarvon and firstly, I'd just like to say thanks to the Nyungar brothers and sisters for allowing me to talk in their country.

I've been involved in Aboriginal Affairs for eighteen years, which is half of my life, and I'm not going to say anything really positive about the media. I thought I'd just get a chance to talk because we're running out of time. But you'd have to be positive too at all times because over the last two hundred years there's been only a negative feeling towards Aboriginal people in this country and we can't be negative because if you put a negative against a negative there's no spark. We have to be positive and if there's a positive and a negative, then there is a spark and there is something that we can go on with.

I'm a Regional Councillor with ATSIC up in Carnarvon, and I'm also a member of the National Indigenous Media Association of Australia. This is the formation of the true warriors of the grassroots Aboriginal cause, because a lot of these people come from the grassroots community and Indigenous media was brought about by Aboriginal people saying, 'We want to do this and we're not going to take another government programme to work with Indigenous media'. It's been going for fifteen or so years now and there are very many fine people who are finding it very, very hard, and have been frustrated over long periods of time, to get support from those who should be helping, namely ATSIC and DEET (federal Department of Employment, Education and Training).

I think you can go so far in blaming the media for the portrayal of Aboriginal people because that's what they deserve. In the past there have been many bad stories, wrong stories, written about Aboriginal people and I'll tell you one in just a little while, about something that recently happened in Carnarvon. But before I do, one positive thing that I'd like to talk about is Indigenous media. Indigenous media is a grassroots initiative and not a government initiative, so things are very bare in the cupboard, because when Aboriginal people want something the government always reaches for the hip-pocket, and says what they think is good for Aboriginal people. As if we don't know how to handle our own affairs. As if we weren't here before the whites came. As if we weren't here for 40,000 or more years and looked forward to another 40,000. But over the last 200 years maybe we aren't going to get that far.

Anyway, I'm a Regional Councillor. On the Regional Council I was doing a show with another girl called Lynette Oxenham, she's a Yamatji girl in Carnarvon, and was doing a show called *Yamatji Talking*, which went for an hour-and-a-half on the local commercial radio station, and we were quite happy with that. Everyone liked the show. Everyone enjoyed the Indigenous music. We aired Aboriginal issues on a commercial radio station. Then the station manager came up to me one day and said, 'We're going to sell this place because we've gone into liquidation'. He gave me one week's notice and one week to me is a long time, because I acted on that. I immediately went out and spoke with all the Yamatji people about the formation of the Yamatji Aboriginal Media Corporation. And we started talking about that, and then I got the ear of the other Regional Councillors who said it was a good idea and within about two or three months we'd bought the place. We established Yamatji Aboriginal Media Corporation, and we own radio station 666–LN which is a commercial radio station and, although we didn't know it at the time, we actually became the first Indigenous Media Association to own a commercial radio station in Australia.

So we sent information about that down to Perth to get in the *West Australian* and the *Sunday Times* and of course we got nothing. There are positive things happening and they are happening in Indigenous media. Indigenous media is a grassroots initiative. You must believe that because that's where our freedom fighters still are, and we're very proud of that. We don't get any positive stories about Yamatji Media and 666–LN in the local newspaper because they see us as black first. On that front, we had a hard time getting advertisers coming over to sponsor us, and it was only through mediation and cajoling that we were able to get the white business houses in Carnarvon to come along and provide advertising revenue to us as an Aboriginal radio station, which they're doing quite handsomely now.

We have to get ATSIC and DEET firmly behind Indigenous media to give us our sponsorship so that we can start to get up and walk on our own two feet. Aboriginal people have got the capacity to do business. It's called Aboriginal business, community business. I think the challenge to the individual journalist is to get close to your local Aboriginal community. Get close to the issues that you're reporting on. Talk to the necessary people. Write down the information that you think is going to be relevant and which is important to all Australians and to take it easy on the blackfellas for a little while.

HELEN CORBETT
United Nations Representative for the Indigenous Women's Corporation, co-founder of the National Committee to Defend Black Rights
These Nyungar women like taking centre stage. My name is Helen Corbett. Some of you in the audience may know me as Helen Boyle, especially those from the east coast of Australia who haven't caught up; I've changed my name. I'm also from Carnarvon and in Carnarvon my name is Ulli to the family.

I'm one of the co-founders of the National Committee to Defend Black Rights, which, some of you would know, is the organization of families who've lost relatives in custody. The other co-founder of that organization was also a Nyungar woman, Rosemary Stack. And we were both living in Sydney at the time, working at Tranby Aboriginal College and that was the headquarters of the organization. Now, in that campaign there were a lot of things that we learned about working with the media. Our initial experience, as has been said by many speakers today, was of not much interest being shown in the issues that we were talking about. The membership of the organization, the Aboriginal families, had the same raw experiences as what we heard about today from the speakers and also from those who haven't spoken yet. We all know what those experiences have been in the community and we know what the relationship was been with the media in trying to portray those experiences and what to do.

After the Royal Commission reported in 1991, it seemed almost like there was a closing of the book by the media as to this particular campaign. There was a perception, not only by the media, but by the Australian community, that the government had done something. They had set up a $3 million, three-year inquiry into Aboriginal Deaths in Custody. It came up with three hundred and thirty-nine recommendations on how to stop further deaths in custody and also to look at ways of how to deal with the underlying issues. But in effect, 1991 was a closing of the book. We've seen since then what effect it's had on the families, and I notice this myself as an individual being involved in that campaign; how we all got burned out. How we still feel today about those issues of how our relatives died and that campaign, and the communities of those families, how they feel, although they may not have lost a relative in custody. We all felt the same. So a lot of us got burnt out in that campaign and we had a rest for a while. As we're saying, there was a closing of the book.

But it's really good for me to stand up here today and to see a meeting like this—and I've been to the two previous Forums in 1992 and 1994. What it does is it gives people like myself, as an individual, hope that someone else is still carrying the torch not just for the families of the people who died in custody but for the whole community. This Forum is not just for the Indigenous community, but for the whole Australian community, because we're talking about human rights issues here—we're not talking about black and white issues. We're talking about human rights issues and that's something we've been saying for a long time. It's not a colour thing. It's a human rights issue. We're human beings too. And so it's good for people like us who are burnt out, to have meetings like this. It's good to have the respect of Indigenous organizations whether they're in media, or whether they're support groups like the Deaths in Custody Watch Committee, and to have them still carrying the torch for us. It's important. Because I know there are still a lot of families out there who are suffering from the effects of this Commission.

But what I'd like to say is that there were many things we learned in that campaign, with respect to our relationship with the media. We had the same problems as people speaking here about how no one was interested. But we developed strategies of how to make the issue of deaths in custody a breakfast item on every Australian's breakfast table for a number of years, right up till the Commission ended. We had media chasing us for news as to what was happening. There are a lot of tactics that we used, although we weren't experts in terms of how to deal with media. We set up teams, Indigenous, non-Indigenous media teams to harass the media every day. We did lots of tricks. For example, we knew when the closing time was for media to put the news out, and we knew that they always go to the police to ask for their comments, so we'd sit up at night at 11 o'clock, and put our media releases through at that time, so that the police spokespeople couldn't have an opportunity to respond, and so it was only our viewpoint of the day that was being printed and not the police's response. That's just one small example that we used. But those are the kind of tactics that we'd like to share with any groups about how we got, for a number of years, the issue of Aboriginal deaths in custody on the breakfast table of the Australian community.

We also had the same experience that other speakers have said, about the international media wanting to play a bigger role than domestic media. As most of you know, I also do a lot international work, and that's where I mainly focus my energies today. But every time I go overseas I get called by media who want to speak to me for two hours on international phone calls, taking interviews about the situation at home. Part of that is to keep in contact with the international arena. The international media are in a less biased position than the domestic media and so they're more willing to do more work. So we can talk about how we dealt with the international media to put our peoples' position on the international arena. The other thing that we did was to look at the different domestic and international agencies which were representative of the communities that they came from, because the media are people from the ordinary community. They have the same prejudices, the same ignorance. And of course there are many who want to do things but they don't know how to.

For instance, with respect to the international agencies, I remember in 1987 we went to the Amnesty International office in London. I took the campaign over a young boy who died in Roebourne. And they laughed at me! Not about the death, but, they said, 'Australia has no human rights abuse record'. And they actually took me into their office, pulled the filing cabinet out and there was nothing on Australia's record of human rights abuse. They then took me to another section and pulled out the Philippines, pulled out Indonesia, filing cabinet after filing cabinet, but nothing on Australia. It took me, and the campaign, many years of persistently keeping at just that organization, Amnesty International, to highlight the issue of deaths in custody. But now, as many of you would know, Amnesty International has been to Australia twice, reporting on the issue. If some of you can remember their first report, it was a big deviation from Amnesty International's standard way of reporting things. They used the one individual's death in prison, but the report said, 'it was a criminal system weighted against Aboriginal people'. They looked at the *systematic* problem, not the individual problem, and that was a major departure by Amnesty International because of the campaign and the pressure that we put on them.

So we have to work out not what the media can do for us, but what we can do. That's the attitude we took, knowing full well, in the first instance, about the bias and the prejudice that we were going to face with the media. Amnesty International is just one example. There are many things that we can share together. There are many other campaigns. I see a lot of people sitting in this room who've been in the game just as long as me, if not longer, and I'm not just speaking about Indigenous people, I'm also speaking about some non-Indigenous people who are sitting in this room that I know of. They've been there as well. It is important to talk about our problems. It is not very often that we get the opportunity to voice our experiences publicly, except in Forums like this, about our relationship with the media. We don't because of the problems we have with the media. But there has to be some way of working out strategies together. There are ways and we've all been using them, not just our organization. There have been many examples. What is needed is combining all those efforts together.

One thing white Australia doesn't like, including media, is having 'their' country being presented in a bad light in the international arena, and I know that and many of you know that. There's an individual here [Michael Mansell] who went on a controversial trip to a particular country and we saw how the media treated that story. I believe that the time is right for us, given that we've got the Olympic Games coming up, that we have to work out some strategy beyond talking about our problems. The opportunity's here now to change things and there is a time-line that we can use—the next five years towards this Olympic Games. It's an opportunity for us not just to work with non-Indigenous media but also with Indigenous media as well. They have a lot of the technical expertise. We in the community have the raw experiences of what's happening to us, and so do they too because they're members of the Aboriginal community— they're us. So they have a big obligation in a sense because they are intimate members of the community, with media expertise on top of that.

But also to the non-Indigenous people of the media, you are also part of the community, because we all live in this country. As I was saying, if there are no rights for us as Indigenous people, how can white Australia stand up and determine what its identity is. That's all I'd like to say. Thank you very much.

GLEN SHAW

I think that's not a bad note to finish on. The main point is that in Australia at the moment there is a huge explosion in the amount of Indigenous people in media. We've got to start using it. If Australia is turning out to be the smart country, we've got to be smarter. We have the capabilities. If we use and resource the Indigenous media the way they should be resourced, those people will then move on into mainstream media and we will be able to tell our own story. Thank you very much.

6 | Telling the Stories: Indigenous Media, Indigenizing Australian Media

> The Indigenous media sector—incorporating radio, television, film, print, and multimedia technologies—is, in itself, an influential cultural resource. The range of Indigenous media being produced across Australia is extraordinary—and remains essentially unknown to most of the non-Indigenous population.... Despite this—perhaps because of it—the Indigenous media sector is the fastest growing in Australia.
>
> (Michael Meadows, 1998: 69)

In this chapter we present the last of the material from the 1996 National Media Forum. It follows two sessions: the first on Indigenous media, focusing in this instance on Aboriginal broadcasting, especially radio stations that are part of the National Indigenous Radio Service (NIRS), a world-class example of a nascent 'broadcast public sphere' for dispersed, remote, and impecunious communities. The second session brought together contributions by Indigenous people working in the 'mainstream'—that is, largely non-Aboriginal—Media. The 'Indigenous media' session was chaired by Jim Remedio, chair of NIMAA, the National Indigenous Media Association of Australia—another organisation that makes up part of Australia's unique bundle of media initiatives in this area, about which both other Australians and other countries ought to know more. The 'Indigenizing the Mainstream' session was chaired by Marjorie Anderson, who was at the time the national co-ordinator of Aboriginal employment and development for the ABC in Sydney. There is a short closing statement by Michael Mansell at the end of this session.

Between them, these sessions illustrate the vibrant and talented diversity of Indigenous media production. But of course much is omitted. In particular there's no mention of the Indigenous print media, perhaps especially the *Koori Mail* (but see Michael Rose's collection of 160 years of Aboriginal print journalism, *For the Record*, 1996). And there's no attention to new media, despite some intensive work in that area by Indigenous people. However, for a very good example of what can be done, including a feature on how it was done, see the CD-ROM *Moorditj: Australian Indigenous Cultural Expressions* (1998). *Moorditj*, a Nyungar word for 'Excellent', was developed by DUIT Multimedia for the Aboriginal Affairs Department of Western Australia as part of the federal 'Australia on CD' project (distributed by VEA: www.vea.com.au/). It includes the work of 110 Aboriginal and Torres Strait Islander artists, introduced by Aaron Pedersen (see Chapter 7) and Justine Saunders. It is also clear that the issues and personalities represented in what follows belong to their period (the mid-1990s). However, we know of no better way to present the *production* side of our subject than through the words of those whose work it is.

1. Indigenous Media

JIM REMEDIO
Chair, National Indigenous Media Association
Welcome to the afternoon session, called *Telling the Stories*. I'm Jim Remedio, Chairperson of the National Indigenous Media Association, a role that I have great honour in carrying. I'm chairing this panel on 'Indigenous Media'. I'd just like to acknowledge the traditional owners of the area, Robert Bropho and Fred Collard and everybody else from this part of the world. I'm from the eastern states and Rob Riley said yesterday he was going to give the ball a 'bounce down' to get started, but I'd just like to say to Rob Riley that we call it a kick-off—and we probably would have run right through him anyway. That's in our game. I'd like to thank the organizers for inviting the National Indigenous Media Association of Australia to the Forum. The Forum theme, 'Telling Both Stories', gives NIMA an opportunity to tell their story and a lot of people here this afternoon are going to be telling their stories as well.

Our story is that of a modern-day messenger. We heard yesterday how Galarrwuy [Yunupingu] spoke about messages being delivered by bark paintings. We feel today that we are the modern messengers, and we deliver the messages in the same spirit that people delivered messages by the bark or by message sticks. That is some of the strength of our organization and we're going to put culture up front wherever we can. Get back to the cultural roots. Get back to people in the communities who are going to be the messengers.

In 1993 NIMA was set up in response to a need by Indigenous communities to have a body which would be truly representative and be truly inclusive of all media associations—whether they be a film production unit, or broadcasting one hour a day on community radio stations, or whether they're a 'BRACS' community [Broadcasting for Remote Aboriginal Communities Scheme], or an Indigenous community such as BIMA in Brisbane. With that in mind, we brought together a mob of people, and we met under the Storey bridge in Brisbane, and I guess a lot of other organizations have met in the same way—sitting in the dust or sitting under bridges. We've come to a situation today where we are operating like everybody else, on a bit of a shoestring, but that hasn't been a problem to us. We're still able to front up to do our programmes with the support of a lot of people out in the broader community as well.

The voice of our people can be heard across the length and breadth of our lands. NIMA broadcasters can now be heard on 83 licensed BRACS community radio stations, seven licensed Aboriginal community radio stations, nine aspirant broadcast groups, 52 individual Aboriginal community groups broadcasting on mainstream community radio stations, including a number of Aboriginal community television broadcasts and production groups.

- The vision of the National Indigenous Media Association is:
- to continue the struggle begun by the people who came before us in the fight against racism, discrimination, and exclusion;
- to develop a quality multi-media service with a strong commitment to the maintenance of language and cultural programming;
- to establish NIMA as a third national authority in Australia and to take our rightful place at the communication table alongside the ABC and SBS.

Whether we are a film production unit, a BRACS community, a journalist on the *Courier Mail*, or a broadcaster on mainstream or community radio, we are out there telling our story in our own voice. We are no longer letting others do the talking for us or telling the story as they see it. We now sing the songs again. We tell the stories. We show the images as we see them and we show them to ourselves and to the rest of Australia and indeed to the rest of the world.

Like many people of my generation, I grew up listening to Slim Dusty. I suppose a lot of people here did as well. After hearing songs like 'Brumby' and reading a bit of Banjo Patterson as well, because of the way they romanticized the country, all I ever wanted to do was to be a ringer. Though I'm a bit big for that! But it's just that romanticizing of the situation in the country that led a lot of us into thinking that there must be some huge equality out there for us, and yet we know that that's not true. I didn't know until I went to the outback country, to Katherine, many years ago, and I could see some of the things that were happening there, that the song just didn't sing about. What old Slim was singing about was a continuation of how colonialism was working. That's why I say that now we sing the songs.

What we have in the place now are these BRACS community stations. People in the last couple of days here have talked about the need for change. We heard this morning about the inherent racism. Racism's like a clock inside people; it is ticking away in this State and indeed in Australia since the early days. Neither politicians nor police are going to change that clock that's ticking away inside them. It's never going to happen; we're always going to be faced with that situation. So if we're going to have change, it's got to come from the grassroots. The grassroots thinking of course is the BRACS communities. BRACS communities are sitting out there in the middle of the country all over the place in the North and North-West and the Torres Strait and they're sending us a message. The voice of Indigenous Australia's becoming very restless. We hear that all the time. We're hoping that people are going to get fully behind BRACS and give them one hundred per cent support in everything that they're doing. They're the ones at the forefront of cultural maintenance and the maintenance of language.

The history of BRACS began after the release of a book by the late Eric Michaels, titled *Out of the Silent Land*. The book told of a big empty hole of silence—the lack of basic communication services in outback communities that people in main rural centres could take for granted. This eventually prompted the Commonwealth Government to act. Telstra then designed a system for Indigenous communities that has become known as Broadcasting for Remote Aboriginal Communities Scheme—BRACS. The system is so successful that Telstra has offered the technology and sold it to other countries for use in their remote communities, and indeed made some millions of dollars.

At present the 83 BRACS stations are classified as community broadcasters under the Broadcast Services Act. The stations were licensed in 1992 and they're up for renewal in 1997. However, being licensed as a community broadcaster required the BRACS licence holders to become signatories to the Community Codes of Practice Agreement. This licence requirement now put BRACS on an equal footing with other national community radio broadcasters. During the past twelve months NIMA has worked closely with BRACS on a revitalization programme including the updating of technical equipment and providing administration services. BRACS stations provide a unique service as they transmit both radio and television. They also have the capacity to develop television documentaries, film local sporting and cultural events, record and preserve oral histories. Stations are also re-transmitting mainstream radio and television.

Culturally relevant programmes popular in Queensland and the Northern Territory include Ron Casey, John Laws, *Home and Away*, *Neighbours*, and *Bay Watch*.... (A bit of a cynical view of things here). The history of Indigenous community radio stations like CAAMA, BIMA, and WAAMA is a tremendous story of frustration and struggle. These stations are based in the main capital cities and large rural centres. They provide a special service to the community. It is not that long ago that the only station was the ABC or commercial channels. If you lived in the country towns, of course, it was worse.

Community stations have had a very hard and frustrating time too. Radio Redfern started with a 15-minute broadcast— and the people who came before us had to really struggle to get that 15 minutes on a community station. The Community Broadcasting people just didn't see the need for Aboriginal broadcasters. They put us in the same category as 'multi-cultural' people, making us 'ethnics' in our own land. So there has been this continual struggle to get community radio airtime. As a result of that, they've been funded by grants from the Community Broadcasting Foundation who fund radio broadcasting and programming and some development costs as well.

One of the things that NIMA's managed to do over the last twelve months is put together a scheme that everybody's quite excited about and that's the National Indigenous Radio Service (NIRS). This radio service has the potential to reach 160 community radio broadcasters as well as 120 Aboriginal broadcasting stations. The NIRS operates on a service very similar to how the Comrad System works on community radio but our system, we believe, is a bit better than the Comrad System or the Community Broadcasting System, because it allows people from places like CAAMA, or TIBA in Darwin, to directly transmit to the satellite or through the up-linking service that NIMA provides. So we can have some programming coming in from say Galiwinku via TIBA into the national system, and it can be heard out there, out in the broader community, by the greater population.

Now, this really has an effect on the broader community people because when you suddenly drive along in a car, whether you're in Bendigo in Victoria or any one of the other capital cities and you twiddle across the dial, you suddenly tune in and you'll hear some language programme coming in from an outback community, and think, 'Well what's this I'm listening to? It's not Italian, it's not Greek...' suddenly you're hit with a new language and then somebody says, 'Well that was Christine Anu playing "such and such"', and then they follow up with some sort of a commercial or a community message about a health meeting that's going to be held next week in that particular centre.

That's got to do something to the overall psyche of the population. If you have a lot of those messengers going through into the mainstream, then you're putting all the problems and so on out on to the broader community as well. They're going to hear Aboriginal music—first re-lease stuff that's coming over community radio as well as our network. You don't get that on commercial stations. The commercial stations in my town in Victoria are still playing 'Goanna's Track'—and that's their contribution to Indigenous music. You'll hear tracks from ten years ago, and plenty of Jimmy Barnes, and they're saying that they're playing Australian content. At least on our network you're going to be hearing 24–hour Indigenous music. Indigenous programming. Programming prepared by these fellas here today. This is all going to have a large impact on the psyche and the thinking of mainstream Australia.

Something else that NIMA has done; we were given the task last year of putting together an industrial (wages) Award which is known as the Indigenous Media Organizations Award. Although that Award is firmly in place, it has caused some difficulties within some communities. The problem is that the top rate of the pay for station managers is around $58,000 a year, and the range from the top to the bottom is really huge. If you think about what we're supposed to do as a caring, sharing people, it's very difficult to have somebody on $60,000 a year in a radio station as a manager and then somebody on $200 a week. As an organization, NIMA has to try to balance that up in some way. By that I mean bringing the minimum rates up, to equal what they should be.

That's what we're working on with the Indigenous Media Award. We've roped in quite a few stations into it. I personally haven't been particularly happy with how that structure has operated in the past, so we're going to make some approaches to the Industrial Commission and try and get some substance built into it. But we've established that Award; it's up there and if people want to use the Union to sort it out, I guess they can.

Just in conclusion, I'd like to say that NIMA, with the support of its members, has achieved this in just three years. Imagine what we'll achieve in ten. This is only the beginning of our vision. Our vision is to have the voice of Indigenous Australia being heard internationally— all around the Pacific and our South-East Asian neighbours, as well as through the networks we are forming through the worldwide body of international broadcasters. Most important, is to provide the medium for the messenger, to pass on the voice of our people in our stories, in our songs, our images, now that technology has caught up with our voice. This is something to remember: technology has finally caught up with what we've been saying all these years and it has enabled our story to be heard across the land, around the nation, all over the world. Until now our voices have been unheard in the wilderness and no one was listening. It is incumbent on governments that now they do not abrogate their responsibilities towards our people. Failure to prioritize funding of Indigenous media is to perpetuate the past government policies, to practise discrimination, exclusion, and violation of human rights. Thank you.

STEVEN BROWN
Waringarri Radio, Kununurra
Firstly, I'd like to thank the Nyungar people for inviting us down here. My name's Steve Brown. I'd like to introduce the panel of speakers for this session. They are: Nooley Preston from Fitzroy Radio Station, Natalie Rogers, Bill Thaiday, Josey Farrer, Russell Bomford, and Joe Edgar.

NOOLEY PRESTON
Wangki Yupurnanapurru Radio, Fitzroy Crossing
Good afternoon. My name is Nooley Preston, 'junior broadcaster'. I'm from Wangki Yupurnanapurru Radio Station and this story I'm going to tell you, a little bit story, and you see on the board over there [points to an Aboriginal painting of a goanna], I know that one. The story comes from early days and people, from the cave where I come from, near to Noonkanbah. On the cave they put that sign for young people and from there the story. That's a story that the people talk about in my language, Walmadjeri, and where I come from, people talk Wangkatjungka and Bunaba.

That story [points to another painting]. That's a story about a witchetty grub. Sometimes we eat them. We eat goanna, snake, everything there is for Aboriginal people. For a long time this was all the people, but the new generation today don't know that sign there. Where I come from, the old people painted a long time ago inside the cave, so that new generations would look at the story. But older people today are all finished, and the new generation takes over. Where I come from we want to teach our young generation language.

That's why we've got a radio in the Kimberley. We speak about everyday stories, but we don't want to lose our language. We're going to keep our language strong in the radio so we can teach the new generation and we have a new generation today. If I passed away, who's going to teach our young children? Nobody. But we're going to teach our children. We're going to put this story in the cassette or in the paper written down, that the new generation can read it when we've passed away.

Some of the people growing up do teach young people, the new generation, how to hunt for the food or water, good water maybe or sometimes a tree—you can see some trees are not good, poison trees. That's what the old people are going out every weekend to teach people, the new generation, and this language we want to teach our new generation. Corroboree as well; we're putting them in the radio so the new generation know the language. Some of us old people, sooner or later, will pass away, but our story will be still there.

A new generation will come up, look at these words, and say, 'Oh, it's a story from that old man'. They will come up and write them down in the paper. That's how we have to keep our culture strong and the language today. From Broome, Derby, Fitzroy Crossing, Halls Creek, Kununurra, Wyndham. We keep our language strong and the culture in it.

Natalie Rogers
Wangki Yupurnanapurru Radio, Fitzroy Crossing
Hello. My name is Natalie. I come from Kununurra but I work at Wangki Yupurnanapurru at Fitzroy Crossing and if you don't know where the Fitzroy is, it's in the Kimberleys. Fitzroy's got a lot of blackfellas there. It's full of blackfellas basically. The majority of the population in Fitzroy is all blackfellas. The local people of Fitzroy are the Bunaba people. There's Wangkatjungka, Walmadjeri, but Bunaba is the main language in Fitzroy. And Fitzroy is practically owned by the traditional people, the Bunaba people. They've got shares in Torunda, the shopping centre there. They've just opened a new Aboriginal roadhouse on the Highway and its Bunaba name means 'White Man's Way'.

And the radio programmes; Nooley does the mornings from 11.05 until 12.00 on the ABC, and that's all in Walmadjeri language. I do the afternoon programme from 4.00 to 6.00. We have just got an extra hour this year from the ABC. We broadcast off the ABC, to Bayulu which is 15 km out of Fitzroy and the signal doesn't go very far, it's only a short way, up to 30 km. You can't hear it very clearly in some communities because they haven't got the right receiver.

My programme is the 4.00 to 6.00 afternoon programme on Wangki Yupurnanapurru Radio. I do interviews and inform the Bunaba people and Walmadjeri people about what's happening outside of Fitzroy or what's happening in Fitzroy. Nooley's programme—the morning programme—is all in the language that I said earlier on and if you were wondering what 'Manangaja' means, Manangaja's a centre down Fitzroy where all them old people go and they do their painting. It's like a meeting place for them. We got KALC there—the Kimberley Aboriginal Law and Culture, which I think is recognized Australia-wide, I don't know.

One of Wangki Yupurnanapurru's aims for this year is to get our licence and broadcast full-time so that we can get on that National Indigenous Media Association satellite service and keep our language and culture strong like these mob. White people are coming into Fitzroy now and all the young people they're ready for basketball and they don't care for language anymore. They'd rather go discoing or whatever, like Nooley said. Nooley was the one who introduced radio in Fitzroy Crossing. He sent to Alice Springs and learned off CAAMA, and he wanted to put one in Fitzroy and he did and that's all I got to say.

JOE EDGAR
Radio Goolarri, Broome
My name is Joe Edgar. I'm from Radio Goolarri which is in Broome. I'd like to firstly thank all the Nyungar people for letting us speak on this agenda. Also the Forum organizers and the Louis Johnson Memorial Trust.

There are several issues that I'd like to speak about today including the state of Indigenous cultural programming at the Broome Aboriginal Media Association (BAMA), the maintenance of Indigenous moral culture and ethics, and how we perceive the Native Title issue. First a brief background of myself and the Media Association that I represent, and a brief overview of the Indigenous media in the Kimberley. I've been employed at BAMA's Radio Goolarri as a broadcaster/journalist since 1992. BAMA was formed in 1980. In 1991 the organization employed two Indigenous trainees and began broadcasting its first programmes; initially an hour per week through the ABC window. Today the organization employs six broadcasters/journalists, a station manager, an administrator, a bookkeeper, and a secretary. Also at hand is a technician/technical adviser who is employed by the Kimberley BRACS revitalization programme.

Operating out of Broome, Radio Goolarri reaches Derby, and all the outlying Aboriginal communities, out-stations, and pastoral communities receive or potentially can receive Indigenous programmes through the windows in the ABC Regional broadcasting network for the BRACS programme, which is currently going through a revitalization phase. In the case of Wyndham in the East Kimberley, it's through Radio War-ingarri in Kununurra. On 22 January 1996 Radio Goolarri began broad-casting 25 hours per week of Indigenous programming, ranging from a children's program to current affairs affecting Indigenous people, com-munity and local news, arts, special music programmes, to sports, and a comedy programme which is a send-up of local issues and people.

We have a 50 per cent Indigenous music policy, which we are wanting to up-grade, but we still need more Indigenous music to be recorded as we continue to play some music over and over again, and we have to resort to non-Indigenous music. The organization does not present any Aboriginal-language programmes other than our five-minute Yaoro language segment on our children's programme. Goolarri covers almost a third of the Kimberley, ranging at times from Wyndham in the East Kimberley to Roebourne in the Pilbarra, so obviously we do not lack for talent for our culture content or language content. On the contrary, because of our wide range of listenership, the diversity of our audience, the lack of sufficient airtime, and problems associated with financial and time constraints on our journalists to conduct interviews and consulta-tions with people outside the immediate vicinity, it would seem a little bit unfair to target one or two language groups within that footprint.

Since gradually upgrading our airtime at least in the last five years, and employing six broadcasters/journalists, and with the anticipated advent of obtaining a community-based broadcast licence sometime this year, Goolarri now has sufficient broadcast time to establish a more comprehensive cultural programme format, although financial support is still being sought. As we all know, cultural programming is a very sensitive issue. Certain codes of ethics and morals need to be observed within the Aboriginal media and these can differ from region to region, from clan to clan. We also have the complex kinship system within those clans and regions, along with sensitive native title issues, and they all contribute to an already diverse cultural situation within today's continually evolving contemporary Aboriginal society.

The observation of strong kinship rules, and other cultural and moral codes of ethics, identify Indigenous media apart from the mainstream. Rules such as substituting common names of those recently deceased, or if you're a male not being allowed to mention the name of your mother-in-law, except as a third party. Or when interviewing a close relative, referring to them as uncle or aunt or whatever relationship you have with them, while, at the same time, being professional. This may seem inappropriate or mushy elsewhere; however in Indigenous media, it helps to strengthen the ties of kinship between the talent and the host and enhances the credibility of media organization.

Possibly the most ardent issue Indigenous media have to contend with is that of Native Title and how it affects everybody. Indigenous media and journalists, as professionals, are entrusted with the role of mediators and attempt to break down the complexities of the government's decision-making processes and laws. Adopting a neutral position can become trying for many Indigenous journalists, especially on the issue of land rights. Being able to grasp the context and decision-making processes of government, and then, in an unbiased manner, having to break that down in laypeople's terms, or in a way that grassroots Indigenous people can comprehend, and be in a position to act or to empower people, takes a lot of skill and experience, considering that they become responsible not only to the Indigenous people but also to the wider community.

Keeping abreast with Indigenous issues is a difficult, time-consuming, and labour-intensive occupation, taking into consideration the vast distances that our programmes cover and the lack of sufficient funding to undertake research and development in order to get grassroots feedback and consultation on issues that affect Indigenous people. And sometimes we have to hitch-hike with other people to get to communities if we can't get a vehicle; it's the lack of that sort of support. These issues may come across as a little bit mushy again to the non-Indigenous component of our society, but are very much topics that need to be and are being brought forward, especially in Aboriginal media in the community, such those that we have in the Kimberley.

Placing some sort of focus or emphasis on the positive aspects of cultural programming and awareness, as we know, only helps further to strengthen and revitalize our already diverse culture. At the same time it assists in fostering better understanding between Indigenous and non-Indigenous Australians. What with the state and influence of the ever-impending tide of multimedia, the multinationals and commercialization creeping ever so rapidly into the most remote parts of the Kimberley, certain important aspects of our culture have been and continue to be lost forever. For instance, there is a saying at home that sport is killing our culture. It's not just the influence of sport. It's the ability of the media to capitalize on its popularity here in Broome, and even in the most remote outback location in the Kimberley. Just about every schoolchild has at least one item of attire, perhaps a T-shirt, a pair of Reeboks or a baseball cap, depicting Michael Jordan or Chuck O'Neill or some other basketball superstar or team, and they're not even Australians. Almost every Friday night, Saturdays and Sundays of the season are dominated by the Wildcats (basketball), the Eagles or the Dockers (Australian football), or the cricket. There's also the cost of local footy matches that take place almost every Sunday of the season. Teams and their supporters travel 500 km round-trip each weekend for these events, for up to eighteen weekends of the year.

Not many are the days of loading the truck and going fishing, hunting, or looking for bush fruit, or gathering your spears and going for long walks, learning the skills and talking the language. Today hunting is mostly done on Nintendo video games and they're talking like New York rappers. Can our culture or our language or our morals and ethics survive? Are our leaders aware of this very loud invasion that is staring us in the face? Are we in a position, if not to stem the tide, at least to come to a compromise and still maintain our culture and identity in this very multiracial community which is Australia? Those are some of the questions that we as media, Indigenous media, are faced with today. Thank you.

JOSEY FARRER
Puranyangu-Rangka Kerrem Radio, Halls Creek
First I'd like to thank the Nyungar people for welcoming us here to their country; Mr Collard and Chris Lewis and Robert Bropho. We are very pleased to be on your land. I'd like to say for myself that as Aboriginal people in the media we are very privileged to be here and to talk about some of the things that we're doing up there.

What was said just a while ago by one of the broadcasters from BAMA Radio tells us what sorts of things that Aboriginal media are doing right around the Kimberley and probably around other parts of Australia. Now those are some of the pretty things about broadcasting and it attracts a lot of the young people because they see broadcasting as modern, it's a Western thing, it's something that's different from a lot of the ways that they were brought up. So a lot of the kids say, 'Oh you know, I'd like to come and do some broadcasting. I'd like to have a go at it'.

With our radio station, Puranyangu-Rangka Kerrem at Halls Creek, we had quite a number of young kids who came in on work experience. They did some of the programmes that they put to air by themselves. Our broadcast trainer, who's a female Aboriginal person who's replaced Mr [Murray] Jennings, sitting there in the front; she's taken that under her wing and was able to get these young kids to go out to do interviews with people, from business people to ordinary everyday Aboriginal people sitting on the creek drinking alcohol, which is a real downfall for our people, and getting some of the stories from them. They asked them questions like 'Why are you out there drinking?' And it's just amazing some of the stories that came back. These are the type of stories that were put on air, and we had a lot of feedback from non-Aboriginal people from around the town that we live in. We don't have that much airtime really, but these kids went out and they did a lot of interviewing, and getting a lot of comments and feedback from non-Aboriginal people, saying things like, 'We didn't know that this was going on. We didn't realize there was a lack of this and a lack of that in town'. And it's just good, they said, it's just good to hear young people's voices coming out of radio.

And to them it looks like a big rosy picture, but the Aboriginal people who work in the media are the ones who are faced with the problems, you know. When we first started out, back in the 1980s, we talked about radio right through the Kimberley. There was a book that was put out that was telling stories about Aboriginal people and why they wanted broadcasting in the Kimberley. A lot of recommendations were put forward but to this day, a lot of those recommendations haven't been fulfilled. Mainly because of lack of funding. The funding bodies don't give us our money's worth. The money that we ask for is to enable us to put out the programmes that we know are needed for our people, because that's the only service that they get via the radio. Sometimes you get old people coming in and saying, 'Look, we want to do some stories. Put that out on air': dreamtime stories, and also educational stories.

We tried working in with the school. Last year we put out a couple of leaflets to the schools; the government school in Halls Creek and the Lunja Community School at Redhill, asking for some feedback. A lot of the kids from the Redhill School, when they gave us the feedback, said, 'We like to hear our stories put on air so that the kids can hear them'. But you know, the other school there, they wouldn't turn their radio on so that the kids could listen to some of these stories. It's a shame really because a lot of those stories are educational. There's meaning in them. As Nooley said about the painting there; it tells a story. *You* can't read it because it's not written up in English letters and in the words that we know because we've been to school, but illiterate Aboriginal people can read those paintings, and it's the same with stories that are put out in the languages. They're educational, but because we don't have funding, that puts us out in regard to the services which we should be giving our people. I'm just directing this comment to ATSIC and to DEET if anyone is here from those bodies!

I remember back in the early years when we all talked about broadcasting, there was a commitment by ATSIC and DEET to come across with the dollars. That happened for so long but now we're chasing them. We're asking where's all this money? We want to be able to produce stories, news, and even current affairs; we want to get them done so that people can speak out in their own language over the air. Sometimes I go in and do broadcasting. I'm not a broadcaster. I'm not trained in any area to tell you the honest truth. I was just a mother. But I've done a fair bit of that and sometimes I go to air. I speak in my language which is the Gidja language and it gives me great pride and pleasure to speak in my language. But too often we're not able to provide a lot of it because of lack of funding. Old people come in, they do stories, they volunteer, but you just can't drag old people around to give stories. You need to be able to give them something back because they're giving you part of their lives.

The media for us are also a means of us communicating with people out there who don't understand about Aboriginal people. It's a way of getting messages across. And we have to present it the way the people want us to. It's mainly what people would call protocol in the Gidja word, and in our custom it's the respect that we show. It's just the way you talk on air. I heard a conversation between two non-Aboriginal people in the local shop. They didn't know who I was—they were new teachers, they'd just been brought in this year to Halls Creek. One fella said, 'Did you hear what was on the news yesterday afternoon? There was somebody rambling off and mumbling', and the other fella said, 'Oh well I thought he might have been talking in some sort of language. It's beats me'. Those are some of the things we need to educate people about, especially the ones that don't have any dealing or don't understand about Aboriginal people and our culture. I just smiled at myself and walked out.

But I'd just like to say in my language to you people... [message in Josey's language]. I'd like to say in English; what I said was 'I am very happy to share with you from our radio station, we came all the way from up there, the North down here to talk to you people in regards to media'. Thank you very much.

Jim Remedio
Thank you Josey, and Josey's made some telling points there. Next we've got that legend in community radio and training, and in country music too I guess: Bill Thaiday.

Bill Thaiday
Waringarri Radio, Kununurra
Is there anybody here from the mainstream press? Anybody reporting on this? You are? Where are you from? Okay. If I said to you, you could ask me a question now, what would you say to me? People continually do this thing. People from the press go ahead and write about us. You

probably wouldn't ask me a proper question anyway because you don't know me, you see. And the press don't know us, they go ahead and do stories about us, never caring who in the hell they hurt.

My name's Bill Thaiday for the people who don't know me. I come from Queensland. I've been working in radio for fifteen years, mainly working with young people. I've worked with Nooley [Preston] for a long time and Bill Bunbury from ABC Radio National as well. He came out to help us with oral history which is very important to Aboriginal radio as it is now. We look at the negative things and the positive things. In December I went to Kununurra and young Steve [Brown] here presents breakfast each morning at 6 o'clock, and he's got a pretty big following for a young fella. There were two white people going to work and they heard his breakfast show. They turned around come back into 'Waringarri' and went in and said, 'Could we see young Steve please'. So they went in there for his autograph and to buy a T-shirt like this one we're all wearing here. So it's getting out there, the positive way we broadcast. Telling our stories as we are today, telling our story hopefully so that we will reach out to people, reach out with understanding, even to those people who are ignorant about us.

This is what is driving the people, the ignorance about Aboriginal people. We can look further into that. Why are these people ignorant? Where did it start from? Journalists are ignorant. How can we get them to do a positive story about us? How can we educate these people before they come out of the journalism courses they've been doing? How can we teach these people before they come out here, because they're going to be faced by our people. And for sure, if our story is going to hit the paper, it's going to be a bad story. No good news will make a story, especially black news. So, in our radio we do oral history and current affairs. Mainly oral history because old people like Nooley and the other old people have got to tell their stories. We've got to tell our stories. We look for a solid rock to stand on and the solid rock in our radio programme is oral history. Maybe even before we do current affairs. It doesn't matter where you place those two programmes, they will always point at each other: oral history and current affairs. This is the current thing that has happened. This is the thing that went on in the past. Did it change? Maybe not. It's only happening in a modern way so the current affairs here is probably what happened back there in history.

We've been giving our message for a long time—a long, long time, maybe even before the day that Cook stuck his little flag down the coast there somewhere in Australia to claim this country for his lousy little king who's sitting over there. And also that early explorer [Dampier] who arrived here on our coast, I think this side [Western Australia]—he never came to my side [Queensland], we might have hit him—anyway, he came here and when he first saw the Aboriginal people he looked at them and he said they were lazy, they were an undernourished, uneducated, unorganized race of people. That's what he said about us. He didn't know a bloody thing. He didn't know. He never took his time to try and understand the Aboriginal people. If he had he would have found it was the most educated, organized race of people in this world. You've only got to go back to the boomerang and you ask yourself a question: who was that old man who worked out the aerodynamics of the boomerang to make it come back? And to make it kill as it goes? So, he [Dampier] was wrong.

In telling our stories on radio we are going to do these sorts of things. We've been doing it for fifteen years now, hopefully so that people outside of us would understand. We're reaching out. We're always reaching out for that understanding. We're reaching out for reconciliation. When you've got bad press coming down on you, you need to reach out. This is where Aboriginal radio comes in. They go in between the lines of every bad story that's printed, televised, or broadcast. This is our job. This is what we're here for. We go in between those lines. 'Hey, hang on; your story yesterday was wrong. That man, he's not so bad. Listen to my story'.

There's two different type of interviews that come out. You get the white journalist's interviews, and our stories. Their story is done from the top with no feeling, just the permission. Our story comes from the heart and the soul, because what we're talking about, we know about that. It is us. It is our story. It is our life. This is where our story differs from the story that the white journalist did. And this is why we have the right to go in between the lines of all these bad stories that are written or broadcast or televised about us.

STEVEN BROWN
Thanks Bill. I'm the breakfast show. It starts about six. It runs till about 9 o'clock. So three hours. We have four broadcasters who work full time and one trainee, a volunteer. We swap shifts every three months; swap shows. We have the brecky show, that's in the morning. The language and culture show from 9.00 till 12.00, and the midday show which is now a request show from 12.00 till 3.00. From 3.00 to 4.00 we have an hour show which Bill sometimes does, and from 4.00 to 7.00 we have things like artists' interviews and profiles. On the brecky show we have Ansett flight details, a field officer's report, TAFE [Training and Further Education]. We get TAFE in every Wednesday, and they come and give up an update on what's been happening, and that's about it, really.

Just a little bit of background on Waringarri. Try not to pronounce the 'g'. Waringarri's been broadcasting 24 hours a day, seven days a week as of about May or June of 1995. We're picking up probably about seven hours satellite time overnight at the moment and that's something we'd like to reduce with more volunteer broadcasters or announcers coming to us—and we do have a very interactive volunteer programme running at the moment already. Last July or August we also established a tourist radio on the FM channel. Like Halls Creek and Fitzroy, we were connected with the ABC, but since just before last year we got our own frequency on the AM channel and our tourist radio is on the FM channel.

Now coming back to a point that Josey [Farrer] made a little bit earlier about funding; I'm not trying to flog it to death, but it's very awkward for any community organization to look at accessing funding, particularly an Aboriginal organization in a remote country town, where you're reliant on sponsorship from white organizations. It isn't easy. Relationships need to be formed and time needs to be spent in order to get the trust and the input from them. On the bigger picture, I suppose, going back to Jim [Remedio]'s earlier comment about the National Indigenous Radio Service, the potential is there for all Indigenous radio stations, community and non-community, to be able to tap into that channel. There's only two options for which way you can go. You either need a retransmission satellite or an ISDN line. Now at Halls Creek, Fitzroy and Kununurra we haven't got an ISDN line. It hasn't been laid in and it's going to be quite a while before it will be, so that only leaves us the other option of accessing a retransmitted satellite which is talking big bucks; big money. That's why funding is important for us, particularly now. I think we've heard throughout the weekend how most people have said, 'Now is the time', particularly with the year 2000 coming on us. This is the time when international media attention will focus on Australia because of the Olympics, and probably that is the perfect platform to actually illustrate what Aboriginal skills there are throughout the country.

Waringarri's role—we've got lots of positives. We have interaction with all government departments in our town. We have updates and information broadcasts from them. We have quite an interactive volunteer network happening, which meets the interests of the people in our town, and we're also broadcasting to a catchment area of probably about 8,000 people in different community outback stations, from Wyndham down to Turkey Creek and across the border into the Northern Territory. The audience we're meeting is enormous in a sense, particularly in the distance that that audience falls in. So it's pretty damn hard to assess what your audience wants, because surveys, being one strategy, are very,

very hard to implement, and it's certainly not done by pen and paper. So as Josey said, there are a lot of difficulties and constraints that the people in Indigenous media are having to face every day. I'll pass back to Bill for a while.

Bill Thaiday

Okay, we're going to cut it now. One of the things that happens too, is that we get a lot of youngsters coming in from school. They come in and offer their services as volunteer broadcasters. We will train them and in the next couple of months we should have more young people, that is black and white people, who come to the station looking for voluntary broadcasts. So it's looking good. I think we're getting our message out, especially in places like Kununurra. Before I left Mount Isa it was a very tough place too. But with Channel Ten and the ABC and the other media associations in Mount Isa, we reached a sort of understanding between us. We learned to share our messages, our stories. Before I left that relationship, between us and those mainstream media, was pretty good. So hopefully we will reach that in the near future just by us going in between every line that these people broadcast or televise about us. I think that's the best way to go. Let them know we're here. We're standing toe-to-toe with them whether you're mainstream media or Aboriginal media, we're going to stand toe-to-toe with them. Thank you for listening.

Jim Remedio

Yes thank you to the speakers. We got a good cross-section of what's happening up to the North of us and, as you can see, we've got some real good commitment there. Thank you fellas.

Now we have Noel Morrish from WAAMA, and Noel has a few things to say. Thank you.

Noel Morrish
Western Australian Aboriginal Media Association
I'd like to welcome everyone here. There's not much I haven't done. I've done just about everything from living off the bush and talking my dialect to going down the Internet. When I was a young fella growing up there was the thing about media; what do media do to people? Well I was in a movie theatre in Narrogin and it so influenced the local population, our people, that they went out and bought toy guns. And the lady in the shop said, 'Do you want me to wrap them?' They said, 'No, we'll strap them on, and while you're at it, you might as well load them up with caps too'. So we go out in the street and have 'High Noon'. Now, every time I go out there and see the TRG [Tactical Response Group] running

around I'm saying to myself, 'When are they going to shoot someone down for going for their mobile?'

Anyway, I don't want to keep you too long. The development of the public radio station Radio 6NR was a big chapter in the Perth Aboriginal community's association with electronic media. It began eighteen years ago when Mike Chitty hosted a programme on 6NR out there at WAIT [now Curtin University]: a 30–minute show called *Aboriginal Voices*, with a format of gospel and country music. It was interspersed with interviews. A year later in 1979, Ken Colbung started a second programme called *Wandoo Bamboo*. In 1981 the two programs merged to form *Aboriginal Radio*. A year later, funding from DEET allowed three Aboriginal trainees to be taken on to produce the programme. In 1984 the ABC began Aboriginal programming on shortwave to remote communities. During this period, Aboriginal radio was the only form of media accessible to the community in the Perth region. Public radio was the only accessible medium for Aboriginal people for training, taking into account that 11,500 Aboriginal people live in the Perth metro area, it's a sizeable part—possibly one third of the State's Indigenous population live right here in the metro area. We have the ability to fly over razor wire, to climb the walls of Fremantle prison and all the prisons and get there to all the people's loved ones. We can't save everybody but we can save somebody, sometime. In 1985 the West Australian Aboriginal Radio Association was founded to look after the interests of Aboriginal broadcasting. The next year saw the foundation of the West Australian Aboriginal Media Association (WAAMA), with funding channelled through the Aboriginal Legal Service. WAAMA then moved from 6NR to share a building with Aboriginal hostels.

Then in 1987 the Association's development as an incorporated body really began. Clare McNamara, a non-Aboriginal radio producer, was appointed as a consultant to develop a training programme, and discussions were begun with major funding bodies. In February 1988 WAAMA went into its current offices in 176 Wellington Street, East Perth. Dennis Eggington was appointed as WAAMA's first full-time director. Four trainees were appointed for a three-year training programme funded by DEET. WAAMA broadcast live from the studio using 6NR. When the place was officially opened by Ernie Bridge, the WA Aboriginal Affairs minister who is himself an Aboriginal person, WAAMA had established programmes on 6NR, the ABC, 100FM, and 6UVS-FM (which is now 6RTR-FM). So we grew. It was becoming clear that there was a definite need in the Perth metro area for an Aboriginal radio station in its own right and WAAMA began the process of obtaining a public broadcasting licence. To prepare for such a move,

WAAMA's Wellington Street headquarters underwent extensive renovations.

We were officially reopened 10 April 1992, and 6AR began broadcasting 24 hours a day, on 8 February 1995, on AM 1170khz. 6AR broadcasts interviews covering a broad spectrum of interests, including health, housing, employment, legal matters, education, sport, culture. Some of these programmes had been sponsored by government departments including Homeswest, Health, and CES. Regular bulletins featuring Aboriginal stories and community news are broadcast eleven times each day during the week. As well as sourcing news ourselves, we're on a network with a national news supplier for the influx of stories concerning community issues, and we're able to feed these stories for national distribution.

Our on-air presenters are all Aboriginal broadcasters. Two of them have been with WAAMA for six years. We have four journalist-trainees who have also been trained as announcers, and can be heard hosting programmes at night and on weekends. Aboriginal music is a major feature of our broadcast, giving the opportunity for many fine artists to get the chance to be heard on radio. So when you've got aspirant Aboriginal musicians out there, someone's got to listen to them and someone's got to play them. We really will take that on. Anyone who's got a tape, who wants it to be played on radio, we'll certainly listen to you. And with our style of programmes we offer listeners a choice from other stations which feature talkback programmes. The listeners are mostly under-25 years of age and most of the music caters for the under-25 population. On Saturday nights is our request programme, and we also get *Deadly Sound*, all the way from Sydney.

Plans are under way for WAAMA to be a fully credited training facility. We're buying a training programme from the eastern states so that when the kids are trained from us, they'll have a certificate that means they can go anywhere in the English-speaking world and work on radio and be fully qualified. In 1995 6AR broadcast from Forrest Place during NAIDOC National Aboriginal Week, when all around Australia everyone joined in and listened to us. Progress has continued towards broadcasting programmes via satellite for two hours each day on the National Indigenous Radio Network, which was officially launched three weeks ago. We expect to commence our broadcast in the not too distant future.

After a year negotiating, funding has been obtained from Screen West, SBS-TV, and the Australian Film Commission for our animated story, called *Bob-tails*, and we are operating a share of something called *Gripping Tales*, so you'll hear some gripping tales from Aboriginal people and all the stories that have been told. Distribution of our video-tapes will be handled by our subsidiary, which is the Aboriginal Education Resource Unit. This was the unit that the WA Education Department threw in the rubbish bin, and we went to the rubbish bin and picked it out, and put it in the shop and made it work; and so this is called recycling. But the same didn't happen to the National Aboriginal Day magazine that I was one of the co-editors or producers of, with stories about Western Australian Aboriginal people who made contributions. Finally the Education Department shut us down. They didn't like what we wrote because we were too controversial. Now the Minister's gone down the gurgler too, so good riddance to the Minister.

I'd like to say WAAMA's in good hands, and is run professionally and this is what ATSIC asked for. They said, 'Can you run this station in a professional manner? You're not on the amateur hour any more.' So we have to have a sound financial structure—which we put in place. We have to have sound management—which we put in place. My wife and my family and I have suffered from the back-stabbing, not from white people, from our own people. There were good people on our committee, but someone got in and poisoned the water and we've had a lot of flak from all over the place. Stories appeared in the newspaper without substance, that we had to take legal action on.

When I first went to NIMA I met people who were thinking the same way as I was thinking. I want rolls of that stuff they call optic fibre. I want a satellite dish, I want the Internet and World Wide Web, and I want people to be in tune with the rest of Australia as computer-literate people. If they can do it in Yuendumu they can do it in Perth, Western Australia. We look forward to another year of outstanding achievement. Our current station manager is Graham Edmond. Graham Edmond gave us worldwide one-day cricket. He gave us all these big shows. He came from Kerry Packer and he said, 'I can help you because I've just done some work with the Maori radio set-up Radio 1 in New Zealand'. Ever since that time things have changed and grown and they're continuing to grow at such a fast rate that sometimes, you know, it's like the grass growing up around you—like a jungle here. Everything's happening.

I'm very happy that I can go home at night and say, 'Gee, the radio, switch it on, listen in'. When our new tower goes down to Point Walter and has its feet encased in a damp area, the station will be clearer and more precise than it's been. If you're getting very bad reception now, it's because our feet are in dry sand up there at Gnangara and we're crackling and every time the lightning strikes we get blown off course I suppose.

But anyway, I'd like to leave you with a video. This video is something because it concerns my son, it concerns a friend of mine who was a senior officer in the WA Police Force. His name was Jerry Collard. Jerry Collard suffered from his wife being put down on the ground at gunpoint by the TRG, to the family breaking up and finally him leaving the Police Force—but he tells his own story. And also my son throws in his badge when the Officer in Charge of Karratha Police covers up for his own son out there at Marble Bar [this concerns a police officer who was not charged after his car hit and killed an Aboriginal woman. His alcohol level at the time was not adequately recorded]. Why my son resigned was because of the words, 'Why didn't you run over more of the gins at Marble Bar?' So I'll switch it on and you can see the story for yourself. It's raw. It's crude. It's ugly but it's true. Thank you. [video-tape played]

JIM REMEDIO
I guess that's a continuation of that clock isn't it? If you had racist assumptions in 1905, the clock's still ticking away in 1920 and in 1996. So Western Australia has real problems, along with some other parts of the country as well. I come from Bendigo. Bendigo's considered to be the whitest town in Australia and, by its very nature, by the amount of Aboriginal people there, it has the same sort of situations. Now I was involved in two cases. One was a death in custody—and I was working in the Juvenile Justice Area at the time and I've actually seen it happen first hand too. We lost the argument on the first day of the inquest when the police won a technical argument to be able to stay in the room while they took evidence at the coronial inquiry. All that meant was that everybody was able to prefabricate or fabricate their evidence so that each one's story was the same all the way through. The judge on that particular day carried on and addressed the jury, which was made up of eleven males and one female, for three-and-a-half hours, an unprecedented time to address the jury. The jury came back after twenty minutes and acquitted the person who'd killed my nephew. So that continuous racism thing is continually happening, and it happens at all levels. Western Australia has got its problems but certainly areas of Victoria have their inherent racism clock ticking away inside too.

Anyway now we've got Neville Khan as our final speaker, from CAAMA.

NEVILLE KHAN
Central Australian Aboriginal Media Association, Alice Springs.
Thanks Jim. Good afternoon ladies and gentlemen. My name's Neville Khan. I work for CAAMA as a journalist/presenter. I think the most important reason for me getting into the media industry business is

because when I was growing up everything I heard about Aboriginal people was, 'Blacks done this', and 'Blacks done that'. I come from a small town in the south-west of Western Australia called Donnybrook. The Aboriginal population is pretty low. Actually, there were only two Aboriginal families there. So if you're an Aboriginal person you can imagine the amount of racism I had to put up with when I was going to school. I was called 'nigger', 'boong', 'coon', every day of the week. And I believe that a lot of it was caused by the actions of the mainstream media and how through their ignorance the distorted picture of Aboriginal Australia was fed to the public and still is today.

In the past CAAMA Productions produced a national programme for ATSIC called *Aboriginal Australia*. This programme I produced, and I presented and reported on it. It looked at issues affecting contemporary Aboriginal Australia from a positive aspect rather than a negative. And of course, one of those issues is Native Title. I think because the mainstream media have given such a distorted picture of Native title that everybody thinks their backyards are going to be handed back to Aboriginal people. In actual fact, there has not been a determination yet, which means no one has successfully claimed their land back through that Mabo legislation.

So what we tried to do with *Aboriginal Australia* was to present from an Aboriginal perspective with all cultural aspects in mind. So without further ado, I'd just like to show you one story that I've done on Native Title. Just have a look. [video-tape played] The reason for showing you these particular stories was to show you the struggle Australia's Indigenous people have had and still have today in relation to being recognized as the original owners of this country. That's even after the Mabo legislation has been implemented. I believe if the mainstream had reported on issues such as Native Title from a positive aspect there would not be that hysteria that surrounds Native Title.

I also believe all journalists working in the mainstream media should at some stage, at the onset of their career, be obliged to attend cross-cultural courses so that when they are reporting on Aboriginal issues, they'll have some sort of understanding about Aboriginal people and our culture and how important Native Title really is to us as the original owners of this land. Thank you.

JIM REMEDIO
Thank you Neville. And thanks to everybody—all the speakers that have participated. I think everybody can see that we've got a good young growing talent. We didn't present everything we should have presented and there's a lot of people we didn't mention. We've got people here

from the *Koori Mail*, independent filmmakers who are strong associate members of NIMA; it's just so large that we really need to have a full day's session to get through what everybody does. It's very hard to cram it all in to a one-and-a-half-hour piece. So the people that missed out and we didn't mention we apologize to you and hope to be able to catch up with you all next time. Thanks very much.

2. **Indigenizing the Mainstream**

MARJORIE ANDERSON
National Co-ordinator of Aboriginal Employment and Development for the ABC, Sydney, and Chairperson of Koori Radio (an applicant for a metropolitan licence in Sydney)
The session we're dealing with now is called 'Indigenizing the Mainstream'. I think it's important that we concentrate on Indigenous media, but also on getting Aboriginal people in the mainstream media as well. I agree with what Colleen Hayward said yesterday when she said that sometimes the only way to change things is from within. Sometimes Aboriginal people who work in the mainstream media feel like they're beating their heads against the wall, but it's all worthwhile when we get programmes up, and we get Aboriginal people within the ABC trained to such a level that people from all over the world want Aboriginal people that have been trained by the ABC to work for them.

First up we've got Gina Williams. Gina's had a long association with media in Western Australia, namely in print with the *West Australian*, in radio with WAAMA and community radio, and for the last six-and-a-half years she has been presenter, senior journalist, and production co-ordinator with Golden West Network's (GWN-TV) Aboriginal Programs Department which produces *Milbindi*. Gina is currently the Federal Secretary of the National Indigenous Media Association and Chairperson of the South-West Aboriginal Media Association. She is also a long-standing member of the Media Entertainment and Arts Alliance. And maybe Gina should tell us what she does in her spare time. Thank you Gina.

GINA WILLIAMS
Federal Secretary, NIMA; Chair, South-West Aboriginal Media Association; representative of the MEAA Union; journalist with GWN commercial TV, Western Australia
A good sleep.... Thank you for the invitation to be able to speak at this Forum. I'd like to pay tribute and respect to the elders on this land on

which I stand. For as long as I can remember I've always wanted to be a story-teller. I've always wanted to be a journalist. At high school I volunteered with my foster Dad in community radio and together we produced radio broadcasts in Maori language. On leaving school I found there weren't a lot of opportunities to work in Indigenous media, so working in the mainstream seemed to be the only alternative. At that time I didn't get a job with the ABC. Starting as a cadet journalist at the *West Australian* newspaper I was one of forty-seven cadets and one of just two Aboriginal cadets. Kirsty Parker was the other one, by the way. Today you can still count on two hands the number of Aboriginal people working in mainstream or commercial media.

As I gained experience, my motivation to work in journalism has changed. I firmly believe that while it's important to have our own strong independent Indigenous media industry, it's equally important to have representation and input into the wider mainstream media. Let's face it, change must also eventually come from the inside. Plus it's wonderful to have some Nyungars running around doing damage. As an Indigenous woman working in mainstream media, I often feel like I'm somewhat of a rarity. The criticism is often been levelled that we're tokens. Well, let this black, female, environmentally-friendly, politically-correct, CFC-free fella tell you that this is not always the case. It's just a shame that there aren't more of us around. Perhaps change would come quicker then.

For the last six-and-a-half years I've worked with GWN's Aboriginal Programs Department. Golden West Network is actually a regional television station; we broadcast throughout the entire area of Western Australia except for the Perth metropolitan area. To my knowledge, we're the only commercial television station which is producing Indigenous programming and we do it without government funding. The main programme I work for, *Milbindi*, was set up in 1987, with the intention of producing just five half-hour episodes. Due to the overwhelming public response, a further eight episodes were compiled in 1988 and by 1989 *Milbindi* went to air for a forty-week series. In 1990 a second Aboriginal community news programme, *Marnum*, was produced, and later that year we commenced radio news on our satellite radio service.

In 1992 *Milbindi* won the Equal Opportunity Commission's Special Award for Excellence in reporting on equal opportunity issues. In 1994 the *Milbindi* crew made it to the Logies as a finalist for the 'Most Outstanding Achievement by a Regional Television Station'. Our show is rebroadcast by Imparja (CAAMA's commercial TV station in the Northern Territory). Unfortunately you need to live regionally to see any of our work. But fortunately, the Aboriginal Programs Department has managed to grow, thanks to the overwhelming support by the entire regional community—and who says that the viewers wouldn't be interested?

While our department is separate from the GWN newsroom, our office is most certainly within earshot, and we have an acute sense of hearing. It's pleasing to see that, at least where I work, things are slowly starting to change—slowly. News journalists following up stories will, where possible, approach us for advice; wording of stories and even pronunciation is checked, again where possible. And 'where possible' is dependent upon our limited time, not theirs. Even vision for stories with a positive slant is borrowed from us, instead of using dated file vision which may otherwise provide a negative image.

In 1991 I was given the opportunity to read GWN's main Six O'Clock News. To think that change in this one newsroom has only taken five years; perhaps there is hope yet. Certainly the fact that colleagues are interested in learning about Aboriginal language, Aboriginal culture, gives cause for hope. So, yes, I do believe that from within we can make a difference. The Aboriginal journalist, producer, cameraman—even the receptionist—can make a person think twice about how they might report issues. Last year I eased my commitment to working for GWN. I left on great terms and I continue to present and file stories. This new-found freedom has meant that I've been able to dedicate time to my position as Federal Secretary of the National Indigenous Media Association. Already I've had a decade as a member of the Media Entertainment and Arts Alliance and in this time the Alliance has been able to provide a lot of support and advice on occasions too numerous to mention.

Just like Colleen Hayward and like our black goddess here [Marjorie Anderson], I too have a real difficulty in understanding why our people work for unemployment benefits. This would have to be the most exciting industry in the universe, but we should not expect people to work just for the love of it. It should no longer be a privilege to work in the media but our right to be recognized as conveyors of stories. Equally, an author would expect to be paid a royalty for their works, yet our elders are met with blank stares when the issue of payment for their priceless stories is raised. The establishment of the Indigenous Media Organizations industrial award, which Jim [Remedio] spoke about earlier, provides a point of reference for those working in the Indigenous media sector, much like the awards set in place by the [Media, Arts and Entertainment] Alliance. Equally importantly, these awards provide recognition for the job that Indigenous people do in the media sector.

Such recognition is about being seen in your community and by your peers as something more than just a professional trainee.

So—'indigenizing the mainstream'?—well I'm not sure. Can we make a difference? I guess we'll find out in time. In the meantime, though, I do look forward to the day when I'm working in a mainstream newsroom that's filled with Indigenous people. Imagine that? Us being the majority. It's a scary thought. Above all I look forward to the day when I can be employed in a position because I'm simply a journalist. I look forward to the day where I'm employed because I'm simply suitably qualified. I look forward to the day when I get a job in the mainstream media because I'm simply the best. Thank you.

MARJORIE ANDERSON

Thank you Gina. I think it's a shame that there doesn't seem to be a lot of people from the mainstream media listening to this because they should be here to hear it. We actually had a case in the ABC where we had a newsroom that was majority-Aboriginal at one stage, and that was our Darwin newsroom. Unfortunately it's not the case now, but it was the case at one stage.

Next up we have Susan Moylan-Coombes. Susan has been in the ABC for eight-and-a-half years. I think she started off there as a producer's assistant and has worked up to be a producer/director and now series producer of *Kam Yan*, which is the programme that has replaced *Blackout*. She's worked on other programmes such as *Blackout, Play School, Backchat, Review*, and now is the series producer of *Kam Yan*.

SUSAN MOYLAN-COOMBES
Indigenous Programs Unit, ABC-TV, Sydney

Thanks Marjorie. I'm actually going to split my talk up into two sections because the other part of this session is about employment and training, which is actually Marjorie's area in television, so I'm doing a little act for her, and I'll also talk about the Indigenous Programs Unit.

I'll start off with the Indigenous Programs Unit. It began back in 1987 and it was then called the Aboriginal Programs Unit, and we made programmes like *First Australians*, which was documentaries; *One People Sing Freedom*, which was a one-off special about the survival of us in 1988; *Blackout* in its various formats, first as a studio-based entertainment programme, which then turned into half-hour documentaries and then a magazine programme. They were all half-hours. Currently we're working on *Kam Yan* which is another half-hour weekly programme. It's looking at Indigenous communities across Australia, hopefully reflecting the diversity of a very rich culture, and full of people who are very colourful and tell some great yarns. Basically we wanted to give a platform and a place for us to tell our stories to the rest of the country. Our brief is to make programmes for a general viewing audience. But also, I think it's important that we have an avenue for black people to be seen on mainstream television. I think that they're very few and far between, apart from programmes like *Blackout* previously, *Kam Yan*, and now SBS's *ICAM* [*Indigenous Current Affairs Magazine*], particularly since that is being run in prime time. *Kam Yan* was actually put on very quickly. We had six weeks to get the programme up—pre-production and production—before going to air. I don't think that the ABC would actually do that to any other programme-making department. But because we are a very talented team within the Indigenous Unit, we were actually able to do that. I applaud the team and I stand here on their behalf.

It is because of Marjorie's area that this has been able to happen. She employs people into the ABC. The ABC has a policy of 2 per cent employment of Aboriginal and Torres Strait Islander people. Currently there are 35 Aboriginal people employed in ABC television, and only six of those are trainees. They are employed in areas such as journalism, directing, producing, staging, archives, make-up, editors, researchers, engineering. I think the employment strategies have changed what we see on our screens. We are creating a change from inside of the ABC, which is sometimes like hitting your head against the brick wall, because it is difficult. As Indigenous people, we are trying to make programmes for Indigenous people and also for the mainstream. It's hard work and some people say, 'Oh but you work in television; it's really glamorous, and you get paid big bucks and so, therefore, you're really powerful people'. But I hate to tell you that we're not. We're actually exhausted people.

I am optimistic and I do see a change on the horizon, particularly with programmes like *Kam Yan*, because it was a programme that came from the Unit. We told the ABC what we wanted to make and because of the very short pre-production period they couldn't really do anything about it. We fought to keep the name because we thought that was import-ant—like 'having a yarn', 'come and chat to us', 'kam yan'; which is what we were inviting people to do. They didn't like the title but the Unit stuck together and we really fought for what we believed in and it stood. We were really pleased with ourselves for doing that.

How do you indigenize the mainstream? Having Indigenous people employed in institutions like the ABC will create a change. It's going to be very slow. There is a high turnover of people because they do get burnt out and it is such a hard place to work in, though I think that is true for any kind of organization of that scale. We need to have people in key roles who can create the change. People who have the power to influence the hierarchy. We need to have cultural awareness for non-Indigenous people who are in key roles, and who are enforcing guidelines and rules on us as Indigenous people making programmes. They say, 'This is how you are supposed to make programmes' and we're saying, 'No, that's not how we want to make programmes'. Marjorie is the one who does all of that, and she does cultural awareness programmes with management, and also with journalists from other organizations, I believe.

The Indigenous Programs Unit has, just recently, had non-Indigenous people working in it. That's a good thing, and I think it's due to the change that's happening within the ABC at the moment. We have a lot of skills as Indigenous programme-makers that we can give to non-Indigenous programme-makers. That's been the feedback that I've had from other producers who we have had come in saying, 'Look, I didn't realize that I was going to learn so much from you', and being out on location and sitting down in the dirt and chatting to people. That is a great thing for them to learn and for us, as programme-makers who are constantly learning on the job, it is good that we get to benefit from their skills as well.

I would like personally to see an Indigenous person sitting on the ABC Board. Since [Senator] Neville Bonner left there hasn't been anyone, and it is very important that we have someone at the top. I would also like to see a quota—there needs to be a percentage of Indigenous programmes being screened on the ABC, as we have it for Australian-made programmes. I would like to see a requirement to be screening Indigenous programmes in prime time between 7.30 and 10.30 at night. One of my biggest gripes about where we are at the moment is that we make these programmes, we put a lot of blood, sweat, and tears into them and they get buried at 10.30 at night. For me that's not good enough. People just don't get to see the programmes. And that's where I think I'd like to leave it. Being short and sweet.

MARJORIE ANDERSON
Thank you Susan. I'll give you that $20 later for making me sound good. In the ABC and I think in other media organizations, Aboriginal people cannot sit back and wait for the mainstream to give them power. I think we have to stand up and we have to take that power. I'm quite often called 'refreshingly direct' by managers in the ABC. I think it's because I do walk in and call a spade a spade when they're doing the wrong thing. So 'refreshingly direct' is a nice way of saying 'a pain in the neck'.

Next up we've got Wayne Coolwell. Wayne Coolwell's been with the ABC for many years, about eleven actually. He's producer/presenter for *Speaking Out*, the Aboriginal programme that's on metro radio and Radio National, and it also goes out internationally on Radio Australia. It's a news and current affairs programme on Aboriginal issues. Wayne has also been on ABC Television as a sports reporter, and he does radio sports as well.

WAYNE COOLWELL
ABC Radio National, Brisbane
Thank you. It's good to be here. I just want first of all to pay my respects to the traditional owners of this country. I'm a Murri from Brisbane, travelling all this way, and thank you to the Forum organizers for allowing me to speak. I'm just delighted to be here because of seeing the leaders yesterday. I think someone mentioned the fact that the young leaders weren't here then, but I think the important thing is that when you see people like Charles Perkins, who isn't burnt out, he's still firing on all cylinders, and John Ah Kit, I'm proud of them, and I'm proud to follow them, and I think they're wonderful Indigenous leaders.

There are a few problems that I've encountered with producing for *Speaking Out*, but I'll mention two. First is the relationship between the executive producer and my role as presenter/producer. The ABC has had a bit of a shift over recent years towards ratings and that's not a bad thing, that's okay, but the ratings become too important. I think they go against the Charter of what the ABC really should be doing, and that's to reflect the diverse culture of this country. There are very good white executive producers who do some wonderful things (. . . if there are any here). But unfortunately there are also those who, because of circumstances or whatever, don't really understand what we're on about. *Speaking Out* is a very important programme. It is heard around this country and actually goes overseas on Radio Australia as well.

This is a situation where the white executive producer, and myself as producer/presenter, become diametrically opposed, simply because of culture and other variables. You have this executive producer who will say, 'Look, make it really interesting. Make sure we have those wonderful white people out there who are going to tune in to *Speaking Out* at 6.30 on a Sunday night, and dress up these issues a little bit. Add a little bit of flair to them and make it palatable for the white people of this country'. My reply to that is simply this: 'If you people can do it—take my job'. It's very difficult for a journalist of over eleven years' standing to dress up issues like Aboriginal deaths in custody as well as infant mortality rates, and all the social justice areas in this country, as well as the political questions that need to be answered. It's my job to be objective and impartial. So I fight with this person, who's a wonderful person but, because of his situation, he's not fully aware of what I'm trying to do. That's one of the main problems with me as the producer and presenter of *Speaking Out*. I would imagine that Susan and other people here probably confront that sort of situation on a daily basis, whether it's television, radio, the print, or whatever.

The other problem that I have is communication within a huge organization like the ABC. I find it really distressing that *Speaking Out* and the *Awaye* programme, as well as television programmes, aren't used as an internal resource more often. After presenting *Speaking Out* for five-and-a-half years, I can say that I've had a handful of phone calls from programme-makers from within the ABC and people outside the ABC asking me questions. These are correct questions about things which are not second nature; people should want to ask straight away about culturally sensitive questions. After such a long time in the media I've seen some bloody terrible things where this consultation doesn't take place and incorrect things go to air or on television. You sit in your lounge-room having a beer or a cup of coffee and you think, 'Oh God, why didn't they just at least make a phone call'. This is the problem with the ABC. I know for a fact that a lot of other programme-makers just don't want to make that phone call. I guess from what I've learned over the years the reason why is that we're all protective of our own programmes. We're all jealous. We love what we're doing and we don't want to share the glory. I suppose that's fair enough; it is human nature— black, white, red, or whatever. I guess Murris do it themselves. You have your programme and you do your interviews, and you produce and you mix it with some music, and do all this la-di-dah sort of stuff, and it sounds fantastic at the end—but the simple thing is that *you've* done it. You know, everyone else can go and get stuffed. You're not going to give any of this away to anybody. But the tragic thing is that we pay for the mistakes that happen all the time. What I really want to say to any professional people here, producers or whoever, is—please just consult with Aboriginal and Torres Strait Islander people about these sorts of issues because, in the long term, we'll all benefit from that, and I think that's the most important thing.

Let me very quickly just say something else. I'm very disillusioned and I don't share the optimism of my colleagues here—my good friends. I think Patrick [Dodson] probably realizes what I'm about to say because I said this at a conference in Townsville last year. After almost twelve years in the ABC, when I joined as a trainee sports broadcaster in 1984, I looked as the media as the great saviour. I thought they were going to come galloping in and change the face of this country. I honestly thought that black and white people were going to get together. And I saw myself as part of that very important role. I thought that here was the knight in shining armour, that the media had this wonderful chance to change all these horrible things, all these negative perceptions around in society, wherever they might be, at whatever public level. No, it hasn't worked. I've got no problem in saying that I don't know where we're headed. I haven't got the answer. I wish I did. But there's a real problem in this country and I don't know what to do about it. The only thing that I can do is, as a good little Aboriginal person, continue on my merry way and produce *Speaking Out* which is heard around the country, and hope that white people tune in and say, 'Oh that sounds all right. Might tune in next week. Good music. Good programme'. That's all I can do and that's all I ever really want to do. I'm getting disillusioned about the fact that the mainstream media aren't going to help us. Never. I've seen too much over the years and so I say we just continue on. If they want to join us, well so be it. Thank you.

MARJORIE ANDERSON
Thank you Wayne, that is an interesting point because I sometimes go through that as well. That doubt about 'am I really making a difference? Are we really making a difference?' I guess I'm the eternal optimist. I think we are making a difference. In television, though, it's a bit easier for us because we've got one network to deal with. In radio, there are five networks, and it makes it much more difficult for Aboriginal people to share their wealth of information. I think Susan would agree with me that television programme-makers tend to use *Kam Yan* and my office a lot and journalists do as well. But that's because we're one network.

The next person coming up is Rachel Perkins. Now Rachel's been involved in the media for over eight years. Rachel worked at CAAMA for three years and she was head of the SBS Aboriginal Unit for three years. She's just graduated from the Australian Film School and has operated her own production company by the name of Blackfella Films since 1993. Rachel.

RACHEL PERKINS
Director, Blackfella Films, former producer, SBS-TV, Sydney
I want to thank the Nyungar people for inviting us here. It's been really good and they've really welcomed us. Specially the Nyungar girls at the back there. They've been giving us cigarettes all day and stuff like that. That's good. [Greeting in Arrernte language]: which means

my name is Rachel Perkins. I'm an Arrernte woman. I'm from Alice Springs.

Blackfella Films is a production company that I'm a director of with another Koori film-maker Michael Riley. It's been going since 1993. But I've been involved in community broadcasting, in television, and with the bureaucracy at SBS. I finally came to be independent because I found that's the way that Aboriginal people can have full editorial control over their work most successfully. Just to tell you a bit about us. We've just finished a 10–minute film called *Pay Back* that I line-produced, directed by a young guy called Warren Thornton, who also worked with CAAMA. It was a real coup for us because we had an almost 95 per cent Aboriginal crew on a drama: the most Koori/Aboriginal crew ever in Australia. That's the area that we're focusing on at Blackfella Films. Aboriginal-controlled film, features, and television drama is really a new front here in terms of Aboriginal media. We've been involved in radio and television for a long time, and the big screen is really the next area to crack I believe.

Our mission at Blackfella Films is to put Aboriginal stories which are, as we all know, ritual stories about our grandmothers and ourselves, onto the big screen. The way to do that is to make them commercially viable. But being an Aboriginal film-maker you have to maintain the cultural integrity of the projects and that's something that will become a bigger struggle for us when we move into the bigger budget productions. To make a $5 million film in this country you've got to sell it in territories around the world. It's got to be commercial, and the big thing that we come up against in this country is that whenever we go in and pitch an idea they say: 'Ah look, black stuff doesn't rate, we're not interested in black stuff. You can keep your little TVs, do your own community video or whatever, but we're not interested in this commercial sense because Coca-Cola just won't advertise with Aboriginal stuff. They don't want to be associated with Aboriginal stuff. The only sponsorship we got for the Aboriginal Rugby Knockout that we did at SBS two years ago was a slab of Coke—that's all we got. 30,000 people went to see it, it went round the countryside on the national broadcaster. Could we get any advertising? No. So that's the situation. That's the reality that we're facing. It is extremely important for us to crack this market and we've got to do it in a good way. We've got to be extremely professional and we've got to be good at what we do, because feature film making is an incredibly difficult craft.

We've got two feature films that will hopefully go into production by the end of 1996. They'll be the first features to be produced through an Aboriginal-owned production company—if we don't get knocked back.

Two feature films have been directed by Aboriginal people. One of them was made by a fellow who's passed away now and he contributed enormously to the Aboriginal creative arts industry. The other one's by another woman.

I'd like to just reinforce what Gina said about working in the mainstream; white people don't like to say, 'Ah but you could do anything, it's great, you've got all these skills and it's fabulous, and you could be employed'. They say, 'Why don't you move out? You could make commercials'. I say, 'Look, I'm not here to make corporate ads. I'm not here to make films about anything else. I'm here as an Aboriginal film-maker'. That's why my community paid for me to go through CAAMA and train, and I really believe that we've been given a mandate by our elders to tell our stories and that's what we're here for. So I'm very committed to doing that, and so is Blackfella Films. We hire Aboriginal freelance people from across the country on contract. They come in and do the job. We put them in key creative roles and we basically run the production.

Feature films are really important to crack because the mainstream is really where the rednecks lie. It's really good to come out here and talk to all you mob but you mob all support us. We're all together. Nobody's going to give us any flak, because we all believe in the same thing. But when you go to the mainstream, it's a different story. It's chokka with rednecks, as you mob all know. The way to change people's attitudes, I believe, is to move them emotionally. Drama is the way to do that. You can put images up on screen like *Gandhi*—that was about a black man— and look, it made people cry. All these racists, they're crying their eyes out. *Malcolm X*, one of the most significant black leaders in this century, had all these whitefellas weeping in the aisles. *To Sir With Love*—another one. They love it. They all love African Americans after that. The power of film is just incredible and that's what we're trying to harness, not just to make money like everyone reckons. I wouldn't mind some money but, you know...

So how do we 'indigenize the mainstream'? We get skilled up. Primarily, we get skills to do the job and do it well. We put blackfellas in key creative roles. Directors, producers, production design, full camera department, accounting, budgeting, production management, all Aboriginal people—and we're doing that. We demand a piece of the action in the feature film industry, because they're so few blackfellas actually directing and producing. We go to industry conferences and it's like going to some dance in the 1960s. You know—when there'd be one blackfella there and they won't let him in. But that's what it's like going to SPA and ASDA conferences these days. There's no blackfellas there. You're the only one. It's like going to some sort of dance hall in Mouri or somewhere in the '60s. I wanted to say that because it's such a new frontier there are not many role models. Lydia [Miller, Executive Officer for ATSI Arts, Australia Council]'s done great work because she's been in *Deadly* and all these fantastic films—that's in the performance side. The only other Aboriginal director [Tracey Moffatt] says she's just a film-maker, she's not an Aboriginal film-maker. That's what I am so I don't take a role model from her. I take it from someone like Spike Lee, who's made five feature films, and is making money. He's employing African Americans in all positions and he's getting black issues out to an international audience.

I just want to read you a quotation from Spike Lee. He's talking about a film, the first film that he made. It won Best Film at Cannes I think. It's called *She's Got to Have It*. He says:

It's not for me to say whether *She's Got to Have It* is a landmark film. I make them, that's all. But I do want people to be inspired by it, in particular black people. Now there is a present example of how we can produce. We can do things the way we want to do. There are no more excuses. We're all tired of that alibi. White man's this. White man's that. Yo—'F' that—it's on us. So let's all do the work that needs to be done by us all. And to all you who aren't down for the cause, move out of the way. Step aside. Besides if you aren't down, you must wear blue-green contact lenses.

I want to say, just to finish up, that we all know what the mainstream media are like and I just wanted to agree with Wayne—they're not going to change very rapidly—none of them are here, you know—so it's up to us to do it, and empower ourselves. That's what Blackfella Films is about and what we want to do; empower ourselves and break into the new frontier of feature film production. Thanks.

MARJORIE ANDERSON
Thank you Rachel. I'm sure Rachel will be a role model for some of our youth coming up. They're starting to get excited about the industry when they see Rachel doing the work that she does. Rachel brought up an interesting fact about whitefellas saying that Aboriginal people don't rate. Now that gets said to me in the ABC all the time. Yet when *Heartland* was made—it was made by whitefellas in the ABC—it rated very, very well. So nobody in the ABC can now turn around and say to me, 'Blackfellas don't rate' because it's just not true. I'd like to thank the Nyungar people for allowing me to chair this session today on the land and I would now like to call on Michael Mansell to come up and close the Forum for us.

MICHAEL MANSELL

Thank you. I feel privileged being a stranger to this country to be given the opportunity to sum up the last couple of days and to formally close the National Media Forum. We've all been privileged to hear many very good and very qualified speakers beginning yesterday and running right through to today. What stood out was not just the diversity of views and experiences in the Aboriginal community around Australia, but the way in which people are able to express their perceptions of the relationship between the Aboriginal community and mainstream media, how the Aboriginal media are making enormous inroads, both for the people in them and among the people who hear about them.

Over the last twenty-four hours, despite our comments and criticisms of the mainstream media, and the way that we are treated by them, I haven't felt that we ought to go away from this Forum with any pessimistic view. In fact, on the contrary, I think a lot of very positive things have come out of this Forum. One of the common features among comments that have been made by people in relation to the mainstream media, which is not negative but a fact of life, is what Rachel summed up at the finish of her talk. Mainstream media are there and they're very, very difficult to change. Reflect upon the fact that some of the most powerful people in this country have cried 'bias' against the media when their views have been presented. Such efforts are futile because even with enormous power—a lot more power than we will ever see—they themselves have been able to bring about very little change within mainstream media. It may well be the nature of the beast, that the media just roll on, on the basis of whatever drives it.

This raises a question out of the very justified comments that people have made at this Forum, about the poor response that the media give us to the very terrible situation of Aboriginal people in this country. There is perhaps a question-mark over whether we should worry about trying to change the media. If we are to get the most out of using mainstream media, it may well be that we have to be like others, and develop new techniques. We have to build up techniques that enable us to get our message through the media, knowing full well that they will be using us for their own benefit, but at the same time we will be using them to benefit the Aboriginal community wherever it is.

I recall watching the display by Greenpeace on the French nuclear tests at Mururoa. They haven't stood back and waited for the media to report. They have their own camera, they have their own satellite networks where they beam direct to commercial TV stations around the world the message that they want published. And they get it. I think there's great lessons in that for us. Let's take Western Australia as an example.

There are no rewards for the worst off, but without doubt the situation of police–Aboriginal relations in Western Australia is by far the worst in this country. And the imprisonment rates and the rates of incarceration of kids, the deaths in custody rates, are the worst in the world. If we want to get that message across to the public, both nationally and internationally, and we find that the local mainstream media, and for that matter the national media, won't run it, then maybe we could look at examples that we see from overseas. In this situation there's nothing wrong with the Aboriginal Legal Service using its resources not just to fund lawyers but also to fund camera-people, to go out and record what's happening in the streets, and give that video to the media, whoever's prepared to run it.

I make that point because it seems to me there have been a lot of comments over the last day or so about people feeling frustrated. We have a cause that most of us can't believe the mainstream media are not reporting. So maybe we have to look at new techniques. We have to bend a little bit, to be able to get our message through the mainstream media. I'm also encouraged by the developments that I see, of Indigenous people within mainstream media, and also in Indigenous media themselves. If you look around the room today and at the panel that sat up here last night—to see Charles Perkins at his best is something I would come 1,000 miles to see. I think it was just unfortunate that more Aboriginal people weren't around to see Charlie but I know that once he throws the shackles of bureaucracy off, he's just bloody brilliant. I think all of you who saw that yesterday would agree. Apart from Charlie and the other people who were up here yesterday, there is an enormous amount of talent in the Aboriginal community. The only reason that talent has not really shown its face to the extent that it should is because people have been deprived of the opportunity. But I see Indigenous people within mainstream media and Indigenous media changing that.

One of the things that I picked up from the reports from people within Indigenous media was the need not to follow; as I said in my own speech yesterday, 'Let's not imitate everything that white people want us to imitate'. One of the speakers [Joe Edgar] really struck a chord with me by talking about the culturalization of Aboriginal kids into Black American culture. I made the point in the audience when I was listening to it that in Tasmania I've told the kids, 'Turn that hat around and point it that way'—because Aboriginal culture is much too important and too rich, and it has a lot more going for it than simply imitating Black American culture—without trying to put down Black American culture.

If you look at the way that Indigenous media presented themselves without any interference from anybody else, I think they are reflecting the uniqueness of Aboriginal people and Aboriginal culture in this country. At the same time as us having been forced to bend to the mainstream to get our message across, I can see the building up of Indigenous media, so that we can present our views in an Aboriginal way back to our communities without having to bend at all. So when I've listened to some of the talks that have taken place here today and yesterday, I have been enormously encouraged that we do have a future. Even though we have enormous problems, as much as anybody else in the world, we are starting to take the bull by the horns and we are starting to turn things around. If nothing else, this Forum shows that we have an enormous amount of talent that we can bring together over a two-day period. If that talent is allowed to develop, the future for Aboriginal people is not going to be gloom, I think it's going to be wonderful.

Part Three | **Reporting**

7 | Mapping the Indigenous 'Mediasphere'

When Australia became modern, it ceased to be interesting.... Aboriginal Australia had provided Europe with a 'photographic negative' of itself.... Once Australia was a sovereign state, and able to deny Aboriginal people citizenship, it was merely one more place filled with whitefellas. 'Australians' were transformed in northern hemisphere theory from dashing blacks living out of time into dull Anglo-Celts living out of place.... No set of nominated individuals exercises the significance outside Australia that Aborigines have done, and continue to do, as a collectivity, via their uptake by forms of social and cultural theorisation dedicated to understanding modernity and postmodernity.

(Toby Miller, 1995: 7–8)

An 'Interest' in Modernity

Founded with modernity, news is a modernizing, modernist discourse, dedicated to progress, reason, truth and the commanding power of empirical, preferably quantitative evidence. News is not at its best, therefore, in dealing with what has been 'negativized' as modernity's 'other'. It has inherited from the militant eyewitness explorers of the nineteenth century the will to oppose the industriousness and democracy of the north to something understood as a natural, pre-modern state from which modernity has been emancipated (see Miller, 1995). Into such a state has been poured, variously, magic or spirituality (non-science), poverty (non-industriousness), childlikeness (non-democracy). The great white explorers roamed Africa, Asia, and Australasia, and some non-territorial 'other' realms as well, such as gender (see Felski, 1995). They found what they were looking for too: contemporary ('surviving') examples of the non-modern. These were valuable, not only to confirm the oppositional structure of the modernist theoretical purchase upon the world, but also in a practical way, as raw material upon which to practise the new sciences of rational government. The idea was for modernity to take in hand the world of magical, childlike poverty, and, by a regime of 'correction and protection,' to govern it for its own good. The idea was to 'improve' both lands and populations by introducing industry, 'development', and productivity ('growth') to their physical and mental 'natural state'.

This is the script into which Aboriginal and Islander people have been written ever since writing was first imported into the Australian continent (see Irving, 1999: 15–16, 111–16). News is not exempt from that will to govern; it is indeed the public, quotidian expression of it. News has therefore always had a hard time seeing Aboriginal people outside of these terms. They have been presumed to inhabit a non-modern universe of spiritual richness, personal childlikeness, and material poverty. They have presented themselves as a problem of governance; success has been expected when they have understood that 'correction and protection' was 'for their own good' (Haebich, 1988; see also Jacobs, 1990). They were the 'other' of modernity and could therefore hardly have been seen as equal participants in its progress and government.

Such a view is not the personal opinion of individual journalists and media professionals—some of them may indeed wish to resist it as soon as they become aware of its operation, as do people in other walks of life. But what is being described here is institutionalized in the fundamental set-up within which news exists—the assumptions about what it is, what and whom it is for, and how it can be accomplished and maintained on a daily basis. In other words, news is one mode in which human intelligence or thinking is practised *collectively*. It is hard for individuals to succeed in it without reproducing in their own individual acts of creativity the structures of thought that have been built in the 'mediasphere' of modernity. Just as an infrastructure of physical built environments has been inherited from those nineteenth-century titans, from railways, roads, and sewers to schools, hospitals, and public houses, so an immense *mental* apparatus has similarly survived into the twenty-first century, and news is part of it. 'Emancipating' Indigeneity from such a situation is going to be a hard slog for everyone involved, not simply a matter of 'self-determination' by Aboriginal people themselves. It is that hard slog, perceptible as a tension between ('unthinking') reproduction of modernist categories, and more innovative efforts to bring together what's useful from both modernist and Aboriginal worlds, that is currently playing itself out in the Australian news media, in academic writing, and in government policy-making alike.

This chapter and the following two report on the ways in which Indigeneity appeared in the Australian media in the snapshot weeks. In this chapter we offer some summary information, the next two chapters extend the discussion begun here. Chapter 8 concentrates on the 'softer' end of the journalism spectrum, reviewing coverage in magazines, TV, radio, and sport; Chapter 9 looks at 'hard' news and its 'remediation' in talkback. Together with the tabular evidence presented here, they provide a general description of factual narration in the Indigenous 'mediasphere' in the mid-to-late 1990s. Ours is not a systematic and replicable approach that treats every item as being of equal interest; neither is it an analysis of a very few 'representative' stories. It attempts to provide a form of analysis that is somewhere between these extremes, communicating our sense of the shape of the mediasphere, the trends, stories, and items that emerge as important over this period. In order to show what is at stake in moving from a statistical to a textual view of the material, we close this chapter with an analysis of some emblematic stories, where kissing, sexuality, gossip, and politics coincide. Finally in this chapter, the question of Aboriginal national status is discussed via an analysis of news stories about, and graphic use of, the Aboriginal flag.

The most compelling result of our survey in numerical terms is a simple discovery: Aboriginality is over-represented in the Australian news media in *factual* stories. While Indigenous *fictional* characters portrayed in popular culture are quite rare, Aboriginality turns out to be a massive *presence* in Australian journalism. Aboriginality, and 'Aboriginal issues', continue to draw headlines, comment columns, and editorial opinion with a frequency unjustified statistically by the population of Indigenous people. Indigeneity has become central for Austalia's status as a nation. It remains as Australia's 'running story', a story that just keeps on going. It is the point around which political debates— debates about social justice, fairness, and the adequacy of social structures—take place in Australia.

The 'Mediasphere'

We have chosen to use the word 'mediasphere' in preference to other more familiar terms, such as 'the media' (alluding to an industry or economic sector), or 'the media-scape' (alluding to the perspective of urban citizens, as in 'city-scape'). For its part, the term 'mediasphere' was coined to associate the media both with Lotman's concept of the 'semiosphere' and with the Habermasian notion of the 'public sphere' (the idea is more fully elaborated in Hartley, 1996). Indeed, we believe that the public sphere is entirely encompassed, like a Russian doll, by the mediasphere, which in turn is encompassed within the semiosphere. The implications of such a view are that the mediasphere needs to be understood as part of the political (public sphere) and the cultural (semiosphere) at once. The mediasphere is not set in opposition to the public sphere, as some public-sphere theorizing would have it (i.e. as a pseudo-realm of mass persuasion, rather than a rational place of public dialogue), nor is it understood as an unfortunate decline from authentic cultural pursuits. Instead, the mediasphere is conceptualized as the very 'medium' that *connects* the world of political and public dialogue with the larger universe of culture. It is this inter-permeation of politics, media, and 'semiosis' that renders so much of what passes for politics as *narrative*, turns 'rational' sciences like government into *drama, story, image, symbol*, etc. At the same time, it shows how those same apparently immaterial objects have very real political impact. Furthermore, the idea of the public sphere interacting with a mediasphere does not require an opposition to be constructed between 'public' and 'private' domains—once again, the mediasphere connects these together.

The Figures

Below we present, as figures, the way that Indigenous issues appeared in the Australian 'mediasphere'. The information was gathered over three 'snapshot' weeks, one each in the years 1994, 1995, and 1996. During these weeks, a sample was taken of national and state newspapers, magazines, television non-fiction, including news, current affairs, infotainment, and radio. An identical sample was not maintained over the three years, partly for reasons beyond our control: some magazines folded in the course of the project, for example, or television schedules changed. However, we were also keen that we should learn as we were working. When it became obvious that the ABC was the site of most radio material, for example, we increased the coverage of ABC stations. The categories also evolved over the course of the three years. A provisional set of categories was established before the project began, encompassing those areas where we expected to find coverage, and which we expected to be important. However, in each year, the distribution of material, and the evolution of our ideas about how it might be ordered, resulted in new categories. For example as well as 'Land Rights', the new category of 'Native Title' was added in 1995. At the end of the three-year period, the survey items were reassessed in the light of these new and evolving criteria, and the extra information was added to relevant items (for example, 1994 items that already showed a move towards Native Title discussions were added to that category).

The sample was taken during NAIDOC week each year. NAIDOC stands for National Aboriginal and Islander Day Of Celebration, but events were held over a week each July. This was obviously not a 'typical' week. The number of stories was liable to be greater than average, and quite possibly the types of stories gathered during such a period would be distinct. More 'scientific' attempts than ours may have aimed to be representative of all coverage (Robert Jackson, for instance, chose a range of different periods from which to sample, in order to overcome the 'bias' of any single period: Jackson *et al.*, 1995: 2). But we did not seek representativeness in this context. The advantage of NAIDOC week was that more stories could be predicted; providing more material for analysing the 'available discourses'.

The sample was coded on Orbis, a freeform text database, part of the Nota Bene software package. We were keen to avoid SPSS or NUDIST (though we did not realize in advance how short the lifespan of Nota Bene would be as a widely used package). Items were coded into multiple categories: labelling a given item with only a single category seemed one of the least workable aspects of traditional statistical analysis (but see Mickler and McHoul, 1998: 123, for a discussion of a different strategy). The coding was conducted in the first year by six research assistants; and in subsequent years by a single research associate (McKee) with more training in the area of Indigenous representation.

Radio 6AR, an Aboriginal radio station run by the Western Australian Aboriginal Media Association, was archived during the second and third survey periods, but was not included as part of the statistical survey. 6AR provided a good example of why we were unhappy with statistical methods of content analysis. Much of the output of the station was not 'Aboriginal content' in origin, although it may have been 'Aboriginal culture' in fact; it specializes in American country and western music, for example. Such output was an important part of constructing 'Aboriginality' in Western Australia simply by being played on 6AR, and to that extent every second of the station's broadcast should have been coded 'Indigenous'. The station was therefore excluded from statistical analysis because this would have introduced a huge burden on the researchers, and it is likely that even reducing the items to those originated by Indigenous performers would have more than doubled the number in the sample (across all media).

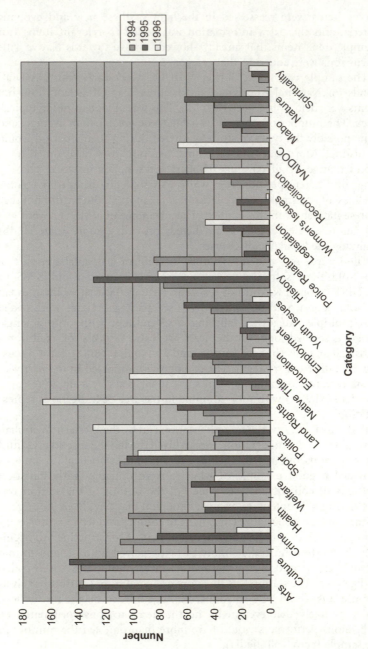

Figure 1. Indigeneity in the Mediasphere

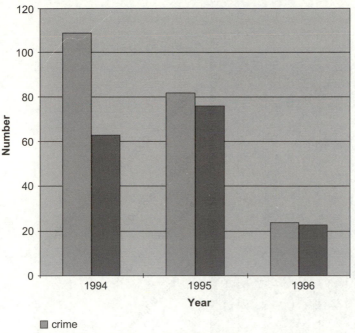

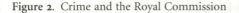

■ crime
■ crime without Royal Commission/Deaths in Custody

Figure 2. Crime and the Royal Commission

Discussion

Figure 1 'Indigeneity in the Mediasphere', shows the distribution of items by category (as those categories developed) over the three years. They were somewhat arbitrary, but were developed for their usefulness of fitting the contours of the representation encountered. 'Arts' included the usual suspects—music, dance, visual arts, and so on. But 'culture' included those elements not normally regarded in such a way—language, social organization, eating habits, and so on. 'History' included elements of many other categories—arts, culture, politics—if they were located in the past. 'Politics' was developed with a specific aim in mind—it referred to traditional party politics (Coalition, Labor, Democrats).

It is possible to make some general comments on this figure. First, it seems that arts specifically, and culture generally, were the most impor-

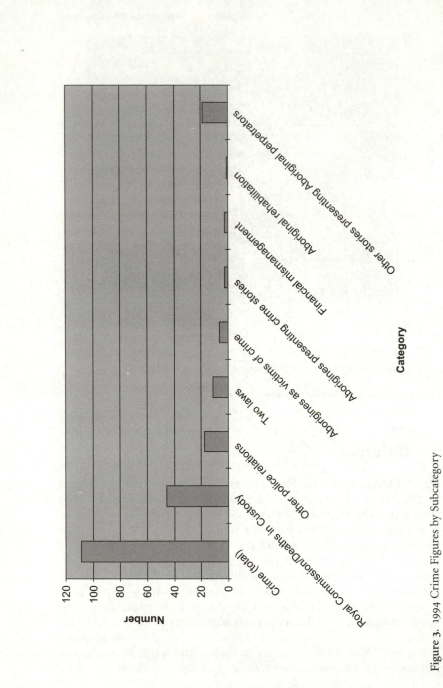

Figure 3. 1994 Crime Figures by Subcategory

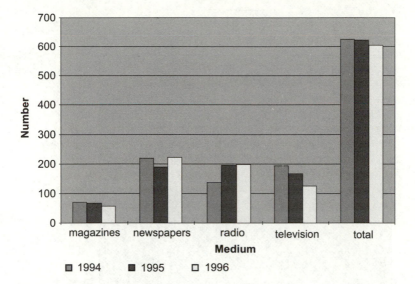

Figure 4. Numbers by Medium

tant ways in which Indigeneity was constructed. Stories about crime presented a poor third, especially in the results for the survey of 1996.

Figure 2, 'Crime and the Royal Commission', shows the number of stories each year that fell into the 'crime' category, and the number of crime stories left after removing those dealing with the Royal Commission into Aboriginal Deaths in Custody and its ramifications. In the first year in particular, the results are telling. Although there were 109 stories categorized as 'crime' in 1994, 46 of these dealt with the report of the Royal Commission, or with examples of deaths in custody. Obviously, there were differences between such stories and those reported by Jakubowicz *et al.* (1994), who argue that crime stories present the 'negative stereotype' of Aborigines as criminals. In fact, a more detailed breakdown of the crime stories in 1994 illuminates this point still further. Figure 3, '1994 Crime Figures by Subcategory,' shows that of 109 stories, as well as Royal Commission stories, there were:

- other police relations stories (for example, an investigation of a police Tactical Response Group after allegations of harassment by Aboriginal actor Rhonda Collard);
- discussions of legislation and history (suggestions that elements of Aboriginal law might be introduced to Australian judicial systems;

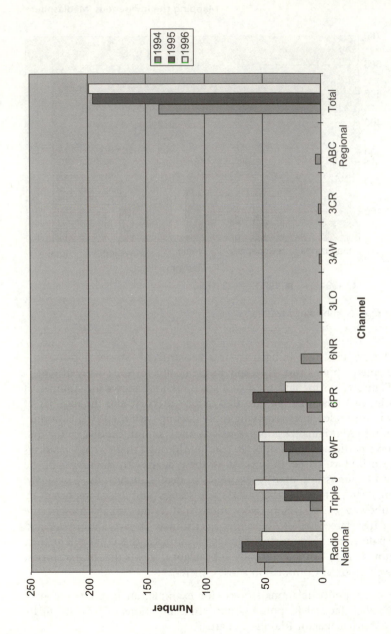

Figure 5. Radio by Channel

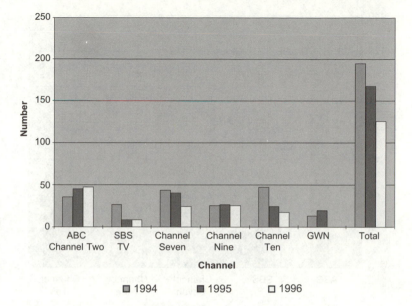

Figure 6. Television by Channel

an Aboriginal man convicted of murder claiming status as a 'prisoner of war');

- Aborigines as victims of crime (an Aboriginal man locked in the boot of a taxicab, for example);
- Aboriginal people presenting stories of non-Indigenous crime (Stan Grant);
- accusations of financial mismanagement (criminal indeed, but not entirely congruent with the 'stereotype' that has worried previous writers).

After these stories were removed, we were left in 1994 with 19 stories presenting Aboriginal people as the perpetrators of crime. This should be compared with 110 stories dealing with arts, and 138 addressing culture.

We would argue against 'representativeness' as a useful concept in doing such a survey, and the results show that the mediasphere was not a homogenous place. With a sample taken for one week across dozens of channels and stations, and across four media, the mediasphere fluctuated according to current stories. The news media tended to identify and follow particular stories (in Walter Lippman's famous analogy of the

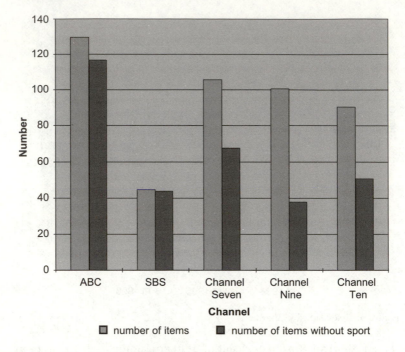

Figure 7. Television by Channel, with and without Sport

1920s, news is like a searchlight, focusing brightly on very small areas of a given society before moving on). Crime stories in 1996 almost vanished, while politics and land rights soared (with the Century Zinc mine and Murrandoo Yanner being most visible at this time). In 1994, Health was a big story during the sample week. Reconciliation was a big story in 1995.

Other investigators with different samples may have found that 'crime' has remained a dominant way of representing Indigeneity. We can state with confidence, however, that this need not be the case. In our sample of national newspapers and magazines, and state-based television and radio, covering dozens of titles and channels for a complete week, conducted over three years, crime was certainly not the most important way of making sense of Indigeneity.

As a final point on crime, though, it is worth noting that to identify 19 stories and label them 'crime' still tells us little about the *story* in these stories, or the functions they might have served. In order to illustrate this point, we take the case of item 'new94150': a front-page headline in the *Sunday Territorian* of 10 July 1994: NT FACES WAVE OF VIOLENCE.

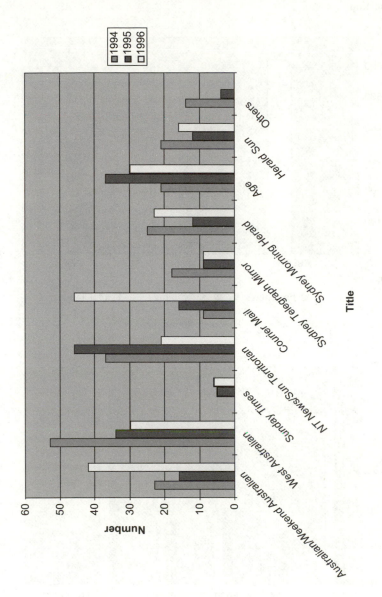

Figure 8. Newspaper, by Title

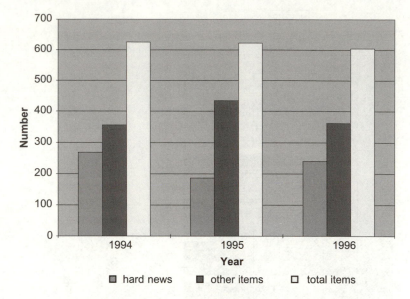

Figure 9. Hard News and Other Forms of Reporting

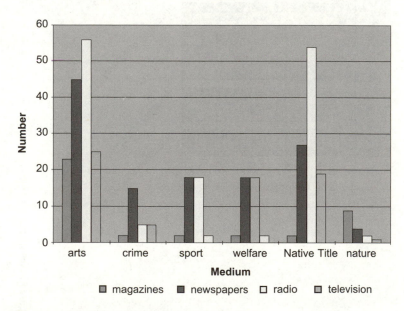

Figure 10. Examples of Subject Matter by Medium

220

This story warned that the next generation of Aboriginal youth might 'unleash an epidemic of violence previously unseen in the Territory'. Reading this headline, it was tempting immediately to categorize the story as 'white fear of Indigenous crime'. However, this was not 'the same old story', for the claims were made by Aboriginal politician Charles Perkins. Illustrated with Perkins's photograph, it was his warning that violence might emerge unless Aboriginal people were 'found jobs and their standards of living raised'. In short, this was not a 'crime' story at all, but one focusing attention on social justice. It may be possible to argue that Perkins played into the hands of those who peddle traditional 'negative stereotypes' by making such a statement. However, Perkins's strategies as an Aboriginal politician should also be respected. He used the crime story genre tactically, in order to get front-page coverage for issues of Indigenous social justice.

So-called 'hard news' stories—health, crime, welfare, land rights, or what we have dubbed stories of 'correction and protection'—fluctuated more than stories involving arts, culture, and sport. Those elements of coverage that occurred in the 'softer' hinterland of news, or across the border in features, lifestyle, and consumer journalism, remained comparatively stable over the three years.

In mapping an Indigenous 'mediasphere', the mismatch between Indigenous and non-Indigenous distribution of stories is notable. In general news coverage (Indigenous and non-Indigenous combined), party politics was vitally important, much more so than its restrained showing in this sample suggests. The Indigenous domain is represented as a consensual field, whether it is in fact or not. Similarly, financial coverage in Australian newspapers, radio, and television presented vastly more coverage of 'employment' for non-Indigenous populations than was the case for Aboriginal people. It seems that while the Aboriginal public sphere was well developed in terms of culture, arts, and sports, it had no public infrastructure in party political or financial terms. The basic construction of Indigeneity in the Australian public sphere is as what Marshall Sahlins once called the 'original affluent society'—people who were culturally rich but politically and economically poor (Sahlins, 1974: ch. 1).

Figure 4, 'Numbers by Medium', shows the presence of Indigeneity in each of the four media analysed. Magazines provided a small but important contribution to the figures each year. Looking at each medium by channel or title, the graphs show how these figures broke down. In Figure 5, 'Radio by Channel', the ABC provided the vast majority of Indigenous coverage. In the case of 'Television by Channel' (Figure 6) SBS provided the least news coverage of Aboriginal affairs. The reasons

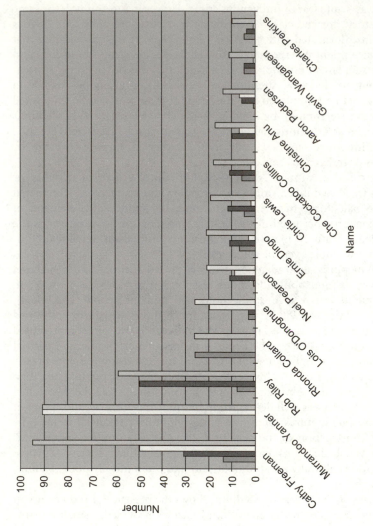

Figure 11(a). Named Individuals in the Indigenous Mediasphere: Indigenous

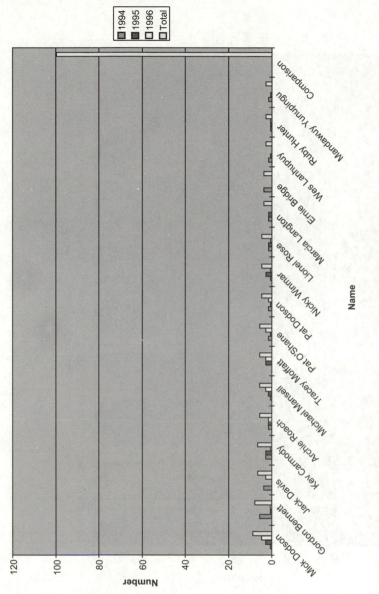

Figure 11(*b*). Named Individuals in the Indigenous Mediasphere: Indigenous (*continued*)

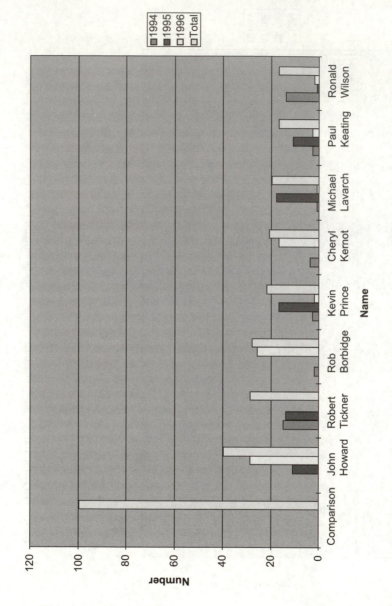

Figure 12(a). Named Individuals in the Indigenous Mediasphere, Non-Indigenous

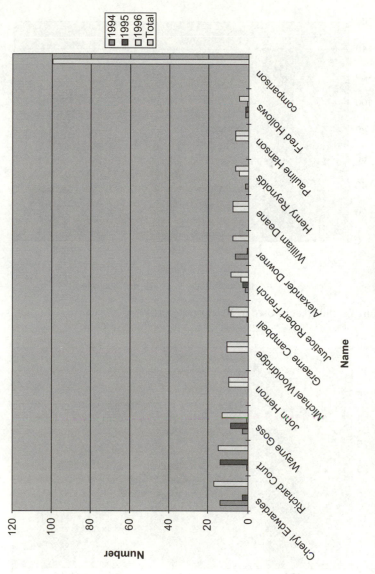

Figure 12(b). Named Individuals in the Indigenous Mediasphere, Non-Indigenous (*continued*)

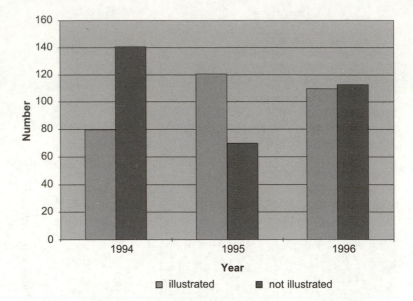

Figure 13. Illustrations Used in Newspaper Stories

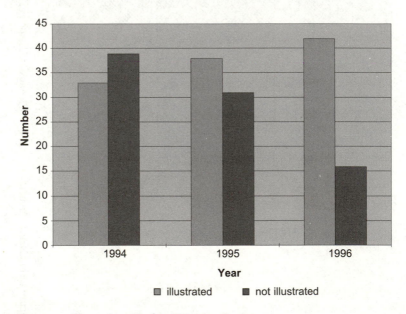

Figure 14. Illustrations Used in Magazine Stories

for this included SBS's focus on 'World News', tending to exclude in advance coverage of Indigenous stories; and the paucity of Australian sport coverage in SBS news reports (as Figure 7, 'Television by Channel, with and without Sport', shows). Sport also greatly inflated the Indigenous coverage of the three commercial stations.

Figure 8, 'Newspaper, by Title', shows that figures fluctuated greatly over the three years, but it was notable that the *Australian* was not the major source of Indigenous stories in any year. Rather, state-based papers (at different times, the *West Australian*, the *Northern Territory News*, and the *Courier Mail*) provided higher levels of Indigenous coverage. Again, the non-homogenous nature of the mediasphere became apparent, with the Century Zinc/Murrandoo Yanner land rights dispute in Queensland in 1996 boosting the representation in that state's paper massively for the 1996 survey period. Unsurprisingly, in those states with large Aboriginal populations (Western Australia and the Northern Territory), Indigenous coverage tended to be higher. It is also notable that the 'broadsheet' newspapers the *Sydney Morning Herald* and (especially) the *Age* in Victoria tended to present more Indigenous stories than their respective popular ('tabloid') competitors.

Arts, culture, and sports stories were important for understanding 'law formation': the kind of news that was not simply concerned with 'anomalies'. It was not hard news, but reassuring and entertaining, serving a different function. It is perhaps hardly surprising if previous surveys have only paid attention to 'hard news', and have then found a focus on crime and welfare, which are central to such coverage. But there was far more to Indigeneity than that. As Figure 9, 'Hard News and Other Forms of Reporting', demonstrates, in each year of the survey, representations other than 'hard news' outnumbered it; in 1995, considerably so. These other elements—arts reviews, fashion reports, sports coverage, and so on—were important to understanding Indigeneity. Yet they have characteristically been ignored in previous writing.

Similarly, Figure 10, 'Examples of Subject Matter by Medium', shows how many stories of various types appeared in each of the four media over the three-year period. It can be seen that if newspapers are chosen as the focus for analysis (as is common in media studies), then quite a particular version of the Indigenous mediasphere will be 'found'. It would exclude the focus on the arts that characterizes radio, for example, in favour of crime. By contrast, looking at magazines would 'produce' a focus on nature greater than that for any other medium. If the Indigenous mediasphere were homogenous across the four media, it could be expected that each of the categories would have the same relative proportions of each medium, as is the case with sport and welfare, for example. For the other categories, this is obviously not the case.

Such areas as 'politics' and 'employment' were under-represented, while arts and culture were over-represented. This suggests a public sphere which was cultural rather than political. That finding is even more pronounced in relation to public figures in the Indigenous media-sphere. Who actually appears to comment on and represent Indigenous issues and questions? As can be seen from Figure 11, 'Named Individuals in the Indigenous Mediasphere: Indigenous', the most visible Indigenous public figures were mostly drawn from the world of sport and entertainment. Cathy Freeman was consistently present, and was the most visible Indigenous person over the course of the three years of this survey. Murrandoo Yanner, Rob Riley, and Rhonda Collard were all strongly represented by particular stories which broke each year (Collard demanded an investigation into police harassment, Riley was charged with driving offences, Yanner was involved in negotiations with Century Zinc). Lois O'Donoghue and Noel Pearson also appeared consistently over the three years, representing a visible Aboriginal political leadership. Beyond this, Indigenous leaders tended to be drawn from the worlds of entertainment and sport. Ernie Dingo, Chris Lewis, Che Cockatoo Collins, Christine Anu, Aaron Pedersen, and Gavin Wanganeen, with Cathy Freeman, might all be characterized as Aboriginal political figures, in the sense of being cultural ambassadors. Although not representative or elected politicians, each made public statements about Indigeneity or Indigenous issues, and was involved in public discussion of the possible relationships between Indigenous and non-Indigenous Australians. With fewer appearances, Charles Perkins, Mick Dodson, Michael Mansell, Pat O'Shane, and Pat Dodson did not have such a high public profile, but were consistently present in the public sphere as Aboriginal politicians (again, as something like 'elders' for Indigenous people, rather than elective politicians). Since the period in which our archive was compiled, Noel Pearson has become prominent in the same role.

By contrast, the non-Indigenous people who are involved in the Indigenous mediasphere can be characterized much more easily: they were party-political politicians (see Figure 12). Since speaking on this subject was their job, it is no surprise to find that prime ministers, state premiers, Aboriginal Affairs ministers and other MPs represented almost the entire profile of this sample. The exceptions were Sir Ronald Wilson (human rights and the 'stolen generation'), Justice Robert French (Native Title), Sir William Deane (the Governor-General), and Fred Hollows (medical matters). If there was a struggle over definitions of

Indigenous issues in the media, and if that struggle is understood to have taken place between definitions produced by Indigenous and non-Indigenous spokespeople respectively, then it should be noted that it was also largely an unequal struggle between politicians and sportspeople. However, we do not know whether the public found Cathy Freeman more convincing than John Howard.

Figures 13 and 14 show the number of stories in newspapers and magazines that were illustrated with a photograph or drawing and those that were not. It is not obviously the case that Indigeneity must be visualized in order to be represented: there was no definite trend in these figures.

Kissing Anu and Pedersen: From Stats to Texts

Item number mag95047 in our archive was a magazine profile of Torres Strait Islander singer Christine Anu, in *Juice* magazine in 1995. It consisted of an interview with Anu, together with a big celebrity picture. Meanwhile, *Star!* magazine from July 1995 published a profile of *Gladiators* presenter Kimberley Joseph. Shown as sexy, sassy, and attractive, Joseph was asked to fill in a questionnaire that the magazine reproduced in her own handwriting. One question left a blank at: 'I want to ___ Aaron Pedersen' (Indigenous TV-presenter, co-host of *Gladiators* at that time). The blank was shown filled in with red pen: 'I want to ... kiss ... Aaron Pedersen.' Pedersen himself appeared in *Studio for Men*, as a new, sexy Aboriginal face, dressed in a stylish suit. Just as he was presented as kissable in *Star!*, so it was that in *Juice* magazine's list of the 20 sexiest people in Australia (1995), Anu took the number 8 slot; just above Anne Fulwood (Channel 10 newsreader) and below Deborah Conway (singer).

There is more to say about these texts than simply coding them in such categories as 'arts (subcategory, music)'. Their place in the semiosphere could not be explained by such means. Naturally, it would be both possible and proper to complete a survey of Aboriginality in the media without ever noticing or finding relevant the appearance of sensualized Indigenous bodies or references to inter-ethnic kissing. Indeed, in terms of the broad coding categories that we employed in this project, all of these articles came under the headings of 'the arts', along with traditional didgeridoo players playing for Melbourne zoo's new wallaby, for example.

But in fact these banal, generic instances of familiar popular journalism can be read as an important turning point for Indigenous media representation, along with the fictional sexualized relationship between (white) Cate Blanchett and (Indigenous) Ernie Dingo in *Heartland* (discussed in Chapter 3). Such images of mutual attractiveness between Indigenous and non-Indigenous Australians have previously been absent in Australian media, even when sexually active and exploitative relationships were common. But there's a world of difference between unadmitted interracial sex at the margins of society, where it may have expressed both colonial power and the far side of the boundary of the social, and its imaging in youth-oriented commercial media. Anu and Pedersen reverse the 'colonial' history of Indigenous sexualization. Their sexiness is that of the 'we' community—they're just stars; hardly helpless (number 1 in the *Juice* list of Australia's sexiest people is Paul Keating: not an exploited object of male lust). Their sexualized status is socially acknowledged; they literally *represent* the Indigenizing of Australia by making Indigeneity 'marriageable'. We shall explore this theme further in Chapter 8.

Law Formation: Hindmarsh and Michael Long

Previous research has focused on crime as the main way in which Aboriginality and the law interact. However, the move to an alternative notion of law, the concept of 'law formation' developed throughout this book out of Yuri Lotman's work, allows for the interaction of Aboriginality, law, and media to be understood in new ways. The media texts of 'law formation' are those which are unsurprising, reliable, and unthreatening: they may include 'banal', repetitive but central texts of 'wedom' such as weather reports, announcements of marriage, horoscopes, diets and recipes. By focusing only on 'hard' news, such material has effectively been downplayed, dismissed as trivial and unworthy of serious attention. And yet 'law-affirming' stories bring out a different kind of Indigeneity, unrecognizable in terms of the approach of 'racism and the media' studies. The case of the Hindmarsh Island story makes the point.

In 1995, a Royal Commission was established to investigate the admissibility of knowledge about 'women's business' in a dispute over the development of a bridge in South Australia. The coverage of the item in newspaper and television news was a typical 'catalogue of anomalies': it dealt with such newsworthy events as revelations, or the transgression of prohibitions (a male minister had seen female knowledge), disruptions (an Aboriginal woman had come forward to say that she knew nothing of these secret knowledges), and challenges (a journalist claimed that an Aboriginal man who had spoken against the women's business had been bribed to speak).

By contrast, magazines were not so concerned with this 'catalogue of anomalies'. They offered rather the space for 'law formation'; for articles that were people-centred, concerned with the structures within society, with family, and with memory. On 17 July 1995, *Who Weekly*'s cover story was 'Once they were N E R D S ! But look at them now. A surprising gallery of famous faces who could hardly get a date at school.' It also featured: 'Blind Love: Inspired by his family and a special mate, Nicholas Killen triumphs over the loss of his sight to pen adventure tales' (56). Into this mix was poured an article called 'Troubled Waters', about Hindmarsh Island.

The first point about it was that it did not present an adversarial binarism in which two sides were set in confrontation, with the aim of discovering truth via 'ordeal by argument'. Instead, 'Troubled Waters' presented three points of view, each with a degree of sympathy:

When 19 year old Doreen Kartinyeri glimpsed a map of Adelaide's Hindmarsh Island for the first time one afternoon in December 1964, the young Aborigine with a deep interest in her ancestry was paralysed with excitement: 'I was stunned,' recalls Kartinyeri... (24)

This opening paragraph was printed underneath a photograph of Kartinyeri, standing before an 'Aboriginal' dot painting, staring at the camera with her arms crossed. The language used was informal, structured as a generically typical introduction to a story in popular journalism. Kartinyeri's reminiscences and personal feelings offered a way into the story. 'Though she is now sixty, and her bespectacled eyes are surrounded by wrinkles, she has a clear vision of the day when she first saw the map.'

The story went on to introduce from Kartinyeri's point of view the couple who were hoping to develop the island: 'Four decades on, Kartinyeri is leading the fight against developers who have big plans for the land.' To begin with, these 'developers' were figures in Kartinyeri's personal narrative, their timescale introduced in terms of her life experiences; while the language of 'leading the fight' made clear that a certain heroism was understood to rest with the Aboriginal woman.

Later in this story, the developers were given a chance to present their story, or rather, and significantly, the female developer was given that chance. While a photograph showed 'Wendy Chapman with her husband Tom', it was only Wendy who spoke: and this became important in the way her point of view was constructed as well. Chapman's story was introduced with a sympathetic sentence similar to Kartinyeri's: 'Meanwhile, Adelaide developers Tom and Wendy Chapman have watched their life's dream ebb away...' (24). ' "We have no income, no assets,

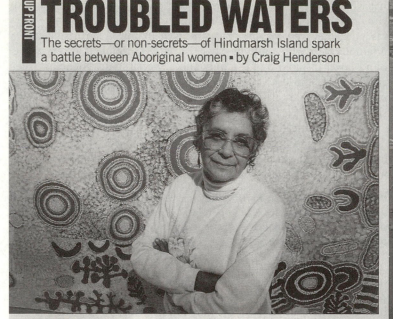

TROUBLED WATERS

The secrets—or non-secrets—of Hindmarsh Island spark
a battle between Aboriginal women ▪ by Craig Henderson

WHEN 19-YEAR-OLD DOREEN Kartinyeri glimpsed a map of Adelaide's Hindmarsh Island for the first time one afternoon in December 1954, the young Aborigine with a deep interest in her ancestry was paralysed with excitement. "I was stunned," recalls Kartinyeri. Though she is now 60 and her bespectacled eyes are surrounded by wrinkles, she has a clear vision of the day when she first saw the map whose contours, she says, mirror the shape of the female reproductive system. "I was able to see with my own eyes what the island meant to the really old Aboriginal women, my great-great-grandmother."

Four decades on, Kartinyeri is leading the fight against developers who have big plans for the island, which is cradled in the mouth of the Murray River, about 80km south of Adelaide. But the building of a multi-million-dollar bridge connecting the island to the mainland at Goolwa has been stalled while the dispute over the island's mystical history goes before the courts.

Hindmarsh is no ordinary land-rights battle. Kartinyeri and her supporters claim the island is sacred ground and home to the Ngarrindjeri tribe's secrets relating to "women's business", which must not be shared with men. In response, at least six women from the same tribe say Kartinyeri's views are rubbish and her claims are groundless. "There is no such thing as women's business and no such thing as men's business," says Ngarrindjeri elder Dulcie Wilson, 63. The dispute has split the tribe of about 2,000 members into bitter factions and led to a royal commission in South Australia (due to begin next week) and a judicial inquiry in Canberra.

Meanwhile, Adelaide developers Tom and Wendy Chapman have watched their life's dream ebb away in the swamp of inquiries and arguments. "It's plunged the whole family into the darkest year of our lives," says Wendy Chapman. "We have

▲ "I learned all these things from my Auntie Rose," says Kartinyeri of the Hindmarsh Island secrets. "Because my mother had died, she felt it was her duty to tell me."

➤ A recent aerial view of Hindmarsh Island. "We knew Hindmarsh Island was there," says Ngarrindjeri dissident Bertha Gollan. "And then all of a sudden, out of the blue, it's all this secret business."

7. Troubled Waters. Law-formation via *Who Weekly*'s narration of 'truth, integrity a

been a victim of political crossfire and point-scoring." In March 1993, the Chapmans signed an agreement with the then-Labor government in South Australia and with the district councils of Port Elliot and Goolwa that a state-backed bridge would be built to connect Hindmarsh with the mainland. Once the bridge was confirmed—with no sign of protest—the couple continued with the first leg of their six-stage project on the partly developed island—a $175 million, 360-berth marina, lagoon and residential development. "To go to the next stage," explains Wendy Chapman, "the requirement of our planning approval was for the bridge to be built."

However, on July 10 last year, before work on the 200-metre, $6.4 million bridge even began, Aboriginal and Torres Strait Islander Affairs Minister Robert Tickner, acting largely on Kartinyeri's claims,

▲ "We have no income, no assets, no nothing," says Wendy Chapman, with husband Tom on the marina at their partly completed development.

slapped a 25-year ban on its construction. Without the bridge, the final five stages of the Chapmans' development are nothing but a pipe-dream, though the mounting debt is all too real. They now owe Westpac Banking Corporation

gossip'. *Source: Who Weekly, No. 177 (July 17 1995)*

no nothing," says Wendy Chapman' (25). The language was obviously as sympathetic to this woman as it had been to Kartinyeri.

The third position to be given a voice and a legitimated point of view in the story was that of a group of Aboriginal women represented by Dulcie Wilson. ' "The state government is only listening to one side", Wilson says.' These viewpoints were spoken as a counterpoint to Kartinyeri's throughout the story: ' "There's no such thing as women's business and no such thing as men's business", says Ngarrindjeri elder Dulcie Wilson.' But the distribution of sympathy between three stances, personalized through three women, prevented the article from being structured as a simple binary: right/wrong. The search for 'truth' seemed to be less important than arriving at an understanding that each side required some sympathy. Nobody was simply wrong, no one isolated as an obvious threat.

Who Weekly's advertising slogan at that time was 'Truth, integrity and a little gossip'. The 'little gossip' was not in opposition to truth, but a necessary corollary to it. The 'truth' which was sought in 'Troubled Waters' was not adversarial and 'legal', but discovered in private, domestic and non-confrontational ways that have traditionally been marked as both private and 'feminine'. The authenticity of speakers, the guarantee that they have a right to speak on these issues, came from locating them within the private and domestic arenas of childhood and the family. So for Wendy Chapman: 'It's plunged the whole family into the darkest years of our lives.' The issue was of Wendy and her children, how the events have affected them. This tendency, moving away from public rights and wrongs to private experiences, was most obvious in the account given of the two Aboriginal women's points of view. No academic, government, or expert voices were called in to judge between the two women's accounts; rather, each was allowed to present a personal story:

'The government took me away and put me in a Salvation Army girl's home at Fullarton...' says Kartinyeri, exhaling cigarette smoke in the lounge room of a friend's home... 'When I was thirteen I got expelled...I knew I had lost my chances at a European education, so I was determined to learn everything I can about my Aboriginal people, which is what I've done...' (26)

It was important that Kartinyeri learned the secret-sacred knowledge which is in dispute 'while Terry and Uncle Nat went shooting or running the net or fishing on the beach'. Similarly, Dulcie Wilson and the Aboriginal women who opposed Kartinyeri's claims were allowed to make an appeal to the same validated space of childhood and family: 'Ironically, the leaders of the rival female factions grew up on the same settlement... [Kartinyeri's story] is nonsense according to some Ngar-rindjeri women who grew up on Point McLeay Mission alongside Kartinyeri' (26, 27).

In this way, *Who Weekly* offered 'gossip' (family and neighbourhood talk) as the mode in which truth was negotiated. To talk about families, about childhood experiences, aunts, uncles, and sitting on the beach together, this was 'gossip'. The photograph of Dulcie Wilson and 'her supporters' that illustrated the story showed them in a group sitting around a kitchen table. In this magazine's coverage of a 'law' issue (Hindmarsh), its generic status as woman's magazine and its avowed (albeit knowingly ironic) commitment to 'truth, integrity and a little gossip' allowed Aboriginality to be written into cultural law-formation via the family and situated talk, rather than just via 'the law'. The 'law' that was ultimately affirmed was that of the primacy of family, of personal experience, and of stories that locate 'truths' somewhere close to 'home'.

Such stories were not concerned with 'one-off exceptional events, but events which are out of time and endlessly repeated' (Lotman, 1990: 152–3). Among the latter, sport figured prominently. Cyclical and regular, with well-known and predictable seasons, sporting events did not occur at the edge of society. They were not like crime, though they were often violent and competitive; they were not like wars, although they featured fighting between opposing sides. Sports served as games and as rituals, working simultaneously to separate people out (winners from the losers) and to bring people together (supporters' communities in particular, the sport-loving community more generally). The distinction present in the umbrella term 'news and sport' made clear that these were not the same thing, but also that they were closely connected. The sports segment that followed the news on each of Australia's commercial television channels provided a series of texts which were involved, once again, in 'law formation': not establishing the boundaries of the 'we' community, but celebrating the very centre of culture. Whereas the gossip of *Who Weekly* was law formation in a feminized space, sport provided a primarily masculinized version of the same work.

Once again, the largely neglected arena of magazine journalism pro-vided examples of Aboriginality being written into 'law formation'. *Inside Sport* published a profile of Aboriginal Australian Rules football player Michael Long: 'True Colours' (July 1995: 69–77). Dealing with Long's experience of being racially abused during a game, the focus of the article was on Long's personal feelings about the experience. Although contemporary legislative issues (the introduction of a Racial Vilification bill) might have been regarded as relevant, in fact this governmental (legal) response to the situation was not mentioned in the course of an extensive interview. Part of the focus was individualized, the personal reaction of Michael Long to the abuse: 'Even though they say these things, they don't really know how it feels to a person. You react to it,' Long said (73). It also became an issue of family. Long said: 'I wouldn't like my kids to play in the AFL and have to put up with the sort of stuff I have' (74):

Some people will never understand where I come from, or where my family come from... They were taken away from their families—they didn't have a choice, and didn't have a say (74).

The arena of childhood reminiscence informed Long's arguments:

As a kid it doesn't cross your mind what colour the other kids are, so it's probably the way you're brought up. It's probably things you hear at school or in the streets... (75).

... or at football matches (although the media were an obvious potential target, Long didn't blame them here). However, he did identify sport as an arena with important influence over children:

[Racial taunts] are not part of football... These are the nineties... [Mal Brown] is saying that sort of thing in the media while kids are looking to him as a role model, so what effect is this having on kids? (75).

Inside Sport refused to turn to the law against racial vilification. There was no discussion, for example, of whether Long felt that making such talk illegal was a useful move (although he did refer to it in passing as a 'crime'). Rather, this was a story about Michael Long's personal responses, appeals to family and memories of childhood, and his acknowledgement of the place of sport in forming communities. Such feature journalism evidently produces a different kind of Indigeneity from 'hard' news. The 'narrative accrual' of Indigeneity in this context may be better suited to Indigenous images than the combative mode of front-page conflict.

Flagging an Imagined Nation

Was there such a thing as an Indigenous nation? It turned out that there was—in the imagined space of the semiosphere. It was insistently, consistently, perhaps even obsessively, labelled with the Aboriginal flag (the Torres Strait flag, by contrast, was never seen). The link between sports and politics via the flag could be seen at its most intense in the furore emerging in the letters pages of the newspapers following Cathy Freeman's victory lap at the 1994 Commonwealth Games carrying both Australian and Aboriginal flags.

During the 1995 survey week, public debate was conducted on the official recognition by the Federal Australian Government of Aboriginal and Torres Strait Islander flags. The news angle of the story was simply that John Howard (then leader of the federal Opposition) had condemned the move. Editorials were supportive of official recognition: 'A flag for reconciliation' (new95051, the *Age*): 'the Essendon footballer Che Cockatoo Collins ran the Aboriginal flag up the . . . flagpole yesterday . . . the flag that was once a symbol of protest has now been officially recognised by the Australian government.' The article went on to suggest that it was the action of Cathy Freeman that made this move possible.

Che Cockatoo Collins himself gave soundbites to ABC Radio National and 6WF: 'the Aboriginal people have always had the flag . . . for it to be recognised is very encouraging for us to know . . .' (rad95002). The story also appeared on Triple J (rad95024). A photograph of Che Cockatoo Collins in front of the flag (new95077) suggested the possibility that he be identified as a sports politician: 'Essendon footballer Che Cockatoo Collins raised a giant Aboriginal flag in Elizabeth Street yesterday—a week after Opposition leader John Howard said the flag should not be officially recognised.' Howard and Collins were linked as political leaders of their respective communities. The flag was likewise featured in the *Age* (new95049), and mentioned in news stories (Radio National, rad95007, 002).

The flag provided a way of recognizing the importance of the 'cultural' rather than simply the economic in dealing with the future of Indigenous and non-Indigenous relations. The *Courier Mail* discussed 'the disgraceful conditions in which many black Australians live', and suggested that 'the root causes of the situation . . . can be found in cultural dispossession; this is why official recognition of the Aboriginal and Torres Strait Islander flags was an essential and sensible step' (new95021). The move to recognise the Indigenous flags officially featured strongly in letters pages, being used to focus discussion on political relations between Aboriginal and non-Aboriginal people. In the *Sydney Morning Herald*, letters were supportive of recognition (new95179, 178, 177, 176, 175). Conversely, in the *Herald Sun* letters tended to attack recognition (new95082, 085, 080, 079), preferring 'unity': 'We should all unite under one flag'; 'dividing the nation'; 'One flag for one people.' Similarly, in the *Sunday Times*, letters worried about divisiveness and the status of the Aboriginal flag: 'the Aboriginal flag belongs in the same category as hotels [and] motels . . .' (new95170). Letters to the *Australian*

8. True Colours. Footballer Michael Long brings Aboriginality, family, and childhoo

MICHAEL LONG'S
TRUE
COLOURS

> "THIS SPORT IS MY LIVING, AND I DON'T THINK ANYONE DESERVES TO BE RACIALLY TAUNTED. IF IT KEEPS HAPPENING, YOU HAVE TO WONDER WHETHER THERE'LL BE ABORIGINES STILL PLAYING IN THE FUTURE."

by ross stapleton

April 25, 1995.

Anzac Day. With 95,000 people shoe-horned into an overflowing MCG, and another 15,000 unhappily locked out, the AFL's greatest contemporary enemies staged one of their greatest battles. Here was Collingwood, without a win after the opening three rounds, frantic for victory; and Essendon, their bitter rival, so far unbeaten. Two hours later, when hostilities ceased, not a single point separated them. But in the dying minutes, as the teams crunched flesh furiously, another drama gatecrashed the arena as Essendon's mercurial Aboriginal mid-fielder, Michael Long, tackled Magpie ruck giant Damian Monkhorst to the ground. In the ensuing fray, Long took exception to being called either "a black bastard" or "a black cunt" (depending on the witnesses surrounding the combatants at the time); Monkhorst subsequently found himself being publicly denounced by Long as racist.

It was a clash that would force a re-evaluation of race relations in Australian sport. The AFL found itself uncomfortably holding a very hot political football – so hot they proceeded to

photo by peter barnes

the 'narrative accrual' of Australia. *Source: Inside Sport No. 43 (July 1995)* followed this pattern. The flag was 'divisive', asserted one letter writer, who was against 'special entitlements' for 'some groups' (new95009; see also 008 and 003) A letter in the *Courier Mail* suggested that the recognition of the flag represented a step towards reconciliation (new95022).

The recognition of Indigenous flags was also noted on Radio National news (rad95111) and 6WF (rad95144). A discussion on the flag on 6PR featured presenter Howard Sattler, federal Minister Robert Tickner, and Labor politician Kim Beazley. Beazley explicitly disarticulated flag and nation:

SATTLER. There are some people who do want a separate Aboriginal nation.
BEAZLEY. I don't think that's on the cards ... what is on the cards is that they get proper recognition for their property rights, for the health and social needs.
(rad95010)

A caller to *Australia Talks Back* said, 'this flag symbolises the long struggle for justice' (rad95152). In an earlier edition of *Australia Talks Back*, guests David Byrne, the deputy director of the Cape York Land Council, Harold Thomas, the designer of the flag, and Tim Rowse, Aboriginalist academic, discussed the recognition of the flag. Callers said that 'we owe them [Aborigines] so very much', that the recognition is 'long overdue' (rad95028) and 'shows Australia to be a tolerant and democratic nation', Tim Rowse said the flag was important for 'new notions of nationhood'.

On Triple J, another talkback elicited comments criticizing the perceived divisiveness of the recognition of the flag—'it's a nation within a nation.' Such opinions were voiced in a talkback show hosted by Aboriginal presenter Jack Beatson (rad95018, 019, 020, 021, 022); his comments favouring the recognition of the flag contextualized such opinions.

During the three years of the surveys, television stations in particular used the flag as a standard icon for Aboriginality. On ABC news (12 July 1996, tv96100) a story about Aboriginal-owned Carey Mining was introduced with a graphic displaying the Aboriginal flag, as was the ABC TV news item on our National Media Forum (16 February 1996). Similarly, Channel Seven news on 12 July 1996 introduced a story on Nelson Mandela with a graphic showing Mandela's face in front of both British and Aboriginal flags (tv96108). It would have been possible to present the story with the Australian flag.

It's not much, but it does seem to indicate a kind of commonsensical, 'de facto' national status for Indigenous Australia.

8 | Reporting Indigeneity: Magazines, Radio, TV, and Sport

The stories that have been told by the old people are still with us... With that, and the land which is our mother, we are a nation.

(Robert Bropho, 1995)

In this chapter, we apply Yuri Lotman's (1990) distinction between 'law-forming' and 'anomalous' stories to the minutiae of media texts. Earlier in this study we applied the distinction to larger-scale structures in the 'universe of Indigeneity'. We believe that the same structure of distinction holds (in a fractal manner) right through from forms (soap opera and news), via genres (features and 'hard' news) to the level of individual stories. 'Law formation' refers to stories where the construction of communities by a ritualized and familiar address to known (banal but central) aspects of cultural life is paramount. A 'catalogue of anomalies' refers to stories about the dangerous, the unfamiliar, and the threatening. In other words, 'law formation' is not the same as 'laying down the law' or speaking authoritatively in a legal speech act. While it helps to affirm the central semiotic structures of a given cultural domain, the stories themselves and the forms in which they appear, may appear 'banal', if by that is meant familiar, everyday, confirming of experience and belief, reinforcing of habits of thought and speech. In what follows we are especially interested in appearances of Indigeneity within the 'law-forming' aspect of media story-telling, since both academic and media attention has hitherto been focused obsessively on the 'catalogue of anomalies'. It follows, perversely, that 'banality' in this context is something of an achievement, not a misfortune.

Rock Art (Indigeneity Outside the Traditional Public Sphere)

'Bad' practice: isolated examples

It is worth starting our analysis with a general point: we have found that most media practice is not racist. This is not to say that all practice is good; but that there are few examples which can be pointed to as obviously racist (McKee, 1997c). A few examples of 'bad' practice can be cited, but they stand as exceptions. For example, there are breaches of the 'AJA code of ethics' (see Chapter 10). This is essentially a voluntary code for journalists who join the union, and it is not binding on employers. As it stood between 1985 and 1995, the AJA code addressed *race* reporting thus:

[Journalists] shall not place unnecessary emphasis on gender, race, sexual preference, religious belief, marital status or physical or mental disability.

It is possible to point to obvious breaches of this code. Nevertheless, our survey reveals a far more complex and multifaceted construction of Indigenous presence than might be suggested by simple accusations of 'racism' or bad practice in the placing of 'unnecessary emphasis' on race. An interesting example came in a magazine that gloried in perhaps the most unrepentantly offensive Indigenous coverage—and which was yet difficult to name 'racist' in the sense of holding to a hierarchy of superiority and inferiority based on racial difference. The magazine was *Lock, Stock and Barrel*, for gun owners.

In an article 'Stranger on the Shore', the editor compared bulldog breeding with Aboriginal breeding. He felt sorry for 'aborigines' [*sic*]—if there were any full pure-blooded aborigines left. Compared with the bulldog who has his 'papers to prove [he is] a pure Staffordshire bull terrier', most Aborigines were 'fair-haired blue-eyed impersonators who have been filching 2 billion dollars from Australians'. '[T]hese half or three-quarter or less aborigines who seek to live off the back of the people who work... are multiraced... they're humans, but they're not abs'. He also asserted that 'abs killed sailors, women and children' (mag94074).

Even here, the situation was not simply about racism: the writer celebrated the lack of distinct races, and suggested that he sympathized with 'aboriginal' people (followed by the usual 'but...'). The article relied on a conception of race that saw only 'pure' genes as determining ethnic identity (mixed genes produced 'humans' not races), felt unashamed in using the term 'ab', and presented a profoundly ethnocentric reading of Australian history—the 'abs' killed 'women and children'. They were not involved in a war of occupation, according to this account. It is simple enough to locate the address of this particular magazine. An advertisement for a book in its 'Lock, Stock and Barrel library' brought together a series of political allegiances. The book *Red Over Black* promised to go 'Behind the Aboriginal land rights', to tell 'the story of Marxist manipulation of the Aboriginal land rights movement' (mag94066). Other books in the library told of the homosexual conspiracy to destroy the family unit, and the Fabian incursion into Australian society. This was designed for a reactionary readership, but even here, it was problematic simply to apply the label 'racism'. The term 'red over black' presumed that Indigenous Australians must have been politically organized by outside forces; and quite clearly the magazine wanted to deracinate Aboriginal people in order to delegitimate their claims for rights. But it did not hierarchize people by race—it was fundamentally an argument seeking to oppose claims for government funding based on racial difference, on the grounds that the claimants were 'multi-raced'. Tolerance was expressed for 'real' Aborigines (who were presumed to be quiet, living outside the city, not making political claims). *Lock, Stock and Barrel* emerged as a profoundly assimilationist journal: an ethnocentric but not a racist position. Its project was political—competing for scarce resources on the basis of arguments about the rights and merits of people understood to be *equal*.

Culture as nature: Ecotouring with the elders

The rest of the magazine sphere constructed quite different forms of Indigeneity, often in celebratory tones. Magazines provided a variety of specific areas in which Aboriginality flourished. One of these was in nature magazines. Indigeneity was routinely associated with nature; for example, in the title sequences of television programmes. *Bush Beat* (tv95134), a nature programme, included a didgeridoo and rock art on its credits. *Landline* (tv95019), the ABC's rural current affairs show, included sheep, sunsets, landscapes, clapsticks, and didgeridoo. The 1994 survey week presented a story that closely linked Indigenous people and nature: a story from Melbourne with visuals of a cute baby wallaby in a zoo and Indigenous dancers in traditional body paint. This received national coverage, and proved very attractive (i.e. readily recognizable) to television as well as to the newspapers (tv94002, 003, 112).

In nature magazines, a particular version of Indigeneity was proposed, bringing together nature, culture, art, and spirituality to create

Indigeneity as a *place*: or at least, as something that could be *visited*. This was the Indigeneity of tourism, and it formed a distinct genre in magazines such as *ANH* and *Geo*. Billy Can tours (mag94068, 069) offered 'the spirit of Australia's top end'; 'Ecotours' provided 'an authentic cultural experience' (mag94067). Readers of *Geo* were invited to 'Experience the spirit of Australia' (mag94057), to go 'Ecotouring with the elders' (mag94023), and 'Experience the wisdom and lifestyle of the traditional Pitjantjatjara people' (mag94013). A culture was on offer, linked directly to nature ('eco-touring'), and to art: the 'Broken Hill Outback tour' offered 'superb Aboriginal rock engravings and wildlife' (mag94055); 'Broken Hills outback tour' (mag95039); 'Australia's Northern Territory...examine an Aboriginal art collection' (mag95037), 'Experience what life was like in Australia 60,000 years ago' (mag95041, all in *Geo Australia*); 'Sharing the dreaming—Australian Academic tours' (mag95048, *Nature Australia*); 'Pitjantjara [*sic*] tours...Experience the wisdom and lifestyle of traditional Pitjantjara people in Central Australia' (mag95043, *Geo Australia*). Aboriginal culture was constructed as nature—'Aboriginal rock engravings and wildlife'. From a non-Indigenous perspective, 'traditional' Indigenous cultures were collapsed into nature, as can be seen in the focus on rock art in both advertisements and editorial. *Geo Australia* (mag95040) presented a story on rock art that linked art, culture, history, and nature. In *Bush Driver*, Aboriginal rock art was presented as part of an article on Carnarvon Gorge (mag95032): 'Its presence has been known to man for at least 20,000 years'.

The transformation (a characteristic of 'law-affirming texts') of 'art' into 'culture' into 'nature' was notable— the emphasis was as much on the 'rock' as it was on the 'art'. Authentic, natural, spiritual culture: the terms collapsed together, inventing a 'real' Aboriginality that could adequately function as the centre of Australianness— 'Experience the spirit of Australia'. Such a construction silently suggested that, by comparison, there must have been something *inauthentic* close by—an Indigeneity that did not follow these terms, one whose 'culture' did not rely on nature, and was thus less deserving of the name 'culture' at all. This tendency could be seen in *Nature Australia*, with a book review of *The Encyclopedia of Aboriginal Australia*. Why should such a review appear in a magazine about nature? The culture of Aboriginal Australia was presumed to be part of nature: from a non-Indigenous perspective, the two collapsed together.

Nature magazines and their advertisements constructed a public, addressed as explicitly white, who wanted to discover Australia, who desired meaning, and who could find it 'ecotouring with the elders'.

Aboriginality was an essentially Australian object, a place that could be visited by white Australians by means of travelling, moving through space and, it was implied, through time. 'Experience what life was like in Australia 60,000 years ago'.

The idea of tourism also constructed Indigeneity as outside the space of everyday life. Tourism was done in time off, time away, from the everyday, and the banal. The search for the 'spirit' of Australia was not an everyday pursuit. It had to be done in spaces and times well beyond backyards and clock time. It was in the language of tourism that one of the few appeals to 'authentic' Aboriginal culture was carried out in the mediasphere; and here, that appeal was relentless.

Bush Driver: the colonial impulse

In another group of magazines, the desire to travel to the authentic (Aboriginal, natural) Australia became explicitly colonial. In '4 × 4' magazines (i.e. magazines about four-wheel drive vehicles), Australia was presented as a natural landscape, a latter-day *terra nullius*, there for non-Indigenous people to enter, indeed to penetrate (mag94007), a right apparently conferred by ownership of a 4 × 4. This idea of a basic right to access to country was colonialist: Indigenous people's cultures and concerns were irrelevant. In a letter to 4 × 4, 'Simpson access' (mag95034), a writer became angry that the Central Land Council had denied access to the Simpson Desert for drivers. In another story in the same magazine, an intrepid (non-Indigenous) explorer crossed the Simpson by camel: 'Ted Colson, in 1936, became the first white man to cross the Simpson desert by camel...Last year, Denis Bartell took Danny Colson for a "Dream Time" trip into his fathers [*sic*] past'. This was a story concerned with non-Indigenous experience, addressing a non-Indigenous audience. It was concerned with exploring, mapping, conquering nature. More than this, the story centred on a non-Indigenous man, but showed him reintroducing an Indigenous man to his family—leading him back to his 'Dream Time'. It presented a non-Indigenous man conquering nature, taking an Indigenous man, and leading him back to his culture. A more precise imagining of non-Indigenous control over and use of both Indigeneity and nature could hardly be imagined. This is a 'law-affirming' story, told at just the moment when that law (*terra nullius*) had just been white-anted by Mabo.

The editorial of 4 × 4 (mag95034) presented a good example of a colonialist approach to knowledge as well as to land and heritage. Indigeneity was something that could be *known* and discussed. Indigeneity was understood as a simple object about which it was suitable to have an *opinion*. Not only did this approach reduce the experiences of all Indigenous Australians across time and space to a knowable object, but it also presumed that everyone was an expert on Indigeneity. So the editor of *4 × 4* ('4word') asked, 'Is Aboriginal welfare working?':

At the risk of being called a bigot, I think I've seen enough to comment... In the past 20 years, around $10 billion... has been spent on Aboriginal welfare... 'Sit down benefits', which we know as unemployment benefits... are doled out to Aboriginal groups under fancy names... but all this has seemed to do is to encourage dependence... Somehow a mutual obligation between us—as the government provider of money—and them as the recipient of this public money, must be established... As well, undoubtedly there are a number of powerful vested interest groups within the Aboriginal welfare organisations ...

The assumptions of this narrative were that Aboriginal people were excluded from the government and the public; that non-Indigenous people paid taxes, while Indigenous people did not; that welfare benefits provided to non-Indigenous people were justified and did not cause dependency (Medicare, education, for example); that non-Indigenous welfare organizations were all neutral and objective.

Esoterica

Closely linked to nature was the idea that Indigeneity in Australia was spiritual. The link could be seen in a *National Geographic* story in 1996: 'Australia's Cape York Peninsula'. At 31 pages and with 21 colour pictures, this was the lengthiest and most detailed item on Indigeneity in that year's magazine survey. The story was illustrated (including the cover) with photographs of Indigenous people in poses that might be named generically as 'National Geographic style' (young, pretty Indigenous girl immersed in river with only her head visible). The story began:

Conjuring an image as old as his ancestors, an Aboriginal teenager dons a mask of mud while swimming in a billabong... for nearly 2000 generations, his people have inhabited this wild and strangely beautiful spike of land... steeped in the supernatural, it endures as a stronghold of native culture.

In the realm of hard news, land rights had by this time been recognized as political. But in the nature/spirituality nexus that provided more Indigenous coverage than any other in magazines, the move to the political had not been accomplished. Indigenous people were resolutely non-material. In describing Indigenous concerns in relation to the land, the spiritual was taken as a suitable frame of understanding, but a peculiarly Western form of spirituality. Magazines like *Simply Living* and

Esoterica provided an important site for constructing Indigeneity. As Julie Marcus has noted, Indigenous culture in such spiritual sites tended to be taken up not in its specificity, but to support non-Indigenous understandings of a general spirituality (Marcus, 1988). This indeed proved to be the case. *Esoterica* presented a story on 'Sacred Site Healing' (mag95033). Indigenous owners of these sites were mentioned, but this was not a story about Indigenous understandings of sacred sites. Rather, the sites were potentially healing in 'non-Western' ways. Similarly, in *Simply Living* (mag95057), a story on a visiting Native American, called Eagle Man, linked Indigenous Australians and Americans (photographs showed an Aboriginal man playing a didgeridoo for him): a generalized Indigeneity. A general sphere of the 'other' to rationalist projects was constructed— for example, Indigenous culture was aligned with 'alternative' medicines (as opposed to Western medicine) (mag94036).

The equation of nature and spirituality with Indigeneity could become clichéd. One television item in 1994 is worth mentioning. The advertisement for the Mitsubishi Pajero car (tv94005, 079) included shots of Aboriginal people intercut with frilly lizards (a fairly direct equation of Indigeneity and nature). The Aboriginal people were painted in traditional ways, but the shots of them were distorted as though in fairground mirrors. They were placed in nature, rendered traditional, and presented in a way that broke up their bodies: a dehumanizing rendition. They didn't get to drive the car; it drove through their country, presumably communicating their spirit to the non-Indigenous driver.

Arts

Aboriginality was represented most visibly in magazines by means of visual art. Stories on nature and Indigeneity have already brought art into the mediasphere. Pictures of Indigenous art objects were particularly visible in art magazines, in reviews and articles, advertisements for exhibitions and competitions (mag94031, 032, 034); (mag95005, 006, 007, 008, 009, 010, 011, 012, 013, 014, 015, 016—all in *Art and Australia*, 069, in *World Art*). Since many Indigenous art traditions have not tended towards the figurative, a series of non-iconic visual representations came to stand for 'Indigeneity', facilitating a break between Indigenous people and Indigenous 'culture'. The latter, not fully embodied in Indigenous people, came to stand as a distinct and available quality— 'the spirit of Australia'—in which individual Indigenous people may have been largely uninvolved. The linking of culture with nature, as effected in the nature magazines, was reciprocated in art magazines. *Art and Australia* (mag95014) moved from art to promote tourism with an advertisement in the same vein as those in the nature magazines. Once again, nature, culture, and art were linked in the concept of 'rock art'.

Outside of the traditional public sphere

Apart from the news journals that form only a small percentage of Australian magazines, and of items in this survey, magazines in Australia tended to construct Indigeneity in ways which caused it to fall outside of the traditional space of the 'bourgeois public sphere'; i.e. somewhere beyond 'rationality' and 'politics'. Most Indigenous items could be placed in realms such as spirituality, nature, the arts. This said less about Indigeneity than about magazines, of course. The magazine universe is not governed entirely by the rationality of the Habermasian public sphere; it may even form a necessary ground against which the rational-political is contrasted. To *confine* Indigeneity to this area is therefore not without political consequences, not only for Indigenous people who are seeking to politicize the Indigenous domain, but also for the very idea of the 'public sphere', which cannot survive as 'rational' and 'political' if it is structured systematically to remove whole populations from its compass.

Sport

The survey of Indigenous items in magazines also suggests that sport was an important part of the Indigenous mediasphere. This was a space in which Indigeneity was visualized as corporeal, in contrast to the 'rock art' and spirituality that signified Indigeneity in art, nature, and tourism journalism. But as with Indigenous coverage in arts magazines, the coverage in sports magazines was insistently visual. Indigeneity was visualized in a series of glossy and attractive colour pictures, whether of Indigenous artworks or of Indigenous AFL players.

An interview with Australian Rules footballer Michael Long in *Inside Sport* (discussed in Chapter 7) was illustrated with a series of colour photographs of the Indigenous body beautiful (he has his shirt off). Football provided a whole series of visualized moments of Indigeneity. Chris Lewis (West Coast Eagles; see also Chapter 4) was presented in a series of colour posters (mag95001, 066). Other Indigenous footballers were presented in colour pictures (mag95002, 003, 004). Sporting pictures were an interesting site in journalism. Their appeal was not to represent a person (they did not simply illustrate stories about an individual). Neither were they simply aesthetic. Rather, they presented moments of spectacular bodily achievement, especially putting bodies into extremes of competitive crisis. They imagined the possibilities of the body. Indigeneity was well written into this discourse.

Westside Football and *Football Action* provided a substantial number of the Indigenous presences in our survey. These tended to be in stories which were not 'about' Indigeneity, although they could be found in items 'about' Indigenous players, and where Indigeneity became important in a variety of ways. Aboriginal footy player Gary Dhurrkay, in his poster-biography in *Westside Football*, for example, gave his 'favourite player' as legendary Aboriginal footballer Maurice Rioli. In fact sport emerged from our survey as a vital part of the wider Australian engagement with Indigeneity, in television and newspapers as well as in magazines. In relation to the presence of Indigeneity in sports magazines, we note simply that this was the space where the most *glossy* photographs of Indigeneity are presented—the site where the Indigenous body is most intensely visualized.

Indigenous bodies were often presented as spectacular, as worthy of being looked at. This occurred when 'traditional' bodies were presented in 'NAIDOC' stories (for example, new95044); and in sports (focus of attention as spectacular, with physical capabilities). The presentation of spectacular bodies, it must be borne in mind, is a generic imperative of sports photography. Presenting the *Indigenous* sporting body within the terms of this genre served to make Indigeneity part of the imagery of the 'we' community.

A 'little black bum' for Australia—marriageability

Indigenous people were shown as being sexy and stylish. In Australian journalism, this is a consistent trope for 'like-us-ness'. Whenever early observers wanted to enlist the sympathy of readers for Indigenous people in town camps, homes, or institutions, for instance, they took pains to describe the girls as pretty and the men as being of 'splendid physique' or manly (Jacobs, 1990: 188). A. O. Neville, Protector of Aborigines in Western Australia in the 1930s, for instance, was given to this rhetorical mode of proposing the 'whiteness' of Indigenous people. In opposition to then prevailing ideas of racial purity, he described mixed-descent Aboriginal people thus: 'Many are handsome, even beautiful, gentle mannered, soft-voiced girls, speaking perfectly enunciated, if somewhat abbreviated English' (quoted in Jacobs, 1990: 193). Neville made the comparison with whiteness explicit:

scores of people, externally indistinguishable from whites, are living like beasts in these camps. In one camp we saw several children with flaming red hair! Dozens of these people taken out of the squalid setting of a native camp and seen differently clad in a wholly white environment, would be accepted without question as people of white parentage. Some of the girls are quite strikingly pretty, and I even saw one who might have sat for Raphael's Madonna. (Quoted in Jacobs, 1990: 195–6. See also the amazing picture of just such a 'madonna' (nursing a white child) that is printed in the 'Stolen Generations' Report: it shows 'Biddy, nursemaid to Mr Mrs J S Gordon of Brewon Station, with John Gordon, Walgett, NSW, 1887' (National Inquiry, 1997: 24)).

Flame-haired madonnas, living like beasts. Redemption is clearly imagined as *romantic* (in both the philosophical and sexual senses of that word). It seems that Australian journalism has at last begun to cotton on to what Neville was trying to show: that Aboriginal people are dehumanized by the context of poverty, not parentage, and that in other environments their 'like-us-ness' would be 'accepted without question'.

The concept of 'marriageability'—of *publicly acknowledged attractiveness*—is thus useful to show how Indigenous people have been represented as being among the 'we' community. Sexiness requires inclusion within the boundaries of 'wedom', because sexual partners are generally chosen from the field of 'neighbour'; i.e. further away from 'self' than 'family', but not so far as 'stranger' (Leach, 1964). But sexual attractiveness is 'liminal' (on a threshold across and between structural boundaries). It works 'anthropologically' as part of the process whereby individuals migrate from family of origin to family of destination, and it works in the media as one of the most important vehicles for transporting meanings to readers (the other is fear: sexuality's opposite). The central structures of a 'we' community—e.g. law, home—need not be especially sexy. Thus lifestyle programmes, or *Better Homes and Gardens*, neither sexualize their own imagery nor do they tell the audience how to be sexy. But the sexualization of Indigenous people in the media serves both 'anthropological' and 'media' purposes. It places Indigenous people in the category of 'neighbour', and it incorporates their image into a communicative regime by means of which meanings are circulated among people who don't know each other, and whose relations with their community are *textualized*. Sexy text is a sure sign of the modern 'We'.

Islander singer Christine Anu (mag95047) stated that upon arrival in Sydney 'I slutted around a bit'; and she was listed as one of the '20 sexiest Australians' (mag95046). Similarly, Aaron Pedersen (Aboriginal TV presenter of *Gladiators*) became sexy—kissed by Kimberley Joseph's

"When I moved to Sydney I rebelled ... I slutted around a bit," says Anu

9. Christine Anu. Sexy text as a sure sign of the modern 'we'. *Source: Juice Magazine No. 29 (July 1995).*

imagination (mag95064), and imaged in stylish, sexy black-and-white (mag95060) (see also Chapter 7). The social pages of the *Australian Women's Weekly* write Indigeneity into the banal space of celebrity. It was Gary Sweet's wedding (the sexiest man in Australia, according to readers of *Cosmopolitan* in 1994), and guest photographs were printed. One showed 'Bill Hunter and his wife, Rhoda Roberts' (the latter is an Indigenous TV presenter). This item was obviously not 'about' Indigeneity (see above); but it extended the Indigenous mediasphere into spaces where it might not be expected: glamorous celebrity, the 'frocks pop'. The social pages in the newspapers were very similar to those in magazines. 'People on Sunday' (new95128) of the *Sunday Territorian* presented photographs of the ATSIC sports awards, including Charles Perkins and others in celebratory suits.

Christine Anu appeared as lithe, young, sexy, and stylish in her video for 'Party', which played during our survey week (tv95135). In a *Sixty Minutes* profile—'Island Girl'—she appeared in a similar way. However this item was also notable for reproducing a series of clichés, including one of the most persistent unsubstantiated rumours in Western journalism (cannibalism), in its construction of Anu's racial identity (tv95166). The voice-over for the programme began with a description of Palm Island—'a great place . . . exotic, hard to believe it's part of Australia'. 'There are rhythms and sounds here that come from a different world'. Anu was quickly placed in a similar position—she has, the voice-over informed Australian viewers, 'exotic looks'. She was shown singing as the voice-over continued to construct its image of her: 'Christine [is] the descendant of fierce seafaring warriors who less than one hundred years ago practised cannibalism'. 'It's obvious where Christine Anu's talent comes from—it's in the blood'. Clips were shown of other Islanders singing.

Aboriginal athlete Cathy Freeman has also migrated to the realm of style. She featured in a variety of advertisements, as 'we' celebrities do. There were newspaper advertisements for Australia Post, featuring her running. She appeared in TV commercials for Ford cars as part of Team Australia. She reached perhaps the innermost ring of the central circle of the 'we' community—the breakfast table—with an action portrait on the box of Kellogg's Sustain cereal (tv95027). In magazines such as *Inside Sport*, Freeman moved from sport to style, selling a deadly brand of sunglasses.

Aboriginality was linked with style and sexuality through fashion. Stories such as 'Designers embrace cultural couture' (new96123, the *West Australian*, Saturday, 13 July 1996: 9) presented precisely this kind of centred, Indigenous identity. Freeman's image also moved into such spaces. 'Fast track to the catwalk' (*New Idea*, 16 November 1996: 16–17) presented a fashion spread:

Cathy Freeman might wow them on the athletics track, but Australia's super-sprinter is moving quickly again—towards a more glamorous look. As she models Aboriginal-inspired fashions by the Balarinji label for *New Idea*... Cathy was inspired by the beauties who surrounded her at the Atlanta Olympics— black athletes including the legendary Florence Griffith-Joyner, who was an inspiration to Cathy in the early days.

Similarly, in *Who Weekly* in 1997 (with another new hairstyle), Freeman appeared in the magazine's list of five great Australian icons, along with Kylie Minogue, 'Roy and HG', Elle Macpherson, and Baz Luhrmann:

'I think everybody should be proud of who they are', says Aboriginal speed queen Cathy Freeman, 24, 'and it should give them strength'. Key word. She is strength; legs, heart, spirit. At the Atlanta Olympics last year, running—as she put it—her 'little black bum off', the rose-tattooed silver medallist won more than can be dangled on a ribbon around her neck .... There's courage and pride in her history. Freeman... caused a major stir when she ran her 1994 Commonwealth Games victory lap in Victoria, Canada, cloaked in the Aboriginal flag ...

The 1996 survey item, 'The A to Z of *Cosmo* babes', could be seen as an oddity, but it was representative of the way Freeman's image functioned in a space of law formation and 'wedom'. Freeman's body provided a direct link between marriageability (publicly acknowledged attractiveness) and national identity, running her 'little black bum off' for Australia. For *Cosmopolitan* magazine:

not only a super-athlete, Cathy is also a super-ambassador for Australia, with a tremendous spirit. Her victory lap with the Aboriginal flag will go down as one of Australian sport's finest moments. We love her!

It is obvious that there was politics involved in this: as she appeared in sites across the Australian media, Freeman's story was consistently 'about' reconciliation and nationhood, and was simultaneously presented as central to Australian culture.

Women's magazines and hierarchies of identity

Women's magazines tended to address issues that were understood to be related to gender, inflected with various age and class components (sex, cooking, emotional problems, fashion, soft furnishings, politics). Women's magazines also dealt with the biological individuals, women, and thus promoted a form of identity politics allusive of the women's

10. Cathy Freeman, reconciling two nations. 'The rose-tattooed medallist won more than can be dangled on a ribbon round her neck ...'. Here she advertises a 'deadly brand of sunglasses'. *Source: Advertisement for eyewear, Inside Sport, No. 55 (July 1996)*, © Oakley.

movement. At some points, Indigenous women were included as women first, where this followed the logic of the 'women's magazine' as the primary identity (mag94044, *New Woman*).

Also interesting was the idea of Aboriginal women's sexuality in *Australian Women's Forum*. The title 'Blood sisters' relied on a certain understanding of Indigeneity (the blood stood for the spiritually in-flected, yet somehow primitive and corporeal Aboriginality); and an overarching female identity: 'sisters'. The presentation of sexuality in this article did not work in the same way as the 'marriageability' of Christine Anu. The point of this article was to construct difference—Aboriginal culture as distinct from white culture. It proceeded in this by writing from a white point of view, from which perspective the differ-ence between 'traditional' sexual practices and 'white' practices was seen as worth commenting on, presumably for the gratification of white readers. There was no attempt to make sense of the ways in which sexuality functioned to structure Indigenous cultures.

Radio's Communities

Turning from magazines to radio broadcasting, we now explore how radio stations moulded themselves in various ways to NAIDOC week. However, this analysis is focused on the ABC (the publicly-funded Australian Broadcasting Corporation) rather than on the more general-ized 'radiosphere'. The reason is pragmatic. In the first year of our survey, a broad range of samples was taken across more radio stations. It was found, however, that most could easily be categorized as 'absence'. For later years of the project, as discussed in chapter 7, resources were focused on cataloguing the ABC, where recognizable forms of Indigene-ity did emerge. We have also not analysed 6AR, the radio station run by the Western Australian Aboriginal Media Association (WAAMA). We begin therefore with an acknowledgement that in popular music stations in (Western) Australia, Indigeneity was almost completely absent during our survey periods. If Christine Anu appeared in the Top 40, she was played, but such appearances were not 'about' Indigeneity. Anu's Islan-der heritage may have seemed an obvious intertext to bring to bear on the playing of such songs; but if so, it was not an intertext that emerged from the editorial decisions of the radio stations themselves.

On ABC-JJJ FM ('Triple J'), ABC Radio National, and ABC 720 6WF (the ABC's metropolitan station for Perth), however, the presence of NAIDOC week did reshape the stations themselves to various degrees. By contrast, on 6PR (Perth's commercial talkback station), the event remained within the confines of news stories, among the catalogue of anomalies that tended to represent external threats to the we-community of the listening audience (see Chapter 9). So how did ABC radio present Indigeneity during the survey weeks in 1994, 1995, and 1996?

Radio National

'And now for our contribution to NAIDOC week' stated the presenter of Radio National's education programme, as the didgeridoo began to play (in 1995—rad95064), going on to present a segment where an Aboriginal writer recalled childhood memories of school. This was how Radio National organized its response to NAIDOC week: regular programming made its 'contribution'. They certainly did—ABC radio consistently presented more special NAIDOC week programming than did any other medium. Some attempt was also made on ABC television, which presented a daily series of shorts in 1995 called *The Dreaming*. These five-minute animations narrated traditional Indigenous stories, and were themselves covered in other media, where their production by Indigenous artists was discussed (tv95038, 053, 055, 076, 087, 108, 129, 151, 153).

In 1996, Radio National included in its *Life Matters* programme a series of three features on the 'stolen generation'.

There's a lot of tragedy being heard by the Inquiry [into removal of Aboriginal and Torres Strait Islander children from their families], there are also stories of remarkable triumphs and alliances between Indigenous and white people... at the Perth hearings... Sadie Canning spoke... and two of the daughters of the missionaries who ran the Mount Margaret mission in the goldfields area of WA... (Geraldine Doogue, rad96099, Radio National, 8 July 1996).

Now, a case study on the impact of separating Aboriginal children from their families... a two-year-old girl from Palm Island was adopted by a middle-aged white couple... and moved to Perth... [In the] early seventies, the girl... increasingly sought out local Aboriginal people... [She] had a learning disability... her father was dead, her mother was institutionalized as an alcoholic, but there was an aunty there. Owen Hanson, an Aboriginal welfare worker... was given the job of taking the girl back to Palm Island... (Geraldine Doogue, rad96112, Radio National, 9 July 1996).

The third of our three-part series about Aboriginal family separation... is about access to records... people trying to find their families, and find out who they are... people can wait for years while the few staff... try to unearth thousands of histories... Dawn Wallem is a... senior Aboriginal policy officer with the WA government's family information service... her father's family was rounded up in the 1920s... he fought in the Second World War... in the late 50s, he separated, retaining custody of three young children... (Geraldine Doogue, rad96131, Radio National, 11 July 1996).

The features involved Indigenous voices, heard regularly throughout the week. On Radio National, the coverage of NAIDOC week appeared in such special features presented within regular ABC programming, and in news stories. There was no disruption to the schedule. NAIDOC offered Indigeneity as an item of exceptional interest. The implications of such placement can be seen by contrasting Radio National with coverage by other ABC stations, Triple J and 6WF.

6WF (ABC Perth metro station)

There are certain aspects of radio programming that don't fit the usual understanding of 'content'. Station idents or IDs, for example, are more like linguistic markers: pausing for breath, and reasserting the 'address' of the radio station as it reminds itself who it is talking to. While radio doesn't exploit the genre of continuity in the pronounced way that TV does, nevertheless, there exist on the radio some items that fit the definition of continuity. The difference between coverage of NAIDOC week on Radio National and the other ABC stations was that the others allowed Indigeneity to seep out of defined programme subject-matter to become part of the audience addressed by the continuity items of their programming.

6WF ran a series of short fillers in 1995, played regularly in the breaks between programmes, and introduced each time with a voice stating: 'As part of NAIDOC week, help us celebrate our rich Aboriginal culture' (rad95086). In one, Robert Bropho (see Chapter 5) spoke on Indigenous stories: 'The stories that have been told by the old people are still with us... With that, and the land which is our mother, we are a nation' (see rad95036, 074, 075 for other examples).

On 6WF and on Triple J, in particular, the amount of time devoted to NAIDOC week was large compared with the presence of Indigeneity in other weeks of the year. The division of media coverage into 'catalogues of anomalies' and 'law formation' proved particularly fruitful in describing the work of radio channels in making sense of Aboriginality. In short, on Australian radio, NAIDOC week was taken as an opportunity to present stories of law formation: there was a focus on 'stolen generation' children (anomalous) and on Aboriginal 'dreamtime stories' (themselves law-affirming stories, of course, within the Indigenous semiosphere itself).

Like Radio National, 6WF presented non-fictional features: a 45-minute tribute to the late Rob Riley in 1996, for example (rad96175), a report by an Aboriginal journalist (Bevan Rankin) on stolen children (rad96164), a discussion on Indigenous sovereignty (rad96193), and so on. Indigenous stories also featured in news bulletins (for example, 145, 146, rad96147). More than this, however, during NAIDOC week, 6WF devoted itself to regular, ritualized presentations of Indigeneity. Indigenous voices were presented in two regular strands. During Peter Holland's afternoon show, a series of stories based on Aboriginal 'sky figures' were read by Robert Matemate (rad96154, 184, 190, 198). Peter Holland introduced them:

NAIDOC week... starting off with a new recording of a booklet which has been released called Aboriginal sky figures... 1993, in a Melbourne hospital ward, Gordon Paxton met Aboriginal elder Gaparangu Napata, also known as Robert Matemate... Aboriginal people and their understanding of the night sky... produced an associated star map... Aboriginal understanding of the movement of planets and stars through the night sky is profound... Robert Matemate tells various stories associated with the sky figures... (Peter Holland, rad96154, 6WF, 8 July 1996).

Robert Matemate, accompanied by a didgeridoo, then told these stories over the course of the week:

Many many years ago, long before the dreamtime, there was a huge giant... the chief of the Nurrubungadeens... (rad96154).

The shape of crocodile is very clear in the night sky... crocodiles are feared by Australia's Northern tribes, and there are many legends about those who have no respect for this animal... an important sky figure to many tribal groups... (rad96184).

this story, which is told in almost the same form by two hundred tribes... demonstrates the extraordinary level of commonality between tribes... (rad96190).

By the Jawoin people of the Northern Territory. The Milky Way... can be seen at all times in the sky... it is associated with moral stories rather than sources of food... for many tribes, the Milky Way is a river... (rad96198).

Similarly, the *Drivetime Show* with Bev East featured an Indigenous story, told daily over the course of the week by Noel Pearson and Karen Kelly:

We're celebrating National Aboriginal and Islander Week, and the drive programme is celebrating it by running a lovely programme called Caden Wallah, about a young Aboriginal boy... read by Karen Kelly and Noel Pearson... (Bev East, rad96168, 6WF, 9 July 1996).

Noel spoke in his Aboriginal language, and Karen spoke in English, telling the story of a young Aboriginal boy who went missing on a farm. Pearson's Aboriginal language was heard daily on 6WF—this was not a substantial amount of coverage compared to the amount of English spoken, but it was by the end of the week a familiar presence.

It would be possible to criticize the ABC for only indulging in such Indigenous community-building during NAIDOC week. Peter Holland, the presenter of 6WF's afternoon show, seemed to suggest that the attempt was a one-off oddity:

to celebrate NAIDOC week...we have a special report by Bevan Rankin, an Aboriginal trainee who spent some weeks with the afternoon programme...[it's] a very special report, which is part of NAIDOC week, and we are very proud of... (Peter Holland, rad96164, 6WF, 9 July 1996).

Triple J (ABC-JJJ—national youth radio)

In 1995, Triple J said:

we're trying desperately not to make a token gesture, so we're handing over whole chunks of the radio to some Aboriginal presenters...tonight, Sean Giles is presenting a special Aboriginal and Islander arts programme from ten, that's in place of *Creatures of the Spotlight*... Tuesday, Christine Anu will be presenting the request show from 7pm at night, Wednesday, Rhoda Roberts will be hosting this morning show, Thursday, Jack Beatson...and on Friday afternoon. Aaron Pedersen will be playing heaps of music...(rad95023).

These features were introduced and moderated by voices stating that it was NAIDOC week, and that special space was being made for Indigenous broadcasters in the light of this fact. Presumably during 'normal' weeks, Indigeneity was not so prominent. Such an interpretation is made by Aaron Pedersen, who presented an afternoon show, and came in for an interview the morning before: 'NAIDOC day is every day for me, kind of disappoints me to focus on one particular week, but I suppose we've got to start somewhere...' (rad95179).

Triple J also included an Indigenous presence in the news (an item on the launch of Aboriginal radio station 6AR in WA, for example—rad95176), and in arts segments (the Australian Film Commission's collection of films *From Sand to Celluloid* was discussed, including an interview with film-maker Sally Riley— rad95178). It was notable that Triple J had a distinctly different news agenda from those encountered on other radio stations. The news/sport section of the Triple J news included an account of 'the third Koori invitational surfing tournament' (rad95177). Youth seems the decisive factor here; attitudes towards 'Koori surfing' were indicative of an identity formed less around 'race' than around age and generation.

But more importantly, Indigeneity appeared on Triple J outside of the quarantined spaces of the 'catalogue of anomalies'. Jack Beatson presented a morning show (rad95146), where he interviewed federal

Minister for Aboriginal and Islander Affairs Robert Tickner (rad95147), and hosted the show's resident scientist as he did his talkback section (rad95148). These features were interesting for placing Beatson, an Aboriginal presenter, as the mediator and central figure in the show, controlling the discourses of visiting experts (especially interesting as he presented different perspectives on the questions being asked of the scientist). Even so, he retained his own 'visitor' status: he was not a regular presenter, but specially invited for NAIDOC week.

Rhoda Roberts presented the morning programme on Triple J on 12 July 1997 (rad95090–100), including Aboriginal songs, and features on the stolen generation:

While most of the welfare and protection boards were abolished by the mid '70s, the socio-economic position Aboriginal people found themselves in as a result of those policies meant that they were in a position where they were still in danger of having children removed under mainstream guidelines. (rad95098).

Pedersen returned to host in 1996:

Good morning, you're with Aaron Pedersen, I'm here as part of NAIDOC week celebrations at Triple J...a lot of Indigenous issues in the news... [including] the reconciliation game... (rad96034).

Outside of news stories, feature articles were surrounded by music. Indigenous songs and Indigenous stories were brought together. Talkback segments were run by an Indigenous host.

Fifty-one weeks of the year, it's white time in Australia— should it be a week of commiserations?...we've seen Pauline Hanson...who told us that Aboriginal Australians get far too much...the new government took on the Aboriginal and Torres Strait Islander Commission with relish. Now the Native Title Act is under scrutiny...where are relations between us going?...are ordinary black and white Australians coming together?...some words from people who have important roles to play in Australia's future... Aboriginal magistrate Pat O'Shane reckons 'There's little to celebrate at the moment...this Federal government is ruining years of hard work'... 'We hear the rhetoric of disharmony, divisiveness...self-centredness, competition and greed...capitalism gives primacy to things over people...when, minutes after assuming office, Prime Minister Howard foreshadowed the closing of Aboriginal community organizations, puts other organizations on notice about special auditors...phrases such as the Aboriginal industry, he is promoting divisiveness...if not hatred ...' (Aaron Pedersen, rad96040).

The morning show hosted by Pedersen in 1996 presented feature stories, like those appearing on Radio National. They were generically recognizable:

And now to another form of Aboriginal expression—Aboriginal artists working in isolated communities have had their artwork stolen and exploited for generations. In some communities, almost everyone is considered to be an artist, but only the most prominent get the reward of global recognition. At Yuendumu near Alice Springs, the Aboriginal-owned arts centre is trying to find ways to bring the benefits of a growing market in Aboriginal art and design to everyone in the community... (rad96005, Triple J, 8 July 1996).

What made these features distinctive to Triple J was the Aboriginal voice introducing them. Also specific to Triple J was the amount of Indigenous music played during the sample week: the Warumpi band (rad96004, 026, 038), Philip Moncrieff (rad96044), Nomad (rad96041), Raven (rad96012), Tiddas (rad96018, 035, 059), Yothu Yindi (rad96057), Amunda (rad96020), The Sunrise Band (rad96032, 050), Blackbella Music (rad96036), and Christine Anu (rad96037). Music was occasionally involved in traditional 'politics':

Philip Moncrieff, this land's worth more than gold or silver, and I totally agree with him—it's certainly not worth Century Zinc. (Aaron Pedersen, rad96044, Triple J, 10 July 1996).

But pop music was also involved in processes of community formation that were indeed political, although it may not make truth-claims, or claim knowledge about society. Playing Indigenous music around the news and features on Indigenous issues, hosted by an Indigenous presenter, created an Indigenous space in the mediasphere, with a particular address. Perhaps the most telling aspect of Triple J's move into NAIDOC week was the station promos, played over the seven days:

Hi this is Christine Anu on Triple J, and happy NAIDOC week. If you're making friends with new nationalities, just remember share a few yarns. (rad96003, Triple J, 8 July 1996, *The Morning Show*, also rad96021, 033, 053).

Ben Perksall from the Sunrise Band also presented a promo, where he spoke in an Aboriginal language before saying: 'Triple J, stay strong, Triple J' (rad96031, Triple J, 9 July 1996, Afternoon Show, also rad96048, 049, 051, 058).

Triple J constituted *itself* as having an Indigenous identity. These promos served as the equivalent of shifters in interpersonal address, establishing who is talking. Here Triple J was talking literally with an Indigenous voice. Triple J and 6WF both employed Indigeneity to identify themselves; and yet, comparing their output with that of the Aboriginal-owned radio station 6AR, it seemed that the audiences they addressed remained conceptualized as non-Indigenous. 6AR included items on Indigenous concerns that were not introduced as 'NAIDOC week' items. These features did not have to be quarantined in such a way. The communities addressed by the ABC stations then, all non-Indigenous, were:

- an audience characterized as national, interested in the serious issues of the traditional public sphere (Radio National);
- state-based, less interested in the traditional public sphere, more 'community' minded in the sense of local rather than national forms of politics (720 6WF);
- a youth audience whose commitment to politics was broadly left-wing and oriented towards issues such as ecology and race (Triple J).

6PR

6PR is a commercial radio station in Western Australia whose output consists mostly of talkback. It has been discussed in detail by Steve Mickler (1992b, 1998), and the items generated in the three years of our survey tended to reinforce Mickler's findings. We said earlier that there are very few examples of explicitly 'racist' practice in the contemporary Australian media, but one broadcaster on 6PR, the morning talkback host Howard Sattler, has regularly been accused of being just that. However, even here, such statements cannot be made without qualification. The station generally did not equate with one host. Other presenters, Ron Edwards for example, were sympathetic to Indigenous stories. Sattler's strategy was to work hard to exclude Indigenous people from his idea of his audience (and thence his idea of the public at large) unless they identified not as Indigenous but as ordinary Australian battlers, in which case they were welcome to phone in to agree with Sattler and back up his points. 6PR did not include any NAIDOC programmes. NAIDOC celebrations and other Indigenous stories appeared in news and news-feature stories, but there was none of the sense that the celebration might interest the community addressed by the radio station. That community was 'the public', and the presenters channelled the voice of this elusive group. The public became, tautologically, the people who listened to the show. Other people were not the public, they were do-gooders, or academics (see rad96064, 067, 068, 069).

In the 1994 radio survey, a major news story was a report into alleged police harassment of three Aboriginal actors. Sattler presented 'balanced' interviews—one with Rhonda Collard, the person involved (rad94105), and one with the secretary of the Police Union in Western

Australia (rad94106). Sattler asked the former if she was sure of her recall of what happened. By contrast, the interview with the police spokesman allowed him to say that the police had been completely cleared (although as representative of the police officers' *union* he was 'defending' his members, not reporting on an investigation).

Rhonda Collard was however given space to discuss the impact of the story on her personal life, using the kind of confessional discourse that suits commercial broadcasting. She was encouraged to come over as an emotional individual—the ideal type for sympathy and identification in talkback media. Similarly, a caller on this topic was allowed to discuss his adopted Indigenous son who was regularly stopped by police, and an Indigenous friend who faced similar harassment until he began to carry a video camera. Again, the space was offered (albeit controlled by Sattler) for callers to take up the discursive positions he favoured (the appeal to individual, emotive experience as the guarantor of truth); and indeed, to go beyond this and offer practical advice for Indigenous people dealing with police (carry a video camera).

At points where Indigenous interests aligned with Sattler's own concerns, he was even happy to encourage Indigenous use of land rights. In one example, Sattler was discussing a proposed billboard tower in the centre of Perth. In the introduction to the story (rad94125), Sattler did not mention any Indigenous concerns. In the talkback section (rad94126), however, space became available for an Indigenous voice. Sattler allowed the speaker to put his position—that the billboard would be on a sacred site and that his people had not been consulted on it. Sattler immediately pulled this into his own discourse: he mocked the idea of the sacred ('Don't look too sacred at the moment'), while encouraging the speaker to make a land rights claim, as the billboard would be an 'eyesore'.

Sattler explicitly used and encouraged a language of 'us' and 'them'; his programme was community building at its most explicit. In an item on a car theft by a group of young Indigenous people, Sattler stated that 'they...don't work too hard for a living...living off the system', while his caller went on to state that 'they try to bring you down...steal cars and kill people' (rad94101). The generalized identity 'they' is obviously several things here, collapsed together as one: 'they' are young, they are criminals; and they are Indigenous.

Sattler's own attitude could be abrasive. Mickler (1992*b*) has documented the ways in which the technology of talkback radio made it possible for Sattler to control the discourses of callers; and Sattler's voice dominated. Sattler, for instance, held Robert Bropho personally responsible for the poor living conditions of Indigenous people, and thus open to personal attack. He was blamed both for representing his people (devoting resources to land rights litigation), and for not representing them to 6PR's satisfaction (improving individual living standards).

Community media

A variety of non-commercial community programmes appeared in the 1994 radio survey (these were not included in later years). The Indigeneity on community radio was constructed quite differently from that on the ABC or commercial radio channels. On 3CR (Victoria's community radio station), *The Koori Music Show* (rad94006), *Not Another Koori Show* (rad94005), and the *Koori Survival Show* (rad94004) were explicitly Indigenous-authored. Similarly, 6NR, a community radio station in Western Australia, offered the Aboriginal request show (rad94088), and a series of programmes named as 'Aboriginal radio'. These included a variety of 'NAIDOC week' features (rad94077, 078, 079, 080, 081, 084). The presenters were Indigenous, the names of the shows proclaiming Indigenous concerns. Their function was community building, identifying a 'wedom' for Indigenous people. The community was addressed through presumed communal musical taste (country and western, gospel), speaking positions that referred to an Indigenous community as 'we', and assumed a variety of political and cultural interests around this identity, and requests that were explicitly aimed at Indigenous people, and so on.

Of particular interest were the different 'NAIDOC week' stories in these programmes, compared to news items on other stations. The NAIDOC stories on 6NR, for example, did not have to explain the importance of NAIDOC in such general, representative terms. Rather, a number of (Indigenous) interviewees explained their participation in particular events. NAIDOC week was not reduced to a single story 'about' Indigeneity. These programmes were all marked as explicitly Indigenous-authored. This label in itself said little about their content or function (see Langton, 1993a; McKee, 1997a), but it did extend the notion of a 'we' community that was explicitly Indigenous.

Television's Banality

Ident-ity

On television, many of the Indigenous items noted during the survey week in 1996 took the form of the ABC station idents. These IDs were part of a large, evolving series designed to address the national ABC audience by showing a rich diversity of people and situations. One example in the 1996 survey week projected Indigeneity as part of that. An Indigenous woman and man were shown, the woman tracing the ABC logo (a shape akin to the sign for 'infinity') in the air. It is worth noting that Channel Seven, in its 'Everyone's home with Seven' campaign—which fell outside of our survey periods—engaged in a similar project, showing a variety of people sitting on sofas, dwarfed within the 'Seven' logo. Aboriginal actor Ernie Dingo was one of these people. Indigeneity was thus included in the construction of Seven's national audience community as well, although in a different way. Dingo represented 'stardom' just as much as he did 'Indigeneity', and, sitting on a sofa, represented a domesticated and suburban form of Indigeneity unlike the more 'traditional' form presented by the ABC.

Banal representations

Television offers great potential for banality. In phenomena such as the *Sale of the Century* (gameshow) and *Neighbours* (soap opera), both stripped across the week's TV schedules, a reiteration of the familiar took place. This was not surprising, shocking, or threatening television, but 'central' to the extent that it worked to show a community to itself in unexceptional ways (McKee, 1997a). How did Indigeneity figure in such spaces? The 1996 survey week included *Australia's Funniest Home Videos*. This programme represented perhaps an apotheosis of 'law affirmation'. Banal and suburban home video versions of Australianness were played out for the purposes of frivolity and hilarity. A studio audience laughed at them. In one cutaway shot during this episode, we saw an Aboriginal man laughing (tv96037). Laughing at a video of a child falling into a swimming pool did not amount to much, but the inclusion of such an image was nevertheless a statement about who could be counted among the 'we' community. Indigeneity was present, and the fact that this is relatively unusual argues for its significance. The fact that such occurrences have never been surveyed by researchers interested in the 'representation' of Aboriginality in the media argues for the importance of 'banality'. It also indicated the need to be more comprehensive about the range of items surveyed, rather than restricting analysis only to predetermined 'serious' items.

In the three years of the survey, Indigenous people took up a variety of positions in the banal sites of the television mediasphere. In particular, a series of Indigenous presenters appeared, placed at the very centre of the most familiar and reassuring television. In 1995, Ernie Dingo was a guest umpire on *The Footy Show*: strongly identified, here and elsewhere in the media, as a footy fan (tv95127). Dingo's appearance as a footy-oriented celebrity rather than as a player placed him firmly within a 'we' community, as a fan. Dingo was also a regular presenter on *The Great Outdoors*, a tourism lifestyle show. In 1994 on this programme, he went shopping for a didgeridoo: an almost literal example of a commodification of Indigenous identity, authorized in this case by an Indigenous person (tv94142).

In 1995, Michelle Tuahine presented *The Investigators* (tv95080), a programme devoted to consumerism. In the same year, Aaron Pedersen was co-host of *Gladiators* (tv95140). In 1994, Rhoda Roberts was presenter of *Vox Pop* (tv94171), taking the same position as the talkback hosts, centred and representative of 'the people', Indigenous and otherwise. Stan Grant took up a similar position as a current affairs presenter on mainstream popular TV, representative of the 'we' community (tv94039, 040). In these examples, Indigenous presenters were all addressing the general Australian community from within.

Don Burke's long-running gardening and lifestyle show *Burke's Backyard* introduced Aboriginality into the 'we' community through its celebrity gardener slot: 'Tonight's celebrity gardener is one of the nicest people you would ever meet—Cathy Freeman'. Don gets together with Cathy (she is wearing a lurid pink, shapeless tracksuit) and they discuss her garden, her dog, the kinds of shrubs she likes, and the important of her Aboriginal identity: 'I mean, we should all be proud of who we are . . . obviously the Aboriginality is a big, a very big part of my life, a huge part' (tv95164). *Healthy, Wealthy and Wise* similarly found it possible to write Indigeneity into the community. An item on education and scholarships included an interview with Robbie Lynch, 'junior 400m champion'. Lynch's Aboriginality was not mentioned: this was an item for concerned parents, thinking about their children's educational needs; sport versus other aspects of school life ('I worked out a programme with my Principal').

'Positive images'

There can be few more banal sites in the Australian mediasphere than daytime television chat shows. These are friendly, relaxed, affable programmes, not solemn, threatening, nor self-consciously serious. The representations of Indigeneity here were interesting because they fitted neatly into a form of representation that has been demanded by activists and academics alike (Bostock, 1993), i.e. 'positive images'. Such images appear on daytime television. *Jenny Seaton Live* presented the familiar daytime Australian mix of advertorial and soft news. During the survey week of 1995, one *Jenny Seaton* story dealt with an emu farm run by an Aboriginal woman. She was interviewed and discussed its organizational aspect while a didgeridoo played in the background (tv95042). The (white) reporter went on to state that this was 'more than just an emu farm . . . [it is] a community . . . based on both the Aboriginal culture and the Christian culture'. The item then became a community profile, and discussed welfare arrangements in that community: 'If you don't work, you don't get paid'. 'Positive images' tend to be understood as involving normative values—and this was certainly the case here. In 1994, the same programme presented a story on 'upcoming citizens'. It focused on three young people, one of whom was Indigenous (tv94101). The address of the programme became clear in the language, and in the studio audience. This was an older audience, warmly embracing an Indigenous 'citizen' caught in the act of community building.

Selling Aboriginality

There has been some concern in academic writing that Aboriginality is being increasingly 'commodified'. But it is equally possible to see the use of Indigenous personalities to sell products as furthering the work of community formation by presenting images around which communities may form. Cathy Freeman was used in this way to sell Kellogg's Sustain—a product obviously relating to her sporting endeavours, where her acknowledged Aboriginality was used to signify Australianness, youth, and achievement (tv95027).

Similarly, McDonalds advertisements (tv94093) were clearly 'commodification', but equally clearly they were 'positive images'. One advertisement in our survey period presented an emotive and attractive international 'we' community consisting of a variety of ages and races, including Indigenous Australians, brought together visually by McDonalds products. International retail brands such as McDonalds seem to arouse mostly hostile reactions among critics, but it cannot be denied that their advertising is 'world-class' in terms of production values and marketing concepts. For Indigenous people to figure in commercial calculations at this level as attractive representatives of Australian national identity is not a defeat.

Assimilation?

Given the history of government policy towards Indigenous people, there remains current in Australia a fear of assimilation: that Indigenous people might suffer a cultural genocide, forced to live non-Indigenous lifestyles. This fear can be used as an excuse to denounce any images of Indigenous people involved in what critics claim to be 'non-Indigenous' cultural practices. As Stephen Muecke has suggested, however, such a fear can be extremely debilitating. If it is insisted that any use by Aboriginal people of non-Indigenous culture represents assimilation, then Indigenous people who might want to go to a university, or get a job, can never do so while retaining any cultural integrity (Muecke, 1992: 182).

A public service television broadcast in 1994 (tv94090) was important from this point of view. 'Where is your child?' used the idea of a threat to children in order to promote respect for others in a 'we' community. Indigenous people were placed at the heart of it. The advertisement shows police officers talking to young people: the police officers in question appear to be Aboriginal. It is not sufficient to dismiss such a text as an example of cynicism or assimilation (as was done by one of the coders working on this ARC project). In its context, such placement of Indigeneity may constitute not 'assimilation' but 'dialogue' between two cultures. At the very least it queries the status of a habituated image of 'police'.

Sport

If the sport stories were removed from *television* coverage of Indigenous people, little would be left. Sport stood with nature and art as one of the areas in which Australian *magazines* consistently represent Indigenous people. In *newspapers*, the presence of sport as the single most prominent and consistently addressed feature outside of traditional hard news lends itself to a substantial coverage of Indigeneity. Sport is clearly a vitally important area in the presentation of Indigenous people.

And yet attempting to make sense of this presence is difficult. For very little has been written on television sports coverage in relation to Indigenous Australians. Indeed, for an area that provides such a high percentage of items, the lack of critical attention to sport is remarkable. A recognizable field of study has provided a social history of Indigenous participation in sport (see, for example, the work of Colin Tatz). But work that analyses media *coverage* of sport, rather than sport itself, has barely even begun. A not untypical (American) approach to this question has been generalized dismissal of the 'racism' of 'stereotypes' which link Indigenous people to physical rather than intellectual accomplishments. This hardly seems adequate.

Sport is most often not 'about' Indigeneity

One of the aims of our work has been to propose a move away from the idea that Indigeneity pre-exists its discursive formation. That is to say, there may be some distance between actual Indigenous people and 'Indigeneity' in the media. By the same token, it should not be presumed that every item that mentions Indigenous people in the media is actually 'about' Indigeneity, nor that it contributes to the construction of 'Indigeneity'. There may be items in which Indigenous people appear that have very little to do with 'Indigeneity' as a public concept in Australia. Are such items part of the 'universe of Indigeneity'? We do not know. If the story is not 'about' Indigeneity, to what extent is it incumbent upon researchers to produce interpretations? These questions become immediately relevant when one is considering items that show or mention Indigenous people in the area of sports.

Radio and television

Take the example of radio. Radio offers the possibility of 'invisible' or unmarked Indigeneity. For example, Cathy Freeman's racing times were presented at the end of one news bulletin (rad95072). Was Indigeneity present in this story? It may have been if the listener knew Freeman as Indigenous, and used that information to make sense of her success. But there was no other textual 'evidence' of Indigeneity. Different media communicate Indigeneity in different ways, most commonly by visual means, relying on certain common understandings of what Indigenous people are supposed to look like, and certain forms of visual art which are taken to be Indigenous (McKee, 1997d). Radio has no access to these markers. Aurally, Indigeneity tends to be communicated through the use of the didgeridoo, but this is not commonly used to mark sports stories. Thus, on sports radio, Indigeneity was communicated largely in names. As a result, Indigenous presence in sports on the radio was almost negligible when compared with television, where Aboriginal football players could be seen even if the commentary didn't single them out. On radio it emerged only at points where, for example, a player was named by the commentators during 6PR's 'Afternoon Football Coverage': 'the self proclaimed Prince of Pockets, Scott Chisholm ...' they began, before giving his statistics (rad96062).

On television, Indigeneity could be communicated in visual ways without comment or naming. Football news and coverage constituted a high percentage of the Indigenous presence on television, but in the vast majority of these items, Indigeneity was not mentioned, identified, or structured in any way. In clips of matches, Indigenous players could be seen participating in games (tv94021, 022, 023, 025, 026, 028, 029, 030, 031, 032, 033, 034, 036, 037, 042, and so on). Similarly, in the sports stories (tv96013, 014, 070, 083, 086, 090, and 097, to name only a few), Indigeneity was present only in the fact that an Aboriginal football player appeared during match footage. None of the stories was *about* Indigeneity: they were not *about* Indigenous players.

Speaking voices

This is not to deny the relevance of Indigeneity in sports coverage, for there was systematic distribution of race in these items. Several times, football players and coaches were interviewed. These were rarely Indigenous. Indigenous speaking voices were therefore rarely heard. The forms in which they communicated were resolutely physical, on the football pitch. Very occasionally, Indigenous sports-people appeared in news items: for example, Mark Ella (star Indigenous rugby player) was interviewed on the setting up of a rugby super-league (tv95141). But this compared to the numerous examples where Indigenous sports people were seen but not heard (tv95125, 126, 128, 131, 133, 136, etc.). Indigenous people rarely spoke on camera because *players* rarely spoke on camera. It tended to be coaches and commentators who did that (for example, tv94031). There were very few Indigenous coaches or commentators in Australia in our survey period. It is not obvious that the 'silencing' of football players represented a concomitant powerlessness. Postcolonial writing has tended to proceed as though this were the case, but with reference to football, being a coach, referee, or commentator was not obviously to hold a more 'powerful' position in the cultural imaginary than to be a player.

We can look at those places where football players have begun to talk—some of the most popular media sites such as *Footy Shows*, which rated remarkably highly—and find Indigenous players speaking in these during the survey weeks. In some programmes, Indigeneity was not present in the studio. Indigenous players were shown in video clips, and Indigeneity was not mentioned. If the studio was the centre, from which clips are shown and the programme anchored, then this centre was white (see *The Footy Show*, tv95158, 159, 160 and *The Sportsworld Footy Panel Show*, tv95155).

However, another such programme, *The Footy Show (WA)*, included Indigenous players in the central community of the show's presenters (Channel Nine, tv95115, 116). In the quiz, one contestant was 'Adrian', apparently Aboriginal. Required to sing a Bee Gees song, he blushed:

'He's going red', said one host. 'That's not easy', said the second. 'Not for him', said the first. In the same show, another player, Jeff Hardy, also appeared to be Aboriginal. He appeared in blackface, as part of a skit on the Jackson Five. Cross-dressing performance (usually gendered) was a vital part of the masculine community-formation of these footy programmes. Here, that cross-dressing was 'racialized', as Hardy and other footballers performed a grotesque version of (American) blackness.

At these sites, where the important place of football players in the cultural imaginary was made explicit, Indigenous players appeared and spoke with non-Indigenous players. Sport may have been stratified so that Indigenous players tended not to become coaches or commentators, but in those sites where the importance of players was made clear, Indigeneity was present.

Explicit Indigeneity

Occasionally stories were 'about' Indigeneity in sport: 'Darwin's Robbie Ah Mat is undaunted by becoming the first Aboriginal footballer to play for Collingwood since the club was rocked by a race row two years ago' (new95124). There was one item in the 1994 survey week where Indigeneity became the focus of a sports story on television (tv94066): 'Racism and sport' was a ten-minute filler on ABC-TV. It made clear the absence of such a perspective in other sports items. Similarly, a Channel Nine news story on Janelle Champion (tv95044), a 'young Australian athlete' (voice-over), and 'Aboriginal junior sportswoman of the year', included her trainer, Ollie Rundle, talking about race: 'we know that sport is the main avenue to help our kids achieve and be off the streets'.

The newspaper story 'Grace of two swans' (new96094, *Sunday Times* [WA], 14 July 1996: 91) discussed the concept of 'Black magic' in relation to Indigenous footballers, in order to puncture a cliché about Indigeneity:

Sydney Swans PR man Stephen Brassel is trying to sell a story. Something he doesn't have to work too hard on these days. Except, this day, we're not convinced. It's the Black Magic thing. The telepathy angle. And it's been done to death.

Telepathy? Black Magic? Get outta here ... When coach Rodney Eade sends the team out for a bit of a kick you can't help noticing that every time Kickett puts his boot to ball, the bloke standing where it lands is O'Laughlin. And vice versa.

...

So how about it. What's the secret? What is it, telepathy? Radar?

'It's . . . vision. Looking around', Kickett said.

Vision? Looking around? That's it? That's the secret?

'No,' says O'Laughlin. 'It's the black skin.'

Yes—that's more like it. The secret. At last, one can almost here the didger-idoos, as O'Laughlin continues, but he can't help laughing as he delivers the punchline.

'It stands out against the white jumpers. Makes it easier to see each other . . .

Indigeneity was introduced, only to be debunked in a joke by Indigenous football players. The final paragraph of this story returned to the radical indifference of most sports coverage: 'Black, white—there's only one kind of magic in football. It's called winning.'

Sport creates 'we' communities

It would be hard to find a more ritualized and predictable community-enhancing event in Australia than football. A variety of 'we' commun-ities (teams and their supporters) compete with 'they' communities (other teams), who are also part of a wider 'we' community (football generally, perhaps defined against a 'they' community such as rugby players and fans). While sports news may continue to catalogue ano-malies (broken bones, surprise wins), the work of sports coverage in the media is largely to ritualize: to analyse results, print league tables, continue familiar daily and weekly work.

AFL coverage, from this point of view, was involved in constructing a 'we' community within which race vanished. Indigeneity was not con-structed, it appeared only to be deconstructed. During the course of this research, coverage would occasionally emerge of alleged instances of racism in the behaviour either of AFL players or fans. Such allegations routinely led to punishment, and pronouncements by the AFL that the game was not, and must never be, racist. Television, radio, and news sports coverage in which race was unremarkable became the ideal for the AFL. The racism stories (which were for the most part narrated in the news pages rather than the sports pages) made the problem of racism, and the issue of race, something that was alien to sport.

It is worth noting a single text that pointed to a notable absence in the construction of a sporting community. Channel Ten's sports news, during the 5.00 p.m. news on 12 July 1996 (tv96095), included coverage of the Sydney Swans playing St Kilda. The story included shots of an Aboriginal supporter. This was unusual in the sports coverage analysed over the three years. Aboriginal people often appeared as players, but rarely as fans and supporters.

Cathy Freeman

During our survey period, Cathy Freeman was the single most consistently present Indigenous figure. In the 1996 week, she was particularly prominent, as Australia prepared for the Atlanta Olympics, but she was also present in previous years. As was the case with Indigenous footballers, Freeman was mostly not presented as an Aboriginal athlete: 'Cathy Freeman has once again lowered her own national record for the 400m . . .' (rad96090, 6PR, 13 July 1996, 9.00 a.m. news). In such stories, Freeman was an athlete pure and simple.

The Olympic Games produced a particular kind of 'we' community around sport: the nation. Spilling out from the usual confines of sports journalism, the Olympics provoked special supplements, guides, and celebrations leading up to the sporting consolidation of national identity. The work of newspapers in relation to this lead-up was particularly interesting. Cathy Freeman became, in the visual rhetoric of the Olympics, 'Australia'. The *West Australian* and the *Weekend Australian* presented front-page banner headlines on the Olympics: 'Australians at the Olympics', proclaimed the *West Australian* (new96120, 13 July 1996), illustrating this with three colour pictures of Olympians, the most recognisable of whom was Freeman. The *Weekend Australian* presented 'Atlanta: the Ultimate Guide', again in a banner headline, again with a photograph of Freeman (new96155, 13–14 July 1996). The *Sydney Morning Herald* presented 'Atlanta 96: 24 page guide to the Games', illustrated with Freeman alone, again in colour (new96065, 13 July 1996). In these moments, where Freeman was drawn out of sport as such to represent '*Australians* at the Olympics', the most powerful work of her image was done. Appearing even in coverage of the Games that did not mention her, Freeman became a visual mnemonic for 'Australia at the Olympics'. Representing the nation, she stood for 'Australia'.

But this did not exhaust Freeman's image: for at the same time that she was (constructed as) fully Australian, she also flagged herself as 'not-Australian'. As a sports celebrity, Freeman was political: in both the sports and hard news sections of the media. Freeman's 'politics' were those of reconciliation, and much of this work was done around the Aboriginal flag (see also Chapter 7). In 1996, the article 'The Gold Prospectors' (new96066, *Sydney Morning Herald*, 13 July 1996: Atlanta 96, 12) presented colour photographs of Australia's best medal hopes. It showed every contestant engaged in their sport. Samantha Riley and Kieran Perkins were in the pool, Megan Still and Kate Slatter in their rowing-boat, and so on. Freeman was the single exception. She was represented standing in the bush, the Aboriginal flag draped around her body. Freeman stood for a delighted reconciliation of nations.

The carrying of flags was still important in the run-up to the 1996 Olympics: a photograph of Freeman in the *Courier Mail* was captioned: 'She has vowed to carry both the Aboriginal and Australian flags on a lap of honour if she wins' (new96213, 9 July 1996: 16). As the *Northern Territory News* observed of this same fact, 'The elegant 400m medal contender is proud of her Aboriginal heritage [and is] keen on promoting her aboriginality [*sic*] in a bid to highlight considerable social problems' (new96049).

Whether she liked it or not, Cathy Freeman operated in the media as a politician, taken to be representative of her people and their 'problems' as well as standing for their potential and success as embodied in herself. Her prominent role promoted a certain understanding of reconciliation. The form of politics in which Freeman engaged was not that of traditional hard news, party politics and the bourgeois public sphere. Nevertheless, she usurped the traditional space of that sphere. Her performance of reconciliation was political, but not quite hard news: sports, but not only sporting. The figure of Freeman with flags of two nations hugged to her body ricocheted around the Australian mediasphere, gaining coverage in hard news sites, sports, lifestyle pages, opinion, discussion, and a telegram of congratulation from the Prime Minister. The Aboriginal flag was a hot topic. The issue of the Aboriginal nation was raised. In the material presence of her body, Freeman reconciled two nations.

9 | Reporting Indigeneity: News and Talkback

How can you call Australia a country if everyone is at a different point in the story?;

(Eric Michaels, in Hay, 1996: 359)

News tends to function with Lotman's 'catalogue of anomalies', telling a community about the threatening, dangerous, and unfamiliar world beyond its boundaries. This distinction is not static and certain, however. Commercial television news tends ever more towards law formation. Here we examine the ways in which news stories, together with mediated feedback to them (via talkback and features), placed and shaped Indigeneity.

A strange tradition of critical media analysis since the work of Hartman and Husband in the 1970s has been to enumerate a series of characteristics that belong to news, and then to criticize news coverage of a specific topic for displaying those very characteristics. Thus, news prefers action and event over background and structure, likes personification and leaders, sensationalism, conflict, binarism, and the like, and it commits the occasional inaccuracy or distortion. It may even be that 'hard' news, chronicling anomalies, is founded on an implicit theory that only in violence (from war to more ritualized conflict) will truth be found. But this is the very approach to reporting for which the media are criticized in relation to coverage of racial issues (Hartman and Husband, 1974: 149–62). In short, the generic imperatives of hard news, rather than any racist impulse, lead to the focus on conflict, the 'negative', and so on. It follows that any research that concentrates only on that genre is sure to find these problems. Indeed, the best that can be hoped for is that such analysis will come to the conclusion that crime news conforms to the status of *news* (as do Mickler and McHoul, 1998: 149).

News Stories 1: Children Found and Lost

NAIDOC stories

Newspaper coverage of Indigeneity may be characterized as largely generic:

- hard news (stories about land rights or Century Zinc, in the news sections, the front of the papers),
- children (in the colour/soft news/family/children sections),
- arts and entertainment,
- sport.

It should not be surprising that Indigeneity is covered in such generic ways: dividing their coverage in generic ways is what news outlets do. While the 'children' genre may appear anywhere in a newspaper, for instance, all the others are routinely rounded up into their own section of the paper, and readers may well choose not to attend to entire sections, for reasons of generic preference.

Our choice of NAIDOC week revealed another genre of Indigenous representation in the news: the 'NAIDOC story'. That is, the 'cute-children-with-painted-faces-smiling-at-the-camera-Reconciliation-story'. It was self-contained and self-explanatory, and (like the children genre generally) staked first claim to any colour slot in the news pages. Several newspapers took the opportunity of NAIDOC week to run 'feel-good' stories involving children and the prospect of reconciliation. The visualization of reconciliation was undoubtedly a smiling Indigenous child, somewhere between 7 and 13. One 1994 NAIDOC story reported that 'Young Islanders jump for joy' (new94201). Not only were such 'non-news' ('positive', 'law-forming', 'community-building', 'wedom') stories focused on children, but there was a particular way of imaging these children. They were often shown in a group, and not named individually (this is unusual practice in newspapers, certainly in news stories). Front-page photographs were often chosen for aesthetic rather than journalistic reasons, as were sports pictures. News photos in general (particularly in the *West* and *NT* newspapers) tended to be prosaic rather than aesthetic, presenting information rather than visual pleasure. Most often they showed (and named) the face of a person involved in a story. The children in 'NAIDOC' stories did not function in this way; they were not there as themselves, but as representatives of 'reconciliation'.

In one story (new94187) about school fund-raising, children functioned not as individual agents, but as a photogenic group: a community
visualized in its youngsters. This allowed for Indigenous people to be
brought together as part of such a community. Similarly, in the Entertainment section of the NT News, a photograph of two children, one
Indigenous, one non-Indigenous, with a piece of Aboriginal artwork,
again represented reconciliation outside of politics. In the 1995 survey:
'Unity message steals the show', for example (new95133), presented an
image of an Indigenous man and child in traditional body paint, with a
didgeridoo, in a story about 'unity' (reconciliation); 'A group of toddlers
drifted into Dreamtime yesterday...' (new95087), accompanied by an
illustration of an Aboriginal man, traditionally dressed and painted,
surrounded by white schoolchildren; 'Members of the Gungganji
dance company help to launch the week of Aboriginal festivities at the
St Kilda town hall with a traditional dance performance' (the Age,
new95049), illustrated with a colour photograph of Indigenous dancers'
faces, wearing traditional make-up. New94154 had a fashion parade to
represent NAIDOC week: 'Daynae struts her stuff.' Fashion parades, like
children, operated outside of politics but, like children, fashion
allowed the discussion of reconciliation. Another NAIDOC story
(new94070) presented a 'multi-racial dance troupe'. Dancing too has
not been associated with the political in a traditional Habermasian
public sphere.

There seemed indeed to be a desire to get beyond history in discussions of reconciliation. A letter to the editor praised a story about two
Indigenous women who were taken away from their families and put
into serfdom. They were 'holding no grudges' (new94135). Grudges
carried the past into the present; the letter-writer felt that the
emergence of such history into the present was unsuitable. The desire
to forget and reconcile was lauded. The story cited was 'Girl's agonies in
torn families' (new94118), on an exhibition being mounted for the
Year of Indigenous People. 'Fostering harmony between two living
cultures' (new94014) presented a photograph of an Indigenous man,
stripped to the waist, shot against misty mountains, playing a
didgeridoo. Reconciliation (fostering harmony) occurred in nature and
was picturesque; Indigenous people appeared in nature, performed
shirtlessly in the arts; this was distinct from the political sphere.
'Traditional' Aboriginal stories were more photogenic in these
terms. Conversely, it might be noted that political stories were less visual
(more verbal), whereas stories on 'culture' stressed the visual
(new94041).

Television and NAIDOC

The NAIDOC genre of story also appeared on television. An SBS *World News* story (tv94152) presented a mixture of Indigenous and non-Indigenous children dancing to didgeridoo music, combining NAIDOC with the visualization of reconciliation. 'Aborigines today celebrated their national day', said Channel Ten (tv94017), with didgeridoos, clapsticks, and dancing children. Linked to this was a story on health: 'In the outback, appalling conditions...[and] Third World health.' The story combined law-affirming with anomalous elements, and perhaps unusually accorded Aboriginal people national status—'their national day'.

Milbindi, an Indigenous-produced current affairs programme on GWN, included an example of the NAIDOC story, showing that this generic impulse was strong in both Indigenous and non-Indigenous authored programmes (tv95149). *Milbindi* covered a NAIDOC event, focusing on the question of culture, on children, and on elements that might be understood as 'positive'. 'Traditional Aboriginal foods and lifestyle' were covered, as was the Bunbury Nyungar baby beauty contest. On the GWN *News Hour* programme, another NAIDOC week story opened with a picture of the Aboriginal flag. Discussing NAIDOC week, the voice-over said that its 'aim is to promote Aboriginal culture [but] some say it goes further' (new95022). Danny Collard suggested that NAIDOC could 'let the wider community know that Indigenous Australians are interested...in reconciliation'.

Channel Seven news presented a flag-raising, and 'happy scenes today with the launch of National Aboriginal and Islander week...fashion parades, painting, dance': the images in this item included body-painted Aboriginal children dancing. This was the NAIDOC story par excellence (tv95031).

NAIDOC: 'culture' versus 'politics'

It is worth contrasting a story presented on SBS news, where the graphic used to illustrate the NAIDOC story showed a picture of Indigenous marchers. This was a story from traditional politics: federal Minister Robert Tickner appeared, calling 'for bipartisan support of Indigenous affairs', while Che Cockatoo Collins raised the flag in Victoria: 'a symbol of Aboriginal struggle, the flag has now been recognized, but Kooris say this only highlights how much further the reconciliation process has to go' (tv95034).

The standard nature of the recurring NAIDOC story became obvious when compared with a few examples of other stories that could be told about NAIDOC. 'Proud parade in city today in celebration of National Aboriginal and Islander Day of Observance Committee week' (new95116); the image illustrating this story showed an Aboriginal man in army fatigues, eating from a tin—'Sergeant Elgan Leedie in the Mall ... for NAIDOC week.' This story presented an explicitly political event (a march). Similarly, 'Hear our voices: call by Aborigines' (new95121) used the NAIDOC event to present political aspirations: 'Aborigines yesterday called for a greater say in the Northern Territory's progress to statehood at a NAIDOC rally.' Television's NAIDOC stories also allowed a space for a political element to NAIDOC week. The most prominent NAIDOC ceremony covered during this week was where a Sydney park was renamed in an Aboriginal language (tv94152 and others).

Visualizing reconciliation

Reconciliation is a political process.

The Council for Aboriginal Reconciliation is the name given to the multi-party and cross-cultural group of Australians who responded to the Australian Parliament's invitation and offer of a unique challenge to establish a process of reconciliation. This process would help to heal the wounds of the past and build the foundations upon which the rights and affairs of Indigenous Australians may be dealt with in a manner that gives respect and pride to all of us as Australians. (Council for Aboriginal Reconciliation, 1994).

The term 'reconciliation' was not prominent in news coverage. Official persons used the term occasionally: Sir William Deane, the Governor-General, said that reconciliation will be impossible unless Indigenous health issues are addressed (new96095, the *West Australian*, 8 July 1996: 6). Similarly, John Howard said that what he wanted in the case of the Century Zinc mine was 'reconciliation' (new96106, the *West Australian*, 11 July 1996: 12).

However, the word 'reconciliation' was less prevalent than a form of visualization that did not use the word. NAIDOC week stories presented a kind of 'positive image'. These stories seemed to be a distinct print genre. Stories such as 'Carnival conveys culture' (new96010, the *Courier Mail*, 13 July 1996: 6) and 'A buzz of activity that works wonders' (new96102, the *West Australian*, 9 July 1996: Today, 6), presented visual reconciliation, without the politicizing effect even of naming it. It was placed into a separate and private realm of interpersonal relationships.

279

More than 4000 Indigenous and non-Indigenous people yesterday gathered in Musgrave park in Brisbane to celebrate the end of National Aboriginal and Islander Day of Celebration Committee week. (new96010).

The photograph accompanying this article was of children. Traditional news values (crime, conflict, the work of public policy) gave way to people being nice to each other, children seeming to offer a privileged way of representing a reconciliation of cultures. Similarly, new96102 presented an account of the Karawara Community Project, attended by Indigenous and non-Indigenous children, represented by a photograph of smiling children.

Christine Jackman wrote in the *Courier Mail* during the 1996 survey week that the term 'reconciliation' had artificially separated cultural from other political concerns:

I suspect many people who say that they are in favour of reconciliation should actually add the caveat 'but only when it doesn't put me out': we'll recognise NAIDOC week, we'll even buy Aboriginal art on a T-shirt or coffee mug, and we feel so warm inside when we can honestly say we like Christine Anu's music—but our sympathies stop dead when it comes to changing our behaviour in any way to accommodate the other perspective. (new96020, the *Courier Mail*, 10 July 1996: 15, 'Time to ponder negotiations').

Jackman identified a tendency to separate the cultural from the political, celebrating the first while denying the second. Hence (to prove her point), the letter writer who was unhappy with the financial component of reconciliation: 'Despite its high profile in the media, has anyone ever defined "Aboriginal reconciliation"? Is it a tangible achievable goal—or just another name for a blank cheque?' (new96160, the *Weekend Australian*, 13–14 July 1996: 18). The same tendency seemed to operate in the preferred figuration of reconciliation as children-sharing-culture. Children seemed naturally to embody a realm outside of adult concerns, especially those of sexuality and politics.

The 'stolen generation': children became political

Children provided the focus for the most extensive single 'hard news' item during the 1995 survey week. This was the release of *Telling Our Story*, a report by the Western Australian ALS (Aboriginal Legal Service,1995), detailing the experiences of children who were taken from their parents. This report was a precursor to, and part of the campaign for, the National Inquiry into the Separation of Aboriginal and Torres Strait Islander Children from Their Families (1997), conducted for federal parliament by the Human Rights and Equal Opportunities Commission.

Most television coverage of the ALS report accepted its terminology. For example, the report alleged genocidal intent. A news item on the Golden West Network's *News Hour* suggested that the practice of removing children was motivated by 'the hope that Aborigines would eventually become extinct'. Aboriginal speakers presented their experiences: Glenys Collard said that 'They took us away as children...' (tv95025). GWN also treated the story as a straightforward political event, covering the response of the state government to demands for compensation in the report).

The release of the report provided an opportunity to make history newsworthy:

It's hard to believe now but for decades our state government forcibly removed Aboriginal children from their families in a misguided attempt to wipe out a whole culture. (tv95049).

This voice-over from Channel Seven's coverage seemed to suggest (erroneously) that the events took place in a past so distant and so different that it was hard even to imagine it. However, the fact that the actions were wrong was accepted, as were the feelings of the children. The television news dwelt on the emotional truth of the situation: 'Imagine being snatched away from your family when you were just two...' said the Channel Seven reporter, addressing a community understood to be equally protective of family and children, and disdainful of the state's intervention in such matters. Coverage on the ABC (tv95057) was more restrained, but also presented the story through emotions. Indigenous singer Archie Roach's song 'Took the Children Away' was played, and there were shots of Aboriginal women crying. The voice-over referred to genocide, but modified this by saying that this was the term used in the report (i.e. reporting it as an allegation).

Similar stories were told in radio news items (see, for example, Triple J, rad95059, 060, 101, 6WF). The editorial content of the stories agreed with the stories told in the report: 'forcibly taken from their families...abuse at the hands of carers ...' (Radio National news, rad95033, see also rad95030, 032). As a prime forum for providing instant reflection on the news of the day, radio was also prominent in picking up the issues of the story in more extended interviews with people involved in the news story. *Verity James* on 6WF said that the history was 'nothing short of kidnap'. Trailing the story, James said that 'it will make you cry, it's the stories of Aboriginal children who've been taken away, kidnapped', and went on to interview Robert Riley, who had an immensely high profile during this week in Western Australia. Riley described the report as an extension of Patrick Dodson's 'underlying issues' report for the Royal Commission into Aboriginal Deaths in Custody.

The release of the report gave history a news value, and politicized the very idea of 'the' family. The media 'translated' that history into news discourse. The testament of emotionally distressed individuals, whose ideals of an unspoilt, uninterrupted family experience were disturbed by outside forces, became the central form of evidence picked up by the news. Robert Riley was also interviewed on 6PR by Ron Edwards, and told just such a personal story (rad95052). His authoritative position as Chief Eexecutive Office, of the Aboriginal Legal Service was enhanced, perhaps entirely superseded, by the fact that he was himself one of the 'stolen generation', and had testified to his experiences in the report:

EDWARDS. Let's now have a yarn to Rob Riley from the Aboriginal Legal Service... nice to speak to you, how're you going? [...]

RILEY. I was eight and a half months old when I was taken away from my mum and dad.

EDWARDS. Why were you taken away?

RILEY. Dad got himself into some trouble with the law, and didn't have the money to pay the fines and was put in jail, and the Native Welfare department determined that my mother wasn't able to provide for me, so I was taken away.

Ron Edwards recapped: 'So from the age of eight and a half months to the age of ten, you never saw your mum and dad.' His tone was unbelieving, and he made clear what an outrage he thought this was:

EDWARDS. Did it make you an angry man?... you had this monstrous injustice inflicted on you for being nothing more than a black baby....

RILEY. It's been something that I've had to deal with over a long time, and I didn't realize how bad the secrets within myself, how deeply they were affecting me... it has made me angry about the policy, I'm not bitter towards the people in their institution because they were doing their jobs... my parents were told at the age of four when they came to visit me that they shouldn't come any more because it would affect my personal development.

EDWARDS. Eugh! (noise of disgust).

RILEY. I went through an identity crisis.

Edwards brought up the possibility that the current generation had nothing to do with the pain:

EDWARDS. How should we handle it from your point of view? Should we feel guilt about it? Or should we say, this event's occurred, and now it's time to make sure we don't repeat that in history?

RILEY. Exactly that... this thing's happened, we can't turn back the hands of time, but what we can do as a community is to not allow the perpetuation of

these policies to continue... the issues of mental health... counselling services... they should support Aboriginal people, support people who are
fighting for this national inquiry... I'm a staunch advocate against what
Cheryl Edwardes [WA Attorney-General] is doing with boot camps [for
young offenders]... to me, this repeats the mistakes of history... kids growing
up in institutions...

EDWARDS. Such a very high crime rate among young Aboriginal people...

RILEY. What I say to the listeners is, I'm not asking for people to condone the
element of the Aboriginal community that get caught up in the criminal
justice system, but this report that we've produced is because of the great
number of Aboriginal people caught up in the criminal justice system... we
saw the need to be able to demonstrate to the powers-that-be the need to
demonstrate this connection, that if they don't see the result of removing
children from their families, the internalized conflict that goes on within the
Aboriginal community... we become very bitter and internalize the conflict
within ourselves...

EDWARDS. When the white community recognize the history, and we understand what happened, then the real process of reconciliation can begin.

Edwards told the story as one of outrageous treatment of individuals
who had been emotionally affected by it: 'Can Aboriginal people forgive
and forget the forcible removal from their families for nothing more
than being Aboriginal?' (rad95050).

This item on 6PR used the release of the *Telling Our Stories* report to
place Indigenous people in the 'battler' category which constituted its
own public. Nevertheless, 6PR's talkback audience were unwilling to
make such a move. The editorial comment on the stolen generation,
such as the stance taken by Edwards, and apparent also in newspaper
and television coverage elsewhere, was strongly resisted. 'Bob', for example, said that Indigenous children were only removed due to the good
intentions of the government, and that Rob Riley was probably removed
from his parents because they were incompetent: 'Do you think it would
have been humane to leave people like Rob Riley with people who
couldn't care for him or give him a good education?' (rad95054). Bob's
was not a lone voice. 'If it hadn't been for white people', 'Betty' called in
to say, 'they [the stolen Indigenous children] would never have been able
to read or write' (rad95051). Mike said that the stolen children policy had
good effects: 'some of them are very high-powered people now'
(rad95058). Fran reminded everyone that: 'There was white children
taken away from their parents too' (rad95055). 'Kerry', working from
the classic 'opinionated' position of generalizing from a supposed personal experience, i.e. her 'personal' knowledge of an act said to have been
perpetrated by someone known to someone known to the caller, came
out with an equally classic white myth:

CALLER. It's not quite as one-sided as what you might think...a lot of these Aboriginal people handed their kids over to the missions, wiped their hands of responsibility...my mother had one working for her...she had twins...she didn't want the girl, so she knocked it on the head. (rad95088).

Ron Edwards continued with his own reading of this history: 'I think the tragedy is that a lot of them were regarded as not having rights at all' (rad95088). Competition occurred between the editorial and 'public' versions of this story.

Fortuitously, a directly comparable story was reported in the same week. Ron Edwards mentioned the possibility of legislation that would prevent parents from smacking their children (rad95083). A series of talkback callers rang in to protest: the state should not be involved in the rearing of children. In short, in relation to 'our' public, the state should not be involved in the family; whereas, in the community of 'they' ('these Aboriginal people'—rad95088), the rules were different. The destruction of 'their' family unit by the state was reckoned by some callers a good thing, because the same rules did not apply to them (a position that also contradicted the callers' demand that Aboriginal political demands should be resisted as privilege, in favour of 'treating everyone the same').

Denying the right to feelings for children

Talkback shows on radio, as well as popular TV news shows such as *A Current Affair*, have tended to construct a public of 'battlers'—battling *for* their own survival, but often enough battling *against* an uncaring state that would remove their rights to private freedom (see Adams and Burton, 1997). The children of the 'stolen generation' were used to bring Indigenous people in Australia into this community. However, the stories told by Howard Sattler on his 6PR talkback show were different. For Sattler, the removal of Indigenous children had to be judged differently from the removal of non-Indigenous children:

CALLER [JANE]. I'm a little bit tired about this Aboriginal thing with these children who were taken away from their parents, now I'm a 70-year-old woman, and I come from Victoria, and we had two Aboriginal children, mum took two Aboriginal children in because one's parents were alcoholics...they were fantastic boys.

SATTLER. Were their parents happy that they came to your mum?

CALLER. They didn't seem to care, it didn't seem to worry them very much, because I didn't think they ever knew much about what was going on anyway...

SATTLER. So the alternative was, they lived down the settlement ... with drunken parents ... So the best thing to do was to put them into a home ... they went to school, they were well clothed.

CALLER. They were better with us then than they were with the darker children ... they just couldn't look after them.

The caller followed the typical 'opinionated' position, generalizing from a personal experience, with no interest in wider structures, causes, or interpretations. Whereas Ron Edwards contested callers' interpretation, Sattler confirmed it, and it became coherent:

SATTLER. Thanks very much for that, I think that story would probably be paralleled in a lot of other homes around Australia ... some people were forcibly taken, that's not on, but in some cases for the good of the children, they were taken.

Similarly, a caller called 'Bev' discusses her situation:

CALLER. There have been a lot of children taken from their families, many years ago, we have an Aboriginal son, we have five other children, and have fostered lots and lots of children in between, but we do have an Aboriginal son, who is now a grown man.

SATTLER. Adopted, is he?

CALLER. Yes, yes, but we knew his mother, and his grandmother, and consequently before he was born, it was decided that this child would be placed, and they decided ...

SATTLER. They decided, which is interesting, because we hear these stories of Aboriginal children being placed, as you say, as a horrendous thing, and how dare this happen to any child, but obviously his natural mother thought that he would be better off with you ...

Howard Sattler and his callers resented that they were being told to feel guilty, even though not a single Indigenous speaker during the week made any such comment, while Rob Riley explicitly rejected that tactic in the passage quoted above. But Sattler and his callers used guilt to exculpate themselves:

CALLER [SHIRLEY]. I cannot feel guilty ... taxpayers have contributed twenty-seven billion over the past twenty seven years ... I don't want to be told I should feel guilty ... I had nothing to do with it. (rad95079).

Sattler agreed: 'we didn't steal it' (rad95077). 'It's not our fault ... we can't turn back the past [*sic*]' (rad95039). Sattler did allow Indigenous people to join the 'public' he constructed in his show, on condition that it was accepted that he knew more about Indigeneity than they did:

CALLER [PETER]. I've got Aboriginal relatives, I'm only a small part Aboriginal, I think that if we organize it so that every Australian is an Australian, and forget Mabo and all the other garbage, the better.

Sattler was happy to go along with that:

SATTLER. I reckon you speak for the majority of Aboriginal people, most people are sick and tired of Mabo, they just want to get on with their lives, they think that issues like Mabo are just going to divide the nation, that they'll be discriminated against because they are Aboriginal people... we're human beings first, secondly we're Australians.... (rad95084)

Sattler knew what 'the majority of Aboriginal people' thought. Indigeneity was fine, as long as it was not presented as such. Sattler's attacks on Indigenous people, and his refusal to allow them into his public unless they renounced Indigeneity, were almost unique in this survey period in any medium.

SATTLER. Oh dear, here he comes again. Clarrie.
CLARRIE ISAACS [Aboriginal activist]. Hello Howard, how you doing?
SATTLER. Yes, Clarrie.
...
SATTLER. None of us in Australia today had anything to do with colonizing Australia, we just happened to arrive here via our mother's womb, and therefore we are Australians.

A point that emerged strongly from our survey was that Indigeneity was taken to be public property. It was a suitable object for untutored 'opinion'. That opinion seemed to offer certain sanctioned solutions— treat everyone the same, forget history.

Policing the family: reshaping stories

During the same week, a rather different story put Indigeneity and parenting at the top of the news bulletins once again. This story showed how the forcible removal of Aboriginal children from their parents was still very much a daily reality in the 1990s. Naturally, no connection was made between this contemporary news event and the 'stolen children' story; indeed, the Aboriginal descent of the man involved was not mentioned. This may have accorded with the journalists' code of practice (see Chapter 10) by not placing 'unnecessary emphasis' on the race of people arrested by the police, but it was certainly a most material fact in the case.

An Indigenous man, Maurin Miller, was charged with threatening his 6-week-old daughter with a knife. At the time of his arrest, he was standing outside King Edward Memorial Hospital for Women in

Perth, holding his daughter and the knife. His reason was given as a lack of access to the child. The incident made all the local TV news bulletins that evening, because they were able to video the moment when Miller was rushed by the police:

His daughter, six weeks old, was rushed into hosptial with a broken arm . . . He was being arrested by police. They said he had a knife and charged him with trying to kill his baby, taken from his de facto Cassandra, seventeen. (Channel Seven, tv95100).

Most of the items contained similar statements (Channel Ten, tv95095). A very clear consensus emerged that obscured the fact that *the police* broke his daughter's arm as they rushed him. But Miller was cast as the one who was responsible for the violence, for threatening to kill his daughter, and for holding her at knifepoint. Only the ABC hinted at the correct 'agent' of the arm-breaking, albeit with an agentless passive verb: 'When Miller was jumped by the police . . . his baby's arm was broken' (tv95112).

That this was not a simple matter of a crazed individual from whom the girl had to be rescued at all costs was also hinted at, but never made explicit, in the news coverage. In every item, a sound-bite was used where Miller said: 'My daughter, I can't help it, but I love her' (see also Channel Nine, tv95103). No reporter followed up on this angle by asking what might have driven someone to snatch their own child in such a dramatic way—far from wanting to harm her, he was trying to keep her. In the light of the concern being expressed throughout the media during the same week about the separation of Aboriginal children from their parents, such an angle was clearly highly newsworthy. Similarly, no reporter asked whether the police were acting within their own 'rules of engagement' for hostage-taking situations, never mind within the boundaries of common sense, when they attacked a person holding a baby in his arms. The wisdom of alternative tactics was not explored, for example trying to talk the situation down, so that the anger and frustration could be defused. No one questioned the advisability of dealing with such a private matter with the full force of the law and in the full glare of TV cameras (very few 'domestics' have in fact been treated this way). Instead, the police version of the event (deleting their own agency in injuring the child) was duly and dutifully reported as the fact. The terrible story was rounded off as Miller meekly accepted his subsequent fate: 'I've got no complaints', he said of his treatment by the police and his bail conditions. It was clear that he would be processed inexorably through the criminal justice system, and another Aboriginal child would be taken away from her father 'for her own good'. Unfortunately, this wasn't clear to the news media, who missed such implications completely.

News Stories 2: Politics, Politicians, and the Economy

Century Zinc—Rights versus Bureaucracy

NAIDOC week stories tended to present 'culture' rather than 'politics'. Indeed, Indigeneity has consistently been 'culturalized':

> [Indigenous people] live in a society—a romantic society... that has burdened them with [a] totalising concept of Aboriginal culture... This is a burden; and it is the Western version of culture, not the Aboriginal, that gives them this... The avenues for this 'being Aboriginal' are paradoxically narrow, and they tend to be over-determined by, precisely, 'the cultural'... While culture is not natural endowment, it is treated as though it is, so that the only 'respectable' ways for Aboriginal people to find identity in this society tend to be through particular forms of culture... 'Aboriginal artist' is in this sense normative, almost tautological, because of the over-determinations of an historical *conception* of culture in general and Aboriginal culture in particular. By contrast, Aboriginal bureaucrat becomes a monstrous term for both the Left radical consensus and the Right. (Muecke, 1992: 17).

What happened when such a monster threatened to leave the realm of 'culture' and enter the realm of politics?

In 1996, a single story dominated the news. The major events covered in the 'Century Zinc' story could be summarized thus: mining company Century Zinc (a subsidiary of RTZ-CRA) wanted to open a zinc mine in far north Queensland. Local Aboriginal groups applied to the National Native Title Tribunal to have their claim on the land recognized. The Native Title Tribunal rejected their initial right to make such an application. Century Zinc nevertheless continued negotiations with local Aboriginal groups. A vote of representatives of these groups was taken: it was 12–11 in favour of supporting the mine. Murrandoo Yanner, the leader of the Carpentaria Land Council, was unhappy with the process by which that result had been gained, and reconvened the group. A second vote was 23–0 against the mine. The Queensland government came out to state that the mine must go ahead. If necessary, they would alter the Native Title Act to enable a compulsory purchase of the land, in order to ensure that the local Aboriginal Land Councils would have no right to negotiate, should they be successful with any subsequent Native Title claim.

The issue of Century Zinc was discussed with remarkably little reference to land *rights*. And this was true of coverage in 1995 and 1996 more generally. There was a shift in the news vocabulary between 1994 and the later years, from 'land rights' to 'Native Title'. Stories changed from debates about rights to complaints about bureaucracy. The *7.30 Report* in 1995 presented a special item: 'Has Mabo worked?' A variety of white voices criticized Mabo: Richard Court, for example, was quoted as saying that 'millions of dollars of investment is stalled by uncertainty caused by Native Title'. 'One thing that farmers and Aboriginal groups agree on' was that Native Title (as it was then legislated) was too complicated. Politics shifted from constitutional to more mundane issues of the economy and legal efficacy. The stories in the news in the 1995 survey week were about Native Title as a legislative question. The ABC discussed amendments to the Native Title Act (tv95056), and reported on discussions between Richard Court (state premier & Western Australia) and Michael Lavarch (federal Attorney-General) over Native Title legislation (tv95077). In a similar item on GWN (tv95066), Lavarch and Court talked, while Indigenous people appeared only as images in file footage, affected by the discussion but not involved in it.

The Century Zinc story was personalized. It became a story about Murrandoo Yanner, who featured in a large number of the stories about the mine. Together with John Howard (Prime Minister), Rob Borbidge (Queensland state premier), and Cheryl Kernot (leader of the Democrats), he became the lead actor in this story (other figures, such as Clarence Waldon, Tim Fischer, and CRA executives appeared in less prominent roles). Yanner was described in a variety of ways, but even in such a 'political' story as Century Zinc, the status of an Indigenous leader was presented as ambivalent and problematic. Yanner was not named as a 'politician', despite his role as the leader of an organization whose aims were expressly political. Rather, he was a 'Man with a mission' (new96117), a 'protester' (new96101), a 'rebel' (new96087), an 'activist' (new96087), a 'radical' (new96087), an 'Aboriginal activist' (tv96018), a 'controversial Aboriginal leader', and a 'fiery Aboriginal leader' (tv96032). He was, in short, a 'warrior from a far country' (new96202).

Aboriginal people were not *excluded* from politics; it was rather the case that the status of Indigenous public figures was difficult for the news media to negotiate. Thus, although Yanner was a protester, rebel, and a 'lethal weapon' (new96087), he was also a 'leader'. The *West Australian* named Yanner 'a significant new leader in Aboriginal politics' (new96117), but at the same time found it necessary to debate Yanner's political legitimacy:

Cape York Land Council deputy director David Byrne says ... 'There is not a hint that he doesn't have the support of the Carpentaria Land Council and a large number of Aboriginal people in the Gulf'. (new96117).

In Channel Seven's 10.30 p.m. news on 9 July 1996 (tv96051), Yanner was equated with Cheryl Kernot through similar language: 'Democrats leader Cheryl Kernot weighed into the row today, but she refused to give an undertaking to hold a senate inquiry.'... 'The Aborigines opposed to the billion dollar project, lead by the outspoken Murrandoo Yanner, met with Democrats leader Cheryl Kernot.' Both Kernot and Yanner were recognized as the 'leaders' of their constituencies.

Yanner was a leader, but not a politician; the reason for this seemed to be that 'politicians' supported the mine. One item stated that ATSIC chair Lois O'Donoghue (another Indigenous 'leader', but not a politician) had at one point evinced support for the mine, and that this had been cited by 'politicians' as showing Aboriginal support for the legislation (new96143). Radio National's *World Today* reported that 'politicians' supported the first and denigrated the second of the votes taken by local Aboriginal groups (rad96113). Politicians were those representing the state (but see Rose and Miller, 1992: 174).

Aboriginal politicians and representativeness

Aboriginality was brought into the field of the political when an item on ABC Radio's *PM*, 'in this Aboriginal and Islander week', discussed the possibility of guaranteed seats for Indigenous people in parliament. John Lester, an Aboriginal politician who stood for the NSW Labor Party in the seat of Clarence suggested that: 'If we are not to be reliant on the goodwill of decision makers ... it's important for Aboriginal people to partake in mainstream society.' The feature went on to discuss the banal divisions and difficulties of representativeness in the political system (rad95112).

The distinction between leadership and politics has turned out to be quite important. Community 'leaders' such as Noel Pearson 'represented' the voice of their people and were routinely accorded this 'right' by news and other media. But without elective office and ministerial responsibilities, such leaders could not act as decision-makers in their own right on issues affecting their community. Thus, although their social reputation may have been much lower than that of 'leaders', 'politicians' could claim both greater legitimacy (they were elected) and greater clout (they allocated resources). There were also sites of elective and decision-making power in the Aboriginal domain, for instance within ATSIC, in some of the Land Councils and other associations. But there were very few Aboriginal politicians in the legislatures and cabinet rooms of the state apparatus. Not being a politician, then, may have been a disadvantage. Critics such as Howard Sattler certainly used it to contest the right of unelected persons to speak for Indigenous people. He became involved in a debate with local activist Clarrie Isaacs on representativeness:

ISAACS. ... I'm the president of the Aboriginal Government of Australia.
SATTLER. When were you elected to that?
ISAACS. I was actually asked to be that in 1990.
SATTLER. So it's not an elected position.
ISAACS. We don't have elections, it's a system of eldership, we ask people to participate and they pass on authority orally, culturally, and it's got everything to do with Indigenous people, and nothing to do with the federal regimes...
SATTLER. It's a separate government.
ISAACS. We've had a democracy of consensus... it's always been our cultural way...
SATTLER. I would have thought the most democratic way to go about it would be to get all the Aboriginal people to have a vote.
ISAACS. We haven't done that for a hundred thousand years. People can live, and they do live, in other countries under a democracy of consensus, where people... you know you don't have this little power leadership it's a totally different system that people here don't understand....
SATTLER. They may tell you to go to hell too Clarrie.
ISAACS. They may say that to you too Howard.

(rad95082).

Sattler's rigorous standard of representativeness did not apply to his own position. No one elects shock jocks. Sattler's 'representative' legitimacy came from his callers:

CALLER [TOM]. ... I hear so many Aboriginal activists, who are supposedly talking on behalf of all the Aboriginals.
SATTLER. They don't, we found that out.
CALLER. They're creating more division than they are trying to get people together.
SATTLER. That's right, they do not represent the Aboriginal people, I've had sufficient numbers of people who don't want to have a bar of those sorts of people call the programme and say, look, we're sick and tired of being identified as different from everybody else, we are just like everybody else, maybe the colour of our skin is different from everybody else, but that's irrelevant, beneath our skin, we're all the same, and we just want to get on with our lives, we just want to pay off our houses, send our kids to school, go

to work and pay our taxes, we do not want to get up and get involved in all this political claptrap...

(rad95080)

Here Sattler proclaimed himself as the representative of the Indigenous constituency, comprising those who refused 'this political claptrap'. Aboriginal leaders such as Clarrie Isaacs 'do not represent the Aboriginal people'; Sattler did.

Representativeness was also raised in a debate about the decision to recognize the Indigenous flag. Against charges that Indigenous people did not want the flag recognized, Tim Rowse, on *Australia Talks Back*, said:

I don't think there is a national representative body of Indigenous Australians... This recommendation is a recommendation of the National Council for Reconciliation... It's an endemic problem in the politics of Indigenous affairs in Australia at the moment that there is no legitimate spokesperson or body for Indigenous people in Australia. (rad95028).

Sattler was not the only media figure who denied Indigenous people the right to function as public figures in the ways enjoyed by non-Indigenous politicians. P. P. McGuinness engaged in a similar project. In an opinion column headed 'Aboriginal "industry" hijacks policy debate', McGuinness applied rules from the private sphere to public figures such as Murrandoo Yanner:

There are many bureaucrats, academics and other professionals who make their living out of Aboriginal policy... there is also a clique of what might be called 'official' Aborigines. Neither the industry, nor the official Aborigines, are necessarily representative of the real interests of Aborigines... Only the determinedly deaf and blind can avoid discovering that there is a great deal of disagreement and dissent among Aborigines, both as regards the system as they experience it and between tribal and clan groups. Finding out what Aborigines actually think is not as easy as simply listening to the official Aborigines... (new96178).

'Politicians' is the name normally given to the 'clique' of 'official' people who speak up for their communities. McGuinness refused it to Aboriginal people. The very ordinary discovery that a nation did not speak with a single voice was characterized not as 'politics' but as 'disagreement and dissent.'

The ambivalent status of Indigenous people in the political sphere could be seen in a report in the *Australian*: 'Report to slate State over cell deaths' (Thursday 11 July 1996: 2; new96133). As part of a story on the failure of the South Australian government to implement the Recommendations of the Royal Commission into Aboriginal Deaths in

Custody, the paper interviewed Tauto Sansbury, NAIDOC's South Australian Aboriginal of the Year, and South Australian chair of the Aboriginal Justice Advocacy Committee:

Mr Sansbury cited as an example of the State Government's lack of respect for Aboriginal groups, that despite being one of three people who contained and helped end a May riot in the State's high security Yatala prison, he has received no acknowledgement from the State Government. He said the Government has not acknowledged their role in ending the 12–hour dispute, or their role in saving the lives of the two prison officers who were bashed and held hostage by 35 inmates. 'Nobody in the State Government has stood up and said three Aborigines solved that riot,' he said.

The story was a feature on the lack of attention by a state government to the Royal Commission's recommendations. It mentioned in passing the work of three Aboriginal people as successful negotiators in a prison riot. This is typical of the way in which the Indigenous contribution to such issues was covered—not as a matter of course but erratically, accidentally. It was hard to see Aboriginal people as performing governmental service or as public representatives of their people in such reporting, even when that role was what was being reported.

Aboriginality, politics, and the arts

The phrase 'Aboriginal politician' only occurs once in our survey sample: 'Western Australia's singing Aboriginal Politician' (new94192), about the Honorable Ernie Bridge, MLA for the Kimberley and first Aboriginal cabinet minister in Australian history. He was Minister of Agriculture, Water Resources, and the North-West in the WA Labor administration in the 1980s and 1990s. Ernie Bridge was well known in the West for two personal obsessions—he was a country singer of note, and he maintained a long-standing vision for a water pipeline to be built from the north of the state to irrigate the arid south. Indeed, he released a country album on this theme, called *The Great Australian Dream* (see *Cultural Studies* (1992): iv and 308). The combination of politician and singer was apparently bizarre enough to be newsworthy on its own. The fact that Bridge was also an Aboriginal person was incidental to the story, although Bridge himself did use the occasion to introduce a particular form of politics: wishing for general acceptance of Mabo legislation.

A racist at last

In the survey weeks, the realm of sport included debates about race, following the case of Arthur Tunstall, a senior official with the Australian team for the Commonwealth Games. Tunstall's position was challenged in 1995: 'Political, Aboriginal and sporting leaders demanded Mr Tunstall's resignation in May after he told a racist joke' (new95076). The editorial of the *Australian* said that 'Tunstall should still stand down' (new95002), while a news story said that 'the wider community' was opposed to Tunstall (new95001). In these stories, Tunstall's offence was repeatedly cited as 'making racist jokes' (new95001). The *Australian* was convinced that they 'show insensitivity to the attitudes of contemporary Australia' (new95002). It was a 'racist joke' in the *Daily Telegraph Mirror* (new95040) and the *Age* (new95047). In a public culture that constantly sought to deny racism, the charge of the racist joke was one of the few examples in our survey weeks where the term was universally applied, from the 'neutral' position of the journalist, to an individual. Once this had been accepted (that he had indeed been associated with 'racist' speech) it was unsurprising that editorials called for Tunstall's removal.

Aboriginal economies

One of the questions we had at the back of our minds as we undertook this research was about the shape of the Aboriginal 'nation' as a straightforward political object. If there was such a thing, what shape did it take in the media? For instance, in the Australian political context, government is divided into various ministerial portfolios—the treasury, foreign affairs, trade and industry, employment, etc. It is already clear that the map of the Indigenous polity is very different from this. Most striking was the *over-representation* of the cultural sphere in Indigenous politics (the most important portfolios appeared to be those in sport, culture, and the arts), and concomitantly the *under-representation* of the economic sphere. If there was an Indigenous economy, it was not reported coherently in the Australian media. So rare was the association of Aboriginal people with finance, wealth-producing economic activity, and with detailed economic issues from trade to employment that it looked almost like a strategy of exclusion (see Partington, 1996: 81–91). Indeed, Indigeneity tended to be placed in *opposition* to the concerns of finance and economics. Indigenous people were consistently presented as spiritual and natural—qualities which were understood to be the opposite of 'material' or 'materialistic'. As Muecke suggested in the passage quoted above, Indigeneity was trapped in 'culture', and that culture was not about making money.

Most newspapers had daily Finance sections. Our survey suggested that Finance was the newspaper section from which Indigeneity was most commonly excluded. Other regular sections where Indigeneity was more or less absent were lifestyle, property, and computer sections. In 1996, for example, there were virtually no Indigenous appearances in these sections. If, as we would want to argue (and see Charles Perkins's speech to the National Media Forum, herein, Chapter 4), there is indeed an Indigenous economy, including Indigenous people conducting their own businesses, stories reporting on this have tended to appear in the general news or even the 'feel-good' feature sections of the paper.

In the media, Indigenous people emerged as only a 'cultural nation'. They had no national status in political and economic terms. Rather, there were lots of unconnected individuals, whose individual or even corporate finances were not linked to each other in any particular way. The notion of 'the economy', suggesting something shared by the members of a nation, some way of making sense of individual and joint finances as part of a single abstract phenomenon, was missing.

'The economy' as a concept is necessarily a fiction. The 'thing' that governments, media, and various competing associations within civil society spend so much of their time worrying about is a model, a textualization of heterogeneous activity. It is reduced as far as possible to numerical form, and in need of constant checking and re-adjustment to keep in any sort of touch with actual economic activity (economic models are not efficient predictors of future economic conditions). Indigeneity appeared in this context not as part of the overall economy, and certainly not as an autonomous economy in its own right (such as a regional or state economy appeared). It appeared as a cost against existing portfolios, and as a potential area of mismanagement, fraud, dependency, unaccountability, and loss. In other words, Aboriginal people and organizations were represented as *recipients* of *someone else's* finance. The appropriate language to use in this context was that of the accountant, the auditor, and the regulator; the perspective was that of surveillance and investigation. There was no counter-balancing discourse of productivity, economic modelling, policy-making, will-formation, and decision-making in terms of an overall Aboriginal economy.

It was not simply the case that the Indigenous economy vanished as it was submerged in the wider non-Indigenous Australian economy. It was rather the case that news discourse consistently constructed Indigenous people as being outside of, and then set in opposition to the Australian economy. The most familiar expression of this model was the dichotomy that was often set up between 'taxpayers' (who contributed to, and were part of the economy) and 'Aborigines' (who were, by definition apparently, not taxpayers, not contributing to the economy, somehow outside of it and relying on gifts from it—see, for example, rad95162, *Country Wide* on Radio National, Friday, 14 July 1995).

The category of 'business' was also encountered in binary opposition to Indigeneity (e.g. new96196, the *Age*, Business section, 8 July 1996, p.C1). Something called 'business'—that is, the consensual opinion of corporate leaders—was set against Aboriginal communities, as where 'business leaders' commented on threats to their plans (the Century Zinc story was reported this way). But stories of Indigenous business success (or failure, for that matter), where reported, were not found in the 'Business' section of the paper, but in general news. For example, see new96122 (the *West Australian*, 13 July 1996: 4), 'Aborigines win mining contract.'

An Aboriginal-owned mining company has won a multi-million dollar contract at a WA gold mine over which it holds a native title claim. Carey mining will have a 25 per cent interest in the $50 million joint venture contract with AWP Contractors at Acacia Resources' Sunshine Dam gold mine, 55km south of Laverton...

This story was news, not Business. Indigeneity was removed from the site in which knowledge of the economy was circulated. It was a news story, less about economic activity as such than about the excitement of 'the first time that a contracting company controlled by Aborigines has taken part in a major resource development'. If there was an Aboriginal economy, its shape had to be constructed by the careful reader from scattered news elements. The media persisted instead with coverage of 'the eternal debate—jobs and economics versus Indigenous rights'—as a reporter put it to Stan Grant on *Eleven AM* (tv96045).

The implications of such an approach and such language could be seen in the case of the Century Zinc case. Editorial voices insisted that the Century Zinc mine had to proceed. In taking such a position, a series of antinomies was employed:

It would be in Australia's best interest for the rich Century Zinc mine... to begin production as soon as possible. The project will provide jobs at a time when Australia needs every job it can get... Uncomfortable as it may be for some Aboriginal activists, what is good for Australia in most cases is good for Aboriginal Australians too... As they have demonstrated via generous allocations of taxpayers' money, Australians generally are anxious for the welfare of their Aboriginal fellow citizens... the nation cannot afford to abandon or have sabotaged projects of this importance because of the unreasonable expectations of one group... The argument here is... how to compensate those who may be adversely affected by it (nes96177, the *Age*, Wednesday, 10 July 1996: A12, 'Let the mine proceed').

With about 800,000 people unemployed and a huge balance of payments problem, Australia cannot afford to be complacent about major development companies. And yet, one of its biggest potential mining projects in Queensland is under threat of stalemate from a small group of citizens—who amount to a minority of a minority... Yanner's objections... have taken on the appearance of a personal campaign rather than a considered representation of soundly based opposition... The dispute not only jeopardises an export venture that Australia badly needs... Direct talks... give Aborigines the chance to get fair compensation... (new96107, the *West Australian*, Thursday, 11 July 1996: 12, 'Australia needs Century Zinc').

If an Indigenous nation and an Indigenous economy were recognized, for example in the way that state and regional economies were uncontroversially understood, quite different kinds of stories would be told. In the discourses actually employed, Indigenous people could only hope for 'compensation'. If they were a nation, they would be in a position to treat, to negotiate, and to arrange terms. Reduced from the status of a nation (with an economy) to 'activists', such an option was not open.

There was one site in the news media in 1996 where the Century Zinc story was covered in a way that hinted at the existence of an already autonomous Indigenous economy. A cartoon in the *Australian* of 10 July 1996 (new96139, p. 12) showed Prime Minister John Howard standing on a beach beside a group of Indigenous people. They were cooking fish over an open fire, and the cartoonist drew the scene to look idyllic. Howard was haranguing them: 'You know, if this Century mine goes ahead, you could all have an education and a job.' Was it possible to imagine an economy that did not function in terms of traditional jobs and tax structures? The high-tech Computer and Technology supplements indeed suggested that the world was rapidly moving to a post-'job' economy, where people worked freelance rather than taking on a stable job-identity with a single employer. And of course the global economy was growing in the knowledge, culture, sport, arts, and information sectors while heavy industry languished. In such a context the Indigenous economy, suggested by this cartoon, may not have been a romantic joke but a possible future (see Leadbeater and Mulgan, 1997).

Accountability

The letters pages in newspapers provided a particular kind of forum. Hard news has its generic rules (politics, crime), as does soft news ('kids jump for joy'). There are also strict terms of debate for letters to newspapers. Surprisingly, perhaps, it was here that Indigeneity and money coincided most consistently. If there was an Indigenous economy, it appeared to reside in the heads of letter-writers. It was possible either to attack Indigenous people for getting too much money; or to defend such funding. The question of 'us' supporting 'them' was often revisited. The right of Indigenous people to benefit from government spending was, in this forum, constructed as being quite outside of citizenship. The ways of discussing such funding made it sound like charity. Common assumptions about the liberal welfare state—that citizens were guaranteed certain rights—vanished. Aborigines were seen as a group outside of such citizenship rights and responsibilities (new94153). The provision of services to Indigenous people was discussed not within the terminology of political science and the state, but that of charity and individual responsibility. There were no such things as an Aboriginal 'economy' or 'politics'—but there certainly was an Indigenous 'industry', made up not of Aboriginal people making things, but of those for whom representing Indigenous issues in public was thought to be personally profitable.

It was a short step from letters-to-the-editor to editorials. A recognizable genre of editorial said that 'money is not the answer' to Indigenous 'problems': for instance one such in the *NT News* (new94119). The writer located the reason for lack of basic social services not in poor provision, which would be a matter of justice for Aboriginal citizens, but in Indigenous culture itself—Aboriginal people were nomadic, and moved away from the services provided for them. It could be 'proved' that vast sums of money have been spent on Indigenous people. This 'money' was counted in ways that would have flummoxed an economist, even an accountant. It became a single lump sum, which had been 'spent' on Indigenous people, and not solved the 'problem'.

A concomitant type of news story was the 'Indigeneity and funding story'. In such stories, repeated in all three years of our survey, Indigenous people and money came together in terms of mismanagement. Thus: the *Age*, 'Why should ATSIC investigate itself?'(new94010); the *Age*, Digest, 'Aboriginal probe: the federal Minister for Aboriginal Affairs, Mr Tickner, has appointed a former Fraser Government minister...to head an investigation into the Victorian Commissioner of the ATSIC, Mr Alf Bamblett' (new94039); the *Courier Mail*, 'CJC Report slams role of Councils' (new94220).

Such stories could be described as a check floating freely without a balance. Accountability was required of organizations and individuals, but Aboriginal organizations enjoyed neither autonomy nor responsibility. Governments are autonomous agencies in action, but they are accountable to their electors. Aboriginal organisations were neither. They were beholden to external bodies, not to their people. The electors likely to have the most impact on Aboriginal organizations were non-Aboriginal; the government agencies most likely to change Aboriginal policy were state and federal cabinets, not ATSIC. Thus a call for *financial* 'accountability' in Indigenous affairs, especially calls from the 'fourth-estate' media, needed to be matched by moves towards autonomy and *political* accountability.

This was an issue facing Indigenous people everywhere. Toronto *Star* journalist Dan Smith wrote of the situation facing Indigenous Canadian communities in the early 1990s:

> Trust. That was still a difficult notion in many aboriginal communities... Many... chiefs and councils were resisting the idea of checks and balances on their power, despite the growing demand from the healing circles and other activist groups for some real accountability in Indian government.... The lack of trust in the Indian leadership and the fear of change without safeguards was alive across Indian country. (Smith, 1993: 238).

He quoted Dene Nation chief Georges Erasmus, co-chair of a travelling Royal Commission on Aboriginal Peoples in 1992:

> 'Two things we hear over and over. In virtually every community we hear the need for healing, of finding ways to make their communities whole again. And there's also the need for accountability. Not the kind of accountability that comes every two years, but being totally involved in the day-to-day government. That's what people want to see out there.' (Smith, 1993: 238).

In Australian terms, the news media's quest for financial accountability in Indigenous issues was addressed to the news media's traditional interlocutor—state and federal government. It wasn't that the media were asking for the wrong thing; it was that the structure in place could not deliver it. Without national status, Aboriginal organizations were not accountable to their own electors, who themselves were not 'involved in the day-to-day government' for which they may have yearned.

Grog is Government

The difficult position of local Aboriginal councils, and a rare insight into some of the problems of the 'Aboriginal economy', arose in the wake of a Human Rights and Equal Opportunity Commission decision to allow Indigenous communities in the Northern Territory not to sell alcohol. The HREOC decided that the ban would not infringe laws against racial discrimination (new95101, 145). Most coverage focused on the HREOC decision itself: 'Banning the sale of alcohol to Aborigines from "dry" communities in the Northern Territory was not racial discrimination, the Federal Human Rights and Equal Opportunities Commission said yesterday' (*Daily Telegraph*, new95042).

But in the context of the HREOC decision, the *Courier Mail* published a column by Aboriginal doctor Professor Grace Smallwood: 'Alcohol ban key to black survival.' Smallwood presented a detailed account of the part played in Black economies by alcohol, noting that the local canteens were often the only source of money for local councils: 'We're the only local authority in the world which has to keep the constituents drunk to operate' (*Courier Mail*, new95030). In other words, an Indigenous professional locates alcohol as an *economic* 'problem' rather than as one associated with the corporeality of Indigenous people themselves (standard 'grog' stories focus on Indigenous people's individual and collective capacity for alcohol).

The *Courier Mail* also quoted Social Justice Commissioner Mick Dodson on the issue. The HREOC judgment stated that: 'When something is done for the benefit of one group of people, to overcome a history of disadvantage, then it may not be regarded as discrimination, even though it does not apply equally to everyone.' Dodson went on to comment that 'the right of the community to self-determine...should not be confused with an individual's human rights' (new95026).

Later items on the same story featured comment from the Northern Territory Hotels and Hospitality Association: the prohibition 'will not work...Territory Hoteliers claimed...they would be put in an "impossible situation"' (new95097; see also 098, 100). As might be expected, this issue was taken up in the letters pages of newspapers:

Run that past me again: Aborigines win right to ban alcohol...how many years ago was it that Aborigines themselves, along with a whole bunch of do-gooders, demanded the removal of discriminatory laws that prevented sales of liquor to Aborigines... (*Weekend Australian*, new95017).

Alcohol was not about health so much as governmentality: for Smallwood it was about economics; for Dodson about collective self-determination; for hoteliers about implementation; for the letter-writer about legal consistency.

ABC television coverage of this story was illustrated with 'suitable' visuals. The images showed Indigenous people playing football, walking, or sitting in the street. They were images of Indigenous people not-drinking, but what they amounted to beyond this negative or absence was a picture of a 'dry' Aboriginal *community*—a 'governmental' rather than 'health' image (tv95015). However, the same images could be used to illustrate the opposite. On the Channel Nine *Today* programme (tv95089), the interviewer, discussing dry days in Tennant Creek, turned to the (white) editor of the local newspaper. The voice-over said that 'There are three hundred identified problem drinkers' and cut to shots of Aboriginal people, not drunk, just walking in the street. The result was a visual implication that the average Indigenous person in the street could illustrate problem drinking. ABC coverage (tv95058) did not talk generally about 'Aboriginal drinking'. Rather, it spoke to the Aboriginal women who organized the dry community, and interviewed them about the reasons for making their choice.

News Stories 3: Crime, Background, and Context

But is it racist?

We turn now to those stories that have attracted most criticism in academic writing—stories involving Indigeneity and crime. Crime news stories are ideal examples of Lotman's 'catalogue of anomalies'. They construct a 'wedom' and a 'theydom' for the community they address. But Indigeneity was not, as an investigation of 'racism' might have predicted, simply constructed as 'theydom'. In our sample, there was no systematic placement of Indigeneity; rather, Indigenous people took up a variety of positions, structured by the form of news. Interestingly, in our survey weeks, the forces of law and order were not unproblematically constructed as 'wedom' either. The way in which two people made the news during our survey weeks may serve to demonstrate that Indigeneity in crime stories was determined by *genre* rather than *gene*.

Rob Riley

In the 1995 survey week, Rob Riley, then Chief Executive Officer of the Western Australian Aboriginal Legal Service (ALS), was charged with a range of offences relating to reckless driving. The story was certainly sensational, not least because of the ALS's role in controversies surrounding Aboriginal juvenile car crime throughout the 1990s. It was also highly personal, the first public indication of a life unravelling. No one suspected how badly at the time, but within a year Riley had hanged himself in a Perth motel.

Earlier in the same week, Riley appeared in quite different stories, being interviewed on 6PR and elsewhere about his personal history on the occasion of the release of *Telling Our Story* (discussed above). The *West Australian* published a profile of Riley: 'A boy's lonely road to kinship' (new95139):

Rob Riley still has the first present his father gave him—elevenpence halfpenny. He was nine when his father gave him the coins and confirmed the one hope he clung to through a lonely childhood—that he belonged to someone...

The article describes Riley's childhood. He was taken from his parents, institutionalized, and sexually assaulted by boys at Sister Kate's Children's Home. He was told he was an orphan, and an only child, but in fact he had six siblings. He 'recalls the day he first met his parents. For the first time he felt a sense of belonging and discovered that he had brothers and sisters.' The item went on to say that Riley 'has been diagnosed as depressive and suffering from anxiety'.

Profiles contradict the assertion that newspapers deal only in 'conflict', 'sensationalism', and stories abstracted from their 'background' and 'context'. Profiles in newspapers (there is no direct equivalent in radio or television) attempt to provide complex information on an individual, usually relevant to a story being told in the hard news sections of the paper, beyond the confines of typical 'news values'. In the 1995 survey week, Riley was presented as an individual with a history, whose personal experiences of genocidal policy had resulted in particular ways of existing: he was at once a major leader of Indigenous people in the West, a seasoned fighter against the legal regime that discriminated against those people, and a damaged individual in himself—'depressive and suffering from anxiety'.

Small wonder that his arrest was the single most reported news item of its week. It was widely covered on TV: 'Riley suspended' (ABC, tv95130), 'Suspended' (Channel 7, tv95123), 'ALS head may step down' (Channel 10, tv95096), 'Riley' (Channel Ten, tv95121), 'Riley' (Channel Nine, tv95102), 'Riley charged' (ABC, tv95110). Radio stations as different from each other as 6PR, ABC-6WF, and ABC Radio National covered the story in generically similar ways. 'Police have charged the head of the Aboriginal Legal Service in Perth, Robert Riley, with refusing a breath test ... reckless driving' (rad95137, see also on 6PR, rad95119, 124). Similar stories are told on Radio National (rad95103, 104, 105) and 6WF (rad95115, 116, 127). All the stories treated Riley as a public figure, representative of the Aboriginal Legal Service. They treated the story in the same way that coverage of charges against a politician might be taken as problematic for his party. The drama was that of the hard fall for those who aspire to great heights: 'Riley is the head of the Aboriginal Legal Service; this morning, he was prisoner Riley' (Channel Seven, tv95099).

One innovation was Channel Seven's use of Peter Blurton to comment on Riley's arrest. Blurton's wife and child had been killed in 1992 when a car containing Indigenous minors was involved in a high-speed chase with the police and crashed into their car (see Chapter 4). Thereafter, Blurton became a media expert on Aboriginal juvenile car crime, until (after this episode) he too was investigated in relation to the income of the Foundation named after his dead family. Using Blurton on the occasion of Riley's arrest seemed tasteless to some, but could also be seen straightforwardly as following news criteria. It was an example of a commitment to a notion of balance, and of a search for conflict—the drama of adversarial political constituencies. The presentation followed standard news values, and the comments elicited from Blurton were clearly his own, not those of Channel Seven.

None of the other channels repeated the angle discovered by Channel Seven, of having Blurton call for Riley's resignation from the ALS. Riley's own position of being 'repentant' was allowed to emerge. Soundbites informed the public that he had no complaints about the way he had been treated by the police. Channel Ten said that 'police are remaining coy about the incident' (tv95094); most channels included a soundbite from the police press conference, listing the charges against Riley. This could be contrasted with ABC's coverage of the charges:

For Western Australian Aborigines, Rob Riley is a respected advocate, a tough-minded champion of Aboriginal justice...he heads up the Aboriginal Legal Service, a huge responsibility as it lends support to Aborigines who find themselves in strife with the law. (tv95113).

Beyond the news, talkback took a different tack, of course. Howard Sattler used the story as an instance of the way in which (he thought) Indigenous people received over-privileged treatment by the police. He said: 'I've expressed amazement that I couldn't get the police to talk about it...' (rad95131). 'Strangely in this case, the police are not prepared to even come on and allege anything...is Mr Riley in some sort of privileged position?' (rad95120). But Sattler took the opportunity in this survey week to emphasize once more his status as not-racist (rad95130). He hated all car thefts, he said, not simply those done by Indigenous people. He attacked an ex-colleague, Peter Newman, as very racist—he used the term 'abs', for example. Sattler disapproved. The boundary was drawn.

Rhonda Collard and problem police

Rob Riley was featured in several items during the week. In each, coverage was generic. It was pretty clear that much of the news coverage of his arrest took its cue from the 'coy' police handling of the affair (you could almost hear the rustle of kid gloves being pulled on by police and news media alike). However, we also found that the status of the police could become problematic in news coverage.

One of the notable events in 1994 was the emergence of Deaths in Custody Watch Committees in a number of states. In the same week, the ambivalent results of the Eadie Report into the harassment of three Aboriginal actors by the Western Australian police's Tactical Response Group were published. Both of these events were important and well covered in the 1994 survey week (new94049, 051, 068, 205, 214; and on the radio: rad94008, 010, 011, 012, 013, 020, 021, 023, 024, 025, 026, 027, 030, 032, 033, 034, 035, 036, 037, 041, 089, 108, 110, 112, 115, 116, 117, 120, 123; and on television: tv94006, 055, 058, 059, 060, 062, 072, 111, 175, 182, 185).

The Eadie Report into the police Tactical Response Group's treatment of a group of Indigenous actors was well-reported, particularly in the newspapers of Western Australia (new94015, 067, 096, 172, 180, 183). Although the report found the police had acted correctly, the media—and particularly the commercial channels—ran stories that problematized the issue (tv94057, 083, 089, 110, 176). On Channel Ten, for example, Rhonda Collard, one of the actors involved, was interviewed. She was still 'haunted' by the events, said a voice-over, and she was presented talking about the experience. Rob Riley was interviewed on the ABC coverage of this story (tv94180). These stories were notable for *not* relying solely on the police point of view. The Eadie Report demanded compensation for the Indigenous people affected, although it stated that the police were 'only doing their job'. However, the editorial decisions to give prominence to Indigenous interpretations of the event, and to take police relations to be a problem rather than a source of copy, set the story apart from 'crime' stories where bad outsiders dealt with good law enforcers.

In the same week, a report published by the Youth Justice Coalition gained some coverage (new94087, 091). This report said that the police paid 'disproportionate attention' to young Indigenous people. It gave the reason for the high rate of Indigenous youth involvement in crime as the fact that the police originated more encounters with Indigenous youth. The report suggested that racism was present in the police force. Even police spokespeople seemed to accept this point. 'Union denies police are more racist' stated one item (new94076), but charges of structural racism were accepted: 'Negative stereotyping [is] part of' the police force training, the union said. 'Racism rife in police' (new94071). The NSW ombudsman stated that 'some [police officers] were genuinely ignorant that they were discriminating' (new94071). The report showed, SBS said, that 'some police officers are still racist and act according to prejudice and stereotyping' (tv94096). SBS used the opportunity to interview an Indigenous former police aide (tv94151). Channel Ten presented the claims of the report in detail, going so far as to show a written list on screen: that police were more likely to stop non-white youngsters, more likely to strip-search them, and that the non--

white young people were less likely to lay a complaint (tv94019). This was followed by interviews with young Asian and Aboriginal men, who agreed with the suggestions; and a soundbite of a police spokesman at a conference who did not deny the charges, but said that they would be investigated.

Another example which made clear the lack of distinct boundaries between 'us' (police/non-Indigenous) and 'them' (criminals/Indigenous) was a story that the Australian Federal Police were running a recruitment campaign specifically oriented towards Indigenous people. Sydney's *Daily Telegraph Mirror* described the campaign: 'Alternative selection criteria... [will] take account of their knowledge, skills and experience' (new95043). The story acknowledged the current exclusion of Indigenous people in the police force, explained as 'cultural difference'.

Features: background and context

In the newspapers of 1995, the *Age* presented a singular series of features: 'Koori Lives.' They were profiles rather than news, with photographs and interviews, putting individuals into the context of particular institutions and communities. 'Yorta Yorta keep sights on protection of sacred areas' (new95191); 'Growing up in the school of hard knocks' (new95190); 'In Robinvale, one looks to the past for inspiration' (new95189); 'Elders remain at the heart of communities' (new95188); 'Back from the fringes to build more bridges' (new95186); 'Seventy seven call her mum' (new95069); 'The family they tried to break up' (new95068); 'Bushman's lesson of respect' (new95067); 'Working to make a world of hope' (new95066); 'A versatile man of many projects' (new95065); 'The future's shaping up for Tony' (new95064); 'A fair brother to his people' (new95063); 'The cash and cultural clash' (new95062); 'Kooris at the sharp bend of history' (new95052); 'Young faces of the Koori future' (new95054); 'Community retains Fitzroy links' (new95055); 'Proud search for heritage knowledge' (new95057); 'Identity rooted in rhythms of age-old culture' (new95058); 'An almost untold story' (new95059).

The limitations and implications of these profiles could be seen by looking in detail at one story: 'Banjo's message: be a friend.' Like the other profiles, it was illustrated, in this case by a photograph of an Aboriginal man with a child on his knee (the generic marker of 'reconciliation'). In an interview, Banjo Clark said: 'I don't know about this reconciliation business they're talking about... I just think, be natural, mate, and be a friend. Everything will fall into place...' The personalizing romanticism of such writing can be acknowledged, but still this was an exceptional series of articles, making a major intervention into news about Indigeneity through their sheer prominence (throughout the news pages of the *Age* throughout the week) and their number. They provided background and context to traditional news stories about crime, alcoholism, etc., personalizing them through the experiences and history of individuals.

Other stories presented 'background' and 'context'. The *West Australian*, for example, carried a story pointing to history and institutions: 'After 100 years of Aborigines being locked up in Perth psychiatric institutes, Graylands Hospital has set up Western Australia's first on-site service to care for their spiritual and cultural needs' (new95144). The idea of 'cultural specificity' seemed to have achieved an acceptable currency in popular journalism. The areas in which recognizable 'background' and 'context' emerged can be named 'culture' (this was the term used in the newspapers) and health. The latter is illustrated by another story, this time in the *Courier Mail*:

Aborigines in communities throughout Queensland are suspicious that Health Department rules that they must give birth in major hospitals are a threat to the land-claim rights of their children. (new95020).

On the same page, another story was headlined 'Nation's shame won't go away':

Australian Aborigines are grossly under-represented in only one welfare group—the age pension. Few live long enough to claim it. (new95019).

The idea of Aboriginal people as 'the nation's shame' was a common one (the phrase has been used in other contexts) to describe the status of Indigenous health. It was a telling phrase: it placed Indigenous people as a specific part of the wider Australian nation, a subset characterized primarily by health. The *Courier Mail* editorial, 'Our shame revealed' (new95021), was worried about 'the disgraceful conditions in which many black Australians live':

We risk being revealed to the world as a society so introverted that the gross disadvantage of a section of our community is of no concern... (new95021).

This story was notable for arguing that the problem was not 'throwing too much money' at Aboriginal people, but that a cultural and political solution was needed.

10 | Journalism: Ethics, Training and 'Indifference'

Aboriginal and Islander people were keenly aware of media images which they felt to be racist . . . Youth worker Shane Phillips told the Inquiry, 'I believe our number one enemy is the media because media are the ones that create all the negative thoughts in people's heads out there.' The [Redfern] community perceives the electronic media in particular as one of the major weapons of their oppression, and one they feel least able to resist.
(Human Rights and Equal Opportunities Commission, 1991: 116, 358)

There is some debate about what journalism is. As an occupation it has been described variously as a craft, a trade, a career (Barker, 1963), even sometimes as an ethnicity—'reporters are born and not made' (Given, 1907: 148). It may also be a profession:

The occupation which one professes to be skilled in and to follow. (a.) A vocation in which a professed knowledge of some department of learning or science is used in its application to the affairs of others or in the practice of an art founded upon it. Applied *spec.* to the three learned professions of divinity, law and medicine: also to the military profession. (b.) In wider sense: Any calling or occupation by which a person habitually earns his living. Now usually applied to an occupation considered to be socially superior to a trade or handicraft. (*Oxford English Dictionary*).

The status of journalism as a profession has been contested by its own practitioners (see Hartley, 1996: 53; Franklin, 1997). However, it has been professionalizing for over a century, both in the USA, where 'J-Schools' have been operating in universities since the early 1900s, and in other Western countries:

From modest beginnings over a century ago, professional associations grouping individuals working in the various media of mass communication have grown in number and importance . . . many organizations soon turned their attention to broader issues concerning the place of their profession in society. Today they are a powerful force in helping to ensure that the mass media contribute to the welfare of the public at large... Their members are men and women whose vital task is to inform and entertain the peoples of the world through the mass media. (UNESCO, 1959: 3).

The professionalization of journalism involved the establishment of bodies whose concerns were not with economic questions such as salaries and working conditions (UNESCO, 1959: 12). This was not trade unionism, for press clubs and other journalistic institutions, coming into being by the 1870s, aimed to 'raise the professional status of journalists', and established the role of professional self-regulation:

A major contribution of the organizations has been their effort to establish standards of professional conduct for those working in the media of mass communication... Disciplinary clauses [are] written into the statutes of professional bodies. (UNESCO, 1959: 21–2).

in 1930 [the International Journalism Federation] established an international court of honour of the press, which was to be based on national courts of honour and codes of ethics in individual countries. (UNESCO, 1959: 13).

Codes of practice do not directly govern the production of news stories. In practice they are mental check-lists for individual journalists to follow or not as their conscience dictates. They may be invoked after the event by others to 'name and shame' a particular breach. But they have no legal force comparable with the sanctions available to traditional professions, whose governing bodies can stop people from practising—doctors and lawyers can be 'struck off the register', priests can be 'defrocked.' Nevertheless, journalism has generated various 'professional' codes of ethics and practice with relevance to the reporting of Indigenous issues, and to these we turn. It should be noted that the discussion below concentrates on the situation in force at the time of our research during the 1990s. While much of the material will remain stable over time (such as codes of practice), some areas may evolve more rapidly (such as the content of training schemes). While it is not an up-to-the-minute 'handbook' it is nevertheless useful, we believe, as an account of the regulatory, educational, and professional-ideological climate that operated in the context of the reporting of Indigenous issues that we have analysed in this book.

Ethics and Laws

AJA Code of Ethics

The Australian Journalists Association (AJA) has amalgamated with the Media, Entertainment and Arts Alliance (MEAA);

308

however, the relevant code remains widely known as the 'AJA code of ethics'.

Members of the Australian Journalists' Association sector of the Media, Entertainment and Arts Alliance (MEAA) are reminded that observance and enforcing of the code of ethics is an important duty.

Respect for truth and the public's right to information are over-riding principles for all journalists. In pursuance of these principles journalists commit themselves to ethical and professional standards. All members of the Australian Journalists' Assocation engaged in gathering, transmitting, disseminating and commenting on news and information shall observe the following Code of Ethics in their professional activities. They acknowledge the jurisdiction of their professional colleagues in AJA judiciary committees to adjudicate on issues connected with this Code.

1. They shall report on the news with scrupulous honesty by striving to disclose all essential facts and by not suppressing relevant available facts or distorting by wrong or improper emphasis.

2. They shall not place unnecessary emphasis on gender, race, sexual preference, religious belief, marital status or physical or mental disability.

During 1995, the AJA released a revised code of ethics for discussion. Expanding somewhat on the 'ten commandments' of the earlier version quoted above, this revised account of journalism's best practice began with a description of journalism's role: 'Journalists describe society to itself. They seek the truth . . .' Thereafter it listed twenty 'standards'. With respect to race reporting, the wording was identical to the old AJA code: 'Do not place unnecessary emphasis on . . . race.' What had changed was the prominence of this injunction. 'Race' came second in the original code; in the revised version it was placed at number fifteen, after clauses on balance, errors, hidden cameras, plagiarism, paraphrasing, disclosure of payments, etc. The AJA is open to complaints from the public about breaches of its code; perceived breaches can be censured. Information on complaints, adjudications, and actions on particular complaints, however, is not available to the public.

International Journalists' Federation Code of Ethics

The International Journalists' Federation Declaration of Principles on the Conduct of Journalists (article 7) states:

The journalist shall be aware of the danger of discrimination being furthered by the media, and shall do the utmost to avoid facilitating such discrimination based on, among other things, race, sex, sexual orientation, religion, political or other opinions and national or social origins.

The statement of the International Journalists' Federation goes further than that of the AJA, because it allows for journalism itself to be actively concerned with combating racism. Instead of avoiding 'emphasis' on race, journalists should avoid 'facilitating discrimination'. The statement has no force in Australia.

The Australian Press Council

The Australian Press Council adjudicates on complaints made by the public about newspaper journalism. If complaints about stories are upheld, the offending newspaper can be required to publish a correction. This 'semi-autonomous' body is funded by the newspaper and magazine industries to deal with complaints made against them. The 'Statement of Principles' of the Press Council begins with an affirmation of the 'freedom of the press'. The basic terms of reference of the Council are to give 'first and dominant consideration to what it perceives to be the public interest'. However: 'Recognising that these are matters of subjective judgement, the Council does not attempt to reduce to a precise and exhaustive formula the principles by which newspapers must govern themselves...'. The Statement goes on to list a range of 'propositions'. Two of these apply to the reporting of racial issues: 'A newspaper should not place gratuitous emphasis on the race, nationality, religion, colour, country of origin, gender, sexual preference, marital status, or intellectual or physical disability of either individuals or groups'. A separate 'proposition' makes a similar point: 'A newspaper should not, in headlines or otherwise, state the race, nationality, religious or political views of a person suspected of a crime, or arrested, charged or convicted, unless the fact is relevant...'. While for the AJA Code of Ethics, emphasis on race should not be 'unnecessary', the Press Council desires that it should not be 'gratuitous'. The Press Council, however, goes on to point out that even 'gratuitous' mentions of race may be acceptable in certain circumstances: 'Nevertheless, where it is in the public interest, newspapers may report and express opinions upon events and comments in which such matters are raised'.

Adjudications in which the Press Council has found that newspapers have contravened its Statement of Principles include: 'Race Identification Breached Principle' (1992: 103 [adjudication number 537]), upholding a complaint against the *Midland Echo* for identifying the race of a defendant in court proceedings; and 'Words Offensive' (1992: 106 [adjudication number 540]), upholding a complaint against the use of the word 'boong'.

The Council has also rejected complaints. In 'Relevance of Race', for example (APC Annual Report, 1992: 81 [adjudication 517]), the Council upheld part of a complaint. The 'Aboriginal Legal Rights Movement' complained against an *Adelaide Advertiser* report of three separate instances, one where six people allegedly attacked a man and a woman, another where four men attacked a man, and a third in which a group of eighty people chased four policemen. 'In all cases the alleged assailants were unnamed but identified as Aborigines': 'In this case, said the paper, it believed race was relevant. The report was published . . . on the eve of a special meeting in Adelaide to discuss police-Aboriginal relations . . .' (81). The Council stated that: 'the value judgement of relevance . . . can be very much a matter of point of view. The Press Council believes that the case for relevance [in this case] can be argued . . .' (81). In 'Racial References Not Gratuitous' (1994: 72 [adjudication number 668]), the Press Council dismissed complaints against the Brisbane *Sunday Mail*: 'There are few current issues of greater public importance and obvious continuity than the place of the Aboriginal people . . . in the Australian community' (72). Bearing this in mind, the Press Council found it necessary to look for some model of objectivity for judging these issues. Avoiding the 'reasonable adult' of various legal and quasi-legal definitions (the ABA and the Human Rights and Equal Opportunities Commission, for example), the Council produced as its independent observer the 'mythical Martian visitor'. This trope was not explained, but given as an example of an innocent reader.

From the viewpoint of the 'mythical Martian', the Press Council decided on the relevance of mentions of race. For example, in one case where a report referred to 'a gang of about sixty Aborigines and Maoris', the Council suggested that:

the numbers involved in the disturbance, its aftermath and the fact that it was relevant to the on-going issue of relations between Aboriginal people, Maoris and the police were sufficient to fulfil the public interest stipulation which is an integral part of the policy. (72).

In relation to another example:

While it is probably true that the racial reference in this article could reinforce the stereotype held by some readers, it is equally true that the article involved a matter of considerable public interest and that readers were entitled to the fullest possible information.

In these two cases, concerns with 'stereotypes' and with 'relevance' appeared to be overcome by appealing to the public's right to know— a stance that overturned the essence of the initial Statement of

Principles. This adjudication also stated that individual articles that breached the code could be leniently read in the context of a newspaper's other coverage of similar issues (1994: 72, 73).

Some complaints were upheld in relation to other aspects of its Statement of Principles than those directly related to reporting of race. For example, 'Words improperly sourced' (APC Annual Report, 1992: 78) concerned an upheld complaint about a story headlined 'Black Violence—Why Whites Shouldn't Feel so Guilty'. An Aboriginal research consultant, Judy Atkinson, complained that she was quoted out of context, to support a thesis with which she did not agree (that Aboriginal society was a violent one even before settlers arrived). This complaint was upheld: there was, however, no complaint about, or comment on, the argument or presentation of the story itself. In 'Column's assertions unsupported' (1995: 123 [adjudication number 794]), a complaint about an article on Aboriginal land claims was discussed in the following terms: 'There is no doubt that the language used in the article is vigorous...but overall it is not beyond the vigour allowable in by-lined pieces...'. But the complaint was partially upheld: 'Robust writing on such a sensitive subject as race relations must surely be coupled with rigorous discipline in accuracy and use of emotive words'. The Council's statistical breakdown of complaints provided a separate category to show the number of complaints made by 'Aboriginal support groups and legal services': 7 in 1992, 2 in 1993, 5 in 1994, 8 in 1995. The number of complaints made by non-Aboriginal bodies or individuals about Indigenous representation was not given.

Australian Broadcasting Authority (formerly Australian Broadcasting Tribunal, formerly Australian Broadcasting Control Board).

The Australian Broadcasting Authority (ABA) oversees the programme content of commercial broadcast media—radio and television. Previously, this work was carried out under the name of the Australian Broadcasting Tribunal in accordance with a set of Program Standards: the Television Program Standards, and the Radio Program Standards. Under the Broadcasting Services Act of 1992, however, the Tribunal became the Authority, and the Tribunal's 'Standards' were replaced with a series of 'Codes of Practice', developed by each broadcasting medium itself.

Both the Standards and the Codes of Practice are concerned with wider issues than the content of programmes. Issues of ownership, production, and technical requirements are also addressed. In fact, there is relatively little attention in either version to textual matters, certainly with regard to Indigeneity. In the 1975 'Program Standards', for example, there was no mention of the coverage of race. The 'General Program Standards' gave some idea of the concerns of the then Tribunal:

Fundamentally these Standards require the observance in programs of good taste and common sense ... no program may contain any matter which is ... contrary to the law ... blasphemous, indecent or obscene ... likely to encourage crime ... likely to be injurious to community wellbeing or morality ... or otherwise undesirable in the public interest ...

Guidelines formulated to deal with the treatment of sex could offer an opportunity for making complaints about race: 'The use of objectionable words and phrases or words which have acquired undesirable or offensive implications, should be avoided' (1975: 8).

The handling of complaints, including those about the treatment of race, has since been taken over by the radio and television stations themselves. If facing a complaint of an unacceptable representation of race, the broadcaster will decide, from its own Code of Conduct, if in fact any breach has been made. It is only if the complainant is unhappy with the broadcaster's handling of the complaint that it can then be taken to the ABA. If the ABA's 'investigation' finds against the broadcaster, an unspecified 'range of sanctions' is available. 'Any action taken depends on the seriousness of the breach' (*ABA Update*, no. 37: 17).

Before 1992, the ABA investigated several thousand complaints in some years (see its Annual Reports). Since the complaint procedure was moved to the broadcasters, the ABA handled only 151 complaints in 1994–5. Breaches of licences or codes were found in only three cases. Only one of these was relevant to ethnicity: '3ZZZ Melbourne (community radio) Serbian language program ... was found to be in breach of radio program standard 3(b) (gratuitous vilification on the basis of ethnicity)' (*ABA Update*, no. 37: 17).

Commercial Television Industry Code of Practice

The 'Commercial Television Industry Code of Practice' governs the representation of Aboriginal people in that medium. A licensee may not 'simulate news or events in such a way as to mislead or alarm viewers', 'induce a hypnotic state in viewers', 'use the process known as "subliminal perception"'. Neither may it 'seriously offend the cultural sensitivities of Aboriginal and Torres Strait Islander people or of ethnic groups or racial groups in the Australian community'. Nor may it: 'stir up hatred, serious contempt or severe ridicule against a person or group of persons on the grounds of age, colour, gender, national or ethnic origin, physical or mental disability, race, religion or sexual preference' (5). Clause 4.3.7 of the Code states that:

news and current affairs programs...must not portray any person or group of persons in a negative light by placing gratuitous emphasis on age, colour, gender, national or ethnic origin, physical or mental disability, race, religion or sexual preference.

In these guidelines, broadcasters face the injunction not to 'offend' Indigenous audiences. This would seem to place some burden of research on them, to discover how such audiences in fact respond to their broadcast material.

There is a standard 'public interest' proviso:

none of the matters in Clause 1.6 will be contrary to this Section if said or done reasonably and in good faith...in broadcasting an artistic work (including comedy...)...for an academic, scientific or artistic purpose or for any other identifiable public interest purpose or...in broadcasting a fair report of, or a fair comment on, any event or matter of identifiable public interest...(5).

Commercial Radio Codes of Practice and Guidelines/Federation of Australian Radio Broadcasters (FARB)

The Commercial Radio Codes of Practice and Guidelines were drawn up in consultation with the National Indigenous Media Association of Australia, and in some ways represent current industry best practice in this area. But it is worth noting that while they were set in place in 1993, they have had little impact on the practice of commercial radio broadcasting.

'Code of Practice One' deals with proscribed material: 'Programs unsuitable for broadcast.' As with the commercial television code, it is stated that: 'A licensee shall not broadcast a program which...is likely to incite or perpetuate hatred against, or...gratuitously vilifies any person or group on the basis of ethnicity, nationality, race, gender, sexual preference, religion or physical disability.' Unlike the television guidelines, however, this statement represents only the introduction to this issue. After six 'Codes of Practice', FARB includes a five-page subdocument, 'Guidelines for the Portrayal of Indigenous Australians (Aboriginal and Torres Strait Islander Peoples) on Australian Commercial Radio'. As well as reiterating general instructions about avoiding vilification, contempt, and ridicule, these guidelines include standards against which transmitted material might be judged. For example, it states that:

It is not up to a broadcaster to question a person's Aboriginality.

Media reports about Aboriginal and Torres Strait Islander peoples should respect the protocols of those peoples.

The document also calls for 'Balance', defined as giving 'an opportunity to reply to the material and should cause the reply to be broadcast', when any 'negative' story is broadcast. 'Positive' portrayals are those which: 'assist [Aboriginal and Torres Strait Islander] communities to maintain and pass on to their descendants their cultures and traditions and facilitate an understanding of Indigenous peoples' cultures among all Australians.... The FARB Guidelines also call for (but do not themselves set in place) 'programs which sensitise non-Indigenous journalists and program makers to the values of Indigenous people'. They do, however, supply a contact list of NIMAA representatives who are available to become involved in such work. They also suggests 'educational material'—*Signposts*, the Office of Aboriginal Affairs' *Rebutting the Myths*, and Lester Bostock's *The Greater Perspective*.

The FARB code lists acceptable and unacceptable terminology, thus providing an explicit set of criteria against which offensive programmes might be measured: unacceptable terms including words such as 'abo', 'boong', 'gin', 'half-caste', and others.

ABC Codes of Practice

At the time of writing the public-service 'national broadcaster', the ABC, had more Indigenous staff, programmes, and reporting than any other broadcasting institution. It is thus surprising to find that in the ABC's own Code of Practice, concerns about the representation of Aboriginal people are present, but there is a substantially less detail than there is in the case of commercial radio broadcasters. Nevertheless, there are several points in the ABC Code in which Aboriginal representation is mentioned. In relation to language, the Code states that: 'Variations of language favoured by different groups of Australians—young or old, well educated or less educated, migrants, Aborigines and others— are equally valid and have their place in programs.' In the most predictable context, paragraph 2.4, headed 'Discrimination', the Code notes that:

The presentation or portrayal of people in a way which is likely to encourage denigration of or discrimination against any person or section of the community on account of race, ethnicity, nationality, sex, age, physical or mental disability, occupational status, sexual preference or the holding of any religious, cultural or political belief will be avoided...

As with other codes, the ABC provides a series of exemptions: 'This requirement is not intended to prevent the broadcast of material which is factual, or the expression of genuinely-held opinion in a news or current affairs program, or the legitimate context of a humorous, satirical or dramatic work.' These exemptions mix the artistic/newsworthy concerns of commercial television exemptions with the 'genuinely-held beliefs' provision of the Race Discrimination Act.

As well as these 'General Program Codes', the ABC also addresses the representation of Aboriginal people in 'Specific Program Codes', which include '3.3. Aboriginal and Torres Strait Islander Programs': 'Program makers and journalists should respect Aboriginal and Torres Strait Islander culture. Particular care should be exercised in traditional matters such as the naming or depicting of Aboriginal and Torres Strait Islander people after death'.

SBS Codes of Practice

The ABC Code of Practice occupies one double-sided A4 sheet. The Special Broadcasting Service (SBS) Codes of Practice are presented in a 35-page booklet. After a general statement of the 'multicultural' mission of SBS, the Code goes on to 'General Program Codes and Policies'. The first of these, 2.1, deals with 'Prejudice, Racism and Discrimination'. In its preamble to these codes, SBS makes the only pro-active statement on this subject:

The SBS seeks through its programming to counter the attitudes of prejudice against any person or group on the basis of their race [and other groups] ... SBS seeks to correct distorted pictures of cultural communities ... through programming which reflects the reality of Australia's demographic pluralism ... which exposes racist attitudes ... strives to eliminate stereotyping by presenting members of different groups in a wide variety of roles and by avoiding simplistic or one-dimensional representations ...

The SBS presents a model of campaigning journalism. Its aim is not neutrally to reflect what occurs in society, but actively to intervene in the name of social justice: 'to correct distorted pictures', 'to counter the attitudes of prejudice'. Such a model of journalism, as having a social agenda, is alien to most of the Codes of Practice here discussed.

A subsection of the SBS Code is addressed to 'Aboriginal and Torres Strait Islander Societies'. This proclaims the need for programming for Indigenous people, and the necessity of Indigenous involvement in the production of such programmes. As with the ABC, it is mentioned that production practices must take account of traditional cultural expectations. Also included is a concern with authorship: 'An Aboriginal or Torres Strait Islander view of Aboriginal or Torres Strait Islander issues is preferable to a non-Aboriginal or non-Torres Strait Islander view'. Such a provision may be seen as provocative in the context of journalism and arguments of free speech. Further comments go on to detail the necessity of Indigenous involvement in the production of Indigenous images. SBS commits itself not to produce 'stereotypes'.

SBS have also commissioned and distributed a booklet by Lester Bostock, *The Greater Perspective*. This provides an extremely detailed 'guideline for the production of film and television on Aborigines and Torres Strait Islanders'. The SBS Codes of Practice should be seen in the context of this work.

ABA Publications

The annual report of the Australian Broadcasting Authority is the only source of information on how its new structure has operated in fact, but it says very little about complaints to do with race. All that can be said from the tables of statistics is that there is indeed a category of complaints in regard to 'Racism', and so the ABA must have been utilizing some criteria to make adjudications on these complaints. In the first half of 1993, commercial television registered no such complaints, but commercial radio was the focus of eighteen complaints of racism. In the 1993–4 report, the categories had changed slightly: commercial radio was then the focus of thirty-two complaints about 'discriminatory broadcasts'; commercial television received no complaints. The categories again evolved for the 1994–5 report: here, commercial television was the focus of 199 complaints with regard to 'Hatred/Ridicule—Discrimination'; and commercial radio of 90 for 'Hatred/Vilification—Discrimination'. The uncertainty of the classifications makes it difficult to compare across years on this subject. In previous years, a category of 'sexism' was employed: presumably it also was subsumed under the 'discrimination' category.

According to the National Indigenous Media Association, in the period 1986–92, 72 complaints were received by the ABA (ABT) about the broadcasting of 'objectionable material' about Aboriginal people on talkback radio stations. It is unclear how this information was gathered. No public statement of the judgments in these cases has been made.

A single ABA judgment on a complaint regarding the representation of race has been made available to researchers, if not publicly circulated. The complainant in this case, Dick Buchhorn, made the judgment available to Michael Meadows of Griffith University, and thus to other interested parties. This document is invaluable in making clear the practice of these codes—how the abstract rules of the Commercial Television stations are read in a particular instance. In this complaint, Channel 7 Brisbane faced a complaint of not having followed Clause 4.3.7 of the Commercial Television Code: 'portraying Aboriginal people in a "negative light"'. According to the complainant, Channel 7 Brisbane had used footage of violence between police and Aboriginal people to illustrate a peaceful Aboriginal protest march. The ABA decided that the complaint should in fact be heard in relation to Clause 1.6.6: 'stir up hatred, serious contempt or severe ridicule'. A second part of the same complaint was then heard in relation to 4.3.7, the 'negative light'.

In addressing the complaint, the ABA posed a question: 'Was it likely in all the circumstances that the broadcast of this program stirred up hatred, serious contempt or severe ridicule against Aboriginal people on the basis of their race?' The ABA considered the impact of these broad-casts on the 'hypothetical viewer'. This viewer would 'not be particularly susceptible to being roused to hatred, contempt and so on . . . an ordin-ary, reasonable person . . .'. This 'reasonable' or ordinary person was however defined as: 'not immune from susceptibility to being stirred up, nor holding racially prejudiced views'. In making its judgment, the ABA attended to the textual details of the material, listing as their concerns:

language, intonation . . . the synthesis of visual and sound elements . . . duration in the proportion to the overall length of the program . . . is the material emanat-ing from the broadcaster in such a way as to carry his [sic] authority . . . 'balan-cing' material within the program . . . [or] in a separate program.

The ABA took several paragraphs to analyse the Channel 7 story in question, noting the language used, the positioning of footage in the story, the authority accorded speaking voices, broadcast context, and so on, finally deciding that: 'the ABA considers the broadcast of this program would have been likely in all the circumstances to stir up hatred against Aboriginal people on the grounds of their race'. The ABA went on to suggest that although the story provoked hatred, it was unlikely to have provoked contempt or ridicule, suggesting that these involved demeaning Aboriginal people, while hatred involved merely presenting them as frightening. The ABA also mentioned a related complaint in which the Aboriginality of a gang of girls involved in an attack was revealed in a news story, taking a similar approach to the analysis of the text, and in this case deciding that:'the reference to the race of the alleged assailants was gratuitous . . . However . . . it is the ABA's view that the reference that did occur was insufficient to portray Aboriginal people in a negative light...'. No comment was made about what action was taken by the ABA in relation to the complaint which was upheld against Channel 7 in Brisbane. But: 'the ABA wishes to emphasise that any breach of the provision set out at Clause 4.3.7 of the code would be viewed as a very serious matter. Broadcasting services should be aware of the importance of continued compliance with this code provision...'.

In a magazine called *ABA Update*, the results of an ABA Research Monograph, *The People We See on TV*, were summarized. 'Just under half (47%) of those surveyed said Aborigines should be shown more often on television': 'One of the issues that arose from the research was the need for more input from Aborigines and Torres Strait Islanders regarding their representation in the media'. Research among Aboriginal populations themselves was cited: '98% agreed there should be more Aborigines and Torres Strait Islanders on commercial radio or television':

the majority of participants felt the media persists in presenting stereotyped and negative images of Aborigines and Torres Strait Islanders... A number of participants cited the example of the drunken, homeless or abusive Aborigine as being a commonly perpetuated stereotype in the media... wanted to see Aborigines portrayed as a regular part of the television landscape, cast in any type of role, not just in a specifically or stereotypically Aboriginal role... (*ABA Update*, no. 5: 4).

The Chair of the ABA suggested that this ABA research

gives [Aboriginal people] powerful tools with which to re-position people's thinking about what the media is, and should be... can use our research to approach the industry both on codes and as part of the new complaints mechanism... can be used as a basis for discussion with the networks, with... local commercial media... These exchanges can then operate beyond anecdote and anger. (*ABA Update*, no. 5: 14, 15).

National Indigenous Media Association of Australia

The National Indigenous Media Association of Australia has produced an Indigenous Media Code of Ethics. It is not overseen in any statutory way (NIMAA is a voluntary association, not a statutory regulatory body). The code deals not with media representations of Indigenous people, but with the practice of Indigenous journalism. It is evidently based on the unrevised version of the AJA code of ethics (the 'ten commandments'), and deals largely with the same issues of journalistic integrity. It calls for 'scrupulous honesty', warns against 'commercial considerations', and so on.

An Indigenous spin is put on this version of the AJA rules. For example, 'personal interests' should be treated with care. Not only is this provision extended to deal with specifically Indigenous concerns—'in the case of family, law, clan, etc. ... they shall state their interest'—but there is also a sense of *inclusion*. That is to say, here, 'personal interest' does not make journalism impossible, but rather is a necessary part of the story, where reporters are seen not to be ('objective') outsiders, but part of the community. Particularly interesting is the intersection of the AJA's code on racism with Indigenous concerns: 'While it is the duty of Indigenous Media to report on Aboriginal and Torres Strait Islander issues, cultures and beliefs, they shall not place unnecessary emphasis on gender, race, sexual preference ...'. The code inevitably points in opposite directions simultaneously: racial identity is the basis of NIMAA, of Indigenous Media, of this reporting; and yet race must not be accorded 'unnecessary emphasis'.

The Indigenous Media Code of Ethics features two points specifically addressed to Indigenous concerns: 'They will actively educate the wider community and media in dealing with Aboriginal Media and issues'; and 'They will observe all tribal, geographical and sacred rights and areas'. This Code is the least enforced of those so far discussed. But, together with the SBS code, it represents a different model of journalism. Indigenous journalists will 'actively educate the wider community'. This is campaigning journalism.

Department of Transport and Communication: 'Statement of Principles'

The Department of Transport and Communication (the federal ministry concerned with the regulation of broadcast media) prepared a 'draft statement of principles for media reporting on Aboriginal and Torres Strait Islander issues' (*ABA Update*, no. 5: 14). This 'Statement of Principles' had no legal or industrial status. It was published purely as advice:

We commend the Statement of Principles to the broadcasting and print media industry. We hope the industry will regard the Statement of Principles as the basic working document for developing their own codes to govern the conduct of the various sectors of the industry... (Michael Lee and Robert Tickner).

The Statement was based on work done at a 'Media and Indigenous Australians' Conference held in Brisbane by the Aboriginal and Torres Strait Islander Commission in 1993. It offered background information mentioning the Council for Aboriginal Reconciliation Act (recognition of prior ownership), the Royal Commission into Aboriginal Deaths in

Custody, and mutual understanding. The Seven 'Principles' dealt with textual, newsgathering, audience, and training considerations.

1. The media 'should not distribute material that is likely to incite or perpetuate hatred...serious contempt...[or which] severely ridicules...';

2. broadcasters should avoid 'gratuitous' reference to Aboriginality;

3. cultural sensitivity would be found in 'seeking advice from the appropriate source'—it deals with the process of newsgathering;

4. 'negative' material should be balanced with 'positive' material;

5. 'negative' comment should be balanced with 'positive' comment;

6. 'The portrayal of Aboriginal and Torres Strait Islander people in the media should facilitate an understanding of Aboriginal and Torres Strait Islander cultures among all Australians and contribute to the maintenance of Indigenous cultures and traditions...';

7. deals with the establishment of 'Appropriate training programs'.

The Royal Commission into Aboriginal Deaths in Custody

The Royal Commission made several recommendations specifically concerned with the representation of Aboriginal and Islander people in the media. Although they have no legislative power, these recommendations have proven to be prominent in recent debates about the representations of Aboriginal people. Recommendations 205 to 212 deal with these issues, suggesting industrial reforms around the funding of Aboriginal media bodies, the establishment of monitoring bodies, awards for excellence in reporting Aboriginal affairs, the establishment of units on Indigenous affairs in university training courses, and so on. These recommendations are notable for making specific, practical, and measurable recommendations, which address many different institutional contexts through which representations of Aboriginality are produced. There is little address to textual matters, and no comment on what would be considered to be good practice in terms of the texts finally produced.

1993 Racial Vilification Legislation

As well as the various Codes of Practice which express the ideals of journalism as a profession, there are in existence legislative measures that impinge directly on the media. Primary among these is the Racial Vilification legislation, which is administered by the Human Rights and

Equal Opportunities Commission. The Racial Vilification Legislation came into effect on 13 October 1995. It provides for complaints to be made about the representation of Aboriginal people in the media:

> It is unlawful for a person to do an act, otherwise than in private, if...the act is reasonably likely, in all circumstances, to offend, insult, humiliate or intimidate another person or a group of people, and...the act is done because of the race, colour, national or ethnic origin of the other person.

The definition of not-private includes those acts which 'cause words, sounds, images or writing to be communicated to the public'. Extensive exemptions are allowed. It is not unlawful to make such statements 'reasonably and in good faith', or if the comments are made as part of an 'artistic work', any 'genuine purpose in the public interest', or of a 'fair and accurate report of any event or matter in the public interest'. Also, it is not unlawful to make offensive comments based on race if 'the comment is an expression of a genuine belief held by the person making the comment'. The complexity of Equal Opportunity Legislation means that the relationships between State and Federal Bodies are difficult to tease out. There are some relevant aspects of the work of several State bodies.

- *Victoria*: The Victorian Equal Opportunity Commission administers the 1995 Victorian Equal Opportunity Act. This does not mention broadcasting or 'vilification'. Although it has a dedicated Koori Department, it has not dealt with any complaints in this area.

- *New South Wales*: The New South Wales Anti-Discrimination Board administers the 1977 New South Wales Anti-Discrimination Act. Division 3A of the Act covers 'Racial Vilification': 'It is unlawful for a person, by a public act, to incite hatred towards, serious contempt for, or severe ridicule of, a person or group of persons on the ground of the race of the person or members of the group' (13). This body primarily works with a non-public conciliation process. Failure of this process leads to a public hearing before the NSW Equal Opportunities Commission. Although figures are not available for the number of complaints made specifically with relation to Indigenous identity and the media in New South Wales, some statistics can be given. Up to mid-1992, 778 verbal and 225 written complaints had been made under racial vilification provisions, including all racial and ethnic groups and all 'public' situations (not just media). In the year 1990–1, there were 8 complaints from Aboriginal and Torres Strait Islander people.

- *Western Australia*: The Western Australian Human Rights and Equal Opportunities Commission administers the 1984 Western Australian Equal Opportunity Act. This has no account of vilification. However, in a useful caveat, the Commission does have jurisdiction over representations of race in job advertising. This is a matter of strictly policing non-representation. 'Under the Equal Opportunity Act (1984), it is against the law to publish or display an advertisement that indicates an intention to discriminate on one or more of the grounds and in an area covered by the Act...The job advertisment should show that the vacancy is open to every qualified person...Job titles should be worded so that they neither openly nor by implication discourage anyone from applying...' (Equal Opportunities, Guidelines for Advertisers). Any complaints directly relating to vilification are passed on directly to the Federal body. There are also provisions under the Western Australian Criminal Code (1913), inserted in 1990, to deal with 'written or pictorial material which is threatening or abusive on racist grounds' (Akmeemana, 1995). Whereas most offences created by such legislation are civil, in Western Australia vilification is a criminal offence. Under section 78 of the WA Criminal Code, 'Publication, etc., of material to incite racial hatred', it is stated that: 'Any person who ...publishes, distributes or displays written or pictorial material that is threatening or abusive and...intends hatred of any racial group to be created, promoted or displayed or increased by the publication, distribution or display of the material...is guilty of a crime and is liable for imprisonment for 2 years...'. This legislation was put in place to deal with a specific instance of racist (Nazi) posters being distributed in the State. It has never been used.

- *South Australia*: The Equal Opportunities Commission of South Australia administers the South Australian Equal Opportunity Act. There is no provision in this Act for vilification. Any complaints relating to vilification are passed on to the Australian Broadcasting Authority, or the Federal body.

- *Queensland*: The Queensland Anti-Discrimination Commission administers the Queensland Anti-Discrimination Act. This makes no mention of vilification. Relevant complaints are passed on to the Federal body.

- *Australian Capital Territory*: The 1991 ACT Discrimination Act includes provisions regarding 'public' vilification: 'by public act, to incite hatred towards, serious contempt for, or severe ridicule of, a person or group of persons on the ground of race...' To 1995 only one complaint had been lodged.

Training Journalists

Journalism's status as profession remains uneasy. There is no widespread acceptance that its practice fulfils the *OED* definition of a profession, i.e. 'knowledge of some department of learning or science is used in its application to the affairs of others or in the practice of an art'. While many journalists accept it as the 'practice of an art', many balk at the idea of that practice as the application of 'knowledge of some department of learning'—i.e. 'journalism theory' as an academic discipline. Thus the question of journalism's status turns upon what is required for entry into it: 'studies' (a profession), 'training' (a craft), 'employment' (a trade), or 'no qualifications' (a democratic right).

Education for the professions—divinity, law, medicine—traditionally occurred in universities. While journalism courses have been running in universities since the first decades of the twentieth century, the acceptability of this move remains problematic:

Both academically and commercially, journalism as a profession has been a bit of a grey area. It's too often thought of as something the talented just 'do', like the arts. And the idea of training is only vaguely acknowledged. But as with a concert pianist or sculptor, to be a success a journalist needs to train assiduously and develop a professional approach. (Clayton, 1992: 8).

Journalism, like medicine or teaching or any other practical profession, cannot be learned wholly from books or in the classroom...the art, the craft, the mystery (to use the medieval term) of journalism can only be learned 'on the job', preferably in the newspaper office. And the best teachers have always been, and always will be, the beginner's own more experienced colleagues. He will find, too, that there is a real sense of fellowship in the profession...(Candlin, 1955: 10).

The classic route of entry into journalism was through apprenticeship or cadetship in a provincial newspaper or broadcasting station: 'Most recruits to journalism have to find their jobs on newspapers in the provinces...Senior men have time, and usually take a great deal of trouble, to teach youngsters their craft' (Barker, 1963: 111). University education of journalists steadily gained ground in the 1980s and 1990s, where it now boasts its own professional association, the JEA (Journalism Educators Association). Nevertheless it retains strong commitments to on-the-job experience, and resists even more strongly the idea that the practice of journalism can comprise the application of disciplines derived from academic learning (see Hamlett, 1999).

In such a situation, it may not be safe to equate what is done in formal training and education with what happens in the newsroom and on the doorstep. However, formal training is well established, and part of it relates to the reporting of Aboriginal affairs. Indeed, one of the Recommendations of the Royal Commission into Aboriginal Deaths in Custody addressed journalism training. It suggested that journalism educators should:

207a. Ensure that courses contain a significant component relating to Aboriginal affairs thereby reflecting the social context in which journalists work.

207b. Consider, in consultation with media industry and media unions, the creation of specific units of study dedicated to Aboriginal affairs the reporting thereof.

How was that challenge taken up by journalism educators?

According to a series of interviews we conducted with journalists identified as 'Aboriginal Affairs' reporters, or who have written stories with an Indigenous focus, the predominant mode of 'training' in newspapers, and especially in the electronic media, was not by means of formal training at all, but of on-the-job apprenticeship. However, those responsible for in-house training indicated that they relied on universities for ensuring that cadets had the basic journalistic skills.

We therefore conducted research into the teaching of journalism in Australian universities. We received responses from twenty-one of twenty-four Australian institutions identified as offering undergraduate and postgraduate degrees in journalism in the mid-1990s. Every journalism degree in Australia mentioned race in its course materials. An adequate generalization was that, overall, the AJA Code of Ethics (no 'unnecessary' mention of race) stood as the basic source, and in some cases the entire content, of journalism educators' attention to the reporting of race. With the exception of Bachelor College no institution featured Aboriginal issues as a separate unit within a journalism degree. At Central Queensland University, a unit was taught on 'Race Issues and Indigenous Media'; but this was not compulsory for journalism students, being rather taught as part of an Aboriginal Studies degree and available to them.

Ethics courses

The most common means of structuring Aboriginality into journalism teaching was as part of a course on 'Ethics', based around the second point of the AJA code of ethics—that 'unnecessary emphasis' should not be placed on race. This was the case at Macleay College, University of South Australia (where it was moved from the elective 'Reporting Minority Issues' to the core ethics course), Queensland University (a three-week block on 'minority' coverage in the media), Deakin, Curtin, Wollongong ('Ethics and Standards') and Murdoch University ('Journalism law and media ethics'). These courses were core units. At Edith Cowan University, Aboriginality was addressed as part of the journalism ethics concern of a 'News/Current Affairs' unit.

Student-led concern

Many respondents suggested that the content of courses was student-led—whether by workshop participation as students produce their own journalism (Bond University), or by the presentation of student papers (Queensland University). Bond's course was workshop based, and relied on that mechanism for Aboriginal issues to be raised beyond a single seminar. Deakin University suggested that most Aboriginal content of the course was *ad hoc*, based on students' interest and, in particular, through Aboriginal students' work on articles about their communities. Queensland University similarly pointed to the journalism produced by students, suggesting that 'every day in the newsroom, Aboriginality will come up as an issue and be dealt with in a progressive way'. Such workshop-led material could be more specifically addressed to Aboriginal issues. Michael Meadows, for example, made clear that at Griffith University students would be set assignments designed to involve all of them in contact with the Aboriginal community: 'assignments where they will have to engage with members of the Indigenous community in Brisbane, and also reflect on the kind of practices they may be using in gathering information from those communities . . .' (Michael Meadows).

Within other courses

The reporting of Aboriginal issues was also mentioned in courses on 'Beginning Reporting' and 'Public Affairs Reporting' (Queensland). James Cook University included one lecture and one assignment as part of the first-year course. The University of Western Sydney featured 'at least one lecture for each of the three semesters' on the reporting of Aboriginal issues. At Murdoch University, Aboriginal Affairs comprised one lecture in the course 'Journalism and Society'. Bond University had one seminar in a foundational journalism course, on interviewing Aboriginal people. Deakin University included Aboriginality in a 'Comparative Journalism' unit. Queensland said that Aboriginality 'infuses the course', citing as examples teaching about news, deviancy, and ideology. Southern Cross had an optional course on Theory (distinct from Practice) that included foundation and film units where race was taught. Students could, however, choose not to take Theory, but to focus on Practice ('practical skills'). Wollongong was seeking to establish a separate Certificate of Multicultural Journalism, and also taught Aboriginality as part of a 'Journalistic Method' course. South Australia included it in 'Issues in Journalism'. Central Queensland addressed Aboriginal issues in 'Introduction to Journalism' courses. At Edith Cowan University, 'cultural diversity' was discussed in the unit 'Language and Culture'. As part of the media studies course at Macquarie, journalism was addressed in a lecture on the reporting of the High Court Mabo decision. At Charles Sturt, lectures on Aboriginal issues were part of the course 'Journalism Research' (in an assignment on discourse analysis, and in two lectures, on ethnographic research and on 'research across cultures'). Within that university's Print Journalism degree, the course 'Basics of Writing' included 'some' exercises on Aboriginal issues, and the course on 'Feature Writing' included teaching on 'community journalism', which had an emphasis on Kooris. Throughout the course, Kitty Eggerking suggested, there was a concern to bring in issues of Indigenous representation.

'Unnecessary emphasis'

Discussion of the 'relevance' of race and when it should be mentioned, based on the AJA code of ethics, can be identified as the core of journalism education in relation to questions of Indigeneity. It was the only aspect common to all university teaching in this area. Of course, the point at which race became 'relevant' was open for negotiation. Monash University said that mention of race should be avoided in 'negative' contexts, but would be necessary in stories about 'reconciliation'. Bond University said race should only be mentioned 'where race itself is an important element of the story...if you withdrew race from the story, you would no longer have a story'. At Deakin, 'if [a] person was attacked because of his race and was giving evidence in the court, you might need to mention that he was attacked because he was an Aboriginal'. Griffith used Bostock's *The Greater Perspective* and the Department of Transport and Communication's Statement of Principles. At Central Queensland, students were taught 'things like, if it's a police report and a description given by someone else, then yes, you have to use it, but I run that by the AJA code...'. At Edith Cowan, they learnt that:

Aboriginality is not mentioned in a news story unless the point is raised by an Aboriginal person, or if the story involves an Aboriginal organisation...even when descriptions are being issued, it is to be avoided unless absolutely proven and pertinent.

Practical issues of approaching/dealing with Aboriginal individuals and organizations

James Cook students were told to 'concentrate on the normal method of going to a spokesperson rather than interviewing individuals on the ground'. Monash used *The Greater Perspective* for sensitivity to cross-cultural dealings. South Australia dealt with 'interaction with Aboriginal people'. Western Sydney mentioned 'the organisations which represent Aboriginal people'. Curtin did not include it in teaching, but said that those students who were interested, 'at the end of their semester of reporting in that particular area, have a fairly good understanding of the range of groups which are relevant'. Griffith suggested that 'the best way of doing that is getting Indigenous people from the community to talk about that...pointing people towards resources'. Edith Cowan wrote this into 'good practice': 'as many viewpoints should be sought as in any case involving non-Aboriginal people'. It recommended that students should approach suitable Aboriginal organizations in order to get a sense of the representativeness of given speakers: 'for example, the ALS, the Aboriginal Medical Service...the Reconciliation Council'. Charles Sturt included 'Kooris' in a course on 'talking to people outside of their experience', and 'research across cultures'. This issue appeared not to be mentioned at Macleay College, Bond, Deakin, Southern Cross, Central Queensland, or Macquarie universities.

Aboriginal Affairs and history

None of the journalism courses included within its structure any substantial body of teaching on the history of race relations in Australia, nor of what might be recognized as 'Aboriginal Affairs', as the Recommendations of the Royal Commission had hoped. Most universities suggested that other courses in the degree structure might cover these topics. There was an idea that this area was reserved for students who were interested in specializing: Deakin University suggested that 'If they were doing something on Aboriginal history', students would be told to 'go and speak to people like Henry Reynolds and other people who have written extensively in that area'. There was a general feeling that this was not the job of journalism teaching; indeed, that it was not possible as part of a journalism course. So, for example, Western Sydney said that 'inside our specialisation there isn't much time to manoeuvre'; Murdoch said, 'I doubt if we'd get down to that sort of depth. It might crop up'. Curtin said, 'No, we don't go into things in that kind of detail'. History was seen as antithetical to journalism—the University of Queensland said that 'all our activity is oriented to dealing with the current situation'. In answer to the question, 'Is there any teaching on contemporary Aborginal Affairs?' Southern Queensland answered, 'Yes. Outside journalism units'. Once again, the exception to this rule was Batchelor College. Wollongong was preparing a course on 'Journalism, History and Structure', to be taught within the journalism degree.

Aboriginal lecturers

There were no permanent Aboriginal lecturers on journalism courses in Australia.

Several universities invited Aboriginal guest speakers on to the courses. Monash used speakers from the university's Koori Studies Centre. South Australia used speakers from within the university, from the Aboriginal community college at Port Adelaide, and from the Office of Aboriginal Affairs. QUT had used Chris Leigh, Sam Watson, and Tiga Bayles, and was considering approaching Aboriginal journalists. Western Sydney had used people from within the university, an Aboriginal employment officer from the ABC, a *Koori Mail* writer, and an Aboriginal photographer. Murdoch had used speakers from the Western Australian Aboriginal Media Association. Queensland had speakers from 'the radio station' and 'the Legal Service'. Southern Cross invited speakers from 'the local community'. Curtin had speakers from within the university. Griffith planned to use Chris Lee from the National Indigenous Media Association. Central Queensland had speakers from its Aboriginal school, Capricornia. Edith Cowan intended to use 'several Aboriginal media people' to address the students. Charles Sturt said that the university's Aboriginal Unit had not been involved in the journalism course, and that: 'It's been hard in Bathurst to get Koori speakers. The local community seem pretty disparate and most don't like talking to the media—we're seen as arch demons'.

Indigenous students

Very few Indigenous students were involved in journalism degrees in Australia at the time of our survey. Policy reviews have insisted on the necessity of promoting Indigenous involvement in media production.

Although substantial numbers of Indigenous people were in fact involved in media production, few came through the standard university system. James Cook had one Indigenous student on a journalism course, as did South Australia, Southern Cross, Western Sydney, and QUT ('one or two'). Murdoch had none; neither did Curtin, Wollongong, Edith Cowan, Macquarie, or Bond ('our fee structure would place our education beyond the reach of most Aboriginals'). Charles Sturt had two, Queensland had 'two or three', Central Queensland 'three or four a semester', Deakin eight ('mainly in first year'), and Batchelor forty-five. Macleay College said, 'We don't ask our students their background'.

The number of graduates from these courses was even smaller: 'a couple' at South Australia, 'two' from Western Sydney, 'five or six' from Deakin, 'a few' from Queensland, 'a few' from Central Queensland, and two from Charles Sturt. Southern Queensland said that some Aboriginal students had graduated, but most left for employment before completing the course. Estimates for Batchelor would run to three figures, as the course had been running for eight years.

Many universities had put structures in place to support and encourage Aboriginal students. To encourage them to take journalism courses, some departments worked to establish links with Aboriginal units within their universities. For example, QUT had:

a program in place where we encourage people of Aboriginal and Torres Strait Islander backgrounds to try to get into journalism, but unfortunately we haven't had a lot of success, they come in and do the original introductory year, then they tend to go off into advertising or public relations... The journalism co-ordinator sits on the entry committee of the Aboriginal school at QUT, and suggests journalism to them.

Aboriginal students on the journalism course at QUT were also provided with 'mentors', 'just so as they get into the course'. Similarly, at Western Sydney: 'the [Aboriginal] liaison unit here is trying to encourage students to choose these options, but we're finding that Aboriginal students are generally choosing things like the education department, visual and performing arts, and so on.' At Deakin also, 'the Koori institute is trying to encourage more [Aboriginal students] to do journalism, because there's a bad need for it'. Curtin was involved in similar work:

trying to formalise a relationship with the centre for Aboriginal studies so that people go up through bridging courses... [and there is] a natural liaison whereby students might proceed to the journalism course... I would want to positively recruit journalism students...

Murdoch wrote to the West Australian Aboriginal Media Association telling them about their journalism course. Western Sydney had also made efforts in other ways: 'I've been trying for a couple of years to get some scholarships up from News Ltd. and Fairfax to get more journalism students here, without much luck . . .' Griffith said that the retention of Aboriginal students would be a major concern in that university's broadcasting course.

Race Issues and Aboriginal Media (University of Queensland)

This unit was not taught as a core unit in the journalism degree, but as part of a Faculty of Arts major in Aboriginal and Torres Strait Islander Studies. It was developed by the Capricornia Aboriginal and Islander Tertiary Education Centre. The unit aimed to produce students who would be able to

analyse the treatment and representation of Aboriginal peoples and issues in the mainstream media in Australia, identify the operation, agenda and strategies of Aboriginal media organisations and their role in Aboriginal communities, and describe and analyse responses of government agencies and commercial media organisations to problems and issues identified in the Report from the Royal Commission into Aboriginal Deaths in Custody.

Aboriginal People and the Media (University of Technology, Sydney)

This unit was taught in the Faculty of Humanities and Social Sciences. It was designed as part of the Aboriginal Studies Major, but could also be taken as an elective in the BA (Communication) degree. It aimed to give students

a critical awareness of racism in the Australian mass media, to develop knowledge of Australian indigenous interventions and mass media alternatives and to develop research skills necessary to enable [them] to identify and evaluate strategies for intervening in the mass communication field to challenge racism and promote intercultural understanding and tolerance. (UTS course handbook, 4).

It addressed 'racism' in the media (4); more specifically, the media's role in 'the production and reproduction of racist power structures . . . racist discourses and representations'. Complaining about racism was compulsory:

There are three assessment tasks. Satisfactory performance in all three tasks is necessary to pass the course . . . Task 2 is to make a complaint about racism in the media... by Week 3 you must have a copy of the offending item and a copy of your written complaint letter. (5).

The course taught 'anti-racist strategies': 'Structural changes, policies and strategies that media institutions can employ to challenge racist media production practices, racist media representations and discourses and racist assumptions about media audiences.'

On-the-job training

Beyond the basics provided by universities, there was very little training in these issues in Australia's news institutions. The formal training of cadets was limited, and was not regarded by journalists to whom we spoke as the most important part of the learning process. Indeed, according to our respondents, in electronic news, no cadetships or formal training programmes in news schools were offered at all. It was assumed that journalists would have a certain set of skills from university training; and other skills would be picked up and honed in the newsroom.

Most of the journalists interviewed for this project had received no formal training in Indigenous affairs. These included Michael Bachelard of the *Canberra Times* (a parliamentary reporter who also wrote most of the stories dealing with Aboriginal issues), Shane Green (State Politics, including Aboriginal issues, at the *Age*), Bill Birnbauer (the *Age*, finalist in the 1996 Louis Johnston Media Awards), and Jill Pengelly, Ethnic Affairs reporter (a post which included Aboriginal stories) at the *Adelaide Advertiser*. None admitted to being unhappy with the absence of training. They were certainly aware of difficulties in the area, but they did not see training as the answer. Michael Bachelard of the *Canberra Times*, for example, said he relied on his 'instincts' about what might be sensitive areas, and they had proved 'OK'. Similarly, Lynn Bliss, the editor's assistant on the *Canberra Times*, suggested that what was needed to cover Indigenous affairs was 'common sense and tact'. Bill Birnbauer, acknowledging that 'as a journalist you don't have training in this area', said that the useful thing is 'experience': 'you do learn... You do things by looking at your experience as a journalist'. Marcus Priest of the *Courier Mail* said: 'the necessary skills cannot be taught'.

Liz Sterel at Fairfax, on the other hand, suggested that the area would 'come up as part of other training courses'. For instance, picking up knowledge about interviewing techniques would provide the journalist with an adequate set of skills to deal with Aboriginal people. Similarly, Rob Boucher at the *Hobart Mercury* said that Indigenous issues are not covered as a specific topic, but are 'built into other areas': such as ethics. Some newspapers did have training programmes in place for new cadets, but these did not address Indigenous affairs. Most dealt with skills— 'feature writing', 'news writing', 'research', and so on (Liz Sterel, Fairfax). However, they also addressed issues. At Fairfax, a 'cadet camp' provided 'intensive training' for the new cadets in basic skills and 'legal training— contempt and defamation'. But Sterel said that Fairfax were not even considering putting Indigenous issues on the cadet training course. At the *Age*, journalists were offered training in various areas. After an initial month for cadets, courses were ongoing. John Lawrence, who formulated this training, said that Indigenous affairs were not mentioned: it was not a 'core' subject, or one of the 'basics'. The 'basics' at this newspaper were skills, and 'defamation law'.

The *West Australian*

In terms of in-house training, the most impressive example of an attention to reporting Indigenous affairs proved to be the *West Australian* (but see Trigger, 1995). Cadetship at the newspaper was for twelve months, during which time cadets learnt skills (such as keyboard), visited government organizations, and so on. As part of this training in 1995, the cadets were taken to meet Robert Bropho at the Cavisham Centre, and Pat Dudgeon at Curtin University Centre for Aboriginal Studies. Peter Beck at the *West* saw the importance of this work largely in terms of simply having the journalists meet Aboriginal people: 'If you meet these people, at least you have some idea about the way they feel, and they [the cadets] will feel less daunted when they have to speak to an Aboriginal leader'. The cadets on these visits discussed community relations problems, and were given a perspective on perceived problems with the media. Beck also suggested that one of the most important aspects of the visit was hearing about differences in opinion between prominent local Aboriginal figures. The *West* also used its award-winning Aboriginal Affairs journalist Karen Brown in training. Brown provided a useful overview of one journalist's sense of what needed to be known by writers in this area:

- *Contacts and protocols.* Basic information about dealing with Aboriginal communities: who to approach, how the hierarchy of communities works, the need for patience and for respect.
- *Range of voices.* Brown said that journalists understood the fact that the Aboriginal community was 'the same as the non-Aboriginal'; that is, it was 'not represented by one voice or one person, or one

group'. No single voice could be understood as 'representative of all Aboriginal people'.

- *History.* Brown gave some basic Aboriginal history to the cadets.
- *Cultural specificity.* Brown gave cadets information about particular customs, and in particular the need to understand that some communities do not mention the names of the recently deceased.
- *Sources and resources.* Brown also supplied information about the best resources in Western Australia, the accessibility and status of various spokespeople and institutions.

The *Northern Territory News*

The *News* trained journalists in Land Rights and Native Title, arranging for lecturers from the Northern Land Council to give background on race relations in Australia. There was no training on cultural interaction for journalists. This would be patronizing, said Nigel Adlam, the editor of the *News*: 'Journalists here deal with black people every day. There's no good telling them how to talk to Aborigines if they go to the shop and they're being served by a black person'. The specific elements of cultural interaction in which they were instructed included the most common one: that care must be taken in naming the recently deceased. Adlam, however, relativized that issue, saying that many Aboriginal people living in Darwin and other urban areas would be upset if names were *not* used in obituaries (out of due respect). Journalists at the *News* were told to be guided by the communities—to call and ask what *they* wanted to do, or to look at the way the information was released by a community. If 'tribal language' was used for 'he is dead', then the name should not be reproduced.

Council for Aboriginal Reconciliation

Perhaps the most important on-the-job training for journalists was that provided by the Council for Aboriginal Reconciliation. Several of the journalists interviewed had attended the CAR project set up to train journalists (and editorial decision-makers) in Indigenous reporting. The course sought to equip journalists with an understanding of cultural differences between Indigenous and non-Indigenous Australians. It did not provide specific training in journalistic skills. An account of this course appeared in the *Report of the Council, 1991–1994*: 'Some Aboriginal people now feel confident and have been reassured from what they have learnt from the media and how to approach them' (Council for Aboriginal Reconciliation, 1994: 219). The journalists similarly saw themselves as having: 'a touchstone—something concrete to hold in our minds as we write about policy which will affect Aboriginal people' (219). The three-day project was repeated several times, working on the theory that to bring together Aboriginal people and journalists would change media coverage. There was little attempt to discuss particular ways in which coverage might be changed, or practical techniques. The benefits of the course were diffuse. Tim Pegler of the *Age* found that it 'confirmed a lot of the things I'd sensed but hadn't been told directly', and taught him respect for the differences between the cultures. Tony Love of the *Adelaide Advertiser* said: 'We learned to be quiet, we learned humility, we learned to listen'.

Making the Grade: News Media and Indigenous Australia

Two videos have been produced to train journalists in the reporting of Indigenous affairs. *Making the Grade: News Media and Indigenous Australia* was circulated to journalism institutions by the Council for Aboriginal Reconciliation early in 1996. The idea that 'good journalism leads to good representations' was made explicit by both interviewees and the presenters of the video, Kerry O'Brien (ABC) and Rhoda Roberts (SBS). Lorena Allen (ABC) called for 'accurate' representation, and 'just a journalist doing their job properly'. She wanted to be 'just another person on the street'. Jeff McMullen (*60 Minutes*) called for the 'same standards' in covering Aboriginal and non-Aboriginal stories. For Stan Grant (Channel 7), Aboriginal people were the 'same as people everywhere else'. Kerry O'Brien summed up this call for Aboriginal stories to be treated the same as all other stories, and for good journalistic practices to be the single rule for all reporting: 'Journalists can't go wrong if they extend to Aboriginal people the same courtesy they'd extend to stories about anyone'.

The same emphasis informed the specific recommendations proposed in *Making the Grade*. It suggested that journalists should 'check facts'. An example of 'bad practice' was given in relation to the arguments that, after Mabo, Native Title claims could affect Australian 'backyards'. Noel Pearson (Cape York Land Council) made the point that a phone call to any of the Land Councils would have established that there was no possibility of such claims. The tape also questioned the 'relevance' of the term 'Aboriginal', and put in place a simple rule: Do not use the word Aboriginal if you would not mention 'Caucasian' in the same context.

Making a Difference

This tape was produced in 1993 by the Centre for Independent Journalism at the University of Technology, Sydney, aimed primarily at journalism students. It took a similar line to *Making the Grade*: that good journalistic practice—specifically, 'balanced' coverage—was the necessary response to questions about Indigenous media coverage. On the other hand, the tape also gestured in quite a different direction: it made clear that traditional news values themselves could be part of the problem. Captions said, 'News is negative' and 'News is conflict'. Also there was the 'need for good visuals' (Debra Bishop, Channel 7 Perth), which determined what stories could be told. Negativity, conflict, and the visual imperative made it difficult for certain kinds of stories to be recognized as news. The recommendations of the tape nevertheless largely involved the promotion of good journalistic practice: to renounce unbalanced 'stereotypes' (Ruska) and seek 'balanced' reporting (caption).

The tape included a clip from *A Current Affair* in 1993, where first an Aboriginal man and then a non-Aboriginal man were sent with hidden cameras into a real estate agent's to ask for properties. The first was told that no properties were available, the second that they were. This story presented a form of journalism that was not simply neutral, but took an active 'investigative' or 'advocacy' role.

The journalists interviewed for this book pointed to some specific ways in which current practice might be improved within the current model of good journalism.

- *Interviewing skills:* Bill Birnbauer from the *Age* suggested that traditional interviewing skills may not be suited to Aboriginal communities: 'you can't just go in and say, Hi, I'm a journalist, tell me your life story. You have to build a rapport and with Aboriginal communities you have to spend a bit more time than you do normally'. This was corroborated by Karen Brown of the *West Australian*, who recalled an instance where it took six weeks to set up a single interview. Tim Pegler from the *Age* suggested that 'the deadlines that a newspaper expects don't correlate with Indigenous communities'. 'It helps to budget for a longer term story'. A similar issue was raised by Jill Pengelly, who suggested that journalists needed to know that Aboriginal communities functioned in specific ways: they didn't always return calls, for example, and were 'not as reliable as . . . government offices or other businesses'.

- *A range of voices:* Several respondents pointed out that there was a tendency to see Aboriginal people as a homogenous group, without realizing that there were differences of opinion in communities. For Bill Birnbauer, this was expressed in terms of 'factions': 'I had no idea how factionalised the Aboriginal community is. You tend to think there's this group and they all have similar thoughts about things'. Marcus Priest worried that some journalists 'have the attitude that all Aboriginal people speak with one voice ... that is, you can grab an Aboriginal spokesman and he represents all two hundred and fifty Aboriginal nations in Australia. This leads to an approach where any difference of opinion leads to a search for who's right and who's wrong—rather than going behind that to see what the issues are. It is simply seen to be the case that one is representative of all Aboriginal people, while the other is unrepresentative'.

- *Cultural restrictions around death:* Tim Pegler gave an example where lack of knowledge about local death customs resulted in a long drive to get a photo of a skull discovered at an Indigenous grave site, only to discover upon arrival that to reproduce the photograph would have violated local Indigenous law. The issue of not naming deceased persons was the most commonly cited cultural difference by all respondents.

- *Teaching different expectations:* Tim Pegler suggested that cadets should not 'impose your own standards or expectations'. He gave the example of families: 'the way an Indigenous family might bring their kids up might be different from the way a non-Indigenous family would—but that doesn't mean that one way is better than the other'.

- *Communicating across cultures:* Marcus Priest listed skills that were necessary in the reporting of Indigenous affairs but which 'cannot be taught'. These included particularly issues of communication, and how to interview people in different cultural relationships. He recommended an awareness of the functioning of body language, and of the specificity of verbal communication in different situations.

- *Sub-editors:* One journalist said there was a problem with sub-editors: that no matter how good a story was, some subs didn't like Aboriginal stories. Another journalist suggested that this was the main problem she had faced. She said her stories had often not been used, and suggested that this was because of the criteria used by the subs: for instance that 'happy stories' or 'good news' were not news.

Thus, no matter how good journalistic practice might be, problems remained when journalism's own priorities came into conflict with what's needed. Some of the areas where conflict occurred were:

- *Good news is no news.* The imperative to understand 'news' as 'bad news'.
- *Newspaper time and community time.* Tim Pegler: 'the deadlines that a newspaper expects don't correlate with Indigenous communities'.
- *'News'* and *'history'.* News is understood to be directly opposite to 'history'.
- *Final say.* Janine McDonald noted that Aboriginal people often asked for final versions of stories to be read to them before they were published. As she said: 'that's not what journalists do as a rule'.
- *Different assumptions.* On *Making the Grade,* Robert Cockburn made the point that 'Just going in with the questions you always ask, just won't work'; he warned against 'lazy journalism . . . assuming that they want what we want'.
- *Identical treatment vs. 'background' and 'context'.* Not mentioning race for ethical reasons could deny precisely the 'background' and 'context' that would explain an event.

Racism and Indifference

The charge is often made that individual journalists, individual news media, or the media generally, are *racist* (see Human Rights Commission, 1991; Jakubowicz (ed.), 1994). But the problem with contemporary journalism might be quite different: the reliance on and use of 'indifferent' discourses to explain the reporting of Indigenous affairs. 'Indifference' in this context means not being swayed by difference, like the traditional blindfold figure of Justice, holding her scales ('balance'). 'Indifference' of this kind in journalism is a modern technique for equalizing an otherwise multivalent population—making everyone the same. As the foregoing account has made clear, this is the prime ideology of professional journalists at all levels in respect of Indigenous reporting. Treating everyone the same is also the mantra of the egalitarian populists whose comments are most frequently cited as racist, from the radio talkback 'shock jocks' to the One Nation party. There is an insoluble problem here: 'indifferent' journalism treats people equally, but it is this very technique that produces the reporting most complained of as 'racist'.

From 'indifference' to 'making a difference'

Batchelor College teaches an Associate Diploma of Applied Science— Broadcasting and Journalism. It is taught to Indigenous students. Its course material suggests what journalism might look like from an Aboriginal perspective: because, of course, to treat everyone the same way, in current journalistic training, is largely to treat everyone as coming from within a recognizably white culture. As well as offering a model of how it is possible to teach journalism with Aboriginality up front, this course also makes clear how the 'indifference' of traditional journalism practices is not, in fact, neutral.

The level playing field does not result in equality of opportunity, nor equality of representation, for all citizens. Indifference does not lead to equality. As Mark Pearson has shown in relation to journalistic interviewing techniques, the impartial application of such skills in fact produces the effect of an unfair representation of cultures that communicate in different ways (Pearson, 1987: 113). An example of this problem can be seen in Batchelor College's teaching of radio editing. Normally, training in 'best practice' would require a student to remove repetition, long pauses, and so on. In Batchelor's unit in radio editing, however, students must be able to 'explain the reasons why editing is done for broadcast material in mainstream or non-Indigenous radio... [and] explain the use of pause, silence and repetition in Indigenous culture as effective way of communicating'. From such minutiae up to the structural issues discussed earlier in this book, 'indifferent' journalism has not served Indigenous people well, whether as producers and journalists, or as readers or subjects of the news.

But to reverse 'indifference' can be equally damaging. It can slip into 'inverse racism', as described by Diana Plater: 'a tendency... to treat some Aboriginal subjects with the sort of reverence usually reserved for the Queen rather than with the usual healthy scepticism' (Plater, 1992: 30). Journalism has to work out what kinds of stories it is going to tell about Indigenous people. The answer isn't reverence, it is recognition. Henry Reynolds has suggested that sovereignty in fact already rests with Aboriginal people; that there already exist an 'Aboriginal nation' and an 'Islander nation' in addition to the 'Australian nation'. Accepting this fact would imply quite a different practice in journalism from the present version. Historically, Australian journalism has presented

Aboriginal people as an underclass, a problem to be addressed and commented upon via discourses of anomaly, correction, and protection. But a news practice emerging from recognition of Indigenous nations would have to deal with Indigenous peoples' *collective* equality with Australia, not simply their equality as abstract legal individuals. Such journalism can be cordial (assuming an alliance is successfully negotiated) without being reverential. It can acknowledge distinctiveness without presuming that this amounts to unequal treatment.

In the hands of Indigenous journalists writing from and for the Indigenous 'nations', such journalism can also be used for the purposes of public accountability, on an equal footing with 'white' journalism. In other words Indigenous journalism can help to create an Indigenous public sphere to hold Indigenous politicians and institutions to account. The need for Indigenous people to 'tell their own stories' in their own idiom would be clear, as would the need to identify, report, and where necessary criticize the Indigenous equivalents of the governmental, civic, and social activities of the Indigenous 'public sphere'. Real 'indifference' would be achieved when the Australian public sphere is itself Indigenized. Indigenous journalism and the accumulated apparatus of Australian journalism may then engage in dialogue, contributing equally to the 'narrative accrual' of Australia.

Primary Sources

Magazines

mag94007. *4x4 Australia*, 19 July 1994, Features, Chaelundi Calling, 31–4.

mag94013. *ANH*, Winter 1994, Adverts, Pitjantjatjara Tours, 75.

mag94023. *ANH*, Winter 1994, Advert, Ecotouring with the Elders, 15.

mag94031. *Art and Australia*, July 1994, Adverts, Cowboy Louie Pwerle, unnumbered.

mag94032. *Art and Australia*, July 1994, Adverts, New Exhibition, unnumbered.

mag94034. *Art and Australia*, July 1994, Features, Review of Aboriginal Artist, unnumbered.

mag94036. *Simply Living/Well Being*, July 1994, Features, Healing aspects of eucalyptus, unnumbered.

mag94044. *New Woman*, July 1994, Features, A Few Good Women, 19–27.

mag94055. *Geo Australia*, July 1994 (vol. 16, no. 3), Adverts, Broken Hills Outback Tours, 8.

mag94057. *Geo Australia*, July 1994 (vol. 16, no. 3), Adverts, Spirit of Australia, unnumbered.

mag94066. *Lock Stock and Barrel*, June/July 1994, Adverts, Red over black, 27.

mag94067. *Geo Australia*, July 1994 (vol. 16, no. 3), Adverts, Discovery, 16.

mag94068. *Geo Australia*, July 1994 (vol. 16, no. 3), Adverts, Pitjantjatjara Tours, 135.

mag94069. *Geo Australia*, July 1994 (vol. 16, no. 3), Adverts, Billy Can Tours, 135.

mag94074. *Lock Stock and Barrel*, June/July 1994, Editorial, Pedigree bull terrier Aborigines, 5.

mag95001. *AFL Football Tips and Techniques*, July 1995, Posters, Nothing succeeds like success, 13.

mag95002. *AFL Football Tips and Techniques*, July 1995, Celebrity Spot, Tony Lockett, 22–8.

mag95003. *AFL Football Tips and Techniques*, July 1995, Celebrity Spot, Tony Francis: Roving the packs, 51–5.

mag95004. *AFL Football Tips and Techniques*, July 1995, Posters, Happy Essendon players, 107.

mag95005. *Art and Australia*, Winter 1995 (no. 32/4), Adverts, Rainbow, Sugarbag and Moon, 446.

mag95006. *Art and Australia*, Winter 1995 (no. 32/4), Adverts, Utopia Art Sydney, 470.

mag95007. *Art and Australia*, Winter 1995 (no. 32/4), Adverts, Black, Bold and Dynamic, 479.

mag95008. *Art and Australia*, Winter 1995 (no. 32/4), Exhibitions, Contemporary Territory, 480–3.

mag95009. *Art and Australia*, Winter 1995 (no. 32/4), Books, Have you looked in McCulloch?, 485–6.

mag95010. *Art and Australia*, Winter 1995 (no. 32/4), Books, Aboriginal artists of the 19 century, 486–8.

mag95011. *Art and Australia*, Winter 1995 (no. 32/4), Features, Eyes on the ball, 490–501.

mag95012. *Art and Australia*, Winter 1995 (no. 32/4), Features, The woodblock painting of Cressida Campbell, 502–13.

mag95013. *Art and Australia*, Winter 1995 (no. 32/4), Features, Bush Art, 526–35.

mag95014. *Art and Australia*, Winter 1995 (no. 32/4), Adverts, Experience what life was like in Australia 60,000 years ago, 570.

mag95015. *Art and Australia* (Sam Fullbrook pullout), Winter 1995 (no. 32/4), Sam Fullbrook (separate catalogue).

mag95016. *Art and Australia*, Winter 1995 (no. 32/4), Queensland Art Gallery Centenary (pull-out catalogue), A corner-stone of Queensland culture, 3–5.

mag95032. *Bushdriver*, July 1995 (vol. 17, no. 6), Travel, Carnarvon—just Gorgeous, 63–6.

mag95033. *Esoterica*, July 1995 (issue 5), Features, Forum in the forest, Sacred Site Healing, 10.

mag95034. *4x4 Australia*, July 1995 (no. 138), Editorial, Is Aboriginal Welfare Working?, 7.

mag95037. *Geo Australia*, July 1995 (vol. 17, no. 4), Adverts, Australia's Northern Territory, inside cover-1.

mag95039. *Geo Australia*, July 1995 (vol. 17, no. 4), Adverts, Broken Hills Outback Tour, 6.

mag95040. *Geo Australia*, July 1995 (vol. 17, no. 4), Features, Rock art warriors, 40–52.

mag95041. *Geo Australia*, July 1995 (vol. 17, no. 4), Adverts, Experience what life was like in Australia 60,000 years ago, 125.

mag95043. *Geo Australia*, July 1995 (vol. 17, no. 4), Adverts, Pitjantjara Tours, 127.

mag95046. *Juice*, July 1995 (issue 29), Features, The 20 sexiest Australians, 12–13.

mag95047. *Juice*, July 1995 (issue 29), Features, Anu style, 66–7.

mag95048. *Nature Australia*, Winter 1995 (vol. 25, no. 1), The Broad Horizon (advertisement insert), Sharing the Dreaming, no numbers.

mag95057. *Simply Living*, Winter 1995 (no. 81), Features, Eagle Man, 26–9.

mag95060. *Studio for Men*, Autumn/Winter 1995, Fashion, The Waiting Game, 116–23.

mag95064. *TV Hits*, August 1995 (issue 84), Put to the test (Features), Kimberley Joseph, 29.

mag95066. *Westside Football*, 20 July 1995 (vol. 17, no. 22), Chlis Lewis, front cover.

mag95069. *World Art*, Winter 1995 (no. 2), Features, The Go-Between, 24–9.

Newspapers

new94010. *The Age* (Vic), 5 July 1994, Letters page, Why should ATSIC investigate itself?, 1.

new94014. *The Age* (Vic), 6 July 1994, Fostering harmony between two living cultures, 2.

new94015. *The Age* (Vic), 6 July 1994, Aboriginal custody rates, 6.

new94039. *The Age* (Vic), 9 July 1994, Aboriginal probe, 1.

new94041. *The Age* (Vic), 9 July 1994, Saturday Extra/Features, The Island Life, 1.

new94049. *Australian*, 6 July 1994, Black deaths lessons go unheeded, 5.

new94051. *Australian*, 6 July 1994, Letters page, Custody deadlines in perspective, 12.

new94067. *Australian*, 5 July 1994, Blacks' claims against police dismissed, 4.

new94068. *Australian*, 5 July 1994, Aborigine dies in custody, 5.

new94070. *Sydney Morning Herald (NSW)*, 4 July 1994, NAIDOC week, 4.

new94071. *Sydney Morning Herald (NSW)*, 4 July 1994, Racism rife in police force: report, 6.

new94076. *Sydney Morning Herald (NSW)*, 5 July 1994, Union denies police are more racist, 6.

new94087. *Sydney Morning Herald (NSW)*, 8 July 1994, Police too vigorous in youth treatment, 2.

new94091. *Sydney Morning Herald (NSW)*, 9 July 1994, Crime drop hits scare tactics (subheading in box) Push for children's ombudsman, 4.

new94096. *Telegraph-Mirror*, 9 July 1994, Koori jail rate alarming, 12.

new94118. *Northern Territory News*, 5 July 1994, Girls' agonies in torn families, 6.

new94119. *Northern Territory News*, 5 July 1994, Editorial, Money not the answer, 10.

new94135. *Northern Territory News*, 7 July 1994, Letters, Holding no grudges, 11.

new94150. *Sunday Territorian (NT)*, 10 July 1994, NT faces wave of violence, 1–2.

new94153. *Sunday Territorian (NT)*, 10 July 1994, Letters page, Doubt over definition, 18.

new94154. *Sunday Territorian (NT)*, 10 July 1994, Arts/Entertainment, People on Sunday, 23.

new94172. *West Australian (WA)*, 5 July 1994, Police internal probe attacked, 1.

new94180. *West Australian (WA)*, 6 July 1994, Ombudsman, 7.

new94183. *West Australian (WA)*, 6 July 1994, Editorial, TRG tactics, 12.

new94187. *West Australian (WA)*, 7 July 1994, Miners' pact with group, 39.

new94192. *West Australian (WA)*, 8 July 1994, Title track strikes Mabo chord, 5.

new94201. *West Australian (WA)*, 9 July 1994, Young Islanders just jump for joy, 1.

new94205. *West Australian (WA)*, 9 July 1994, Watchdog has real bite, 15.

new94214. *Courier Mail*, 6 July 1994, Custody death reforms 'slow', 6.

new94220. *Courier Mail*, 9 July 1994, CJC report slams role of councils, 7.

new95001. *Australian*, 10 July 1995, Critics await next gaffe as Tunstall keeps Games post, 3.

new95002. *Australian*, 10 July 1995, Editorial, Tunstall should still stand down, 8.

new95003. *Australian*, 10 July 1995, Focus Extra, Howard runs his strategy up a flag poll, 9.

new95008. *Australian*, 13 July 1995, Letters page False claim on Aboriginal flag, 10.

new95009. *Australian*, 13 July 1995, Letters page, Flags are never reconciliatory, 10.

new95017. *Weekend Australian*, 15 July 1995, Letters page, Alcohol ban, 24.

new95019. *Courier Mail*, 10 July 1995, Nation's shame won't go away, 7.

new95020. *Courier Mail*, 10 July 1995, Birthplace birthrights, 7.

new95021. *Courier Mail*, 10 July 1995, Opinion, Our shame revealed, 12.

new95022. *Courier Mail*, 10 July 1995, Opinion, Can they legally do this?, 12.

new95026. *Courier Mail*, 12 July 1995, Blacks to decide alcohol sale bans, 7

new95030. *Courier Mail*, 13 July 1995, Perspectives, Alcohol ban key to black survival, 19.

new95040. *Daily Telegraph Mirror*, 10 July 1995, Sport, Tunstall's outburst: attack on me over the last several weeks is disgraceful, 73.

new95042. *Daily Telegraph Mirror*, 12 July 1995, Alcohol sale ban backed by law, 16.

new95043. *Daily Telegraph Mirror*, 12 July 1995, Indigenous police to swell ranks, 24.

new95044. *Daily Telegraph Mirror*, 13 July 1995, Dancers celebrate history, 13.

new95047. *The Age*, 10 July 1995, Athletes angry as Tunstall keeps Games job, 5.

new95049. *The Age*, 11 July 1995, An Aborigine's pride flying high, NAIDOC, 5.

new95051. *The Age*, 11 July 1995, Opinion-Analysis, A flag for reconciliation, 13.

new95052. *The Age*, 12 July 1995, Koori Lives, Kooris at the sharp bend of history, 1.

new95054. *The Age*, 12 July 1995, Koori Lives, Young faces of the Koori future, 8.

new95055. *The Age*, 12 July 1995, Koori Lives, Community retains Fitzroy links, 8.

new95057. *The Age*, 12 July 1995, Koori Lives, Proud search for heritage knowledge, 8.

new95058. *The Age*, 12 July 1995, Koori Lives, Identity rooted in rhythms of age-old culture, 8.

new95059. *The Age*, 12 July 1995, Features, An almost untold story, 13.

new95062. *The Age*, 13 July 1995, Koori Lives, The cash and cultural clash, 6.

new95063. *The Age*, 13 July 1995, Koori Lives, A fair brother to his people, 6.

new95064. *The Age*, 13 July 1995, Koori Lives, The future's shaping up for Tony, 6.

new95065. *The Age*, 13 July 1995, Koori Lives, A versatile man of many projects, 6.

new95066. *The Age*, 13 July 1995, Koori Lives, Working to make a world of hope, 6.

new95067. *The Age*, 13 July 1995, Koori Lives, Bushman's lesson of respect, 6.

new95068. *The Age*, 14 July 1995, Koori Lives, The family they tried to break up, 10.

new95069. *The Age*, 14 July 1995, Accent / Koori Lives, Being mother is the top job, 10.

new95076. *Herald Sun*, 10 July 1995, Vote silences critics—Tunstall, 9.

new95077. *Herald Sun*, 11 July 1995, Proud moment for Che, 7.

new95079. *Herald Sun*, 11 July 1995, Editorial page, One flag for one people, 12.

new95080. *Herald Sun*, Letters, 12 July 1995, I agree wholeheartedly, 14.

new95082. *Herald Sun*, 12 July 1995, Letters, Flag issue merely a smokescreen, 14.

new95085. *Herald Sun*, 13 July 1995, Letters, We should all unite under one flag, 14.

new95087. *Herald Sun*, 14 July 1995, Dream time replaces the sandpit on Koori day, 32.

new95097. *Northern Territory News*, 12 July 1995, Ban on grog sales impossible: pubs, 3.

new95098. *Northern Territory News*, 12 July 1995, Alcohol limit: 'expect effects', 3.

new95100. *Northern Territory News*, 12 July 1995, Liquor rules 'won't work', 4.

new95101. *Northern Territory News*, 13 July 1995, Tennant grog ban plans get go-ahead, 4.

new95116. *Northern Territory News*, 14 July 1995, Proud parade in city today, 28.

new95121. *Northern Territory News*, 15 July 1995, Hear our voices: call by Aborigines, 4.

new95124. *Sunday Territorian (NT)*, 16 July 1995, Robbie helps break the ice, 1.

new95128. *Sunday Territorian (NT)*, 16 July 1995, People on Sunday, various, 29.

new95133. *West Australian (WA)*, 10 July 1995, Unity message steals the show, 1.

new95139. *West Australian (WA)*, 11 July 1995, A boy's lonely road to kinship, 9.

new95144. *West Australian (WA)*, 12 July 1995, Aborigines to get cultural support, 9.

new95145. *West Australian (WA)*, 12 July 1995, Watchdog backs curb on alcohol, 34.

new95170. *Sunday Times (WA)*, 16 July 1995, Comment/Letters, Flags place, 32.

new95175. *Sydney Morning Herald (NSW)*, 10 July 1995, Letters, Flags that symbolise Australia, 12.

new95176. *Sydney Morning Herald (NSW)*, 10 July 1995, Letters, Flags that symbolise Australia, 12.

new95177. *Sydney Morning Herald (NSW)*, 10 July 1995, Letters, Flags that symbolise Australia, 12.

new95178. *Sydney Morning Herald (NSW)*, 10 July 1995, Letters, Flags that symbolise Australia, 12.

new95179. *Sydney Morning Herald (NSW)*, 10 July 1995, Letters, Flags that symbolise Australia, 12.

new95186. *The Age*, 15 July 1995, Koori Lives, Back from the fringes to build more bridges, 10.

new95188. *The Age*, 15 July 1995, Koori Lives, Elders remain at the heart of their communities, 11.

new95189. *The Age*, 15 July 1995, Koori Lives, In Robinvale, one looks to the past for inspiration, 11.

new95190. *The Age*, 15 July 1995, Koori Lives, Growing up in the school of hard knocks, 11.

new95191. *The Age*, 15 July 1995, News/Koori Lives, Yorta Yorta keep sights on protection of sacred areas, 11.

new96010. *Courier Mail*, 13 July 1996, Carnival conveys culture, 6.

new96020. *Courier Mail*, 10 July 1996, Perspectives, Time to ponder negotiations, 15.

new96049. *Northern Territory News*, 8 July 1996, Sport, Cathy has green light on dual flags, 4.

new96065. *Sydney Morning Herald (NSW)*, 13 July 1996, Atlanta 96, Atlanta's Top 10 clashes, 4.

new96066. *Sydney Morning Herald (NSW)*, 13 July 1996, Atlanta 96, The gold prospectors, 12.

new96087. *Herald Sun*, 13 July 1996, Rebel with a big cause, 15.

new96094. *Sunday Times (WA)*, 14 July 1996, Sport, Grace of two swans, 91.

new96095. *West Australian (WA)*, 8 July 1996, Health linked to Aboriginal reconciliation, 6.

new96101. *West Australian*, 9 July 1996, Century mine protesters fire salvo over project, 4.

new96102. *West Australian (WA)*, 9 July 1996, *Today/Freewheeling*, A buzz of activity that works wonders, 6.

new96106. *West Australian (WA)*, 11 July 1996, Howard to let zinc mine talks take their course, 12.

new96107. *West Australian*, 11 July 1996, The Issues: Australia needs Century project, 12.

new96117. *West Australian (WA)*, 12 July 1996, Man with a mission leads the way, 2.

new96120. *West Australian (WA)*, 13 July 1996, Australians at the Olympics, 1.

new96122. *West Australian*, 13 July 1996, Aborigines win mining contract, 4.

new96123. *West Australian (WA)*, 13 July 1996, Designers embrace cultural couture, 9.

new96133. *Australian*, 11 July 1996, Report to slate State over cell deaths, 2.

new96139. *Australian*, 10 July 1996, Opinion, cartoon, 12.

new96143. *Australian*, 9 July 1996, ATSIC chief attacks Howard, 1.

new96155. *Weekend Australian*, 13–14 July 1996, News, Atlanta 96, The Ultimate Guide, 1.

new96160. *Australian*, 13–14 July 1996, Opinion, Reconciliation, 18.

new96177. The Age, 10 July 1996, Opinion, Let the prime proced, A12.

new96178. *The Age*, 10 July 1996, Opinion, Aboriginal 'industry' hijacks policy debate, A13.

new96196. *The Age*, 8 July 1996, Business, Delay threat to Century project, C1.

new96202. *The Age*, 13 July 1996, News Extra, Warrior from a far country, 19.

new96213. *Courier Mail*, 9 July 1996, Sports, Full speed, 16.

Radio

rad94004. 3CR (Vic), 5 July 1994, *The Koori Survival Show*, culture.

rad94005. 3CR (Vic), 4 July 1994, *Not Another Koori Show*, welfare, land rights, women's issue.

rad94006. 3CR (Vic), 7 July 1994, *Koori Music*, politics.

rad94008. Radio National, 4 July 1994, *AM*, Features, Deaths in custody.

rad94010. Radio National, 4 July 1994, *News*, 4 p.m., Death in custody.

rad94011. Radio National, 4 July 1994, *News*, 4 p.m., Aboriginal actors harassed.

rad94012. Radio National, 4 July 1994, *News*, 7 p.m., Aboriginal actors harassed.

rad94013. Radio National, 4 July 1994, *News*, 8 p.m., Aboriginal actors harassed.

rad94020. Radio National, 6 July 1994, *News*, 6 p.m., Royal Commission into Aboriginal Deaths in Custody.

rad94021. Radio National, 6 July 1994, *News*, 7 p.m., Royal Commission into Aboriginal Deaths in Custody.

rad94023. Radio National, 5 July 1994, *AM*, Newspaper headlines, WA Police investigation.

rad94024. Radio National, 5 July 1994, *News*, 6 p.m., Police harassment.

rad94025. Radio National, 5 July 1994, *News*, 6 p.m., Custody deaths.

rad94026. Radio National, 5 July 1994, *News*, 7 p.m., Police harassment.

rad94027. Radio National, 5 July 1994, *News*, 7 p.m., Boot camps.

rad94030. Radio National, 5 July 1994, *News*, 7 p.m., Royal Commission into Aboriginal Deaths in Custody.

rad94032. Radio National, 5 July 1994, *News*, 12 noon, Police harassment.

rad94033. Radio National, 5 July 1994, *News*, 12 noon, Watch committee.

rad94034. Radio National, 5 July 1994, *News*, 12 noon, Police harassment.

rad94036. Radio National, 5 July 1994, *News*, 1 p.m., Police harassment.

rad94037. Radio National, 5 July 1994, *News*, 1 p.m., Custody deaths.

rad94041. Radio National, 5 July 1994, *News*, 3 p.m., Boot camps.

rad94077. 6NR/Aboriginal Radio (WA), 9 July 1994, *Gospel broadcast*, NAIDOC week.

rad94078. 6NR/Aboriginal Radio (WA), 9 July 1994, *Gospel broadcast*, NAIDOC week.

rad94079. 6NR/Aboriginal Radio (WA), 9 July 1994, *Gospel broadcast*, NAIDOC week.

rad94080. 6NR/Aboriginal Radio (WA), 9 July 1994, *Gospel broadcast*, NAIDOC week.

rad94081. 6NR/Aboriginal Radio (WA), 9 July 1994, *Gospel broadcast*, NAIDOC week.

rad94084. 6NR/Aboriginal Radio (WA), 9 July 1994, *Gospel broadcast*, Young women's course.

rad94088. 6NR/Aboriginal Radio (WA), 9 July 1994, *Request Show*, Aboriginal music.

rad94089. 6NR, 4 July 1994, *Healthwise*, Aboriginal death in custody.

rad94101. 6PR (WA), 4 July 1994, *Howard Sattler, Features/Talkback*, Lockridge, land rights.

rad94105. 6PR (WA), 5 July 1994, *Howard Sattler, News feature*, Eadie Report.

rad94106. 6PR (WA), 5 July 1994, *Howard Sattler, News feature*, Eadie Report.

rad94108. 6PR (WA), 5 July 1994, *News*, 12 noon, Watch committee.

rad94110. 6WF (WA), 5 July 1994, *Peter Kennedy*, Eadie Report.

rad94112. 6WF (WA), 5 July 1994, *Peter Kennedy*, Eadie Report.

rad94115. 6WF (WA), 5 July 1994, *News*, 6 p.m., Eadie report.

rad94116. 6WF (WA), 5 July 1994, *News*, 6 p.m., Deaths in custody watch committee.

rad94117. 6WF (WA), 6 July 1994, *Peter Newman*, Soapbox, Custody deaths.

rad94120. 6WF (WA), 6 July 1994, *Richard Utting*, Feature, Custody death.

rad94123. 6WF (WA), 6 July 1994, *AM*, Deaths in custody watch committee.

rad94125. 6PR (WA), 7 July 1994, *Howard Sattler, Feature*, Billboard tower.

rad94126. 6PR (WA), 7 July 1994, *Howard Sattler, Talkback*, Billboard tower.

rad95002. Radio National, 10 July 1995, *News*, 1 p.m., Che Cockatoo-Collins.

rad95007. 720 6WF (WA), 10 July 1995, *News*, 8 a.m., Che Cockatoo-Collins.

rad95010. 6PR (WA), 10 July 1995, *Howard Sattler, Talkback*, Aboriginal substance abuse.

rad95018. Triple J (WA), 10 July 1995, *Angela Katerns, Morning Show*, NAIDOC week.

rad95019. Triple J (WA), 10 July 1995, *Angela Katerns, Morning Show*, NAIDOC week.

rad95020. Triple J (WA), 10 July 1995, *Angela Katerns, Morning Show*, Gondwana.

rad95021. Triple J (WA), 10 July 1995, *Angela Katerns, Morning Show*, Jack Beatson.

rad95022. Triple J (WA), 10 July 1995, *Angela Katerns, Morning Show*, Jack Beatson.

rad95023. Triple J (WA), 10 July 1995, *Angela Katerns,/Morning Show*, Jack Beatson.

rad95024. Triple J (WA), News, 10 July 1995, *News*, 11 a.m., Che Cockatoo-Collins, 246.

rad95028. Radio National, 11 July 1995, *Australia Talks Back*, Aboriginal flag.

rad95030. Radio National, 11 July 1995, *News*, 2 p.m., Stolen generation.

rad95032. Radio National, 11 July 1995, *News*, 6 p.m., Stolen generation.

rad95033. Radio National, 11 July 1995, *News*, 7 p.m., Telling our stories.

rad95036. 720 6WF (WA), 11 July 1995, *Grapevine*, Naming in the Kimberley.

rad95039. 6PR (WA), 11 July 1995, *Gary Carbol*, Topics of the day.

rad95050. 6PR (WA), 11 July 1995, *Ron Edwards*, Aboriginal forgiving.

rad95051. 6PR (WA), 11 July 1995, *Ron Edwards*, Aboriginal issues.

rad95052. 6PR (WA), 11 July 1995, *Ron Edwards*, Rob Riley.

rad95054. 6PR (WA), 11 July 1995, *Ron Edwards*, Japanese Aboriginal situations.

rad95055. 6PR (WA), 11 July 1995, *Ron Edwards*, Removal of white children.

rad95058. 6PR (WA), 11 July 1995, *Ros Broadfield, Aboriginal dispossession.*

rad95059. 720 6WF (WA), 11 July 1995, *Liz Berski (for Peter Kennedy)*, Aboriginal compensation.

rad95060. 720 6WF (WA), 11 July 1995, *News*, 6 p.m., Aboriginal compensation.

rad95064. Radio National, 11 July 1995, *Education programme*, NAIDOC week.

rad95072. 6PR (WA), 12 July 1995, *News*, 7.30 a.m., Cathy Freeman.

rad95074. 720 6WF (WA), 12 July 1995, *Richard Utting*, Mining in the Pilbarra.

rad95075. 720 6WF (WA), 12 July 1995, *Richard Utting*, Uniting church apology.

rad95077. 6PR (WA), 12 July 1995, *Howard Sattler*, Stolen cars.

rad95079. 6PR (WA), 12 July 1995, *Howard Sattler*, White guilt.

rad95080. 6PR (WA), 12 July 1995, *Howard Sattler*, Aboriginal issue.

rad95082. 6PR (WA), 12 July 1995, *Howard Sattler*, Aboriginal week.

rad95083. 6PR (WA), 12 July 1995, *Howard Sattler*, Aboriginal week.

rad95084. 6PR (WA), 12 July 1995, *Howard Sattler*, Aboriginal question.

rad95086. 720 6WF (WA), 12 July 1995, *Verity James*, Aboriginal dreaming.

rad95088. 6PR (WA), 12 July 1995, *Ron Edwards*, These Aboriginal people.

rad95090. Triple J (WA), 12 July 1995, *Angela Katerns/Morning Show*, NAIDOC week.

rad95091. Triple J (WA), 12 July 1995, *Angela Katerns/Morning Show*, From little things, big things grow.

rad95092. Triple J (WA), 12 July 1995, *Angela Katerns/Morning Show*, Atlanta Olympics.

rad95093. Triple J (WA), 12 July 1995, *Angela Katerns/Morning Show*, Stolen generation.

rad95094. Triple J (WA), 12 July 1995, *Angela Katerns/Morning Show*, Stolen generation.

rad95095. Triple J (WA), 12 July 1995, *Angela Katerns/Morning Show*, Link-up.

rad95096. Triple J (WA), 12 July 1995, *Angela Katerns/Morning Show*, Stolen generation.

rad95097. Triple J (WA), 12 July 1995, *Took the children away*, song.

rad95098. Triple J (WA), 12 July 1995, *Angela Katerns/Morning Show*, Stolen generation.

rad95100. Triple J (WA), 12 July 1995, *Angela Katerns/Morning Show*, new music.

rad95101. Triple J (WA), 12 July 1995, *Angela Katerns/Morning Show*, Stolen generation.

rad95103. Radio National, 13 July 1995, *News*, 9 a.m., Rob Riley.

rad95104. Radio National, 13 July 1995, *News*, 10 a.m., Rob Riley.

rad95105. Radio National, 13 July 1995, *News*, 1 p.m., Rob Riley.

rad95111. Radio National, 13 July 1995, *News*, 6 p.m., Flags.

rad95112. Radio National, 13 July 1995, *PM*, Parliamentary representation.

rad95115. 720 6WF (WA), 13 July 1995, *News*, 8 a.m., Rob Riley.

rad95116. 6WF 720, 13 July 1995, *Richard Utting*, Mabo.

rad95119. 6PR (WA), 13 July 1995, *News*, 8.30 a.m., Rob Riley.

rad95120. 6PR (WA), 13 July 1995, *Howard Sattler*, Rob Riley.

rad95124. 6PR (WA), 13 July 1995, *News*, 10 a.m., Native Title.

rad95127. 720 6WF (WA), 13 July 1995, *News*, 10 a.m., Rob Riley.

rad95130. 6PR (WA), 13 July 1995, *Howard Sattler*, Peter Newman.

rad95131. 6PR (WA), 13 July 1995, *Howard Sattler*, Rob Riley.

rad95137. 6PR (WA), 13 July 1995, *News*, 3 p.m., Rob Riley.

rad95144. 720 6WF (WA), 13 July 1995, *News*, 6 p.m., Aboriginal flags.

rad95146. Triple J (WA), 13 July 1995, *Morning Show*, Treaty.

rad95147. Triple J (WA), 13 July 1995, *Morning Show*, Robert Tickner.

rad95148. Triple J (WA), 13 July 1995, *Morning Show*, Scientist call in.

rad95152. Radio National, 14 July 1995, *Australia Talks Back*, Aboriginal flag.

rad95157. Radio National, 14 July 1995, *Australia Talks Back*, Aboriginal dispossession.

rad95162. Radio National, 14 July 1995, *Country Wide*, Native Title.

rad95176. Triple J (WA), 14 July 1995, *Angela Katerns/Morning Show*, 6AR, media broadcasting.

rad95177. Triple J (WA), 14 July 1995, *News*, 11 a.m., Koori surfing.

rad95178. Triple J (WA), 14 July 1995, *Angela Katerns/Morning Show*, Hidden pictures.

rad95179. Triple J (WA), 14 July 1995, *Angela Katerns/Morning Show*, Aaron Pedersen.

rad96003. Triple J (WA), 8 July 1996, *The Morning Show*, Christine Anu.

rad96004. Triple J (WA), 8 July 1996, *The Morning Show*, My Island Home.

rad96005. Triple J (WA), 8 July 1996, *The Morning Show*, Aboriginal artists.

rad96012. Triple J (WA), 8 July 1996, *Afternoon Show*, Anguwai.

rad96018. Triple J (WA), 8 July 1996, *Afternoon Show*, Music, Tiddas.

rad96020. Triple J (WA), 8 July 1996, *World Music Show*, Music, Amunda.

rad96021. Triple J (WA), 8 July 1996, *World Music Show*, Music, Christine Anu.

rad96026. Triple J (WA), 9 July 1996, *The Morning Show*, Music, The Warumpi Band.

rad96031. Triple J (WA), 9 July 1996, *Afternoon Show*, Music/promo, The Sunrise Band.

rad96032. Triple J (WA), 9 July 1996, *Afternoon Show*, Music, Sounds of the Yolngu.

rad96033. Triple J (WA), 9 July 1996, *Afternoon Show*, Music, Christine Anu.

rad96034. Triple J (WA), 10 July 1996, *Morning Show*, Whole programme, Aaron Pedersen.

rad96035. Triple J (WA), 10 July 1996, *Morning Show*, Music, Ignorance is bliss.

rad96036. Triple J (WA), 10 July 1996, *Morning Show*, Music/Promo, Barunga music festival.

rad96037. Triple J (WA), 10 July 1996, *Australian Music Show*, Music, Barunga music festival.

rad96038. Triple J (WA), 10 July 1996, *Morning Show*, Music, Warumpi band.

rad96040. Triple J (WA), 10 July 1996, *Morning Show*, Features, NAIDOC week.

rad96041. Triple J (WA), 10 July 1996, *Morning Show*, Music, Nomad.

rad96044. Triple J (WA), 10 July 1996, *Morning Show*, Music, This land's worth more than gold or silver.

rad96048. Triple J (WA), 10 July 1996, *The Afternoon Show*, Station promo, Aboriginal promo.

rad96049. Triple J (WA), 10 July 1996, *The Afternoon Show*, Station promo, Aboriginal promo.

rad96050. Triple J (WA), 10 July 1996, *The Afternoon Show*, Music, The Sunrise Band/Bukula.

rad96051. Triple J (WA), 10 July 1996, *The Afternoon Show*, Promo, Aboriginal promo.

rad96053. Triple J (WA), 10 July 1996, *The Afternoon Show*, Station promo, Christine Anu.

rad96057. Triple J (WA), 13 July 1996, *The Afternoon Show*, Music, Sunset dreaming.

rad96058. Triple J (WA), 13 July 1996, *Evening Show*, Promo, Aboriginal language.

rad96059. Triple J (WA), 13 July 1996, *Evening Show*, Music, Ignorance is bliss.

rad96062. 6PR (WA), 7 July 1996, *Afternoon football coverage*, Player of the Year, Scott Chisholm.

rad96064. 6PR (WA), 8 July 1996, *Howard Sattler, Talkback*, Inebriated Aborigines.

rad96067. 6PR (WA), 8 July 1996, *Howard Sattler, Talkback*, Homeswest.

rad96068. 6PR (WA), 8 July 1996, *Howard Sattler, Talkback*, Racism.

rad96069. 6PR (WA), 8 July 1996, *Howard Sattler*, Promo for Jenny Seaton, Native Title.

rad96090. 6PR (WA), 13 July 1996, *News*, 9 a.m., Cathy Freeman.

rad96099. Radio National, 8 July 1996, *Life Matters*, Features, Stolen generation.

rad96112. Radio National, 9 July 1996, *Life Matters*, Features, Stolen generation.

rad96113. Radio National, 9 July 1996, *World Today*, Century Zinc.

rad96131. Radio National, 11 July 1996, *Life Matters*, Features, Stolen Generation.

rad96145. 6WF (WA), 8 July 1996, *News*, 10 a.m., Century Zinc.

rad96146. 6WF (WA), 8 July 1996, *News*, 11 a.m., Century Zinc.

rad96147. 6WF (WA), 8 July 1996, *News*, 12 noon, Century Zinc.

rad96154. 6WF (WA), 8 July 1996, *Peter Holland*, Features, NAIDOC week.

rad96164. 6WF (WA), 9 July 1996, *Peter Holland*, Features, NAIDOC week.

rad96168. 6WF (WA), 9 July 1996, *Drive Show (Bev East)*, Features, NAIDOC week.

rad96175. 6WF (WA), 10 July 1996, *Morning Show*, Features, Riley's story.

rad96184. 6WF (WA), 10 July 1996, *Peter Holland*, Features, Aboriginal sky figures.

rad96190. 6WF (WA), 11 July 1996, *Peter Holland*, Features, Aboriginal sky figures.

rad96193. 6WF (WA), 12 July 1996, *Morning Show*, Features, Aboriginal sovereignty.

rad96198. 6WF (WA), 12 July 1996, *Peter Holland*, Features, Aboriginal sky figures.

Television

tv94002. Channel Ten (Vic), 5 July 1994, *Eyewitness News*, Wallabies in Melbourne.

tv94003. Channel Seven (Vic), 5 July 1994, *Nightly News*, 6 p.m., Wallabies in Melbourne zoo.

tv94005. Channel Ten (Vic), 5 July 1994, Advert, Pajero.

tv94006. ABC (Vic), 5 July 1994, *Late Edition*, Deaths in custody.

tv94017. Channel Ten (Vic), 8 July 1994, *News*, 5 p.m., National Day under attack.

tv94019. Channel Ten (Vic), 8 July 1994, *News*, 11 p.m., Youth concerns.

tv94021. Channel Seven (Vic), 5 July 1994, *News*, 11 a.m., Sport, Rugby.

tv94022. Channel Nine (Vic), 5 July 1994, *News*, 6 p.m., Sport, Footy.

tv94023. Channel Seven (Vic), 5 July 1994, Sport, *News*, 6 p.m., Bulldogs vs. Tigers.

tv94025. Channel Seven (Vic), 4 July 1994, Sport, Tigers/Crows.

tv94026. Channel Seven (Vic), 6 July 1994, *Eleven AM*, Sport, Football.

tv94028. Channel Ten (Vic), 6 July 1994, *Sports Tonight*, Football.

tv94029. Channel Ten (Vic), 7 July 1994, *Eyewitness News*, Sport, Football/Cockatoo Collins.

tv94030. Channel Nine (Vic), 7 July 1994, *National Nine News*, Sport, Football/Essendon.

tv94031. Channel Seven (Vic), 8 July 1994, *Nightly News*, Sport, Football—Richmond.

tv94032. Channel Seven (Vic), 9 July 1994, *News*, 5 p.m., Sport, Football.

tv94033. Channel Nine (Vic), 9 July 1994, *News*, 6 p.m., Sport, Football—Cats/Demons.

tv94034. ABC (Vic), 9 July 1994, *News*, 7 p.m., Sport, Football—Cats/Demons.

tv94036. Channel Nine (Vic), 10 July 1994, *News*, 6 p.m., Sport, Football—Brisbane/Sydney.

tv94037. Channel Nine (Vic), 10 July 1994, *The Footy Show*, Match footage, Great marks.

tv94039. Channel Seven (Vic), 4 July 1994, *Real Life*, Whole show, many items.

tv94040. Channel Seven (Vic), 7 July 1994, *Real Life*, All segments, several items.

tv94042. Channel Nine (Vic), 4 July 1994, *Today*, Sport, Football.

tv94053. ABC, 7 July 1994, *Open Learning/Aboriginal Studies*, Aboriginal health, a holistic approach.

tv94055. ABC, 4 July 1994, *Late Edition*, Custody death.

tv94057. ABC, 5 July 1994, *First Edition, News Headlines*, Police internal probe.

tv94058. Channel Nine, 5 July 1994, *News*, 6 p.m., Custody deaths.

tv94059. ABC, 4 July 1994, *News*, 7 p.m., Report findings.

tv94060. ABC, 4 July 1994, *News*, 8.30 p.m., Eadie Report.

tv94062. Channel Nine, 4 July 1994, *News*, 5 p.m., Ombudsman's report.

tv94066. ABC, 8 July 1994, *ABC Moments*, Racism and sport.

tv94072. GWN, 5 July 1994, *Newshour, News*, Royal Commission Findings.

tv94076. GWN, 5 July 1994, *Marnum*, Aboriginal events.

tv94079. GWN, 8 July 1994, Advert, Mitsubishi Pajero.

tv94083. Channel Ten, 4 July 1994, *News*, 5 p.m., Eadie Report.

tv94087. Channel Seven, 4 July 1994, *At Home*, At Home.

tv94089. Channel Seven, 4 July 1994, *News*, 6 p.m., Compensation.

tv94090. Channel Seven, 4 July 1994, Advert, Where is your child?

tv94093. Channel Seven, 4 July 1994, Advert, McDonalds.

tv94096. SBS, 4 July 1994, *World News*, NSW police racism.

tv94101. Channel Seven, 5 July 1994, *Jenny Seaton Live*, Chat, Upcoming citizens.

tv94108. 268, Channel Ten, 5 July 1994, *Good Morning Australia*, Features, Boxing.

tv94110. Channel Ten, 5 July 1994, *News*, 5 p.m., Collard case.

tv94111. Channel Ten, 5 July 1994, *News*, 5 p.m., Custody watch.

tv94112. Channel Ten, 5 July 1994, *Late News*, Rock wallabies.

tv94129. Channel Ten, 6 July 1994, *Sport Tonight*, Rugby.

tv94142. Channel Seven, 8 July 1994, *The Great Outdoors*, Features/Lifestyle, Kakadu.

tv94151. SBS, 8 July 1994, *News*, Youth justice report.

tv94152. SBS, 8 July 1994, *News*, NAIDOC celebration.

tv94171. SBS, 10 July 1994, *Vox Populi*, Features, Lake Victoria.

tv94175. ABC, 4 July 1994, *News*, 7 p.m., Black deaths.

tv94176. ABC, 5 July 1994, *News*, 7 p.m., Collard complaint.

tv94180. ABC, 5 July 1994, *Newsbreak*, Collard complaint.

tv94182. ABC, 5 July 1994, *Late Edition*, Overrepresentation.

tv94185. ABC, 6 July 1994, *First Edition*, Deaths concern.

tv95015. ABC, 11 July 1995, *First Edition*, Alcohol Report.

tv95019. ABC, 10 July 1995, *Landline*, Title, title sequence.

tv95025. GWN, 11 July 1995, *Newshour*, Compensation.

tv95027. GWN, 11 July 1995, *Newshour*, Adverts, Sustain.

tv95031. Channel Seven, 10 July 1995, *News*, 6 p.m., Flag raising.

tv95034. SBS, 10 July 1995, *World News*, NAIDOC week.

tv95038. ABC, 10 July 1995, *The Dreaming*, Doombi.

tv95042. Channel Seven, 11 July 1995, *Jenny Seaton*, Emu farm.

tv95044. Channel Nine, 11 July 1995, *News*, 6 p.m., Sport, Champion.

tv95049. Channel Seven, 11 July 1995, *News*, 6 p.m., The lost children.

tv95053. ABC, 12 July 1995, *The Dreaming*, Mar the cockatoo.

tv95055. ABC, 11 July 1995, *The Dreaming*, Jumpa jimpa.

tv95056. ABC, 11 July 1995, *News*, 7 p.m., Senate review.

tv95057. ABC, 11 July 1995, *News*, 7 p.m., Lost generation.

tv95058. ABC, 11 July 1995, *News*, 7 p.m., Alcohol control.

tv95066. GWN, 12 July 1995, *Newshour*, Mabo.

tv95076. ABC, 12 July 1995, *The Dreaming*, Two willy willes.

tv95077. ABC, 12 July 1995, *News*, 7 p.m., Title talks.

tv95080. ABC, 11 July 1995, *The Investigators*, Your Problem, Mitsubishi motors.

tv95087. ABC, 12 July 1995, *The Dreaming*, The black snake.

tv95089. Channel Nine, 13 July 1995, *Today*, Tennant Creek/alcohol.

tv95094. Channel Ten, 13 July 1995, *News*, 5 p.m., Charged.

tv95095. Channel Ten, 13 July 1995, *News*, 5 p.m., Custody bid.

tv95096. Channel Ten 13 July 1995, *News Update*.

tv95099. Channel Seven, 13 July 1995, *News*, 6 p.m., Riley charged.

tv95100. Channel Seven, 13 July 1995, *News*, 6 p.m., Father free.

tv95102. Channel Nine, 13 July 1995, *News*, 6 p.m., crime, alcohol.

tv95103. Channel Nine, 13 July 1995, *News*, 6 p.m., Miller.

tv95108. ABC, 13 July 1995, *The Dreaming*, Biri.

tv95110. ABC, 13 July 1995, *News*, 7 p.m., Riley charged.

tv95112. ABC, 13 July 1995, *News*, 7 p.m., bail granted.

tv95113. ABC, 13 July 1995, *7.30 Report*, Rob Riley.

tv95115. Channel Nine, 14 July 1995, *The Footy Show (WA)*, Quiz.

tv95116. Channel Nine, 14 July 1995, *The Footy Show (WA)*, Quiz, Adrian.

tv95121. Channel Ten, 14 July 1995, *News*, 5 p.m., Riley.

tv95123. Channel Seven, 14 July 1995, *News*, 6 p.m., Suspended.

tv95125. Channel Seven, 14 July 1995, *4 Quarters*, Title sequence, Nicky Winmar.

tv95126. Channel Seven, 14 July 1995, *4 Quarters*, Sports news/Who's hot, Wanganeen.

tv95127. Channel Seven, 14 July 1995, *4 Quarters*, Features, Kids kick ball.

tv95128. Channel Seven, 14 July 1995, *4 Quarters*, Features, I'd like to see that.

tv95129. ABC, 14 July 1995, *The Dreaming*, Becoming a koala.

tv95130. ABC, 14 July 1995, *News*, 7 p.m., Riley suspended.

tv95131. ABC, 14 July 1995, *News*, 7 p.m., sport, Last chance.

tv95133. Channel Seven, 14 July 1995, *AFL Coverage*, Aboriginal players.

tv95134. Channel Nine, 15 July 1995, *Bush Beat*, Titles and credits, Rock art.

tv95135. Channel Ten, 15 July 1995, *Video Hits*, Music clip, Christine Anu.

tv95136. Channel Seven, 15 July 1995, *AFL Saturday*, Fremantle vs. Hawthorne.

tv95140. Channel Seven, 15 July 1995, *Gladiators*, Aaron Pedersen.

tv95141. Channel Ten, 15 July 1995, *Sports Tonight*, Sports, Packer's Union.

tv95149. GWN, 16 July 1995, *Milbindi*, Community news.

tv95151. ABC, 15 July 1995, *The Dreaming*, Creeks sing.

tv95153. ABC, 15 July 1995, *The Dreaming*, Gelong and his mother.

tv95155. Channel Seven, 16 July 1995, *Sportsworld* Footy Panel, Sports features, Footy players.

tv95158. Channel Seven, 16 July 1995, *The Footy Show*, Title sequence, Aboriginal player.

tv95159. Channel Seven, 16 July 1995, *The Footy Show*, Sports features, Swans singing.

tv95160. Channel Nine, 16 July 1995, *The Footy Show*, Title sequence, Football players, including Aboriginal.

tv95164. Channel Nine, 16 July 1995, *Burke's Backyard*, Celebrity gardener, Cathy Freeman.

tv95166. Channel Nine, 16 July 1995, *Sixty Minutes*, Features/Current affairs, Island girl.

tv96013. Channel Ten, 7 July 1996, *News*, 6 p.m., Sport, football.

tv96014. Channel Ten, 7 July 1996, *Sports Tonight*, Sport, football.

tv96018. ABC, 8 July 1996, *First Edition*, Century Zinc.

tv96032. Channel Seven, 8 July 1996, *News*, 10.30 p.m., Century Zinc.

tv96037. Channel Nine, 8 July 1996, *Australia's Funniest Home Movies*.

tv96045. Channel Seven, 9 July 1996, *Eleven AM*, News discussion, Century Zinc.

tv96051. Channel Seven, 9 July 1996, *News*, Mine talks.

tv96070. Channel Seven, 10 July 1996, *News*, Sport, AFL.

tv96083. Channel Nine, 11 July 1996, *A Current Affair*, Welcome invasion.

tv96086. Channel Seven, 11 July 1996, *Today Tonight*, Commercial break, AFL advert.

tv96090. Channel Nine, 11 July 1996, *The Footy Show*, End credits, More than a game.

tv96095. Channel Ten, 12 July 1996, *News*, 5 p.m., Sport, Clash.

tv96097. Channel Seven, 12 July 1996, *Eleven AM*, Sport, Swans.

tv96100. ABC, 12 July 1996, *News*, 7 p.m., Trade off.

tv96108. *Channel Seven*, 12 July 1996, *News*, 6 p.m., Mandela.

References

Aboriginal Legal Service (1995), *Telling Our Story: A Report by the Aboriginal Legal Service of Western Australia on the Removal of Aboriginal Children from their Families in Western Australia* (Perth: Aboriginal Legal Service).

Adam, Phillip, and Burton, Lee (1997), *Talkback: Emperors of Air* (Sydney: Allen & Unwin).

Akmeemana, Saku (1995), 'Memorandum: Racial Vilification in Other Jurisdications', for Zita Antonius, Federal Human Rights and Equal Opportunities Commission, June.

Allen, Rod (1998), 'This is not Television . . .', in Jeanette Steemers (ed.), *Changing Channels: The Prospects for Television in a Digital World* (Luton: University of Luton Press), 59–71.

Anderson, Benedict (1991), *Imagined Communities: Reflections on the Origin and Spread of Nationalism*, rev. edn. (London: Verso).

Ashley, Laura and Olson, Beth (1998), 'Constructing Reality: Print Media's Framing of the Women's Movement, 1966–1986', *Journalism, & Mass Communication Quarterly*, 75/2: 263–77.

Attwood, Bain (1996), 'Mabo, Australia and the End of history', in Bain Attwood (ed.), *In the Age of Mabo: History, Aborigines and Australia* (Sydney: Allen Unwin), 117–35.

——— and Arnold, John (eds.) (1992), *Power, Knowledge and Aborigines* (Melbourne: La Trobe University Press).

Australian Press Council (1992–5), *Annual Reports* (Sydney: Australian Press Council).

Balzer, Marjorie Mandelstam (1999), *The Tenacity of Ethnicity: A Siberian Saga in Global Perspective* (Princeton: Princeton University Press).

Barker, Dudley (1963), *The Young Man's Guide to Journalism* (London: Hamish Hamilton).

Bennett, Tony (1998), *Culture: A Reformer's Science* (London: Sage Publications).

——— Emmison, Michael, and Frow, John (1999), *Accounting for Tastes: Australian Everyday Cultures* (Cambridge: Cambridge University Press).

Beresford, Quentin, and Omaji, Paul (1996), *Rites of Passage: Aboriginal Youth, Crime and Justice* (Fremantle, WA: Fremantle Arts Centre Press).

Bostock, Lester (1993), *From the Dark Side: A Survey of the Portrayal of Aborigines and Torres Strait Islanders on Commercial Television* (Sydney: Australian Broadcasting Authority).

355

References

Bunbury, Alison, and Hartley, John (1994), *Telling Both Stories: Media Forum Report 94* (Murdoch University: Centre for Research in Culture and Communication).

——, ——, and Mickler, Steve (1993), *Telling Both Stories: Reporting on the Media Forum* (Murdoch University: Centre for Research in Culture and Communication).

Burnum Burnum (1988), *Burnum Burnum's Aboriginal Australia: A Traveller's Guide*, ed. David Stewart (Sydney: Angus & Robertson).

Candlin, E. Frank (1955), *Teach Yourself Journalism*, 2nd edn. (London: English Universities Press Ltd).

Chesterman, John, and Galligan, Brian (1997), *Citizens Without Rights: Aborigines and Australian Citizenship* (Cambridge: Cambridge University Press).

Clayton, Joan (1992), *Journalism for Beginners: How to Get into Print and Get Paid For It* (London: Piatkus).

Continuum (1998) *Special Issue: Philosophy and Cultural Studies*, ed. Niall Lucy, *Continuum*, 12/2 (July).

Council for Aboriginal Reconciliation (1994), *Walking Together: The First Steps, Report of the Council for Aboriginal Reconciliation to Federal Parliament, 1991–1994* (Canberra: Australian Government Printing Service).

Cultural Studies (1992), *Special Issue: Dismantle Fremantle*, ed. Ien Ang and John Hartley, *Cultural Studies*, 6/3.

Cultural Studies (1998), *Special Issue: The Institutionalization of Cultural Studies*, ed. Ted Striphas, *Cultural Studies* 12/4 (October).

Davidson, Alastair (1997), *From Subject to Citizen: Australian Citizenship in the Twentieth Century* (Cambridge: Cambridge University Press).

Deloria Jr., Vine (1988 [first published 1970]), *Custer Died For Your Sins: An Indian Manifesto* (Norman, Okla.: University of Oklahoma Press).

Dodson, Patrick (1994), 'Preface', *Walking Together: The First Steps. Report of the Council for Aboriginal Reconciliation 1991–94 to Federal Parliament* (Canberra: Australian Government Printing Service).

Donald, James (1998), 'Perpetual Noise: Thinking about Media Regulation', *Continuum: Journal of Media and Cultural Studies*, 12/2: 217–32.

Donzelot, Jacques (1979), *The Policing of Families* (New York: Random House).

During, Simon (ed.) (1999), *The Cultural Studies Reader*, 2nd edn. (London and New York: Routledge).

Edgar, Joe (1996), 'Indigenous Media: Radio Goolarri', in John Hartley and Alan McKee (eds.), *Telling Both Stories: Indigenous Australia and the Media* (Perth: Arts Enterprise, Edith Cowan University), 111–12.

Edmunds, Mary, and James, Roberta (1992), *Black and White and Read All Over: Discourse, Media and Attitudes* (Canberra: Aboriginal Studies Press for the Australian Institute of Aboriginal and Torres Strait Islander Studies).

Fedler, Fred, Carey, Arlen, and Counts, Tim (1998), 'Journalism's Status in Academia: A Candidate for Elimination?', *Journalism and Mass Communication Educator*, 53/2 (Summer), 31–9.

Feldmann, Jules (1951), *The Great Jubilee Book: The Story of the Australian Nation in Pictures* (Melbourne: Herald & Weekly Times).

Felski, Rita (1989), *Beyond Feminist Aesthetics* (Cambridge, Mass.: Harvard University Press).

—— (1995), *The Gender of Modernity* (Cambridge, Mass.: Harvard University Press).

—— (1998), 'Images of the Intellectual: From Philosophy to Cultural Studies', *Continuum: Journal of Media and Cultural Studies*, 12/2: 157–71.

Franklin, Bob (1997), *Newszak and News Media* (London: Arnold).

Giddens, Anthony (1998), *The Third Way: The Renewal of Social Democracy* (Cambridge: Polity Press).

Gitlin, Todd (1998), 'Public Sphere or Public Sphericules?' in Tamar Liebes and James Curran (eds.), *Media, Ritual and Identity* (London: Routledge), 175–202.

Given, John L. (1907), *Making a Newspaper* (New York: Henry Holt and Company).

Griffiths, Tom (1996), *Hunters and Collectors: The Antiquarian Imagination in Australia* (Cambridge: Cambridge University Press).

Haebich, Anna (1988), *For Their Own Good* (Perth: University of Western Australia Press).

Hamlett, Tim (1999), 'A Theory of Journalism: Why and by Whom?', in Jacqui Ewart (ed.), *Journalism Theory and Practice: Proceedings of the 1998 Journalism Education Association Conference* (Central Queensland University: Journalism Education Association), 59–70).

Hargreaves, Ian (1999), 'The Ethical Boundaries of Reporting', in Mike Ungersma (ed.), *Reporters and the Reported: The 1999 Vauxhall Lectures on Contemporary Issues in British Journalism* (Cardiff University: Centre for Journalism Studies), 1–15.

Hartley, John (1992), *The Politics of Pictures: The Creation of the Public in the Age of Popular Media* (London and New York: Routledge).

—— (1996), *Popular Reality: Journalism, Modernity, Popular Culture* (London: Arnold).

—— (1999), *Uses of Television* (London and New York: Routledge).

—— and McKee, Alan (eds.) (1996), *Telling Both Stories: The Report of the National Media Forum* (Perth: Arts Enterprise, Edith Cowan University).

Hartman, Paul, and Husband, Charles (1974), *Racism and the Mass Media: A Study of the Role of the Mass Media in the Formation of White Beliefs and Attitudes in Britain* (London: Davis-Poynter).

Hay, James (1996), 'Afterword: The Place of the Audience: Beyond Audience Studies', in James Hay, Lawrence Grossberg, and Ellen Wartella (eds.), *The Audience and its Landscape* (Boulder, Color.: Westview Press), 359–78.

Hollinger, David (2000), 'The Ethno-Racial Pentagon', in Stephen Steinberg (ed.), *Race and Ethnicity in the United States* (Malden, Mass. and Oxford: Blackwell Publishers), 197–210.

Holston, James and Appadurai, Arjun (1996), 'Cities and Citizenship', *Public Culture*, 8: 187–204.

Human Rights and Equal Opportunities Commission (1991), *Racist Violence: The Report of the National Inquiry into Racist Violence in Australia* (Sydney: Human Rights and Equal Opportunities Commission).

References

Irving, Helen (1999), *To Constitute a Nation: A Cultural History of Australia's Constitution*, rev. edn. (Cambridge: Cambridge University Press).

Jackson, Bob, Stanton, Michelle, and Underwood, Rod (1995), 'The Portrayal of Aboriginal People in West Australian Newspapers: Less than a Lily-White Record', paper presented at the Australian and New Zealand Communication Association Conference, Perth.

Jacobs, Pat (1990), *Mister Neville: A Biography* (Fremantle, WA: Fremantle Arts Centre Press).

Jakubowicz, Andrew (ed.) (1994), *Racism, Ethnicity and the Media* (St Leonards, NSW: Allen & Unwin).

Jennings, Karen (1993), *Sites of Difference: Cinematic Representations of Aboriginality and Gender* (Melbourne: Australian Film Institute).

Johnston, Elliott (1991), *Royal Commission into Aboriginal Deaths in Custody. National Report: Overview and Recommendations* (Canberra: Australian Government Publishing Service).

Jull, Peter (1994), 'Mabo Politics in a "First World" Context', in Murray Goot and Tim Rowse (eds.), *Make a Better Offer: The Politics of Mabo* (Sydney: Pluto Press, 203–16).

Keating, Paul (1993), 'Native Title Bill 1993: Prime Minister's Second Reading Speech', *Commonwealth of Australia. Parliamentary Debates. House of Representatives.* No. 11, 16 Nov. 1993: 2877–83.

Langford, Ruby (1988), *Don't Take Your Love to Town* (Ringwood, Vic.: Penguin Australia).

Langton, Marcia (1993a), '*Well, I heard it on the radio and I saw it on the television...*' *An Essay for the Australian Film Commission on the Politics and Aesthetics of Filmmaking by and about Aboriginal People and Things* (Sydney: Australian Film Commission).

—— (1993b), 'Rum, Seduction and Death: Aboriginality and Alcohol', *Oceania*, 3: 195–205.

Edmund, Leach (1964), 'Anthropological Aspects of Language: Animal Categories and Verbal Abuse', in E. H. Lenneberg (ed) *New Directions in the Study of Language* (Cambridge, Mass.: MIT Press).

Leadbeater, Charles, and Mulgan, Geoff (1997), 'The End of Unemployment', in Geoff Mulgan (ed.), *Life After Politics: New Thinking for the Twenty First Century* (London: Fontana Press).

Lloyd, John (1998), 'Are Intellectuals Useless?', *New Statesman* (30 Oct.), 11–12.

Lotman, Yuri M. (1990), *Universe of the Mind: A Semiotic Theory of Culture.* (Bloomington and Indianapolis: Indiana University Press).

Lumby, Catharine (1997), *Bad Girls: The Media, Sex and Feminism in the 1990s* (Sydney: Allen & Unwin).

—— (1999), *Gotcha: Life in a Tabloid World* (Sydney: Allen & Unwin).

McKay, George (1998), *DiY Culture: Party and Protest in Nineties Britain* (London: Verso).

McKee, Alan (1997a) '"The Aboriginal Version of Ken Done..." Banal Aboriginal Identities in Australia', *Cultural Studies*, 11/2: 191–206.

—— (1997b), 'Putting the Public into Public Toilets', *Continuum*, 11/3 (December), 85–101.

—— (1997c), 'The Lack of Racism in Contemporary Australia', in Geoff Gray and Christine Winter (eds.), *The Resurgence of Racism: Hanson, Howard and the Race Debate* (Monash: Monash Publications in History), 139–48.

—— (1997d), 'Films vs *Real Life*', *UTS Review*, 3/1: 160–82.

—— (1999), 'Researching the Reception of Indigenous Affairs in Australia', *Screen*, 40/4 (Winter), 451–4.

—— and Burns, Lynette Sheridan (1999), 'Reporting on Indigenous Issues: Some Practical Suggestions for Improving Journalistic Practice in the Coverage of Indigenous Affairs', *Australian Journalism Review*, 21/2: 103–16.

MacKillop, James (1998), *Dictionary of Celtic Mythology* (Oxford: Oxford University Press).

Macquarie (1994), *Macquarie Aboriginal Words*, General Editors Nick Thieberger and William McGregor (Sydney: The Macquarie Library).

Marcus, Julie (1988), 'The Journey out to the Centre: The Cultural Appropriation of Ayers Rock', *Aboriginal Culture Today* (Special issue, *Kunapipi* magazine 10/1 and 2), 254–74.

Marris, Paul and Thornham, Sue (eds.) (1999), *Media Studies: A Reader*, 2nd edn. (Edinburgh: Edinburgh University Press).

Meadows, Michael (1992a), *A Watering Can in the Desert: Issues in Indigenous Broadcasting in Australia* (Brisbane: Institute for Cultural Policy Studies, Griffith University).

—— (1992b) 'Portrayal of Aboriginal Australians: Reporting or Racism?', in John Henningham (ed.), *Issues in Australian Journalism* (Melbourne: Longman Cheshire), 89–97.

—— (1994), 'Reclaiming a Cultural Identity: Indigenous Media Production in Australia and Canada', *Continuum*, 8/2: 270–92.

—— (1998), 'Into the New Millennium: The Role of Indigenous Media in Australia', *Media International Australia, incorporating Culture and Policy*, No. 88: 67–78.

Media and Indigenous Australians Conference (1993), *Transcript of the Media and Indigenous Australians Conference* (Canberra: Australian Government Publishing Service).

Media International Australia incorporating Culture and Policy (1999), Special themed section on 'Media Wars', No. 90 (Feb.).

Michaels, Eric (1994), *Bad Aboriginal Art: Tradition, Media and Technological Horizons* (Sydney: Allen & Unwin [originally published by the University of Minnesota Press]).

Mickler, Steve (1991), 'The Battle for Goonininup', *Arena*, 96: 69–88.

—— (1992a) 'Visions of Disorder: Aboriginal People and Youth Crime Reporting', *Cultural Studies*, 6/3: 322–36.

—— (1992b) *Gambling on the First Race: A Comment on Racism and Talkback Radio – 6PR, the TAB and the Western Australian Government* (Perth: Louis Johnson Memorial Trust and the Centre for Research in Culture and Communication, Murdoch University).

References

Mickler, Steve (1996), 'Watching the Watchdogs', in John Hartley and Alan McKee (eds.), *Telling Both Stories: Indigenous Australia and the Media* (Perth: Edith Cowan University), 75–80.

—— (1997) 'Talkback Radio and Indigenous Citizens: Towards a Practical Ethics of Representation', *UTS Review*, 3/2 (Nov.), 46–66.

—— (1998), *The Myth of Privilege: Aboriginal Status, Media Visions, Public Ideas* (Fremantle, WA: Fremantle Arts Centre Press).

—— and McHoul, Alec (1998), 'Sourcing the Wave: Crime Reporting, Aboriginal Youth and the WA Press, Feb 1991–Jan 1992', *Media International Australia incorporating Culture and Policy*, No. 86: 122–52.

Miller, Toby (1995), 'Exporting Truth from Aboriginal Australia: "Portions of our past become present again, where only the melancholy light of origin shines"', *Media Information Australia*, 76: 7–17.

—— (1998), *Technologies of Truth: Cultural Citizenship and the Popular Media* (Minneapolis: University of Minnesota Press).

Morrison, David E. (1998), *The Search for a Method: Focus Groups and the Development of Mass Communication Research* (Luton: University of Luton Press).

Morton, John (1996), 'Aboriginality, Mabo and the Republic: Indigenising Australia', in Bain Attwood (ed.), *In the Age of Mabo: History, Aborigines and Australia* (Sydney: Allen & Unwin), 117–35.

Muecke, Stephen (1992), *Textual Spaces: Aboriginality and Cultural Studies* (Kensington, NSW: University of New South Wales Press).

Myers, Fred R. (1991, first published 1986), *Pintupi Country, Pintupi Self: Sentiment, Place and Politics among Western Desert Aborigines* (Berkeley: University of California Press).

National Inquiry into the Separation of Aboriginal and Torres Strait Islander Children from Their Families (1997), *Bringing Them Home: The Report of the National Inquiry into the Separation of Aboriginal and Torres Strait Islander Children from Their Families* (Commonwealth of Australia, Sydney: Human Rights and Equal Opportunity Commission).

Neumann, Klaus (1998), 'Remembering Victims and Perpetrators', *UTS Review*, 4/1: 1–17.

Osborne, Thomas (1998), *Aspects of Enlightenment: Social Theory and the Ethics of Truth* (London: UCL Press).

Partington, Geoffrey (1996), *Hasluck versus Coombes: White Policies and Australia's Aborigines* (Sydney: Quakers Hill Press).

Pearson, Mark (1987), 'Interviewing Aborigines: A Cross-Cultural Dilemma', *Australian Journalism Review*, 9:1/2, 113–17.

Pearson, Noel (1994), 'From Remnant Title to Social Justice', in Murray Goot and Tim Rowse (eds.), *Make a Better Offer: The Politics of Mabo* (Sydney: Pluto Press), 179–84.

Peterson, Nicolas and Sanders, Will (eds.) (1998), *Citizenship and Indigenous Australians: Changing Conceptions and Possibilities* (Cambridge: Cambridge University Press).

Plater, Diana (1992), 'Guidelines on Reporting Aboriginal and Torres Strait Islander Issues', in Diana Plater and Kitty Eggerking (eds.), *Signposts: A Guide to Representing Aboriginal, Torres Strait Islander and Ethnic Affairs* (Sydney: Australian Centre for Independent Journalism, UTS).

Ray, Robert B. (1995), *The Avant Garde Finds Andy Hardy* (Cambridge, Mass.: Harvard University Press).

Read, Peter (1988), *A Hundred Years War: The Wiradjuri People and the State* (Canberra: ANU Press).

Reynolds, Henry (1996), *Aboriginal Sovereignty: Three Nations, One Australia?* (Sydney: Allen & Unwin).

Rose, Michael (1996), *For the Record: 160 Years of Aboriginal Print Journalism* (Sydney: Allen and Unwin).

Rose, Nikolas, and Miller, Peter (1992), 'Political Power beyond the State: Problematics of Government', *British Journal of Sociology*, 43/2: 172–205.

Rowse, Tim (1992), *Remote Possibilities: The Aboriginal Domain and the Administrative Imagination* (Darwin, NT: North Australia Research Unit, Australian National University).

—— (1993), *After Mabo: Interpreting Indigenous Traditions* (Melbourne: Melbourne University Press).

—— (1996), 'The Political Identity of Regional Councillors', in Patrick Sullivan (ed.), *Shooting the Banker: Essays on ATSIC and Self-Determination* (Darwin, NT: North Australia Research Unit, Australian National University), 42–69.

Sahlins, Marshall (1974), *Stone Age Economics* (London: Tavistock).

Smith, Bernard (1980), *The Spectre of Truganini: The 1980 Boyer Lectures* (Sydney: ABC Books).

Smith, Dan (1993), *The Seventh Fire: The Struggle for Aboriginal Government* (Toronto: Key Porter Books).

Stanner W. E. H. (1969), *After the Dreaming: The 1969 Boyer Lectures* (Sydney: ABC Books).

Stokes, Geoffrey (1997), 'Citizenship and Aboriginality: Two Conceptions of Identity in Aboriginal Political Thought', in Geoffrey Stokes (ed.), *The Politics of Identity in Australia* (Cambridge: Cambridge University Press), 158–71.

Trigger, David (1995), ' "Everyone's agreed: the *West* is all you need": Ideology, Media and Aboriginality in Western Australia', *Media Information Australia*, 75: 109–24.

—— (1998), 'Citizenship and Indigenous Responses to Mining in the Gulf Country', in Nicolas Peterson and Will Sanders (eds.), *Citizenship and Indigenous Australians: Changing Conceptions and Possibilities* (Cambridge: Cambridge University Press), 154–66.

UNESCO (1959), *Professional Associations in the Mass Media: Handbook of Press, Film, Radio, Television Organizations* (Paris: UNESCO).

von Sturmer, John (1984), 'The Different Domains', in Australian Institute of Aboriginal Studies, *Aborigines and Uranium* (Canberra: Australian Government Publishing Servce), 218–37.

References

Wark, McKenzie (1997), *The Virtual Republic: Australia's Culture Wars of the 1990s* (Sydney: Allen & Unwin).

Yunupingu, Galarrwuy (ed.) (1997), *Our Land is Our Life: Land Rights – Past, Present and Future* (St Lucia: University of Queensland Press).

INDEX